Modern Sci-Fi Films FAQ

Modern Sci-Fi Films FAQ

All That's Left to Know About Time Travel, Alien, Robot, and Out-of-This-World Movies Since 1970

Tom DeMichael

APPLAUSE
THEATRE & CINEMA BOOKS
An Imprint of Hal Leonard Corporation

Published in 2014 by Applause Theatre & Cinema Books
An Imprint of Hal Leonard Corporation
7777 West Bluemound Road
Milwaukee, WI 53213

Trade Book Division Editorial Offices
33 Plymouth St., Montclair, NJ 07042

The FAQ series was conceived by Robert Rodriguez and developed with Stuart Shea.
Printed in the United States of America

All images are from the author's personal collection.

Book design by Snow Creative Services

Library of Congress Cataloging-in-Publication Data

DeMichael, Tom.
    Modern sci-fi films FAQ : all that's left to know about time travel, alien, robot, and out-of-this-world movies since 1970 / Tom DeMichael.
       pages cm
    Includes bibliographical references and index.
    ISBN 978-1-4803-5061-8 (pbk.)
1. Science fiction films—History and criticism. 2. Motion pictures—History—20th century. 3. Motion pictures—History—21st century. I. Title.
    PN1995.9.S26D46 2014
    791.43'615—dc23
                                                                        2014026831

www.applausebooks.com

Dedicated to Russell Emery Otvos, whose life was like the greatest sci-fi film
one could ever imagine: wild, brilliant, out-of-this-world,
and ending much too soon

Contents

Foreword

On a hot afternoon in 1955, my pal Bruce and I hurried into the Hawaii Theater on Hollywood Blvd. to see a new color movie, *Conquest of Space*. We were eight years old. I loved sci-fi fantasy films, but this one was different. There were no aliens. It didn't involve time travel or space invasion. *Conquest of Space* was an earnest attempt at depicting how scientists might actually travel to a very, very, very distant Mars. "Reeling" by on the giant screen, we saw a giant circular space station in orbit one hundred miles up, seemingly in orbit above me over Hollywood. Wow! And that was just the beginning. Awesome rocket ships of various shapes flew about. Crew members enjoyed and then struggled with zero-g. Finally, the movie ended with a skillful landing and joyful liftoff from the desolate red surface of Mars. The theater seats had been designed to comfortably rock backward, which I did in perfect sync as the movie's crew members were pushed back during blastoff. I felt I was with them. This was so fun!

Imagine my surprise upon learning that everything I had seen on the screen was made only four blocks from the Hawaii Theater, within the mighty Paramount Pictures giant, dark soundstages. I had a strong imagination and wanted to make my own movie magic. At that time there were no books or classes that taught visual effects. But the local studio effects artists and technicians whose work I'd admired were more than willing to discuss how they did it. In most cases, they had never been asked my questions and were actually appreciative that someone was interested, even if I was just a kid.

I had to teach myself how to use basic tools to build my miniature sets, such as saws, hammers, pliers, clamps, glues, paints, and woods. I also learned about stories, film directing, acting, editing, high-speed cameras, close-up lenses, and lighting choices. Choices? I'd believed that movies just happened. But with choices came the intoxicating opportunity to actually see what I imagined in my mind's eye. Given my financial and skill limitations, technically real-looking shots were often impossible. That didn't deter me so long as I felt an emotional reaction when seeing it projected.

When I read the script for *Star Wars*, I understood George Lucas's intent. He wanted to show young, rebellious heroes battling authoritarian forces across landscapes of highly emotional, visual wonders. What kid wouldn't want to see that? When we finished a year later, I quickly jumped on to Steven Spielberg's sci-fi mystery *Close Encounters of the Third Kind*. Channeling my childhood imagination had given me a career.

Since then, I've supervised the visual effects for many sci-fi films, including more *Star Wars, ET, Terminator 2, Jurassic Park, AI* and *Super 8*. I'm always looking into the future for the Next Big Thing in visual effects, and many of my quests, as well as those of others, are found in this book. I hope you will enjoy it and enjoy rediscovering your own childhood adventures as much as I have mine.

Dennis Muren

Dennis Muren *is an American film special-effects artist, most notable for his work on the films of Steven Spielberg, James Cameron, and George Lucas. He has won nine Academy Awards.*

Acknowledgments

Like the movies themselves that this book addresses, there are many, many people who are involved with putting this project together. It may be my name on the spine, but quite a number of others have added their knowledge, direction, and skills to the book you now hold in your hands (or tentacles, depending on your orientation).

I am eternally grateful and offer my thanks to the following folks:

- Illusion master Douglas Trumbull from *2001: A Space Odyssey, Close Encounters of the Third Kind, Blade Runner, Brainstorm, Silent Running,* and many more
- Producer Kevin Conran and concept artist Thom Schillinger from *Sky Captain and the World of Tomorrow*
- Concept artist Greg Broadmore from *District 9*
- Brandon Alinger from The Prop Store, Los Angeles
- Claryn Spies from Yale University Library
- Heather Wisner from *Makeup Artist* magazine
- Marybeth Keating, Wes Seeley, Gary Morris, and John Cerullo from Hal Leonard Publishing for their incredible patience, direction, and backing along the way
- Rob Rodriguez for his never-ending guidance and trust

and, for who they are and what they make me . . .

- Wife Paula, sons Anthony and Alex, their friends Ian and Dana, my dear old Daddio (who left us just before he got to proof the manuscript), and grandson Charlie
- Tom Edinger for his encouragement and never-wavering friendship
- And to all the sci-fi film fans around the world, who have made the last forty years in sci-fi films an out-of-this-world treat . . .

Introduction
Where Have We Been, Where Are We Going?

S ir Isaac Newton—a man not unaccustomed to the world of science—is quoted with saying something to the effect of, "If I have seen further it is by standing on the shoulders of giants." In the realm of science fiction films, those so-called "giants" are the classic films made prior to the year of 1970 (at least as far as this book is concerned. When you write your book, you can determine what years are "classic" and what years are "modern").

With shoulders broad and sturdy, films like *Metropolis, The Day the Earth Stood Still, This Island Earth,* and others laid a foundation on which today's sci-fi films are being built. Excluding remakes—which, in most cases, can't hold a ray gun to the originals—many of the science fiction movies of the last forty years have blazed new vistas. They've reached farther into the future, traveled longer into the past, soared deeper into the vastness of the cosmos, and delved further toward man's consciousness than the classics did.

Much of today's science fiction cinema doesn't come easy, as technology—both in the world-at-large and in the hands of current filmmakers—is broader and more accessible than ever before. Yesterday's dreams have become today's realities.

The scientific concept of a laser beam wasn't even thought of in the 1930s—today, you can carry one in your pocket to highlight your corporate presentation. In 1950, the thought of landing a manned spaceship on the moon was a Hollywood dream—today, it's a historic event of more than forty years in the past. The first computer brain—ENIAC—made more than five thousand additions per second when it was first introduced in 1949, even though it weighed twenty-eight tons and occupied eighteen hundred square feet—enough space for a quaint three-bedroom home. Today, your laptop computer is four million times faster, nearly nineteen thousand times lighter, and eighteen hundred times smaller.

What passed for amazement to the general public in 1950 is beyond mundane in today's world. Filmmakers are continually challenged to instill awe into the moviegoing experience in order for today's sci-fi films to make any impression. It's no wonder they are dependent on three-dimensional images that are generated by farms of high-powered computers and augmented by multi-layered digital sound.

With that in mind, it's no surprise that today's sci-fi blockbuster can cost up to $300 million to produce. And that's still no guarantee for success—witness Disney's 2012 production of *John Carter*. Based on the Edgar Rice Burroughs sci-fi character who visited Mars in his novels of one hundred years ago, the film was budgeted at the above-mentioned dollar figure—only to lose 200 million of those greenbacks with poor box-office results. (Why the company chose to delete the key sci-fi words—of Mars—from the generally known title, virtually assuring the film's failure among fans of the series and the genre, is anyone's guess.) Couple that with Disney's 2011 sci-fi disaster, *Mars Needs Moms*, which cost $150 million to make and lost 130 million smackers at the box office, and Mickey found himself stuck eating government cheese.

That being noted, most of today's sci-fi films still make a sizable impression on audiences. Director James Cameron's *Avatar*, a futuristic story with deep eco-logical roots released in 2009, was another of those mega-budgeted films. But the public ate it up; it grossed more than $700 million in America, with another $2 billion overseas. The blue-hued Na'vi were a big hit around the world.

A phenomenon unique to today's sci-fi films (among other genres) is the sequel or, plural, sequels. Monster and horror films relied on sequels as a staple to their success—consider Universal Pictures' eight *Frankenstein* films, six *Dracula* films, six *Mummy* films, five *Wolfman* films, and three *Creature* films of the 1930s through the 1950s. Add in Toho of Japan's *Godzilla* franchise, the *Freddy Krueger/Nightmare on Elm Street* flicks, *Halloween/Michael Myers* entries, *Hellraisers*, *Friday the 13th* series, ad nauseam.

Modern sci-fi films have spawned repetitive sagas for *Star Trek* (ten films, not counting the 2009 reboot), *Alien* (seven films, if 2012's *Prometheus* is considered), *Star Wars* (six films), 1968's *Planet of the Apes* (five), *Predator* (five), *Terminator* (four), *The Matrix* (three), and *Jurassic Park* (three, with a fourth in the works for 2014), among others.

Why sequels? Is there a burning need to tell a seemingly endless story about the USS *Enterprise* and its crews, going where no man has gone before? Is there a crying demand to follow the tales of more DNA-created dinosaurs than you can shake a stick at (if that's your idea of fun)? Do we need five films about an alien that comes to earth in search of human prey?

The simple answer is: no. But the real answer is: ye$. As much as we love C-3PO and John Connor and Cornelius, the fact is, we must remember Hollywood is the heart of the movie business—emphasis on the word "busi-ness." The studios and distributors have shareholders to satisfy, families to feed, Hummers to keep gassed up. Their challenge is to bring more money in the door than goes out.

If C-3PO and John Connor and Cornelius help to make that happen, then that's all right. We don't mind. The modern sci-fi film gives us two hours (give or take) where we can forget about our troubles, sit back, crunch some popcorn, and get lost (the last part is something my wife tells me to do quite often).

This book on modern sci-fi films, then, brings the yang to the yin of classic sci-fi films. With it, the full circle of movie magic and all things out of this world comes together. That is, until the next batch of sci-fi films take us where we've never been before.

I can't wait—can you?

After Words Collide

The Literary Roots of Modern Sci-Fi Films

Wrapping Your Arms Around All These Authors . . .

T he task of tracing the roots of sci-fi films from the last forty or so years is daunting, to say the least. To coin the old riddle: How does one eat an elephant? (Assuming there happens to be one in the fridge ...) The answer is: One bite at a time. We might take the same tack in getting a grip on the world of sci-fi cinema and where it all starts.

Many of the films—successful and otherwise—came from the fertile minds of Hollywood's finest (and not-so-finest) screenwriters. Perhaps an equal, or more, amount of those films were born from the novels, novellas, and short stories from the world's community of sci-fi authors. Being a rather large community, it would be prohibitive to attempt a review of its sum total. Suffice it to say, this chapter can only try to gain a better view of those writers whose work has been translated into major cinematic works since 1970. If your favorite sci-fi writer has been neglected, my apologies—but you can include him or her when you write *your* book.

And, just a reminder: This is a book on sci-fi films, not sci-fi authors (Another time, perhaps.)

Common Traits of the Species, Scribner Fantastica

Trying to codify the makeup of a sci-fi writer is near impossible, just as it's difficult to describe the typical poker player or music teacher. They come in all shapes and sizes, ages and styles. However, a very broad and general profile could be assembled for the science fiction writer, albeit taken with an enormous grain of sodium chloride.

It goes without saying the sci-fi writer has a mind that's wired in a truly unique way. They see and write of things that aren't there, that don't exist. In many cases, they never did and never will (but who can really say?). Call it imagination; call it inspiration; call it insanity; whatever they have, it takes the reader where he or she has never been before.

The sci-fi writer often has a sense of advanced intelligence, natural and/or acquired. While the concept of owning a high IQ can vary, there's no denying many of the authors have scientific backgrounds (duh!) excelling in fields of medicine, mathematics, physics, astronomy, and more. Their ability to apply scientific principles—real and bogus—in fantastic ways through their storytelling becomes the very crux of sci-fi stories.

Like it or not, most sci-fi writers are male, although a handful of women have made their mark in the field. Sidestepping the fantasy worlds of *Harry Potter* novels and the *Hunger Games* books, by J. K. Rowling and Suzanne Collins, respectively, female writers of true science fiction have found themselves in a quandary (although the film versions of those above-mentioned literary series have found a large and loyal viewership). Just as women strive for legitimacy in the real world of science, so do they fight for a voice in writing science fiction. Just don't forget: Mary Shelley was a twenty-one-year-old novelist when she brought the man-made monster known as *Frankenstein* into the world nearly two hundred years ago. There's room for everyone.

Turning Verbiage into Visuals

From the days of the Golden Age of science fiction and before (figure 1950 and prior) came groundbreaking authors such as Jules Verne, H. G. Wells, Edgar Rice Burroughs, and Aldous Huxley, among others (subjects of a future book on classic sci-fi films). Around that same time, more standard bearers like Isaac Asimov, Robert A. Heinlein, Richard Matheson, and Philip K. Dick paved the way for writers like Arthur C. Clarke, and Frank Herbert.

But often, the time between story publication and film production has been substantial. For example, more than forty-five years separated Dick's short story "Minority Report" and its loose cine adaptation by Steven Spielberg. Forty years elapsed between the novel and cinema versions of Heinlein's *Starship Troopers*. Almost twenty years passed between the print release of Herbert's novel *Dune* and the less-than-successful David Lynch film version.

In other cases, film deals seem to have been signed at nearly the same time the literary publication occurred. Only in his twenties, Michael Crichton published his first novel, *The Andromeda Strain*, in 1969. It hit the silver screen just two years later. The same gap separated the book and film of his 1972 work *The Terminal Man*. Ditto for Crichton's fabulously famous *Jurassic Park* and its sequel, *Jurassic Park: Lost World*, in the 1990s.

Who Are These People?

Robert A. Heinlein

Born in 1907 in Missouri, young Robert Heinlein was only three when Halley's Comet roared across the night's sky. No matter that he probably didn't notice it; the event just might have made some impression with him, as he became fascinated with astronomy. Similarly, he found novels of science fiction to his tastes, as he consumed everything by Wells, Verne, and Burroughs.

At age seventeen, Heinlein joined the Naval Academy, setting his sights on a career as a naval officer. But he contracted tuberculosis and retired in 1934, considered unfit for the military for medical reasons. A quick sampling of college at UCLA and a failed attempt to enter local politics in California in 1938 left him broke and unsure how he would make a living of any kind.

Robert A. Heinlein.

Noting an ad for new authors in a pulp publication known as *Thrilling Wonder Stories*, Heinlein spent four days writing a story called "Life-Line." But he felt it was too good for the magazine and instead submitted it to a rival publication, *Astounding Science-Fiction*, edited by John Campbell Jr. The story became the first of many to be printed in the magazine. Yet Heinlein wrote only as he pleased and found himself willing to quit writing within a few years. But his passion for science fiction was great, and he quickly returned to write for the myriad of pulp sci-fi mags of the day, as well as beginning to create larger literary works.

When World War II drew America into its grip, Heinlein became an aviation engineer for the war effort. Not surprisingly, he penned a letter to the navy, suggesting they get into the business of space exploration. Reaching the upper echelons of President Truman's administration, the proposal was trash-canned when the navy discovered their ships wouldn't be practical in launching space-craft. Their loss would become the air force's eventual gain.

After the war, Heinlein and his wife Virginia settled in Colorado, where the somewhat paranoid author figured they were safe from nuclear attacks on major American cities. He continued to deliver short stories and novels in the science fiction genre, but he had another goal: Hollywood.

Working with Alford "Rip" van Ronkel and James O'Hanlon, Heinlein wrote the screenplay for 1950's *Destination Moon*, as well as acting as technical advisor. Produced by George Pal, the film was one of the first real sci-fi epics and won the 1951 Academy Award for Special Effects.

One of several juvenile novels written by Heinlein, *Space Cadet*, was adapted for early 1950s television as *Tom Corbett: Space Cadet*. The show made the rounds on all major networks for several years, but Heinlein had no active role in writing or advising for its production.

One of the author's major works was *The Puppet Masters*, a 1951 novel originally published in serial form in *Galaxy Science Fiction* magazine. The story of an alien invasion fought by American agents and set in the near future, it smacked of the Communist paranoia that prevailed across America at the time. It would take more than forty years before the novel was adapted for the screen, as a 1994 film starring Donald Sutherland that, by the admission of one of its screenwriters, was "God-awful."

Another novel in the 1950s was Heinlein's *Starship Troopers*. Once again, it was serialized in an abridged format, this time in 1959's *The Magazine of Fantasy and Science Fiction*, before full publication. Despite some views that the story of a young man's experiences in joining the military and fighting in an interstellar war against "bugs" glorified war, the book won the 1960 Hugo Award for best sci-fi novel. (*Starship Troopers*' adaptation into a 1997 film is noted elsewhere in this book.)

Heinlein had been working for years on a huge story that he called—at different times—*A Martian Named Smith*, *The Heretic*, and *The Man from Mars*. Finished in 1960, it was published the next year as *Stranger in a Strange Land*. Inspired by the character of Mowgli in Kipling's *The Jungle Story*, Heinlein's

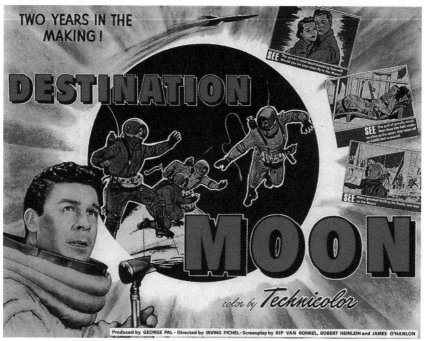

Destination Moon half-sheet—1950.

book told of a human, born and raised on the planet Mars, who came to Earth as an outsider. Once again, the book was a great success and controversial, with themes of politics, religion, and sexuality raising some eyebrows (not to mention the book's sacred Martian tradition of eating the corpses of deceased loved ones. Ick. Obviously, Heinlein never met my Aunt Trudy—he would definitely pass on dessert). Still, it was considered the best sci-fi novel of the year, taking another Hugo Award. Yet, while the title has been used in numerous (mostly unrelated) TV shows across the years, and many have considered it, *Stranger in a Strange Land* has never been made into a big-screen movie.

In the 1960s, Heinlein and his wife decided that Colorado Springs was no longer safe from nukes. It might have been due to the fact that NORAD and the Air Force Academy had headquartered themselves basically next door to the author since he had moved in, making the area an ideal site for "ground zero" in a nuclear strike.

Settling near Santa Cruz, California, Heinlein continued to write (and win awards, as he took yet another Hugo for *The Moon Is a Harsh Mistress*" in 1967). Regarding all things lunar, when astronaut Neil Armstrong placed man's first step onto the moon's surface in July 1969, Heinlein joined fellow sci-fi author Arthur C. Clarke as commentators with news anchor Walter Cronkite on CBS-TV's live coverage of the historic event.

Poor health vexed the author in the 1970s and 1980s, including issues with peritonitis, a stroke-like transient ischemic attack, and carotid bypass surgery. Still, Heinlein wrote when he could, although much would not be released at the time. Published novels included *The Number of the Beast, Friday,* and *To Sail Beyond the Sunset,* his last in 1987.

Heinlein died at age eighty in 1988, with his novels and collections of stories continuing to sell and amaze sci-fi-fans around the world.

Richard Matheson

A prolific writer of sci-fi novels, short stories, as well as film and television screenplays, Richard Matheson's work has influenced other notables like Stephen King and Dean Koontz. He was born in New Jersey in 1926 and first published as a child, with stories and poems in the *Brooklyn Daily Eagle* newspaper. Like many, Matheson finished high school and entered the army infantry during World War II.

After the war, he earned a degree in journalism and, always interested in the fantasy genre, wrote a short story called "Born of Man and Woman." He sold the tale to *The Magazine of Fantasy and Science Fiction* in the summer of 1950, the first of many for magazines like it and *Galaxy Science Fiction,* among others.

Matheson penned his first sci-fi novel in 1954, *I Am Legend.* It is the story of Robert Neville, the last living man on Earth and his fight against a world of zombie-like vampires (or are they vampire-like zombies? Whatever.). Inspired

"This may be the most terrifying novel you will ever read."

—William Campbell Gault
Prize Winning Mystery Novelist

25¢

GOLD MEDAL BOOK

417

I AM LEGEND

Richard Matheson

Richard Matheson's first sci-fi novel—1954.

by the 1931 version of *Dracula* with Bela Lugosi, Matheson figured if one vampire was scary, an entire world of them would be heart-stopping.

The novel became the basis for three attempts at creating a heart-stopping film (although countless more movies, including director George Romero's 1968 classic *Night of the Living Dead*, used the story's basic premise). In 1964, Matheson himself wrote the screenplay for an adaptation called *The Last Man on Earth*, starring Vincent Price, although he was less than pleased with the final film. *The Omega Man*, with Charlton Heston, was made in 1971, with significant changes from Matheson's original story. (The 2007 version of *I Am Legend* is covered elsewhere in this book.)

In 1953, Matheson saw an innocent-sounding film called *Let's Do It Again*. In it was a scene where Ray Milland's character left in a hurry and mistakenly grabbed someone else's hat. Placing it on his head, he found it to be much bigger than he expected, as it hung over his eyes and ears. Matheson wondered what might happen if a man discovered the same problem, but with his own hat. With that thought, the author wrote the novel *The Shrinking Man*, published in 1956. Universal-International Pictures liked the story and bought it, agreeing to the provision that Matheson be allowed to write the screenplay. Released in 1957 as *The Incredible Shrinking Man*, it was a huge success and earned the first Hugo Award for Outstanding Movie.

The following years found Matheson writing for Hollywood, including adapting many of his short stories for the *Twilight Zone* television show and working with director Roger Corman on many of his campy film adaptations of Edgar Allan Poe stories. Later in the 1960s, the author wrote scripts for *Star Trek* and, into the 1970s, *Rod Serling's Night Gallery*.

The April 1971 issue of *Playboy* magazine printed Matheson's short story of a highway driver menaced by a trucker and his relentless eighteen-wheeler. Simply titled "Duel," it was purchased and produced as a made-for-TV movie, with Matheson adapting his story for the screenplay. It was directed by a young filmmaker named Steven Spielberg.

In 1975, his *Bid Time Return* novel—a story of a love-smitten man who travels in time back to the nineteenth century to find a stage actress whose picture has captured his attention—won the World Fantasy Award for Best Novel. Five years later, Matheson would write the screenplay for its film version, called *Somewhere in Time*, starring Christopher Reeve and Jane Seymour.

Richard Matheson remained busy for sixty years, continuing to pen novels, short stories, and screenplays. Early in 2013, it was announced that, aged eighty-seven and with his son Richard Jr., Matheson would write the script for MGM's remake of *The Incredible Shrinking Man*. Sadly, he passed away in June of that year.

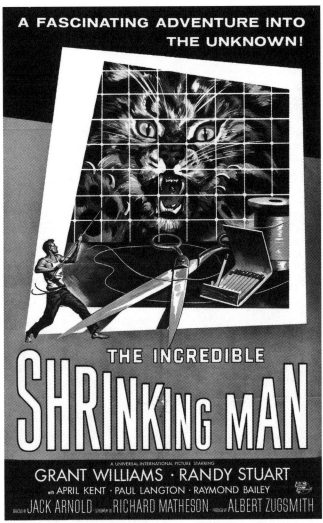

The Incredible Shrinking Man one-sheet—1957.

Philip K. Dick

Despite the fact that he was a prolific writer of sci-fi for more than thirty years, the world would not see a Philip K. Dick story on the silver screen until three months after his passing in 1982. *Blade Runner*, starring Harrison Ford, was the first of quite a few posthumous productions highlighting the author's work.

Born in Chicago in 1928 with a twin sister named Jane, Philip Kindred Dick soon found his life to be one of extreme and unique challenges. His sister died just six weeks after birth, which, along with the divorce of his parents when he was only five, may have contributed to deep periods of anxiety and mental instability. Dick and his mother relocated to California, where he discovered science fiction at the age of twelve. A voracious reader, his tastes ran from pulp sci-fi magazines to works of authors like James Joyce and Gustave Flaubert. He graduated high school and attended the University of California at Berkeley studying philosophy, albeit briefly, before quitting in 1949.

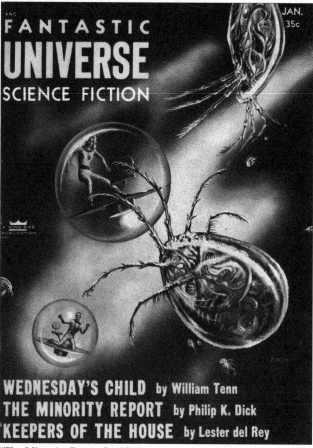

"The Minority Report"—1951.

Working in several music shops, Dick began to write science fiction with the encouragement of sci-fi editor and co-founder of *The Magazine of Fantasy and Science Fiction* Anthony Boucher. The young author was soon selling many of his short stories to the large number of sci-fi mags of the time.

When he met famed sci-fi writer A. E. Van Vogt in 1954, Dick was advised to write novels rather than short stories, as they simply paid more. While that may have been the case, Dick often found himself in a financial bind, at one point with the Internal Revenue Service. Several times, he received monetary help from fellow sci-fi author Robert Heinlein.

Dick's stories often touched on themes of government subversion, raising the eyebrows of the FBI and other law officials. He frequently received unexpected visits from Bureau agents in the fifties, and after a suspicious house break-in 1971, it was suggested that Dick move out of Marin County in Northern California.

As a sci-fi writer, Dick won the 1963 Hugo Award for Best Novel, *The Man in the High Castle*. Offering an alternate view of history, it told of America after World War II, but with the Axis coming out on top. The United States found itself split between German, Japanese, and Italian control. The Hugo was the first of many kudos for Dick's sci-fi writing.

By his own admission, Dick was not a writer who focused on the technology of sci-fi. Rather, he concentrated on people and their problems—the human predicament—despite the time frame. In a 1978 interview in *The Aquarian*, he said, "it doesn't matter if it's centuries in the future, the predicament is still the same." The author often sided with the everyday person—the little man—rather than superman-like characters.

In the last few years of Dick's writing, after a prolonged period of substance abuse, he was strongly influenced by what he believed was an extraterrestrial encounter. A seemingly innocent pendant worn by a delivery girl bathed Dick in a beam of pink light—the author felt reborn and experienced a series of hallucinations. The result was a series of three somewhat autobiographical novels known as the *VALIS Trilogy*, as well as a one-million-word diary/journal he called *Exegesis*.

In 1982, after several strokes, Philip K. Dick died at the age of fifty-three. Curiously, his stories began to reach Hollywood just at that time, with *Blade Runner, Total Recall*, and *Minority Report* (all covered in depth elsewhere in this book) hitting the big screen in the twenty years to follow. Other films derived from Dick stories include:

- *Screamers*, in 1996, based on the 1953 short story "Second Variety"
- *Impostor*, in 2002, based on the 1953 short story
- *Paycheck*, in 2003, based on the 1953 short story
- *A Scanner Darkly*, in 2006, based on the 1977 novel
- *Next*, in 2007, based on the 1954 short story "The Golden Man"
- *The Adjustment Bureau*, in 2011, based on the 1954 short story "Adjustment Team"

Additionally, *The Man in the High Castle* was announced in development as a four-part TV series by the Syfy Channel in 2013, as well as the BBC's possible production of *Flow My Tears, the Policeman Said*, Dick's 1975 novel. The folks at Disney announced an animated version of *King of the Elves*, another early short story by the author, although a release date was never mentioned.

Michael Crichton

Unlike many writers of sci-fi who found their efforts at attending college to be unsuccessful, Michael Crichton took his schooling about as far as one could go. He achieved a bachelor of arts degree in anthropology (Phi Beta Kappa and summa cum laude) from Harvard, as well as earning a medical degree from the same institution, plus postdoctoral work at the Salk Institute and visiting writer at MIT. Suffice it to say, sci-fi writers come in all forms.

Michael Crichton was born in Chicago in 1942 and grew up on Long Island in New York. By age fourteen, he had published a piece on travel in the *New York Times*. But his desire to major in English at Harvard was dampened when a teacher condemned his style of writing. Crichton switched to anthropology, then entered Harvard Medical School. To support his education, he wrote and sold several novels under pseudonyms.

He never sought licensing to practice as a doctor and wrote his first sci-fi novel in 1969. Titled *The Andromeda Strain*, it combined his medical knowledge with a thrilling story of scientists who must save the world from a deadly alien microorganism. It quickly reached the top of the booksellers' charts and introduced Crichton to the world as the next great sci-fi author.

Michael Crichton.

Two years later, Universal Pictures and director Robert Wise adapted Crichton's novel, featuring a low-impact cast including Arthur Hill, Kate Reid, and David Wayne. The film earned two Oscar nominations, for Best Art Direction and Best Film Editing, and featured special visual effects by Doug Trumbull, who had masterminded the visuals in 1968's *2001: A Space Odyssey*. The novel was again adapted in 2008 miniseries on the SciFi Channel.

Crichton's next foray into sci-fi was *The Terminal Man* in 1972, first serialized in three issues of *Playboy* magazine. The story concerns an epileptic computer programmer named Benson, whose seizures leave him dazed and confused. Doctors implant electrodes and a microprocessor into his brain in an experimental attempt to control his attacks with pleasurable pulses. The procedure works but backfires, as Benson finds he can control the pulses on his own. Unfortunately, Benson also becomes extremely violent as a result.

The novel was adapted for the silver screen in 1974, with George Segal in the title role. Crichton wrote a screenplay, but producers had director Mike Hodges write a final version for shooting. In general, the novel and movie made little impact, and, in fact, the film was never even released in the United Kingdom.

Around the same time, Crichton entered the film world head-on, writing and directing the sci-fi film *Westworld*, for MGM. (The film is covered in-depth elsewhere in this book.)

The author then broke from the genre, writing *The Great Train Robbery*, *Eaters of the Dead*, and *Congo*, among others in the late 1970s and early 1980s. Crichton also stayed with cinema, writing and directing the film version of Robin Cook's *Coma* in 1978, a 1981 sci-fi film about cosmetic surgery, the world of fashion modeling, and a computer company that creates 3-D models of the models called *Looker*, and a 1984 sci-fi film starring Tom Selleck, Kirstie Alley, and KISS bassist Gene Simmons called *Runaway*.

A novel about the discovery of an enormous alien spacecraft deep in the Pacific Ocean, *Sphere*, was published in 1987 and became a Barry Levinson–directed film in 1998. As 1990 approached, Crichton was about to score his biggest hit yet.

Originally conceived as a screenplay about a college student who diddled with dinosaur DNA, Crichton reworked the idea to include a unique theme park, and he wrote a novel called *Jurassic Park*. Published in 1990, it became a smash motion picture in 1993, with two sequels (his *Lost World*, the follow-up novel, was published in 1995) and a third scheduled for 2014 has been reset for an undisclosed date. (The original movie is covered in-depth elsewhere in this book.)

Ever busy, Crichton wrote *Rising Sun* in 1992, made by director Philip Kaufman the next year. His novel on sexual harassment, *Disclosure*, was published in 1993 and directed the following year by Barry Levinson. Crichton also created and executive produced the highly popular NBC-TV series *ER*, which ran for fifteen seasons beginning in 1994.

In 1996, Crichton produced and cowrote the screenplay for *Twister*, a film directed by Jan De Bont that turned the natural weather phenomenon of a tornado into a snarling, Godzilla-like monster, bent on killing everything and everyone in its path. Starring Bill Paxton and Helen Hunt, it took in more than $240 million at the American box office.

Timeline, published in 1999, involved a team of archaeological students who traveled back in time to the fourteenth century in France during the Hundred

Years War to rescue their professor who has gone before them. The 2003 film, directed by Richard Donner, lost a bundle at the box office.

Entering the twenty-first century, Michael Crichton continued to publish novels steeped in speculative science fiction, medicine, genetics, technology, and more. He published *Prey* in 2002, *State of Fear* in 2004, and *Next* in 2006. Continuing to write, he had finished *Pirate Latitudes* and begun work on *Micro* when he surprisingly succumbed to lymphoma and throat cancer in 2008, at the age of sixty-six. The incredibly productive author had sold more than two hundred million books in a diverse career that spanned more than forty years.

Even more authors and their stories . . .

Aye, Robot(s)

In the annals of sci-fi literature, there have been two different—and unrelated—storylines with the same title of *I, Robot*. Even though they are from separate authors (three, to be exact), they do share some connections.

In 1939, Eando Binder penned a short story called "I, Robot." Actually, that's not true—two writers, brothers named Earl and Otto Binder, wrote the story. Combining their first initials created the pen name of "Eando" (E and O, get it? Hey, I didn't make this up, so don't come down on me . . .). The story was first published in *Amazing Stories* magazine, with nine more in the series to follow.

The title robot was named Adam Link, who relates the sad story of his creator's accidental death, for which the cyborg was wrongly blamed. Despite its innocence, the story closes with Adam deciding to shut himself down for good . . . until the next story came along.

Fast-forward twenty-five years, and the great ABC-TV anthology series *The Outer Limits*, adapted some of the Binder stories into a one-hour episode called "I, Robot." The 1990s version of the series remade "I, Robot" once more.

Nineteen-year-old Isaac Asimov, a fledgling sci-fi writer himself, happened to meet the Binders at a sci-fi society meeting in 1939. He told the brothers how much he enjoyed their story of Adam Link, and a short time later, Asimov began writing a series of short stories about a robot named Robbie (which happened to be the title of his first story). When published in a 1940 issue of *Super Science Stories*, it was oddly retitled "Strange Playfellow."

In total, ten short stories were published between 1940 and 1950, in *Super Science Stories* and *Astounding Science Fiction* magazines. When they were combined as a single collection in 1950, Asimov wanted to call the book *Mind and Iron*. His publisher wanted *I, Robot*. When the author pointed out that Eando Binder had already published a story with that title, the publisher made a crude sexual suggestion about Binder, and *I, Robot* was a done deal.

Emerging from the Asimov stories was a basic building block in sci-fi literature: The Three Laws of Robotics:

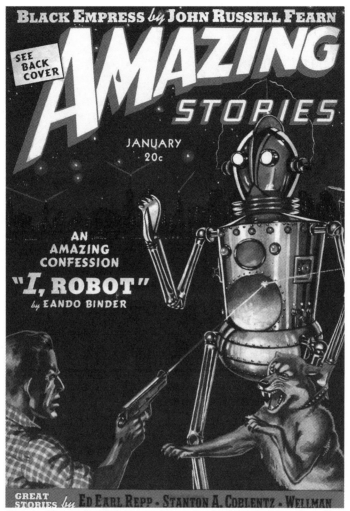

Cover of January, 1939 issue of *Amazing Stories* magazine, featuring "I, Robot".

1. A robot may not injure a human being or, through inaction, allow a human being to come to harm.
2. A robot must obey the orders given to it by human beings, except where such orders would conflict with the First Law.
3. A robot must protect its own existence as long as such protection does not conflict with the First or Second Law.

These tenets would be used, abused, and adapted by dozens—if not hundreds—of sci-fi authors and screenwriters from that point on. When Twentieth Century-Fox produced the big-screen film called *I, Robot* in 2004, the Three Laws were established early on in the flick. (The film is covered in-depth elsewhere in this book.)

The Clumsy Guy in the Sky

Author Walter Tevis was hardly a workaholic, prolific writer like some of his peers. But as one might guess, what might have been deficient in quantity was certainly balanced by great quality.

Born in 1928 in San Francisco, Tevis received undergrad and grad degrees in English lit from the University of Kentucky. He taught high school while publishing mainstream short stories in magazines like *The Saturday Evening Post*, *Esquire*, and *Playboy*. He eventually became a professor at Ohio University for many years and died from lung cancer in 1984, at the age of fifty-six.

His first novel, *The Hustler*, was published in 1959 and told the story of a brash pool shark who sought the best players around, including Minnesota Fats, to reach the top. It became a classic film, stark and gritty, starring Paul Newman in 1963.

That same year, Tevis published his next novel, a sci-fi story about an alien who came to our planet in an effort to save the population of his ravaged world. *The Man Who Fell to Earth* was received as one of the finest sci-fi novels ever written.

Director Nicholas Roeg originally wanted sci-fi author Michael Crichton to star in his 1976 cinema production of *The Man Who Fell to Earth*. Tevis' main character, Thomas Jerome Newton, was described as being very tall, and Crichton, at six foot, nine inches, clearly fit the bill. Cooler heads prevailed, and rock star David Bowie was cast in his first film role as Newton. Candy Clark, Rip Torn, and Buck Henry rounded out the lead characters. Receiving mixed reviews upon its release, *The Man Who Fell to Earth* has taken on a cult following in its more recent years. In 1987, ABC-TV aired a made-for-TV version of *The Man Who Fell to Earth*, intended as a pilot for a regular series. The enthusiasm was underwhelming, and that ended that.

Hey! How Ya Dune?

Despite creating a substantial body of sci-fi work, both novels and short stories, Frank Herbert only had one of those works adapted into a major motion picture. Its source is a well-known and well-read mainstay in sci-fi lit, having been translated into many languages and selling an amazing twenty million copies.

Frank Herbert's *Dune*, the first of his six novels in the Dune universe, was published in 1965, following six years of research. Starting as a magazine article on the US Department of Agriculture's use of grasses to reduce the erosive effects of wind on sand dunes, the novel evolved as Herbert discovered he'd amassed a drawer full of material and it might make a great sci-fi story. It did, as *Dune* won the 1966 Hugo Award, as well as the Nebula Award for best novel. The book was an early nod to ecological concerns, as well as politics, philosophy, and religion.

The author was born in 1920 in Washington State, growing up as an avid reader of books, including the Rover Boys, Wells, Verne, and Burroughs. He possessed great natural intelligence but never finished college—he wished to take only courses that interested him.

Herbert lied about his age in 1939 to begin a career in journalism as a writer, copy editor, and photographer for several Washington newspapers. After serving in the Navy Seabees during the war, he began to sell short stories to pulp magazines and in 1952 sold his first sci-fi short story. Titled "Looking for Something?" it appeared in *Startling Stories*.

Frank Herbert.

More sci-fi short stories followed, with Herbert publishing his first sci-fi novel, *The Dragon in the Sea*, in early 1956. The story of life on a futuristic submarine originally appeared in a series as "Under Pressure" in *Astounding Science Fiction* in late 1955.

The original *Dune* was published in eight installments, showing up in *Analog Science Fact/Science Fiction* from 1963 to 1965 as *Dune World* and *The Prophet of Dune*. When Herbert reworked the parts into a four-hundred-page novel, it was then rejected by as many as twenty publishers. One, however, was willing to take a chance. Chilton—yes, the folks who publish all those fix-'em-up car manuals—gave the author an advance of $7,500 to publish a hardcover edition of *Dune*.

Warp ahead nearly twenty years. Despite several aborted efforts in the 1970s to bring the saga of *Dune* to movie theaters, the process finally began to take shape in the early 1980s. Producer Dino De Laurentiis purchased the film rights and selected talented and quirky David Lynch to write, direct, and bring it to life. Young actors like Kyle MacLachlan and rock star Sting were cast against Oscar winners like Jose Ferrer and Linda Hunt.

The production was big, bold, and—a bust, at least in America. Budgeted at $40 million—a lot in those days—it grossed only $31 million. While it did better in the international markets, *Dune* still left a bad taste in Lynch's mouth. The studio insisted the film run no more than two hours and seventeen minutes—anything longer would eliminate one showing per day in theaters. Despite the fact that the complex and expansive story of *Dune* required more screen time, Lynch was forced to deliver a film of 137 minutes in length.

In 2000, the SciFi Network broadcast a three-part miniseries—nearly four and a half hours in length—called *Frank Herbert's Dune*, which received a much more positive response, including winning two Emmys in technical categories. Three years later, the cable network presented *Children of Dune*, crafted from Herbert's *Dune Messiah* and *Children of Dune* novels.

The author, however, would never get to share in those triumphs, as he died in 1986 after an extended bout with cancer.

Just Wild About Harry

Harry Harrison, born in Connecticut in 1925, grew up in New York with an interest in art and illustration. But life during the Great Depression meant frequent moves from apartment to apartment. The nomadic lifestyle would stay with Harrison and his family for much of his life.

He discovered science fiction from the multitude of pulp magazines he read and became one of the original members in the Queens, New York, chapter of the Science Fiction League. Started by sci-fi visionary and editor Hugo Gernsback, the league was designed to further the fascinating world of science fiction. Harrison began to write and draw for sci-fi publications in his early teens.

Drafted into the US Army Air Corps, Harrison's intelligence tests found him ranking very high and placed him as a specialist with power-aided, computerized (albeit very rudimentary) gun sights. After the war, he attended several art schools, focusing on illustration and cartooning.

Harrison was soon working with comic art greats like Wally Wood and began to draw for EC comics like *Weird Science* and pulp mags like *Worlds Beyond*. Harrison's first story, "Rock Diver," was printed in the magazine in 1951, and he was soon editing some of the sci-fi publications he had drawn for. As a freelancer, he was also writing most of the *Flash Gordon* comic strips through the 1950s and 1960s, while he and his family moved between Mexico, Great Britain, Italy, Denmark,

Harry Harrison.

and then San Diego, California. Harrison finally landed back in the UK for good in the mid-1970s.

Along with short stories and essays, Harrison published a series of sci-fi stories with great humor, most notably *Bill, the Galactic Hero* in the 1960s and the *Stainless Steel Rat* in the 1980s.

The author's first novel, *Plague from Space*, was published in 1965. The following year, a story of overpopulation and food shortage in the near future—*Make Room! Make Room!*—appeared on bookshelves. It would become the basis for the 1973 sci-fi film *Soylent Green*, starring Charlton Heston and Edward G. Robinson. (The film is discussed in depth elsewhere in this book.)

Harrison continued to write past the age of eighty, passing away in England in 2012.

Logan Can Run, but He Can't Hide

Imagine a world in the future where, in order to keep the population and limited resources in check, folks are required to die at the age of twenty-one. Authors William F. Nolan and George Clayton Johnson did, and, in 1967, *Logan's Run* was published as a novel.

Nolan was born in 1928 in Kansas City, where he fell in love with science fiction by the master, H. G. Wells. Nolan attended the KC Art Institute and joined Hallmark Cards as an illustrator. He and his family moved to Southern California in 1947.

The young man scuffled around, not sure what he would do for a living. He began to hang out with writers like Ray Bradbury, Richard Matheson, and Charles Beaumont, among others. At their urging, Nolan began to write and soon published some of his work in pulp magazines. In 1956, he wrote "The Darendinger Build-Up" and sold it to *Playboy* magazine for $500. William F. Nolan was officially a writer.

George Clayton Johnson was born in a Wyoming barn in 1929. Spending much of his childhood in an orphanage, he found reading was his passion. A dropout before reaching high school, Johnson shined shoes and tried his hand as a draftsman in an aerospace plant. A friend named Jack Russell encouraged him to try his hand at writing with the paper and pencils he brought home from the plant.

Together, they wrote a story that would be turned into a screenplay for a film that would become *Ocean's Eleven* in 1960 (and remade in 2001). It would appear that George Clayton Johnson was also—officially—a writer.

Hanging out with the same bunch of sci-fi writers as William F. Nolan, Johnson began to write for television. His first short story, "All of Us Are Dying," first appeared in a 1961 issue of *Rogue*, a men's magazine in the mold of *Playboy*. TV producer Rod Serling had already used the material in an episode of *The Twilight Zone* called "The Four of Us Are Dying." Johnson would eventually write eight episodes for the popular sci-fi and fantasy show, including the classic "Kick the Can."

As the 1960s progressed, the country and the world were rocked by the Vietnam Conflict, college campus unrest, and widening social and cultural differences between generations. Noting these events, Nolan imagined a society that would send people who reached the age of forty to their death and wrote an outline called "Killer Man, Killer Man, Leave My Door." He then teamed up with Johnson to turn the concept into a novel. The writing took just three weeks.

Logan's Run focused on Logan, a "Sandman" in the future who must eliminate those who have reached their expiration date. Those who refuse to go along with the government's policy become "runners," trying to stay one step ahead of Sandmen like Logan. The entire story changes when Logan turns twenty-one and becomes a runner himself.

The book was a hit, and within the decade, plans were made to turn *Logan's Run* into a feature motion picture. Released in 1976, the MGM film starred Michael York, Jenny Agutter, Farrah Fawcett, and Peter Ustinov. As has often been the case, many liberties were taken with the original story. As a result, Nolan and Johnson were disappointed when they saw the final result. It was not what they had written.

Audiences weren't particularly impressed either. With a budget of $9 million (a hefty sum in the mid-1970s), *Logan's Run* grossed $25 million. By comparison, *Star Wars*, released the following year, was produced for $11 million and brought nearly $220 million to the domestic box office in its initial run. Even so, *Logan's Run* was good enough to earn a Special Achievement Oscar for visual effects. It also spawned a CBS television series in 1977, albeit for a one-season run of fourteen episodes.

Nolan and Johnson kept writing in their separate ways. After the film's release, Nolan wrote two more Logan novels (without the aid of Johnson), as well as a novella and comic book series in the Logan universe. He also continued to write a large body of short stories, as well as poetry and essays. Johnson, who had written the screenplay for "The Man Trap," the very first *Star Trek* episode aired in 1966, was not as prolific. He still wrote some short stories and essays, but largely assembled compilations of teleplays and stories from his work with *The Twilight Zone*.

Thumbing a Ride to Alpha Centauri

Douglas Adams' *The Hitchhiker's Guide to the Galaxy* is a franchise unto itself. The life span of the work includes novels, a radio series, a TV series, an album, a computer game, stage productions, and a major motion picture.

Adams was born in Cambridge, England, in 1952. At the age of ten, he received a top mark for one of his written compositions and at age nineteen entered St. John's College. Though he eventually earned bachelor's and master's degrees in English lit, Adams really wanted to make folks laugh. While at St. John's, he had joined Footlights, a comedy club for students. He also started his own comedy trio with whom he could write and perform.

After a short and failed partnership with Monty Python's Graham Chapman, Adams took a number of odd jobs while he searched for work writing radio comedy. He wound up at BBC Radio 4, where he met producer Simon Brett. The two agreed the time was right for a sci-fi comedy show on the radio.

Adams claimed the idea for the *Hitchhiker's Guide to the Galaxy* show came to him while he was in a drunken stupor somewhere in Austria in 1971. But being in a drunken stupor, he really wasn't sure. No matter, the first series of six episodes featured Earthling Arthur Dent, who discovered

Douglas Adams.

from his friend Ford Prefect (based on the name of a real British motorcar) that the world was about to be demolished in order to make room for an intergalactic highway. Conveniently, Prefect was actually an alien who wrote for a travel guide called *The Hitchhiker's Guide to* . . . you-know-where. The duo barely escaped annihilation on one of the demolition spacecraft, made their way onto a hijacked spaceship—and then it got really weird. The shows were broadcast in early 1978; a second season—delayed multiple times—aired two years later.

By 1982, the shows had been rerun several times on BBC, broadcast in North America on National Public Radio (NPR) and the Canadian Broadcasting Company (CBC), as well as translated into German, French, and other languages. Quite obviously, *The Hitchhiker's Guide to the Galaxy* was an international hit.

Adams was convinced, reluctantly, to write a novel from the radio series. Completing it in 1979, he would eventually write four more books in the series (which he would refer to as "A trilogy in five parts"):

- *The Restaurant at the End of the Universe* (1980)
- *Life, the Universe and Everything* (1982)
- *So Long, and Thanks for All the Fish* (1984)
- *Mostly Harmless* (1992)

The books didn't come easily. Occasionally, Adams had to be locked into a hotel room with his editor for weeks at a time in order to make (and often miss) deadlines. The writer had overextended himself, at one time becoming a script editor for the BBC's sci-fi TV series *Doctor Who*, as well as writing a children's show called *Doctor Snuggles*.

Almost immediately, efforts were started to make *The Hitchhiker's Guide to the Galaxy* into a movie. In 1982, Columbia Pictures brought in Ivan Reitman to produce the film and Douglas Adams began to write the screenplay. By 1986, Reitman had gone off to make *Ghostbusters*, and Adams' script had been rewritten into an abominable mess. In 1992, Adams met with movie producer and former Monkee Michael Nesmith. It was rumored that James Cameron was interested in directing. But there was no studio interest in making the film. By 1997, Adams had selected Spyglass Entertainment for a production company and Jay Roach to direct, but he was deep into the *Austin Powers* spy spoofs, and his schedule was very tight. In 1998, Disney purchased the film rights, and it was decided that, as rumors suggested, Jim Carrey would not play Arthur Dent—he was not British. By 2000, Adams had finished a new screenplay, but Roach admitted studios had been hesitant to take the next step in production. The idea of a very expensive sci-fi comedy was intimidating; at one point, Roach referred to it as "Monty Python in space."

Everything came to a crashing halt in May 2001 when Adams had a massive heart attack and died at the age of forty-nine. Yet Roach was still determined to get the film made, and by the end of 2002, a rewritten script was ready. A few months later, Jay Roach had moved on, and the commercial/music video team of Hammer and Tongs (actually Nick Goldsmith and Garth Jennings) was recommended to produce and direct. With the pieces finally in place, *The Hitchhiker's Guide to the Galaxy* would shoot the next year and hit the screens in April 2005.

The public reaction to the film that took nearly twenty-five years to make was lukewarm. Produced on a budget of $50 million, *The Hitchhiker's Guide to the Galaxy* grossed those same amounts, domestically and internationally.

One would hope that somewhere in the galaxy, Douglas Adams was smiling.

The Father of Cyberpunk

Among the vast and diverse worlds of sci-fi is cyberpunk. Many have labeled it as "high tech, but low life." Usually set in the near future, cyberpunk often offers a dystopian view of society (think the opposite of "utopian"—that's right, the land of bleak and dreary). Sometimes, computer hackers, petty thieves, those cast out on the street will fight back against the government and the system that put them where they are.

The writer who was the first to venture into these worlds was William F. Gibson. Born in South Carolina in 1948, Gibson was a young boy when his father died suddenly, leaving the type of traumatic impact that seems to strike many sci-fi authors. Like them, Gibson immersed himself in reading science fiction and dreamed of being a writer one day.

As a teen, Gibson was sent to Arizona to attend a private boys' school. Still a voracious reader, he stumbled onto counterculture Beat writers like William S. Burroughs, Jack Kerouac, and Allen Ginsberg. Their style suited Gibson's tastes to a "T."

But at age eighteen, his mother also passed away. With no family and the military draft sending young Americans to Vietnam, Gibson moved to Canada, where he ended up making his residence permanent—even though his name was never called for military service.

In the 1970s, the author-to-be earned a degree in English from the University of British Columbia, and he took a renewed interest in the sci-fi that thrilled him as a boy. What's more, he found himself intrigued by the radical movement of punk music, with bands like the Boomtown Rats, the Sex Pistols, and the Screamers adding to the mix.

As a result, Gibson wrote a short story, "Fragments of a Hologram Rose," in 1977, publishing it in a small sci-fi magazine for new writers, *Unearth* (and receiving the princely sum of twenty-seven dollars for it). Four years passed before he published another short story, "Johnny Mnemonic," in *Omni* magazine.

That story, like many from Gibson, is set in a fictional area between the cities of Boston and Atlanta known as "The Sprawl." The title character is a mule of sorts; hijacked data is stored in a drive implanted in his head and delivered to those who will pay for it. Johnny comes up against the Japanese Mafia known as the Yakuza, and with the help of a tough cyborg girl named Molly, he escapes an assassin sent to eliminate him.

Sony Pictures budgeted $26 million to put *Johnny Mnemonic* on the big screen in 1995. Starring Keanu Reeves, the movie took large liberties with the original short story (to no one's surprise), and Gibson—having written the screenplay—wasn't really pleased with the final cut. Neither were filmgoers, as the flick grossed only $19 million, leaving somebody short a few bucks.

Gibson's short story "New Rose Hotel" appeared in a 1984 issue of *Omni* magazine. Set in the Far East, it features an unidentified narrator relating a story of corporate espionage, seduction, and murder. In the end, the narrator is left to hide from an assassin in the New Rose Hotel.

Fifteen years later, *New Rose Hotel* was made as a small art film featuring big-name talent like Christopher Walken and Willem Dafoe. Surprisingly, director Abel Ferrara, who also wrote the screenplay with Chris Zois, stayed close to Gibson's short story, and the author was pleased with the result. But with no real distribution to speak of, *New Rose Hotel* grossed just $20,000. (For some major movies, that's just the cost for on-set coffee.)

Among William Gibson's extensive body of work, *Neuromancer* stands out as the best for many. Published in 1984, the novel takes place in the locales of *New Rose Hotel* and *Johnny Mnemonic*—Japan and the Sprawl. The main character, Henry Case, is a digital cowboy—a computer hacker. But he's caught hacking his own employer and, as punishment, has his nervous system rearranged to make access to computers impossible. Drug addicted and suicidal, Case is saved by, and starts to work for, an enigmatic individual named Armitage. Case is teamed up with Molly (yup, the same character from *Johnny Mnemonic*). Together, they discover the power behind their actions is Neuromancer—a powerful AI (artificial intelligence.)

The novel scored a first among sci-fi literature, winning the "Triple Crown" of a Nebula Award, a Hugo Award, and the Philip K. Dick Award in 1985. Since then, more than seven million copies have been sold. The world of cyberpunk had become a force to consider in sci-fi.

Almost immediately, rumors began to circulate around the production of a film version of *Neuromancer*. And thirty years later, the rumors persist, but they are still speculation. Gibson himself admits that most of the talk is just "noise," even though director Vincenzo Natali—having helmed sci-fi flicks like *Cube* in 1997, *Cypher* in 2002, and *Splice* in 2009—has been attached since 2007. An advance poster from late 2012 infers the film may still become reality, but—unlike the very genre from which *Neuromancer* comes—seeing is believing.

Three, Two, One . . .

Contact was the product of a scientist—it was the only science fiction novel he wrote, although he penned sixteen other nonfiction books, some that became best sellers. He was one of the most visible and well-known men in his field, winning awards for his television broadcasts. His name was Carl Sagan.

Sagan was born in Brooklyn, New York, in 1934. As very young boy, he visited the 1939 New York World's Fair—an experience with technology that made an enormous impression on him. Before long, Sagan was combing the public library and museums, seeking any knowledge he could on astronomy, the stars, and the then-unexplored vastness of outer space.

With bachelor's and master's degrees in physics and doctorates in astronomy and astrophysics, Sagan performed research and taught at prestigious schools like Harvard and Cornell. He was also associated with NASA from its very start, advising in both manned and satellite space programs. It was Sagan who conceived the idea of attaching messages of greetings to the Pioneer 10 and Voyager space probes, both of which continue to travel billions and billions of miles into deep space today.

As a writer, Carl Sagan brought an ease and accessibility to science for the common reader. The Time-Life science series book *Planets*, was cowritten by Sagan in 1966, and his book on the development of human intelligence, *The Dragons of Eden*, won a Pulitzer Prize in 1978. The creator and host of the widely popular 1980 PBS television series *Cosmos*, Sagan and the show won numerous awards, including two Emmys, a Hugo, and a Peabody.

Carl Sagan was a supporter of SETI—the Search for Extraterrestrial Intelligence—and, with his wife Ann Druyan, wondered in 1979 what might be the result if aliens actually responded to one of SETI's radio signals? Their answer was a movie treatment for *Contact*. But as is often the case, developing the project became a long, drawn-out nightmare, and Sagan forged ahead and turned the treatment into a novel, earning the author an unprecedented $2 million advance from publisher Simon and Schuster. Published in 1985, *Contact* sold nearly 1.75 million copies in its first two years. It would eventually make its way to the big screen in 1997 (the film is covered in depth elsewhere in this book.)

Regrettably, Sagan would not see the release of *Contact*. With three bone marrow transplants for an anemia-like disease called myelodysplasia, he succumbed to pneumonia in late 1996 at the age of sixty-two. In 1980, sci-fi master and fellow scientist Isaac Asimov wrote that Carl Sagan was one of only two people in the world who was smarter than he was—high praise, indeed.

Carl Sagan.

The Baroness James of Holland Park, or . . .

P. D. James, is well known for her finely crafted detective novels featuring Adam Dalgliesh of Scotland Yard. Writing fourteen Dalgliesh mysteries since 1962, James strayed in 1992 to pen *The Children of Men*, a book she claimed was not sci-fi. But considering it is set in a (once again) dystopian society in the future, that sounds science-fiction-y enough for us.

James was born in Oxford, England, in 1920 (the P. D. stands for Phyllis Dorothy) and grew up in Cambridge. She had to quit school at sixteen and, despite a desire to attend college, began working. She married, and when her husband returned from WWII suffering from mental illness, James began work with the National Health Service.

She eventually shifted to the Home Office in the UK, which is responsible for national security, law enforcement and crime prevention, and immigration. It was great training for someone who wanted to write crime novels. Having a lifelong affair with reading books, she began to write one of her own in the 1950s.

Incredibly, her first submission to a publisher resulted in an acceptance, and *Cover Her Face* was published in 1962. Her husband died two years later, and even though she continued to write and publish crime novels, she also stayed with the Home Office until retiring in 1979.

The genesis for *The Children of Men* evolved from an article that outlined the fact that for some unknown reason, fertility in humans had experienced a dramatic decline in the last twenty years. James combined that concept with the fact that most life forms on Earth eventually die out—what if that happened to man? (Now there's a pleasant thought to keep.) The result in 1992 was a novel that she believed was a "moral fable," rather than a sci-fi novel. *The Children of Men* became a major motion picture in 2006 (covered in depth elsewhere in this book.)

P. D. James has been awarded the Order of the British Empire, honored as a Life peer with a seat in the House of Lords in Parliament (thus, the title of Baroness James of Holland Park), as well as receiving numerous literary prizes and honors, all of which are well earned.

Say "Hello" to *The Host*

Novelist Stephenie Meyer earned her notoriety (and a boatload of money) by writing the immensely popular *Twilight Saga* books. She broke away from the world of hormone-crazed vampire and werewolf teens long enough in 2008 to write a sci-fi story of alien occupation called *The Host*.

Born in Connecticut in 1973, she earned a bachelor of arts degree in English from Brigham Young University. While Meyer dreamed of being a writer, her reality was being a wife and mother of three young boys. But her persistence in pursuing a literary agent for her *Twilight* story paid off, and she suddenly found herself with a three-book contract and an advance check of three-quarters of a million dollars. Suddenly, Meyer had a new reality.

The series established Meyer as a writer of fantasy in the mold of J. K. Rowling, and her ravenous teenage

Stephenie Meyer.

characters rivaled Harry Potter and his mates at Hogwarts. Meyer also wanted to write an adult story, and, finding herself completely bored on a road trip from Phoenix to Salt Lake City, she began making up a story.

The resulting novel was *The Host*, published in 2008 with a first printing of 750,000 copies. Not surprisingly, it was released at the number one position on the bestseller list and stayed there for half a year. The story revolved around a race of aliens known as Souls, who invaded Earth. Wanderer, one of the Souls, took over the body of a young woman named Melanie, who didn't take very kindly to being inhabited by an alien.

By the fall of 2009, Meyer had sold the film rights for *The Host*, with Andrew Niccol—writer and director of 1997's *Gattaca* with Ethan Hawke and Uma Thurman—set to perform the same tasks with *The Host*. The release of the film, budgeted at $40 million, was anxiously awaited in early 2013. Audiences, however, were disappointed with it, as *The Host* grossed only $26 million domestically and another $21 million overseas.

Meyer promises more *Twilight* novels (from the perspectives of other characters than Bella) and more novels in the *Host* series, which, inevitably, promises to become more movies for hungry film fans.

2

The Future Is Closer Than You Think

The Worlds of Tomorrow

Will You Still Shove Me—Tomorrow?

It's mostly human nature that prompts us to expect the future will be better than the present—at least we can hope. Historically speaking, we know that technology tends to make a natural transition to processes or devices that are smaller, faster, more efficient, or somehow better than previously known. Sociologists and psychologists may believe that humans simply wish for a better life for our children than we experienced.

On the other hand, sci-fi films often opine that we've blown it (or blown it up, as suggested by Charlton Heston's Taylor in the climax of 1968's *Planet of the Apes*). The flicks largely predict our future will present a dystopian society, full of crime, doom, and despair. Movies that focus on tomorrow tend to imply that while the technology may be advanced, our behavior will not be. Often, the world has destroyed itself with excesses of greed, gluttony, or war. In other words, we've screwed everything up, so it's "That's it! Everyone out of the gene pool!"

Occasionally, a film will portray a future world where leisure time can be technologically enhanced (witness the vacation concepts of 1973's *Westworld* or 1990's *Total Recall*). But future sci-fi films tend to demonstrate a world where society (and/or the government) has cleaved itself into haves and have-nots. Much like the pre-1900 world for real, the suggestion in these flicks is that the middle class does not exist—there's only the upper and lower classes. Consider the 1993 *Demolition Man*, where there's a clear distinction of those who live above ground in bland serenity or those who fight to survive underground. Similarly, 2013's *Elysium* placed the fortunates on a luxurious space station, while the unfortunates struggled back on Earth.

Alternately, some sci-fi films offer a world where everything seems to be a lost cause. The 1973 *Soylent Green* delivered a society devastated by overpopulation and diminished natural resources. *The Terminator*, in 1984, offered a future where humans fought for their lives against machines that sought to eliminate them. In 1999's *The Matrix*, a similar concept had a machine-controlled world creating a false façade for humans trapped in it. The multiple film versions of the George Orwell novel *1984*, depict a sad society controlled by a totalitarian government.

The rare exceptions—sci-fi films that propose a utopian future world—are few and far between. After all, what good is a movie that has no conflict, no drama, no pain? Woody Allen's very funny 1973 *Sleeper* has a future where everyone sits around, getting high with their Orb and dallying in the Orgasmatron. But behind that society is a government that goes bananas when a single unaccounted-for human appears to gum up the works.

If anything, future sci-fi films may act as a dire warning to those of us in the present. Our task is to make sure those dastardly predictions of future failures don't turn science fiction into science fact. Or maybe our task is to just sit back, be entertained, and pass the popcorn.

I suggest you take the latter.

A Clockwork Orange

Synopsis

- 1971—British/Warner Brothers—137 min./color
- Director: Stanley Kubrick
- Original music: Walter (now Wendy) Carlos
- Film editing: Bill Butler
- Production design: John Barry
- Based on the 1963 novel by Anthony Burgess, who developed a special vocabulary, Nadsat, for the book. (Definitions appear in parentheses.)

Cast
- Malcolm Mcdowell (Alex De Large)
- Patrick Magee (Mr. Alexander)
- Warren Clarke (Dim)
- Adrienne Corri (Mrs. Alexander)
- Miriam Karlin (Cat Lady)
- James Marcus (Georgie)
- Aubrey Morris (Mr. Deltoid)
- Sheila Raynor (Mum)
- Philip Stone (Dad)
- Anthony Sharp (Minister of the Interior)
- Michael Tarn (Pete)
- Steven Berkoff (Det. Constable Tom)
- David Prowse (Julian)
- Clive Francis (Joe the Lodger)

Alex treats his Droogs to some ultra-violence in *A Clockwork Orange.*

Somewhere in the near future, a group of tough teenaged thugs relax in a milk bar called the Korova, quaffing molocko (milk). The leader of the group is the belligerent Alex, and his droogs (pals) are Dim, Georgie, and Pete. Anxious for a "bit of ultraviolence" (graphic and exciting brawling), they roll a drunk and beat up a rival group of toughs who are about to rape a woman.

Not to be outdone, Alex and his droogs motor to the home of author Mr. Alexander, where, wearing disguises, they break in. After severely beating Alexander, Alex cuts away the wife's knit jumpsuit while delivering a rousing chorus of "Singin' in the Rain." Alex puts "the old in-out in-out" (sexual intercourse) to Mrs. Alexander as his droogs restrain the couple.

The delinquents leave their home, and Alex rounds out his evening by playing with his pet snake and listening to Beethoven in his room. Alex really loves and respects only one thing in life—the music of "old Ludwig Van." "Pee and Em" (his parents) are hard-pressed to do anything about their vile and renegade son.

He misses school the next day and receives a visit from the truancy officer, Mr. Deltoid, who threatens Alex with prison if he continues his evil ways. Of course, Alex immediately picks up two teenage girls in a record shop and brings them home for a doubly-quick "in-out in-out."

That night, the droogs resent Alex's treatment of Dim, and they attempt a revolt. But Alex shows them who's the boss by cutting Dim's hand with a knife, and the mutiny quickly subsides. They break into the home of an eccentric "Catlady," where things get out of hand and Alex beats her with a giant phallic sculpture. As the police arrive, Dim smashes Alex in the face with a milk bottle and the droogs escape, leaving Alex holding the bag.

Alex is roughly handled at the police station, and when Mr. Deltoid informs him that the lady has died, Alex is sent off to prison. Once there, he plays the model prisoner while fantasizing about vile and bawdy activities all along. With a new political party in office, the Minister of the Interior inspects the prison. He offers a parole to anyone willing to take part in a new experimental treatment to tame pathological criminals—the Ludovico technique. Alex steps forward and accepts the challenge.

But it seems to be more than he bargained for, as he endures injections and a straitjacket while being forced to "viddy" (watch) incredible atrocities on film. Ironically, the music accompanying these sessions is all Beethoven. At first, Alex thinks the films are "real horrorshow" (good or great), but the Ludovico technique takes hold, and he soon becomes repulsed by the scenes. The treatments have become the ultimate torture for Alex, for he can no longer bear the music of Beethoven.

As a result of the treatments, the mere thought of violence now makes Alex physically sick. At a demonstration for prison officials, Alex takes the physical abuse and sexual temptation from the hired help while he responds by becoming ill. Those watching seem pleased with the results.

No longer considered a threat to society, Alex is now a free man. But Pee and Em have rented his room to Joe, and Alex is not welcome. Now homeless on the streets, a tramp recognizes Alex as his former assailant, and he is beaten by the tramp and his associates. The police break up the ruckus, but Alex is no better off, as the cops happen to be Dim and Georgie. They savagely beat and nearly drown Alex, leaving him for dead in the country.

He comes to the home of Mr. Alexander, now a crazed and widowed invalid. Attended to by Julian, his beefy bodyguard, Alexander takes the broken and bleeding Alex in. Alexander opposes the government's new direction and sees Alex as a victim of their abuse. But Alex makes the mistake of innocently crooning "Singin' in the Rain" while showering, and Mr. Alexander now knows who this young lad is.

Drugged with wine, Alex falls face-first into his meal of spaghetti and wakes up locked in an upstairs bedroom. With Julian's help, Alexander has set up an enormous set of loudspeakers and pumps thousands of watts of "Ludwig Van" into Alex's room. The torture is madness to Alex's "gulliver" (head), and he decides to "snuff it" (commit suicide) by jumping out the window.

But he survives and winds up in the hospital, where the government now admits Alex became a "victim" of the overly zealous doctors and their wayward treatment. Pee and Em now want Alex to come home, and the Minister of the Interior offers him a lucrative position. While newspaper photographers snap PR pictures of Alex and the Minister, the lad dreams of erotic encounters once again. He says, "I was cured all right."

Afterwords

The novel of *A Clockwork Orange* was not much of a literary success when it was first published in 1962. Yet in 1965, the then-manager of the Rolling Stones, Andrew Loog Oldham, had thoughts of Mick Jagger and the other tough-guy rockers being ideal to play Alex and his droogs in a film version. But Oldham couldn't secure the rights, and it's hard to imagine any way this film could have been made before the graphic violence and sexual revolution that opened up the cinematic world in the late 60s.

Still, in early 1968, movie producer Si Litvinoff approached director John Schlesinger about a film version of *A Clockwork Orange*. In a letter sent to Schlesinger, Mick Jagger was once again mentioned for the role of Alex, and, incredibly, the Beatles were keen on creating the soundtrack. Goo-goo-ga-joob, indeed.

Author Anthony Burgess drew much of the book's premise from his personal experiences, as his wife was brutally beaten and robbed during World War II. The pregnant woman lost her child from the ordeal and eventually died. Burgess claimed the only way he was able to produce such a brutal work was first to get himself into a state of near drunkenness. (The graphic sex and violence in the book are much stronger than depicted in Stanley Kubrick's film.)

The Alexander home invasion and rape scene didn't come easily. If it had been shot in a purely realistic manner, the scene wouldn't have had the same surreal quality of the rest of the film. Crews sat for five days as director Kubrick searched for a solution. Malcolm McDowell had the answer—he sang the famous "Singin' in the Rain" during the assault, giving the scene its needed absurdity, but chose that piece because it was the only song he knew *all* the words to.

It's said that artists often suffer for their craft—one scene in *A Clockwork Orange* proved that to be true. The uncomfortable sequence where Alex is forced to watch films of murder and mayhem while receiving eyedrops required actor McDowell to be strapped to a chair with his eyes held open with metal clips. Even with a real doctor applying the eyedrops, the result was a painful case of scratched corneas. After they healed in a few days, Kubrick insisted on one more retake for an extreme close-up. When a stunt man refused, McDowell found himself back in the chair. Recalling the recent discomfort, the resulting terror in his face was real.

Mr. Alexander's bodyguard, Julian, was played by David Prowse, who had played the monster in Hammer's *Horror of Frankenstein* in 1970. He would later become the monster in *Frankenstein and the Monster from Hell* in 1974 and, of course, the evil Darth Vader in the *Star Wars* trilogy of the 70s and 80s.

Unfortunately, the social impact of the film in Britain instigated a series of copycat crimes in the early 1970s. The offenses prompted Kubrick to consult with Scotland Yard, and at the decision of the director—not the British government—*A Clockwork Orange* was pulled from distribution in the UK in

1974. Shortly after Kubrick's death in 1999, the film was returned to open British distribution.

The box office in America seemed to accept the ultraviolent activities of Alex and his droogs. Made for slightly more than $2 million, *A Clockwork Orange* grossed more than $26 million for Warner Bros. during its initial release. Contemporaries also thought favorably of the film, nominating it for a Best Picture Oscar and Kubrick for Best Director.

THX 1138

Synopsis

- 1971—American/Warner Brothers—88 min./color
- Director: George Lucas
- Original Music: Lalo Schifrin
- Film Editing: George Lucas
- Art Director: Michael Haller

Cast

- Robert Duvall (THX)
- Donald Pleasence (Sen)
- Don Pedro Colley (Srt)
- Maggie Mcomie (Luh)
- Ian Wolfe (Pto)
- Sid Haig (Nch)
- James Wheaton (Voice of Omm)

Somewhere in a bleak dystopian future, life is devoid of emotion—even sex is illegal. Yet an omnipresent video screen—known as OMM 0910—always asks "What's wrong?" And no matter what the answer, the remedy is a prescription of drugs. Everyone is bald and clad in simple white clothing, except for the metal-faced robot police force, which wears black.

THX 1138 is a man who works in a plant that assembles these police officers. Efficiency and productivity are keys, with workers constantly being scrutinized and reminded from a massive, monitor-filled control room. The work is dangerous, with an ever-present risk of a radioactive disaster. A successful shift is considered to have dozens, rather than hundreds, of casualties.

A telephone booth–like kiosk acts as part confessional and part visit to a psychiatrist. THX reveals his errors at work and his own maladies, as a vacant voice hidden behind an image of Christ offers empty empathy and insincere encouragement.

THX has a female mate, LUH 3417, who shares his barren and sterile apartment. He relieves his sexual needs by automation while watching a nude dancer on a holographic screen, then changes channels to a robot cop beating someone.

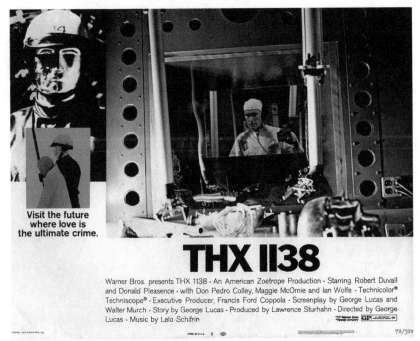

Visit the future
where love is
the ultimate crime.

THX 1I38

Warner Bros. presents THX 1138 · An American Zoetrope Production · Starring Robert Duvall
and Donald Pleasence · with Don Pedro Colley, Maggie McOmie and Ian Wolfe · Technicolor®
Techniscope® · Executive Producer, Francis Ford Coppola · Screenplay by George Lucas and
Walter Murch · Story by George Lucas · Produced by Lawrence Sturhahn · Directed by George
Lucas · Music by Lalo Schifrin

70/320

US lobby card—*THX 1138*.

LUH switches some of her meds with those of THX, despite warnings of dangerous interactions. THX confesses that he thinks he's dying from the meds and vomits, while the home video screen claims to understand everything. THX collapses and LUH tries to comfort him, and, even though it is illegal, they make love. The couple believes they are not being watched, but they are.

A male monitor named SEN 5241 changes LUH's shift, but THX believes a supervisor is not supposed to do that. SEN then arranges for THX to be his new roommate. Angered, THX reports the illegal shift change as a programming violation.

THX makes a critical error while handling radioactive material at the plant, due to an interfering mindlock order from the control room. The area is evacuated, but the mindlock on THX is quietly removed, and the danger passes.

Robotic police take THX into custody for suspected drug evasion and illegal sexual activity. At his trial, a prosecutor considers him incurable and recommends immediate destruction. THX seems to have a persuasive defense attorney as, while he is found guilty of the charges, he is sentenced to detention and conditioning.

In the lockup, THX is corralled by robot police, who prod at him with taser-like poles and run him in circles until he collapses. He is scanned, tested, and injected, then isolated. Technicians are inexperienced with their gear, throwing switches that place THX in various awkward and tormenting body positions.

LUH is allowed to see THX, and she reveals she is pregnant. The couple make love once more and then are separated by robot police, who take THX away. He is confined with several inmates, including SEN, who claims to have a plan for something escape. THX sits in silence.

PTO, an elderly inmate, rants about theological ideas, while inmate NCH upends and stomps an android police officer. SEN shares food with THX, claiming a bond with him and spouting thoughts of dissent. THX returns the biscuits and walks into the blank distance with SEN following.

They come upon a man—SRT 5752—who claims to know the way out, but the doorway opens to masses of thousands of people moving aimlessly through the tunnels. SEN gets caught up in the crowds and is separated from THX. It seems that SRT is actually a hologram who wants to be real.

THX and SEN are reported missing, with a reward for their return. SEN rides a train, then walks empty corridors. But he seems frightened by the experience and returns to the train. SEN confesses to OMM 0910 that he wants to go back to where he was before. A monk confronts him, and SEN assaults the man. He then plays with some children until police pick him up.

THX and SRT move quietly among banks and banks of electronic racks, evading police who are searching for them. The pair then hide in a morgue, where the other bodies show evidence of organ harvesting—the government seems bound to make a buck in any way it can. THX and SRT are found out and run.

A database confirms that LUH was consumed and her name reassigned to fetus 66691—most likely, her unborn child. Police prepare to apprehend THX, but he and SRT evade them, each escaping in a sleek sports car.

SRT has some difficulty in driving and immediately smashes into a concrete parking lot column. THX fares better, weaving among cars on the open highway until his vehicle overheats and shuts down. Once cooled, the car roars off again, breaking through gates and entering a restricted area. Heading into a dead end at more than two hundred miles an hour, THX crashes the car, and a motorcycle cop in pursuit piles into the wreck.

THX runs, followed by police on foot. He climbs an exit ladder, and as the officers are about to arrest THX, the allotted budget for his case is exhausted, and they merely cease the chase. Emerging from the underground world, THX sees the setting sun for the first time in his life.

Afterwords

For George Lucas, college in the late 1960s wasn't about pulling all-nighters, or panty raids, or tuning in and dropping out, as suggested by Timothy Leary. At the University of Southern California film school, Lucas was focused on making movies. For the annual student film festival, he wrote, directed, and submitted a seventeen-minute bleak, dystopian view of the future called *Electronic*

Labyrinth THX 1138 4EB. Everyone who saw it was convinced that they had seen something special.

One of those viewers was director/producer Francis Ford Coppola, who believed the young filmmaker's sci-fi short should be made into a feature film. With his encouragement, a script was completed and casting began.

Finding performers willing to shave their heads for a film role wasn't easy. Although Robert Duvall realized his hairline was on its way out anyway, no actress wanted to become a billiard ball of the future. A pretty stage actress from San Francisco named Maggie McOmie survived multiple auditions—and the shave of a lifetime—to get the part of LUH. Extras were recruited from a local drug rehab center, where they didn't mind having their heads shaved for the sum of thirty dollars a day. Character actors like Donald Pleasence and Don Pedro Colley rounded out the cast (and heads.)

Lucas would have liked to use Japan as the film's background, but that would have blown the budget. Since San Francisco's BART—Bay Area Rapid Transit—system was not yet opened to the public, it was chosen for its maze of long and empty tunnels. Additional locations like the Lawrence Livermore National Laboratory—a serious center for nuclear weapons research—and the Marin County Civic Center, designed by Frank Lloyd Wright, added to the futuristic appearance of *THX 1138*.

Two high-priced sports cars were used for the escape scene, both Lola T70 coupes from the late 1960s. The car driven by THX was originally owned by actor James Garner, who had to sell it when movie studios insisted the actor give up all of his racing interests. In 2007, the Lola was sold to a car collector in Belgium.

The final scene of Robert Duvall's character escaping the underground world, silhouetted against a golden sunset—wasn't Duvall at all. A filmmaker and good friend of Lucas, Matthew Robbins, put on Duvall's costume, a bald head cap over his flowing long hair, and appeared—uncredited—as the freed THX.

With a budget of $800,000, *THX 1138* barely grossed that amount back upon release in March of 1971. Film distributor Warner Bros. weren't sure what they had on their hands when the movie was finished, so it became the second feature in a lot of double-billed movie theaters.

In 1977, Lucas had great success with a little film called *Star Wars*, so Warner Bros. rereleased *THX 1138*. As Lucas is prone to do with his films, he added new real and computer-generated footage in 2004, releasing a very limited theatrical run before the DVD hit the stores.

THX 1138 has since become acknowledged as the first movement in a symphony of filmmaking from George Lucas, recognized as a cult classic by many sci-fi fans.

Westworld

Synopsis

- 1973—American/Metro-Goldwyn-Mayer—88 min./color
- Director: Michael Crichton
- Original music: Fred Karlin
- Film editing: David Bretherton
- Art director: Herman Blumenthal

Cast

- Yul Brynner (Gunslinger)
- Richard Benjamin (Peter Martin)
- James Brolin (John Blane)
- Norman Bartold (Medieval knight)
- Alan Oppenheimer (Chief supervisor)

An airport in the near future is the site of a TV reporter interviewing people returning from their vacations. But they aren't just any vacation—the Delos resort offers full-bore realistic experiences in adult amusement parks, themed as Roman World, Medieval World, and Western World. Each park provides guests with total interaction, thanks to advanced, lifelike robots. Even at a cost of $1,000 a day, it's worth it.

Another group of visitors arrives at Delos, including Peter Martin, who's never been there before, and his friend John Blane, an experienced veteran of the park. Color-coded trams take the visitors to their respective theme parks.

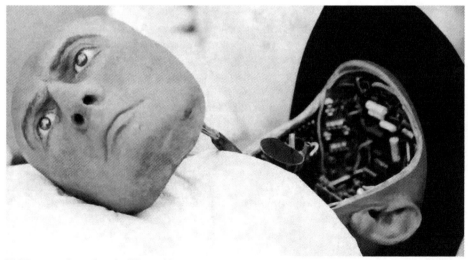

Yul Brynner loses face in *Westworld.*

Martin and Blane arrive at Westworld, where they select authentic clothing, hats, holsters, and weapons from the Wild West of the 1880s. Behind the scenes, all activity is monitored and controlled by technicians and computers.

Westworld visitors arrive by stagecoach, surrounded by authentic buildings, townsfolk, horses, and even ladies-of-the-evening. Martin and Blane visit the local saloon; Blane is fully engrossed in the experience, but Martin feels it's just silly.

A robot gunslinger insults Martin, but he's hesitant to respond. Blane urges his friend to kill the gunslinger, and Martin finally faces off against him. They draw and Martin guns the gunslinger down. The body is dragged away. Martin fears he might shoot a real human, but the guns have sensors that can tell the difference between them and the robots.

The next stop for Martin and Blane is the brothel at the end of the street. While a bank robbery erupts in gunfire outside, the pair selects two lovely robot ladies, taking them upstairs for some fun.

Later, as Martin and Blane sleep, maintenance vehicles clear the street that's littered with the bodies of dead robot cowboys. They're taken to a repair facility for upgrade or replacement. The chief supervisor notes that all three worlds are starting to show evidence of increasing malfunctions. It's almost as if the robots are becoming infected with some sort of computer virus.

The next morning, Blane's shaving routine is interrupted by the same robot gunslinger that Martin killed in the saloon. Obviously repaired, he holds Blane at gunpoint, until Martin bursts in and—once more—shoots the gunslinger dead. The lifeless body crashes out the window and tumbles to the street below.

Curiously, Martin is thrown in jail for murder, despite the protests of his friend. Blane sends over a tray of food, which happens to have instructions for Martin on how to escape from jail. He blows out a wall of the building, and Blane shoots the robot sheriff dead as the two tourists escape on horseback. They figure anything goes in town, now that the law is gone.

Another guest is given a sheriff's badge at his request, while Blane is bitten by a robot snake out in the desert; something that's not supposed to happen. Tech designers are at a loss to explain the malfunction.

A wild bar fight breaks out in the saloon. Martin and Blane have a grand and drunken time getting their punches in on the robot cowboys. The sheriff comes in and, instead of breaking up the fracas, joins in the fisticuffs.

The robot gunslinger is in the repair shop, undergoing a sensory update. On another table, a wench from Medieval World is inspected for faulty circuits, having wrongfully rebuffed the amorous advances of a guest. No problem is found, and the decision is made to keep the parks open, for fear of deterring the confidence of the visitors.

In Medieval World, a guest engages the Black Knight robot in a violent sword fight, with the Queen looking on. Losing his shield, the guest is run through and killed by the Black Knight—a malfunction on a major scale.

Back in Westworld, the now-repaired gunslinger confronts Martin and Blane, while the control center notes the robots are not responding to commands to shut down. The gunslinger draws on Blane and shoots him dead. The robot smiles wickedly, as Martin fears he will be the gunslinger's next victim. He runs for his life as the gunslinger fires and follows. The other two parks are experiencing similar catastrophic breakdowns.

Martin rides horseback into the desert, and the gunslinger tracks him. The guest tries to ambush the gunslinger, but his highly sensitive aural circuits hear the breathing, and the robot turns the ambush around.

Martin comes across a technician who is fixing a flat tire on his vehicle. He fears Martin is a robot, until he sees that he's a tourist. He has nothing but discouraging words for this cowboy guest, telling him he doesn't have a chance against the robot gunslinger. But Martin may have an idea up his sleeve.

He rides into Roman World, where evidence of carnage is all over the area. Martin slips down a darkened service tunnel, arriving at the repair shop. He finds large vials of acid as the gunslinger enters the shop.

Pretending to be one of the robots lying in wait for repair, Martin attacks the gunslinger as he walks by. Dumping an entire bottle of acid into the robot's face, it begins to smoke and melt away. Martin thinks he's safe, but the gunslinger comes after him. Even though his six-shooter has a dead battery, the robot refuses to quit.

Now in Medieval World, Martin is able to avoid the robot, as its vision system cannot distinguish Martin's heat signature from those of the wall torches. With one quick move, Martin grabs a torch and sets the gunslinger ablaze.

Finding a damsel in chains, Martin frees her. But when he tries to sooth her with a drink of water, she short-circuits in a shower of sparks—she, too, is a robot. Martin turns to leave, coming face-to-face with the charred body of the gunslinger. It topples lifeless onto the floor, then slowly turns over—faceless and aflame.

Stunned but safe, Martin sits and considers his once-in-a-lifetime vacation.

Afterwords

While *Westworld* is an entertaining sci-fi film about the near future, it also holds a unique position in the history of cinema and special effects. Today, the availability and use of computers to create and alter images is taken for granted. But forty years ago, computers were bigger than refrigerators and only used by scientists and space flight technicians. *Westworld* cautiously stuck its toe into the waters of computer-generated images in feature film for the first time.

Writer/director Michael Crichton's script called for several minutes of the world as seen through the eyes of Yul Brynner's robot cowboy. The technology and equipment to create such an effect simply didn't exist then—at least for movies.

Logically, NASA's Jet Propulsion Laboratory in Pasadena, California—which had the appropriate computers and experience in processing images—was asked if they could do the job. Of course they could—all it would take is nine months and $200,000, neither of which Crichton had at his disposal. The director then turned to experimental filmmaker John Whitney Jr., who agreed to tackle the task for $22,000 and complete it in four months' time. It was a deal.

Essentially, special computer programs were written to look at a frame of film and turn it into numeric values based on various parameters (a simple case of digitizing, although hardly simple for 1973). Then those values were turned back into an image, but with the values expressed as a series of rectangles. (Today, the process is very common—known as "pixelization," it's used to blur your TV screen, like when some nut runs naked across a soccer field.)

It was very tedious work for Whitney, as every ten seconds of film took up to eight hours to process. Plus, he had to deal with issues concerning proper color and contrast balance. But in the end, the scenes in *Westworld* were something never seen before, and they were the start of a whole new way to make sci-fi movies.

Special contact lenses—large and coated with an 80 percent reflective mirror finish—were developed for the robot characters. Unfortunately, Yul Brynner was accidentally hit in the eye with the wadding from a blank gunshot, which resulted in a scratched cornea. It made wearing the lenses incredibly painful and irritating. Shooting schedules had to be rearranged until the actor's eye healed and he could once again wear them.

Released in time for the Thanksgiving holiday in 1973, *Westworld* grossed more than $3 million. As Michael Crichton's first directorial effort, the film did well on its budget of $1.3 million. Well enough for a sequel in 1976 called *Futureworld*, although Crichton was not involved. In 1980, CBS-TV broadcast the brief five episode series of *Beyond Westworld*.

Soylent Green

Synopsis

- 1973—American/Metro-Goldwyn-Mayer—97 min./color
- Director: Richard Fleischer
- Original Music: Fred Myrow
- Film Editing: Samuel Beetley
- Art Director: Edward C. Carfagno
- Based on the 1966 Harry Harrison novel *Make Room! Make Room!*

Cast
- Charlton Heston (Detective Thorn)
- Leigh Taylor-Young (Shirl)
- Chick Connors (Tab Fielding)

Charlton Heston and Edward G. Robinson in *Soylent Green*.

- Joseph Cotten (William R. Simonson)
- Brock Peters (Chief Hatcher)
- Paula Kelly (Martha)
- Edward G. Robinson (Sol Roth)
- Leonard Stone (Charles)
- Lincoln Kilpatrick (The Priest)
- Whit Bissell (Governor Santini)
- Roy Jenson (Donovan)

New York City has gone from being a quaint nineteenth-century burg as imagined in sepia-toned pictures to an enormous metropolis choked with waste and pollution. By the year 2022, it is overburdened with forty million inhabitants. Manufacturers have addressed the desperate need for food by developing a line of plankton-based products known as Soylent Red, Soylent Yellow, and the new Soylent Green.

Old and grizzled Sol Roth—a police case researcher in his retirement, known as a "book"—lives with Detective Richard Thorn in a dilapidated and overcrowded apartment building. Electricity is scarce for the pair, so Roth makes their own by pedaling an exercise bike hooked up to a generator.

William Simonson is an affluent attorney and politician, living in luxury with his bodyguard Tab Fielding and paid mistress Shirl (women of Shirl's type are known as "furniture"). The two go grocery shopping for their boss at a dingy store, where a small slab of beef is regarded as a rare and expensive treat. But while they're out, a thug slips into Simonson's apartment and—on the orders of someone else—savagely beats the man to death.

Thorn investigates the murder, availing himself to the food, liquor, and soap kept by Simonson, packing the items in a satin pillow case. The corpse is picked up by a waste disposal team, who will dump the body in a site outside the city limits—no funeral, no burial. Their truck drops Thorn back home with loot that amazes Roth and brings him to tears. The detective also has brought recent oceanographic survey reports from Soylent.

At police headquarters, hundreds of people are lining up to collect death benefits on those who have recently passed away. Thorn offers the opinion to Chief Hatcher that the Simonson murder was an assassination, with Fielding somehow involved.

Throngs of people collect jugs of drinking water and rations of Soylent Green, while Thorn visits Fielding's apartment. The ex-bodyguard isn't around, but Martha—his furniture—is and lets Thorn in. The detective is impressed at Fielding's somewhat opulent lifestyle, but leaves quickly.

Thorn savors a fine meal and fresh fruit prepared by Roth, something the old man hasn't had in a long time. His nosing through the files on Simonson reveals he was a director of Soylent. Roth is also intrigued at a spoonful of strawberry jam that Thorn took from Fielding's apartment—not many bodyguards can afford fruit spread at $150 a jar.

The detective returns to Simonson's place, finding Shirl and a roomful of furniture—just some friends of hers. Thorn slips off for some private time with Shirl, and then he intervenes when Charles, the building manager, starts knocking some of Shirl's friends around for loitering. When they leave, Thorn sticks around for a hot shower and something to eat.

A local church acts as a refuge for the poor and needy. Knowing Simonson spoke to the priest there, Thorn presses the harried soul to reveal what the rich man had to confess. The priest can only shudder and collapse on the altar in shock and exhaustion.

Hatcher is anxious to close the Simonson case, but Thorn insists it remain open. He fears his boss has been bought off by someone who wants the truth buried. Thorn gets stuck with riot duty, as Governor Santini quietly meets with security chief Donovan in a small tent that acts as a tree sanctuary. When the governor finds that Thorn won't close down the Simonson case, he orders Donovan to close down Thorn—permanently. Meanwhile, Fielding kills the priest during confession.

At an outdoor food mart, Thorn and other officers attempt to disperse the crowd when the allotted supply of Soylent Green runs out. A riot breaks out, and front-loading vehicles scoop dozens of people into their truck beds. Simonson's assassin slips through the crowd, stalking Thorn, and unsuccessfully tries to shoot him dead. He wounds the cop, but is crushed under the scoop of a riot control truck.

Thorn catches Fielding at the bodyguard's apartment, beating him up and warning him to stop harassing the cop. But Fielding will not reveal who was behind the Simonson murder, or if he was involved in setting up the rich man for death.

Sol Roth visits a private book exchange, where other elderly scholars meet. His study of the oceanographic surveys has revealed some startling facts, but there is no proof. It's possible that Simonson also discovered these details and that may have been the motive for his elimination.

Having enjoyed a full life and deciding to end it, Roth visits a center where death is provided to those who want it. Surrounded by soft music and wonderful images of nature, Sol is sent peacefully to the hereafter. Thorn arrives at the center, too late to stop his friend's procedure, and is only able to offer a tearful goodbye. However, Roth is able to share Simonson's secret with Thorn before he expires. But there must be proof.

Thorn makes his way down to the dock where the dead bodies are loaded into disposal trucks, and he quietly hops on the back of one. At a waste disposal plant, Thorn watches as the bodies are dumped under the eyes of armed guards. Inside the plant, he follows the corpses as they are conveyed into processing tanks—where he is horrified to find they are turned into Soylent Green. Thorn is discovered and evades security, hopping a truck back to the city.

Fielding and his thugs find Thorn, shooting it out among dark and deserted streets. The bodyguard wounds Thorn and follows him into a church crowed with the sick and destitute. A blood trail leads Fielding to Thorn, who kills the villain with a knife.

Hatcher finds the injured Thorn. As he is taken away for treatment, the cop urges his Lieutenant to spread the word that "Soylent Green is people!"

Afterwords

As is often the case in Hollywood, the film version of *Soylent Green* strayed a bit from Harry Harrison's 1966 novel *Make Room! Make Room!*—starting with the title itself. Harrison's title inferred an increasing population and the need for space and food. But the execs at MGM felt the title might confuse moviegoers into thinking that Danny Thomas—star of the longtime TV show called *Make Room for Daddy!*—was bringing his popular program to the silver screen.

Harrison also noted that story points like the wafer-like Soylent Green and female companions known as "furniture" did not even appear in his book. (Actually, his word of "soylent" was an amalgam of "SOYbeans" and "LENTils.") Ye, the author felt the overall message that continued overpopulation and abuse of natural resources would result in a less-than-rosy future was delivered. As such, he found himself 50 percent pleased with the film version of his book.

One of the most impressive parts of *Soylent Green* comes right up front, in the form of a two-minute montage of images that effectively shows the growth—and decay—of America across its history. What starts as roomy, sepia-tinged photos of people and places in the early days of the country transforms into scenes of crowded and hurried masses, filling every nook and cranny of the screen.

The montage was assembled by filmmaker Chuck Braverman who, at only twenty-four years of age in 1968, had assembled an amazing film montage called "American Time Capsule"—Two hundred years of American history in less than three minutes. (Find it on YouTube—it's brilliant.) By age twenty-eight, Braverman was hired to build the opening sequence that would set the tone for the upcoming story in *Soylent Green*.

Following meetings with director Richard Fleischer, Braverman spent six weeks researching the photos needed. Another two to three weeks were spent shooting the images on what's known as the Oxberry animation stand, just like Saturday morning cartoons (before the days of digital animation and sending everything overseas to Korea for low-cost animating). With reviews and approvals, the whole process took Braverman about two and a half months.

Director of cinematography Richard Kline understood Fleischer's desire to present a world that was gritty, grimy, and gray. He used a clever method to convey that mood by building a huge box in front of the camera lens. Inside it, he injected a smoky haze and a little fan to circulate the smog. Shooting through it, the effect was perfect.

Although ticket sales numbers from the seventies are not as complete and available as they are for more recent films, the domestic box-office gross for *Soylent Green* was still impressive. The film took in more than $8 million (in a day when a movie ticket was about $1.75). It also had stiff competition that year, as blockbusters like *The Sting*, *American Graffiti*, and *The Exorcist* were released.

Blade Runner

Synopsis

- 1982—American/Warner Brothers—117 min./color
- Director: Ridley Scott
- Original Music: Vangelis
- Film Editing: Marsha Nakashima, Terry Rawlings
- Production Design: Lawrence G. Paull
- Based on the 1968 Philip K. Dick novel *Do Androids Dream of Electric Sheep?*

Cast
- Harrison Ford (Rick Deckard)
- Rutger Hauer (Roy Batty)
- Sean Young (Rachel)
- Edward James Olmos (Gaff)
- M. Emmet Walsh (Bryant)
- Daryl Hannah (Pris)
- Joe Turkel (Tyrell)

- Brion James (Leon)
- Joanna Cassidy (Zhora)
- William Sanderson (Sebastian)
- Morgan Paull (Holden)
- James Hong (Chew)

By 2019, the Tyrell Corporation developed sophisticated, humanlike robots—called replicants—for use as slave labor in space. Following a mutiny by a group of rogue replicants, Earth banned them, and special police units—called Blade Runners—were assigned to kill, or "retire," any replicant found on the planet.

Los Angeles, now a dark, fire-belching metropolis, is home to Tyrell. Holden, a Blade Runner, tests an employee named Leon for emotional reactions. A query about Leon's mother prompts him to calmly shoot Holden.

Amid flying cars called spinners, billboards soar high over the city and offer the promise of a new life to those who travel to the off-world colonies. A police officer named Gaff interrupts the dinner of Rick Deckard, a retired Blade Runner, bringing him to headquarters and the office of his old boss, Bryant.

Four replicants have found their way into LA, and Bryant wants Deckard to retire them. His attempt to refuse the job is ignored, under the threat of nasty consequences. The pair view a videotape of Holden's Voight-Kampff (VK) test of Leon; the results show he's one of the replicants.

The replicant's leader is Roy Batty, a new Nexus-Six model from Tyrell. The others are Zhora, a beautiful killing machine, and Pris, a female model designed for pleasure. They are human in every way, except they lack emotions (the basis of the VK test). Fearing the replicants could develop emotions over time, they're built with a four-year life span.

Sent to the Tyrell building, Deckard meets Dr. Tyrell and his pretty assistant, Rachel. The doctor doubts the effectiveness of the VK test and desires a test on a human subject, offering Rachel. After more than one hundred questions, Deckard determines that Rachel is a replicant—an advanced model programmed with memories. Even she doesn't know she is a replicant.

At Leon's apartment, Deckard and Gaff find dozens of photos. Nearby, Roy Batty meets up with Leon, who couldn't retrieve his photos with the police at his place. They find an old Chinese man named Chew, who makes synthetic eyes. The old man can't answer their questions about replicant life spans, but a designer named Sebastian at Tyrell can.

Refusing to believe she is a replicant, Rachel surprises Deckard at his apartment. She even offers a childhood photo as proof, but Deckard insists otherwise, and she quickly leaves. Meanwhile, Pris charms her way into the seedy apartment of Sebastian, who builds robotic toys for a hobby.

Deckard reviews the photos from Leon's apartment and finds the image of a tattooed woman. He also takes an animal scale he found at Leon's to Chinatown, where it's identified as a fake snake scale from a maker named Abdul Ben Hassan. He sold the item to a nearby strip club owner named Taffy Lewis.

Harrison Ford in *Blade Runner*.

At the club, Deckard decides to call Rachel, but she turns down his invitation to join him. He lies his way into the dressing room of Zhora, who is a dancer at the club. But she spots Deckard as a fraud, attacks him, and runs out onto the street. He chases after Zhora and retires her in a storefront, with gunfire from his double-triggered blaster. Only then does he see that she was the tattooed woman in the picture.

Bryant commends Deckard on his skill in retiring replicants and reminds him that Rachel makes four more to go, not three, as the Blade Runner insists. Deckard spots Rachel on the rainy streets, but Leon finds him first and pummels the ex-cop. Preparing to finish Deckard, Leon is shot dead by Rachel.

Back at Deckard's apartment, Rachel realizes she's a replicant and wants to escape. Deckard admits he wouldn't track her down, since she saved his life in the tussle with Leon. Unfortunately, someone else would. Rachel lets her hair down and spends the night with Deckard.

Pris leads Roy to Sebastian's place, where the replicants convince the toymaker to connect them with Dr. Tyrell. Roy and Sebastian find Tyrell in his penthouse, and the replicant asks for an extension on his life, fearing his life span will be ending very soon. The doctor considers Roy "the prodigal son," but altering the life span of the replicants is not at all possible. Batty viciously kills him, then turns to eliminate Sebastian.

Bryant informs Deckard about the deaths of Tyrell and Sebastian. The Blade Runner places a call to Sebastian's apartment in the Bradbury Building, claiming to be an old friend when Pris answers. She hangs up and Deckard drives there, where Pris hides by pretending to be one of Sebastian's toys. She suddenly attacks Deckard with some impressive acrobatic moves before he retires her with his blaster.

Batty catches up with Deckard, finds Pris' dead body, and begins to hunt down the Blade Runner in the building. Enormously strong, Roy pulls Deckard's gun hand through a wall, dislocates two fingers (one for Zhora and one for Pris), and lets go. Roy mourns Pris' death, crying as he kneels by her body.

Deckard loses his blaster and climbs out onto the roof of the building, where Batty follows him. The Blade Runner makes a dangerous jump to another building, hanging onto a girder as he doesn't quite make it. Roy jumps with plenty of room to spare, and as Deckard loses his grip, the replicant grabs his wrist and pulls the ex-cop to safety.

Holding a dove in his hands, Batty sits with Deckard, recalling memories soon to be lost forever. The replicant releases the dove and expires, while Deckard merely stares.

Back at his apartment, Deckard finds Rachel under a sheet on his bed. Fearing she's dead, he's overwhelmed to find she's only asleep. They leave together in the elevator.

Afterwords

The legend and legacy of certain sci-fi films seem to loom larger than the films themselves. Often, movies are released to lukewarm reception from the public and the media, but as time goes on, viewers take a new and different look. The result is a very popular film, occasionally achieving a near-religious cult status (no sacrilege intended). *Blade Runner* is one such film.

Despite his admitted love of movies, author Philip K. Dick had no love for where they came from—Hollywood was not his cup of tea. Yet he was warm to the idea of turning his novel *Do Androids Dream of Electric Sheep?* into a feature film.

After initial interest from then-nascent director Martin Scorsese in 1969 came up empty, five years passed before screenwriter Robert Jaffe took a shot at penning a script. Dick's reaction was to wish he could take a shot at Jaffe.

Then in 1977, a writer named Hampton Fancher teamed up with producer Michael Deeley in an attempt to bring Dick's story to the screen. After completing a total of ten drafts, the duo convinced Ridley Scott—fresh from the success of 1979's *Alien*—to direct. Just two weeks before production on *Blade Runner* was set to begin, David Peoples was brought in to polish the script.

Filmways Inc. originally put up the $15 million production budget, but backed out as they neared bankruptcy. A triumvirate of The Ladd Company, Asian producer Sir Run Run Shaw, and Tandem Productions picked up financing for *Blade Runner*. Tandem thought they were getting a piece of an action-adventure project in the *Star Wars* mold. But with production progressing, they got nervous as they realized that wasn't the case.

A caveat of the financing agreement allowed Tandem to take over the production of *Blade Runner* if it went 10 percent over budget. When it did, they did and offered a rough-cut sneak preview to a few selected cities. Those attending didn't like what they saw at all, and Tandem, now thoroughly scared, ordered changes to be made without consulting Ridley Scott (who was summarily angered and, technically, removed from the picture).

In making *Blade Runner*, the director was telling a story forty years in the future, while making it in a cinematic style of forty years in the past. Featuring a dark and smoky dystopic future, it may have been the first sci-fi film noir. Scott pictured Rick Deckard as the sort of character Humphrey Bogart could have played.

In reality, Fancher had pictured classic tough guy Robert Mitchum as the lead, while Scott was partial to Dustin Hoffman. Ultimately, Harrison Ford—post–Han Solo but pre–Indiana Jones—got the part. Almost immediately, the actor found himself at odds with the perfectionist director.

With Ridley Scott, patience ran thin. Fifteen to twenty takes were normal, as was taking over five hours to set up one shot. In another instance, art director David Snyder and his crew worked for months to build a street set for Scott, spending more than $1 million on it. When the director arrived, he took one quick look, suggested it was very good—for starters—and left. Snyder and his team were stunned.

After all the tension and hard work, audiences were probably a bit overwhelmed with *Blade Runner* upon its release. They may have objected to its leisurely pacing or complex story and exposition. Whatever the reason, with a budget that eventually grew to $28 million, it grossed almost that exact amount domestically. Overseas numbers seemed nonexistent, with only a half-million dollars.

However, the life of *Blade Runner* continued. For a tenth anniversary in 1992, a somewhat revised *Director's Cut* brought in nearly $4 million in limited release. In 2007, a *Final Cut* that ran in only a dozen or so theaters took in $1.5 million.

Along with an early release to the cable market years ago, as well as VHS, DVD, and Blu-Ray rentals and sales, *Blade Runner* has become one of the biggest and most iconic sci-fi films in the last forty years. With that in mind, talk of *Blade Runner 2* abounds, as Ridley Scott promises it will happen . . . sooner or later.

The Running Man

Synopsis

- 1987—American/Tri-Star Pictures—101 min./color
- Director: Paul Michael Glaser

- Original music: Harold Faltermeyer
- Film editing: Mark Roy Warner, Edward A. Warschilka, John Wright
- Production design: Jack T. Collis
- Based on the 1982 novel *The Running Man*, by Richard Bachman (Stephen King)

Cast
- Arnold Schwarzenegger (Ben Richards)
- Maria Conchita Alonso (Amber Mendez)
- Yaphet Kotto (William Laughlin)
- Jim Brown (Fireball)
- Jesse Ventura (Captain Freedom)
- Erland Van Lidth (Dynamo)
- Marvin J. Mcintyre (Harold Weiss)
- Gus Rethwisch (Buzzsaw)
- Professor Toru Tanaka/Charles Kalani Jr. (Subzero)
- Richard Dawson (Damon Killian)
- Mick Fleetwood (Mick)
- Dweezil Zappa (Stevie)

The year is 2017, and the world finds itself in bad shape. Food is hard to come by, and the reigning government is a fascist police state. Television is controlled by the state, and its most popular program is a life-and-death game show called *The Running Man*. Despite the oppression, a small element of underground resistance seeks to topple the regime.

Officer Ben Richards pilots a police helicopter over a group of Bakersfield citizens, rioting for a chance to get some food. Richards refuses an order to open fire on the unarmed crowd, knowing they're just hungry. His fellow officers subdue the righteously rebellious cop, then train their gun sights on the people below.

Richards end up in prison, framed for the deadly assault in Bakersfield. Prisoners are fitted with explosive neck collars. If they venture outside the computer-controlled perimeter, they are decapitated. Richards and his friend Laughlin stage a brawl, allowing them to escape with a third partner named Weiss.

The three men slip into Los Angeles, now a broken metropolis where enormous screens broadcast *The Running Man* to keep the poor and homeless brainwashed. The trio connect with members of the underground movement, led by Mick. He carefully removes their deadly collars while revealing his plan. If the TV network's satellite uplink can be located and jammed, then the truth about the government can be told. Richards wants no part of the revolution and just wants to leave the city behind.

The TV network, ICS, is home to the slick and, ultimately, slimy host of *The Running Man*, Damon Killian. Adored by millions of viewers, Killian is never far from his towering bodyguard, Sven. But Killian's ratings have leveled off, and his bosses at the Justice Department want a new angle for *The Running Man*. Killian thinks Richards will fill the bill nicely and wants him.

Ben Richards returns to his brother's apartment, which is now occupied by the pretty Amber Mendez, who is a songwriter for the network. Richard's brother is gone, and she fears this "Butcher of Bakersfield"—as Richards is called by TV news—will kill her. But all he wants is some money and a plane ticket in order to escape to Hawaii, and Amber will make a perfect cover.

But Richards is ratted out by Amber at the airport and arrested after a spirited chase. Taken to ICS, the ex-cop meets with Killian, who offers him a guest spot on *The Running Man*. If Richards refuses, Laughlin and Weiss—also captured—will go in his place. Nowhere near the fit and muscled specimen that Richards is, the two would quickly perish on the show at the hands of the deadly Stalkers. With no real choice, Richards reluctantly agrees.

Back at her apartment, Amber watches a phonied-up TV news story, claiming Richards killed several people during his capture at the airport. Maybe his claims to her of innocence and being framed by the government were really true.

It's showtime, as the Stalkers arrive and lithe dancers add to the broadcast spectacle. The studio audience is huge, and street-bound bookies take bets on which Stalkers will strike first. In a network hallway, Amber is somewhat remorseful as Richards passes by on his way to run for his life. She quietly slips into the video library, where she finds the unedited recording of Richards' refusal to shoot in Bakersfield. She now knows the truth about him.

As the TV audience watches, Richards is strapped into a rocket sled and readied for release into the Game Zone. But the evil Killian has lied, revealing that Laughlin and Weiss will be joining Richards in the game. Speeding through a maze of tunnels, the hapless trio end up on the streets and head into the first Zone.

Subzero is the first Stalker sent after the men, wielding a razor-bladed hockey stick and swiftly gliding after his prey on ice skates. As remote cameras watch, Richards, Laughlin, and Weiss narrowly escape beheading by the evil Asian master. But Richards deftly catches the villain in a dragline of razor-wire and Subzero is killed, to the shock of the studio audience.

Unfortunately, Amber has been caught with her hands in the video library and, branded as Richards' girlfriend and lover, finds herself joining the three men in the Game Zone. At the same time, two more Stalkers are sent after the Runners. Buzzsaw carries a deadly chain saw and rides a motorcycle, while the massive Dynamo casts bolts of electricity from his speedy motorized vehicle.

Slipping past the ever-present cameras, Weiss and Laughlin are still intent on finding the satellite uplink. As Richards and Laughlin keep the Stalkers occupied, Weiss and Mendez find the uplink box. Weiss breaks the pass code for the device and forces Amber to memorize it, before Dynamo kills Weiss with a shocking bolt of lightning.

Buzzsaw lassos Richards with a bolo, but is stripped from his bike when Richards wraps the cable around a concrete block. The brawly pair wrestles hand-to-hand with a whirring chain saw between them, but Richards gets the upper hand and kills Buzzsaw with it.

He then turns his attention on Dynamo, drawing him away from Amber and forcing his car to overturn. The rotund Stalker pleads for a commercial break, while Richards won't kill the helpless man. The audience is appalled at the showing of mercy.

Arnold Schwarzenegger is *The Running Man*.

Richards finds Laughlin, mortally wounded by Buzzsaw. The dying man urges him to get back to the underground with Amber and the code. In a private video conversation, Killian offers a Stalker deal to Richards, who angrily refuses.

The final Stalker is Fireball, equipped with a jet pack and flamethrower. But the audience is starting to favor Richards over the Stalkers. The betting on the streets also starts to go Richards' way, as the bookies reluctantly take their money.

With Fireball hot on their trail, Richards and Amber run through a maze of underground corridors. When they separate, Amber stumbles across the dead, decaying bodies of supposed winners from previous seasons of *The Running Man*. Cornered by Fireball, Amber escapes as Richards breaks his fuel line and sets him ablaze.

With Richards three-for-three in kills, the popular Captain Freedom is called out of retirement to finish off Richards. Again, Killian has a scheme—Richards' and Amber's faces will be superimposed on body doubles, and when Captain Freedom kills them, Richards will appear to be eliminated. The plan is hatched, and the audience cheers when Richards is killed.

The real Richards and Amber are found by the resistance and share the pass code with Mick. Amber has secreted a tape of the real Bakersfield footage—when it's broadcast by the resistance when the uplink is finally cracked, the audience immediately knows that Killian and the government are liars.

The underground forces charge the ICS network, with Richards leading the way. The audience scramble for their lives, as government guards open fire on everyone. In an empty hallway, Dynamo corners Amber, with nasty intentions. But an errant gunshot sets off the overhead sprinklers, and Dynamo is electrocuted in his own suit.

Richards comes face-to-face with Killian in a now-empty studio. When the villain urges his enormous bodyguard to take care of Richards, Sven decides he's also had enough of Killian and leaves him to Richards. Tossed into one of the game sleds, Killian is dispatched through his own maze of tunnels, emerging and crashing into a billboard for Cadre Cola. Killian and *The Running Man* have been permanently canceled.

As the crowds in the streets and around the city cheer, Richards enjoys an embrace with Amber.

Afterwords

Producer Rob Cohen had his hands full in trying to bring *The Running Man* to the screen. It was a process that took three and a half years, from acquiring the film rights to the American release in theaters. Writer Steven deSouza had to prepare fifteen drafts of a shooting script before hitting on the right one.

Five people held the title of director before someone finally took proper control. One spent $700,000 trying (unsuccessfully) to set the action in a shopping mall; another quit after finding he disliked "this kind of film"; a third wanted to rewrite the script in a way that would portray American culture as a disease to the world; a fourth took eight days to put the production four days behind schedule and nearly half a million dollars over budget.

In the end, former *Starsky and Hutch* TV star Paul Michael Glaser arrived to put things right for Cohen. In the meantime, actors like Christopher Reeve and Patrick Swayze were considered for the role of Ben Richards before Arnold Schwarzenegger (who did not approve of Glaser's style in directing *The Running Man*) came on board.

One series of effective scenes involves dispatching the runners (and, finally, Killian) onto the streets via a cage-like sled and a labyrinth of slick pipelines, subjecting the rider to tremendous speeds and G-forces. The actual effect was achieved using a shortened tunnel that held a full-sized sled, which was ridden by Schwarzenegger, Alonso, Dawson, and anyone else who had to hit the road. A miniature was also constructed, with a camera rig that traveled the entire length at very high speeds. Sharp editing of the two sources resulted in a very effective ride—for the actors and the filmgoers.

The Stalkers were played by members of the athletic world, including Football Hall of Fame running back Jim Brown as Fireball, pro wrestlers Professor Toru Tanaka (actually Hawaiian-born boxer and martial arts expert Charles Kalani Jr.) as Subzero and Jesse Ventura as Captain Freedom, Olympic wrestler (as well as opera singer and computer whiz) Erland van Lidth as Dynamo, and powerlifter and former *World's Strongest Man* competitor Gus Rethwisch as Buzzsaw.

In terms of curious casting, two members of the underground resistance stand out. Top pop band Fleetwood Mac cofounder and drummer Mick Fleetwood appears in *The Running Man* as the shaggy-haired leader of the organization (Fleetwood also guest starred as an alien in a 1989 episode of TV's *Star Trek: The Next Generation*). Dweezil Zappa—cracking-good guitarist and son of music genius Frank—shows up as a youthful gun-toting member of the movement.

It's difficult to say if any film ever featured not one but two future state governors, as *The Running Man* did. On minuscule campaign funds and against all odds, Jesse Ventura was elected governor of Minnesota in 1999, sitting for one term. Star Arnold Schwarzenegger, taking advantage of the unseating of California governor Gray Davis in the fall of 2003, replaced him with 56 percent of the vote. He was reelected for a full four-year term in 2006.

Total Recall

Synopsis

- 1990—American/TRI-Star Pictures—113 min./color
- Director: Paul Verhoeven
- Original music: Jerry Goldsmith
- Film editing: Carlos Puente, Frank J. Urioste
- Production design: William Sandell
- Based on the 1966 Philip K. Dick short story "We Can Remember It for You Wholesale"

Cast

- Arnold Schwarzenegger (Douglas Quaid/Hauser)
- Rachel Ticotin (Melina)
- Sharon Stone (Lori)
- Ronny Cox (Vilos Cohaagen)
- Michael Ironside (Richter)
- Marshall Bell (George)
- Mel Johnson Jr. (Benny)
- Roy Brocksmith (Dr. Edgemar)
- Ray Baker (Bob Mc Clane)

Safe in their spacesuits, a man and woman enjoy the romantic view of the canyons and mountains of Mars. But one false step sends Douglas Quaid tumbling down the mountain, shattering his visor as he comes to a stop. The rapid change in pressure causes his face to expand in a grotesque and deadly manner. But it's only a dream, as Quaid awakes in his bed with a start. His wife, Lori, comforts him, despite the fact he has the same dream every night—always with a mysterious woman.

Late in the twenty-first century, things on Mars are not well, as violence erupts over the mining activity there. There is concern over the discovery of alien artifacts in the Pyramid Mine. But the administrator of Mars, Vilos

Cohaagen, vows to control the rebel uprising. Doug would like to live on Mars, but Lori is against it.

The big and brawny Quaid works construction. On his morning commute, he watches a commercial for ReKall—a company that implants memories for virtual vacations. Despite the advice from his coworker Harry to not do it, Quaid visits ReKall to take a virtual trip to Mars. A pushy salesman named McClane convinces him to add the option of an alternate identity, and Quaid picks a secret agent mission.

As he's strapped into the implant chair, Doug assembles a virtual female companion from a list of options. But before the implant can take place, he flies into a frenzy—claiming his cover has been blown and his name isn't Quaid. The technicians finally sedate him. McClane orders Quaid's memory cleaned of any traces of his visit to ReKall.

Not knowing how he got there, Quaid finds himself in a Johnnycab taxi with a robotic driver. Harry and some coworkers meet Doug at the subway station and try to kill him, claiming he "blabbed about Mars." But the muscled Quaid is able to kill them first and is stunned at the mayhem he created.

Thinking he's safe at home, Doug finds Lori trying to kill him. Forced to talk, she admits she's not his wife but only a plant from "The Agency." His memory has been erased, and her job was to ensure it worked. It seems Quaid's whole life has been a dream.

Doug slips out of the apartment before Richter, Lori's real husband, and his band of thugs can catch him there. Following a bloody shootout, Quaid escapes by jumping onto a moving subway train. Richter then takes a video call from his boss, Cohaagen, who insists on getting Quaid back to Mars alive before he experiences "Total Recall."

Doug checks into a cheap hotel room, where a mysterious call advises him to wrap a wet towel around his head, since Richter can track him via a bug planted in his head. The caller—a former agent associate of Quaid's on Mars—leaves a suitcase for him outside. With it, Doug grabs a Johnnycab and barely eludes Richter.

Opening the suitcase, Quaid finds Martian money, IDs, and a handheld device that can create a mirror image of whoever holds it. There's also a video of himself that

Dean Norris, Rachel Ticotin, and Arnold Schwarzenegger in *Total Recall.*

explains his name is really Hauser, a longtime member of Mars intelligence, and he has a great deal of incriminating evidence on Cohaagen. The recording instructs Quaid on how to remove the bug in his head—a painful extraction through his nose. In closing, Hauser urges Quaid to make his way to Mars and expose Cohaagen.

Richter and his men have followed their prey to the Red Planet. Quaid arrives disguised as a large, red-haired woman, but his mechanized costume begins to malfunction at the immigration center. Richter watches as the fake woman's head opens like a blooming flower. Quaid tosses it to the villain's men, and it explodes.

Gunfire from Richter breaches a window in the pressurized building, and Quaid has to hang on as people are sucked into the vacuum of Mars' atmosphere. As emergency doors seal the hole, Quaid escapes once more.

An angry Cohaagen meets with Richter, insisting on compliance with his orders to find Quaid before Kuato, the rebel leader with psychic powers, does. Quaid's evidence on Cohaagen could help the rebels topple the empire he's built on Mars.

Quaid checks into the Hilton, where he has left a note for himself to find Melina at a bar known as the Last Resort. He quickly grabs a cab driven by Benny as rebels begin shooting up the area, safely arriving in the sleazy red-light district called Venusville. Many of the locals are psychic mutants, a result of damaging radiation.

At the Last Resort, Quaid turns down the company of Mary, a three-breasted woman, and finds Melina. She is, incredibly, the same woman that kept appearing in his dreams. She calls him Hauser, and it's clear they have been together before. When he tries to explain about Quaid and Lori and why he doesn't remember who Melina is, she is angered, unsympathetic, and throws him out.

Back at the hotel, Quaid receives a visit from Dr. Edgemar of ReKall. It seems that everything that has happened to Quaid since the implant chair is a dream in his mind and he's now trapped in it. Edgemar will try to get him out and brings Lori into the room, who tries to convince him she is really his wife.

Doug almost buys the story, but a telltale drop of sweat on Edgemar's face says otherwise. Quaid kills the man as Richter's men burst into the room. They subdue him and place him in cuffs.

The group waits for an elevator, and when it opens, Melina is there and armed with a machine gun. Shooting the men, she and Lori go at it in a hand-to-hand fight. Melina is knocked unconscious, and Lori tries to charm Doug. He wants none of her and shoots her, claiming it's "a divorce."

Melina and Doug run for it, as Richter finds his men and his wife dead. The pair slip into a taxi, luckily with Benny behind the wheel. They crash into Venusville, with Richter and one of his men right behind. Melina, Doug, and Benny duck through a hidden panel at the Last Resort, and a riot erupts when the bad guys can't find the trio.

Cohaagen orders Richter and all troops out of the area, as it's sealed and the ventilation system is shut down. As a result, the mutants will suffocate. Meanwhile, the rebels take Melina, Doug, and Benny to their underground headquarters. George, one of the leaders, turns out to be Kuato. The mutant is a grotesque, childlike head and hands, conjoined to George's midsection.

Kuato reads Quaid's mind, where he sees the alien artifact that Cohaagen is hiding. It's a reactor capable of creating a viable atmosphere for Mars, making Cohaagen's empire of selling breathable air worthless.

Explosions rock the caverns, as Cohaagen's soldiers attack the rebels. Doug, Melina, Kuato, and Benny escape the gunfire, but Benny suddenly shoots Kuato down—the cabbie is on Cohaagen's payroll. Before he dies, Kuato urges Quaid to start up the reactor. Richter shows up to take the survivors to Cohaagen.

The chief villain claims everything has been part of a plan; a plan that Hauser and he formed, including creating Quaid to find Kuato. Quaid doubts it, until he watches a video of Hauser that confirms his allegiance with Cohaagen.

Doug and Melina are forced into implant chairs, where they will be reprogrammed as compliant members of the Agency. Quaid's massive strength comes to the rescue, as he breaks free of his shackles. He kills the techs, frees Melina, and the pair make their way to an elevator.

The mutants are nearly dead, as the air in Venusville is just about gone. Doug and Melina try to find the reactor, but Benny drives them into a corner of the mines with a deadly drilling machine. Quaid disables it at the last minute and kills Benny.

Doug and Melina reach the reactor, but Richter and troops are lurking close by. They surround Quaid and empty their guns into him. But he merely laughs, as they've been shooting only at a holographic image, created by the gadget Quaid had in his suitcase. The real Doug returns fire, with Richter and a few gunners running for their lives.

Melina suckers a few more soldiers with a hologram, as Richter attempts to escape in a freight elevator. Doug jumps on and fights with him. As Richter hangs over the side, his arms are caught between the dock and a guard space. They're severed and he falls to his death.

Quaid finds the starter for the reactor, but Cohaagen stops him at gunpoint. He prepares to shoot Doug, but Melina arrives to shoot Cohaagen first. Wounded, the villain detonates a bomb to destroy the reactor. Before it can go off, Doug throws it out of the area, blowing a hole in the wall.

With rapid depressurization, the three are being sucked into the void of the Martian atmosphere. Doug and Melina are able to hold on to a cable; Cohaagen isn't as lucky and dies an ugly death as he's pulled into the vacuum of Mars.

At the last minute, Quaid is able to start the reactor, and massive blasts of air save Melina and Doug. The people in Venusville recover as well, with the skies of Mars turning azure blue. But Doug can't tell if it's real or part of a dream. If it is a dream, Melina urges him to kiss her quickly before he wakes up, and he does.

Afterwords

Having penned the story and screenplay for 1980's *Alien*, Dan O'Bannon and Ronald Shusett got together for another sci-fi script ten years later. It would be an action story set in the future about the blurred line between reality and virtual reality. But getting to that point wasn't particularly easy.

Shusett had first acquired the rights to Philip K. Dick's "We Can Remember It for You Wholesale" in the mid-1970s and had the interest of Disney Studios first, then producer Dino De Laurentiis. David Cronenberg—writer and director of films like 1981's *Scanners*, 1983's *Videodrome*, and 1986's *The Fly*, among others—worked with Shusett, writing a dozen drafts of a script. But Cronenberg wanted a sci-fi film faithful to the original story, while Shusett had envisioned *Raiders of the Lost Ark Go to Mars*. Obviously, the two weren't on the same page.

Actors like Richard Dreyfuss, William Hurt, and Patrick Swayze were attached at one point or another to star in the film, retitled as *Total Recall*. Sets for the production were being built in Australia when De Laurentiis' company went belly-up in bankruptcy.

Arnold Schwarzenegger, with big sci-fi hits like 1984's *The Terminator* and 1987's *The Running Man* and *Predator* under his belt, became the obvious choice to star. The selection immediately transformed Dick's meek main character into a muscular action hero. Schwarzenegger used his superstar leverage to hand-pick Paul Verhoeven to direct *Total Recall*.

Verhoeven had proved his skill in making an action sci-fi film with plenty of excitement and mayhem with 1987's *RoboCop*. *Total Recall* would be no different, with a high quotient of bloody violence and special visual effects. In fact, the sci-fi film distinguished itself as being the last major production to rely mostly on miniatures, scale models, and physical visual effects. Computers would soon take much of a movie's FX into the digital realm.

One memorable scene involved Arnold's character using the mechanical masquerade of a large woman in an attempt to evade security guards. Special makeup FX designer Rob Bottin painted himself into a corner with Verhoeven, first suggesting the elaborate female disguise, then realizing he had no idea how he would accomplish it.

Following the tedious search for a female that was large enough to conceivably contain the bulk of Arnold, Bottin located actress Priscilla Allen. Even then, her head was too small to believably fit Schwarzenegger's noggin inside. After many sculpts, the false head reached enormous proportions—still, not having enough room inside for all the mechanical gear needed to make it open up in sections.

The final head was cast in latex with steel reinforcements inside to prevent warping (insert appropriate "warped mind" joke here). At a hefty twenty pounds and loaded with steel, the appliance was now too dangerous for the real actor to wield, so a false Arnold head and torso had to be made as well to fit inside.

Once completed, with mechanics and bearings attached on the outside rear, the head disguise weighed seventy pounds. Children's clay was used to fill the minute cracks in the slices before they opened up. Seven off-stage operators were employed, each controlling the opening of one pair of facial sections. The resulting effect was astounding—and used no computers.

A scene in Venusville brought Quaid face-to . . . er, face with a three-breasted hooker named Mary. The awkward role was played by actress and journalist Lycia Naff, who was originally told she would have four breasts. Fearing the character might bear too much resemblance to a cow, the boob count was reduced by one—to Naff's udder relief (sorry).

When *Total Recall* was finally released as a summer spectacular, the many years of waiting for Shusett and O'Bannon paid off. Produced on a budget of $65 million, it grossed nearly $120 million in America, making it one of the Top Ten moneymakers in 1990. Overseas, the film took in more than $140 million, for a total of over $260 million.

A remake in 2012 once more proved that Hollywood should leave well enough alone. Starring Colin Farrell, the $125 million-budget film brought in a paltry $59 million. Overseas, the take was better, to the tune of $139 million.

Demolition Man

Synopsis

- 1993—American/ Warner Brothers—115 min./color
- Director: Marco Brambilla
- Original music: Elliot Goldenthal
- Film editing: Stuart Baird
- Production design: David L. Snyder

Cast

- Sylvester Stallone (John Spartan)
- Wesley Snipes (Simon Phoenix)
- Sandra Bullock (Lenina Huxley)
- Nigel Hawthorne (Dr. Raymond Cocteau)
- Benjamin Bratt (Alfredo Garcia)
- Bob Gunton (Chief George Earle)
- Glenn Shadix (Associate Bob)
- Denis Leary (Edgar Friendly)

Los Angeles in 1996—the iconic Hollywood sign is in flames, chaos rules. A busload of citizens has been kidnapped by arch-criminal Simon Phoenix, who has them stashed in an abandoned warehouse, surrounded by police searchlights. Only one person can stop him—Officer John Spartan, a rough and reckless cop known as the Demolition Man.

Sylvester Stallone and Wesley Snipes in *Demolition Man*.

Spartan rappels from a hovering helicopter to the roof, rushing into the building to face Phoenix. The villain is crass, belligerent, and defiant against Spartan. He sets the building on fire, and Spartan, despite his own feelings, carries Phoenix to safety as the building explodes.

But the hostages are found dead—Spartan and his rash methods are blamed for the killings. Both he and Phoenix are sentenced to incarceration by means of cryogenic confinement. The officer is placed in a large clear cylinder, immersed in a thick fluid, and flash frozen for the next seventy years.

Thirty-six years pass, and life in San Angeles—the metroplex that now encompasses the former cities of Los Angeles and San Diego—is quite dull. Lieutenant Lenina Huxley, eager for action, finds everything quiet . . . and a bore. The perky officer immerses her interests in the twentieth century, when life and living were wild, harsh, and brutal. Her fellow officer Alfredo Garcia understands none of it.

But in the world underground, people scratch for food and existence. The scruffy Edgar Friendly, keeping an eye on the people above, leads them in their daily struggle to survive.

A parole hearing at the CryoPrison goes wrong, and Simon Phoenix finds himself defrosted and escapes to the streets. He kills two guards and the warden, which sends the police department into a frenzy. They just aren't prepared to deal with the long-obsolete "murder-death-kills."

Phoenix kills a doctor and steals his car, then finds he is somehow fully trained in operating the ultramodern computer kiosks in the city. He immediately finds a data file on Edgar Friendly, but a voice from somewhere suggests that Phoenix's job is to kill him.

Simon Phoenix is confronted by six SAPD officers. Unfortunately, they are no match for his martial arts skills and are quickly dispatched. But Phoenix needs weapons to carry out his assigned task.

Elegant and educated Dr. Raymond Cocteau, the architect of the new lifestyle in the city, addresses the ongoing problem of subversives like Edgar Friendly. Associate Bob, his manservant, informs him of the sudden appearance of Simon Phoenix. Cocteau instructs Police Chief George Earle to do whatever is necessary to eliminate Phoenix.

Huxley convinces a hesitant Chief Earle to defrost John Spartan, since he was the only one who was ever able to capture Simon Phoenix. Understandably, Spartan is a bit cranky when awakened from his thirty-six-year nap. He is no happier to find that cigarettes, alcohol, contact sports, and swearing have all been deemed illegal. In fact, cursing violators are fined with a chiding computer voice and a citation. Top radio stations play nothing but old commercials. While he wants no part of this new world, Spartan doesn't relish a return to the CryoPrison. Reluctantly, he accepts the assignment.

Phoenix finds an enormous cache of weapons in the Hall of Violence in the San Angeles Museum of History. When Spartan arrives, the two tear up the building with gunfire of all kinds. In an underground exhibit of old Los Angeles, the fighting turns hand to hand, and Phoenix escapes into a public park.

Unexpectedly, Phoenix comes upon Cocteau and Bob and tries to shoot them. But something prevents him from pulling the trigger, and he runs when Spartan shows up. But before Phoenix leaves, Cocteau quietly reminds him of his assignment to kill Friendly. Spartan is formally introduced to Cocteau, who knows of the cop's reputation. Gratefully, he invites Spartan and Huxley to dinner—at Taco Bell.

The survivor of the Franchise Wars, Taco Bell is now the only restaurant chain around. With an upscale piano bar and valet parking, it's not the same place Spartan remembers. The testimonial dinner is interrupted by Friendly and his scraps, who assault a delivery truck for food. Spartan takes them on and subdues them, cutting the cables to a large tent and trapping them under it. Huxley is impressed.

As the evening comes to an end, Huxley offers to perform sex with Spartan. But it's hardly a performance, as physical contact is frowned upon and Huxley provides two helmets that will do all the work without any touching. But Spartan is old school and offends Huxley with his old-fashioned ideas.

He is thrown out and returns to his own apartment, where he reviews surveillance tapes from the day and believes there's something fishy between Phoenix and Cocteau. Spartan also finds he has learned how to knit during his stay in cold storage.

The next day, a review of Phoenix's files shows he has been taught something other than knitting during cryostasis—all sorts of martial arts, weaponry, and other skills to make a bad man even badder. Spartan confronts Cocteau with the facts and receives no explanation.

Accompanied by Huxley and Garcia, Spartan ventures down into the underground world to capture Phoenix. Instead of aggressive scraps, the trio finds frightened and crowded masses of people trying to survive. Friendly corners Spartan, assuming he is to be apprehended. The officer clues Friendly in as to the real problem—he is on Cocteau's hit list.

Meanwhile, Phoenix has convinced Cocteau to defrost a number of additional criminals to carry out his assignment, and the leader agrees. The group of thugs ambushes Spartan, Friendly, and the others.

Phoenix escapes to the streets, where he steals a police car. Spartan and Huxley give chase in a vintage Olds 442 muscle car stashed underground. They weave dangerously through traffic, exchanging gunfire.

Spartan jumps to Phoenix's vehicle, and they wrestle. Along the way, Phoenix proudly reveals the hostages back in 1996 were already dead at the warehouse, so Spartan's actions didn't kill them. Phoenix is finally thrown from the vehicle, and Spartan, unable to activate any of the auto's automatic features, crashes into the pond in front of the SAPD station.

Chief Earle is both outraged at Spartan's ongoing destructive ways and in fear of the oncoming crowd of scraps, led by Friendly. To Spartan's amusement, Officer Garcia has joined the underground. Spartan grabs two guns from the scraps and, with Huxley, takes off after Phoenix.

At Cocteau's headquarters, even Phoenix has grown tired of the leader's heavy-handed, controlling ways. Although he is prevented from killing Cocteau, nothing stops Phoenix from ordering one of his defrosted villain partners to do the job. Cocteau is shot dead and unceremoniously tossed into his own fireplace.

Spartan and Huxley arrive at Cocteau's control center and are immediately assaulted by Phoenix's men. They are quickly subdued, and Spartan thoughtfully incapacitates Huxley with her own glow rod. He wants Phoenix all for himself.

With the help of Associate Bob, Phoenix begins to revive eighty more criminals from the CryoPrison. Spartan crashes the party, as he and Phoenix exchange gunfire. But Phoenix grabs Spartan in the jaws of a crane used to transport the cryo-cylinders. He toys with the policeman, but doesn't notice a broken hose that sprays liquid nitrogen onto one of the jaws.

Spartan breaks free of the brittle metal trap and takes on Phoenix in hand-to-hand combat. The villain gets the upper hand, but becomes soaked in cryofluid. Jumping to safety, Spartan breaks a capsule that acts as a catalyst for the cryogenic process. From toe to head, Simon Phoenix freezes solid, and for good measure, Spartan kicks his head off, shattering it into a million pieces.

As the cryo-facility explodes in a ball of flames, Spartan escapes. Chief Earle is despondent over the loss of Cocteau, but Edgar Friendly proposes getting together to set things right, with Associate Bob lending a hand.

John Spartan breaks the law by kissing an appreciative Lenina Huxley.

Afterwords

The opening scene in *Demolition Man* immediately tells the viewer that things are not right with the world, as the iconic Hollywood sign is in flames high in the hills above Los Angeles. Visual effects supervisor Mike McAlister enlisted the Image Engineering FX house to create the sequence.

A miniature of the letters—hardly "miniature" at seventy-five feet long and ten feet high—was rigged with propane gas lines to control the flames that appeared to be engulfing the sign. A motion-controlled camera filmed the helicopter move that weaved its way past the sign. That shot was digitally combined with a real shot of the Hollywood Hills, with searchlights and fires in the distance added as well. The finished shot made for a chilling tip on what would come next.

That exciting scene involved the first confrontation between John Spartan and Simon Phoenix—in an old building where the villain held his hostages. The result of their meeting ended up with the structure blown to bits and the two men sent to the CryoPrison, where they remained on ice for nearly forty years.

An actual Los Angeles building—the abandoned downtown Department of Water and Power facility—was chosen for destruction. Even though it was already tagged for a common piece-by-piece dismantling, filmmakers convinced the city to allow the massive and impressive total destruction of the building. Two hundred pounds of dynamite were strategically placed by a professional demolition company, augmented by sixty-five gasoline bombs set by the special effects crew. In a flash, the building ceased to exist—all captured on film.

Part of the world of 2032 in "San Angeles" is accomplished with futuristic vehicles, courtesy of General Motors. Many automakers create "concept cars," which are one-of-a-kind vehicles that are built to showcase a new design or technology. GM provided the makers of *Demolition Man* with their 1992 GM Ultralite, equipped with a rounded carbon-fiber body and a three-cylinder engine that provided gas mileage of an amazing one hundred miles per gallon. The car barely weighed fifteen hundred pounds.

General Motors loaned another seventeen concept vehicles for the film, worth nearly $70 million. The Warner Bros. production team also built twenty copies of the Ultralite from body molds provided by GM. The cars were made of fiberglass, plastic, a steel chassis, and a small gasoline engine.

Demolition Man was originally slated for martial arts stars Steven Seagal and Jean-Claude Van Damme. But the two couldn't come to terms on who would be Spartan and who would be Phoenix. So they both dropped out. Then, with Stallone on board as Spartan, it was thought that Asian action superstar Jackie Chan would be the perfect villain. However, it was feared that Chan's fans would be disappointed to see their fave as a bad guy, so Wesley Snipes stepped in. Lori Petty was chosen to play Lenina Huxley with Stallone, but she left the shoot after only a few days and was replaced with Sandra Bullock.

Stallone needed a hit at the box office after subpar films like *Lock Up* in 1989, *Oscar* in 1991, and *Stop! Or My Mom Will Shoot* in 1992. Each of those flicks brought in less than $30 million in domestic ticket sales. *Demolition Man*, on the other hand, grossed $58 million in the US, with another $100 million overseas. The total of nearly $160 million put the film in the Top Twenty–grossing films of 1993.

12 Monkeys

Synopsis

- 1995—American/Universal—129 min./color
- Director: Terry Gilliam
- Original music: Paul Buckmaster
- Film editing: Mick Audsley
- Production design: Jeffrey Beecroft

Cast
- Bruce Willis (James Cole)
- Madeleine Stowe (Dr. Kathryn Railly)
- Brad Pitt (Jeffrey Goines)
- Jon Seda (Jose)
- Maximilian Schell (Dr. Goines)
- David Morse (Dr. Peters)
- Frank Gorshin (Dr. Owen Fletcher)
- Joseph Mckenna (Wallace)

A young boy watches the shooting of a man in an airport. In a dingy prison, a crane pulls James Cole from his cell, and he dons a complex suit with a plastic outer shell—looking much like an astronaut. He steps into a small airlock, then climbs into an elevator that starts upward.

Cole emerges from a manhole onto a snowy street. The city is deserted and crumbling. Wild animals prowl the sidewalks, and Cole collects insect specimens in sample jars as he surveys the area.

Technicians vigorously scrub down Cole upon his return, and he stands before a panel of doctors and scientists. The prisoner sits in a metal chair, confined and raised fifteen feet up a wall. A sphere with video monitors nears his face, as the panel debriefs Cole on his journey to the surface.

In 1990 Baltimore, the beeper of psychiatrist Kathryn Railly interrupts the words of a poet addressing a gallery of fans. Embarrassed, the doctor leaves quickly. Railly has been summoned to an overcrowded police station to examine a mental case. Restrained and considered violent, it is Cole.

Railly speaks with Cole, trying to find out why he assaulted five police officers. He's only concerned about the year—he thinks it's 1996. Railly informs him it's 1990—the year he wants is in the future. To Cole, 1996 is the past, and he needs to make a phone call.

Taken to a mental hospital, Cole gets the tour from inmate Jeffrey Goines and then meets with the psych ward doctors, including Railly. Cole explains that five billion people die in 1996 from a deadly virus, with only 1 percent of the world's population surviving. Claiming that his arrival in 1990 was a mistake, Cole just needs to make a phone call and leave a message for the scientists in his present.

Railly allows Cole to make the call, but unfortunately, the person on the other end has her hands full of screaming kids and knows nothing about James Cole. It occurs to him that he's supposed to be in 1996, not 1990—that's why the number didn't work.

While the patients sleep, Goines offers to help Cole escape. With a very important father, Jeffrey claims to have a lot of pull on the outside. But his ravings begin to wake the others, and guards carry Goines away.

A television report exposes the incidence of animal cruelty in the name of science, while Cole scribbles away on a magazine. Goines slips him a key, and, although heavily sedated, Cole makes a failed attempt to escape while Jeffrey creates a wild and noisy distraction.

Cole is confined in a solitary cell, while Dr. Fletcher reprimands Railly for her poor judgment in not keeping the patient restrained in the first place. The lecture is interrupted when it's discovered that Cole has vanished.

He disappears back in the future, seated in the chair on the wall, and the panel of doctors tries to make sense out of a distorted message they believe Cole sent. They quiz him about his activities during his trip in time, asking about an organization called the Army of the Twelve Monkeys. They show him pictures, including one of Jeffrey Goines, a face Cole recalls.

The scientists make one more attempt at sending Cole back in time, but now he ends up—naked—in a trench during World War I. Soldiers ask about his missing clothes, and Cole is stunned to see Jose, his cellmate from the future, carried by him on a stretcher. Suddenly, Cole is shot in the leg.

In 1996 Baltimore, Dr. Railly delivers a speech on "Madness and Apocalyptic Visions" from the campus of a local college. She discusses the strange discovery of a World War I French soldier who suddenly spoke fluent English and claimed to be from the future—on the screen behind Railly is a picture of Jose.

During a post-lecture autograph signing, a pushy man named Dr. Peters suggests the ravings of the lunatics in her speech might just be true. In the parking lot, a stranger abducts Railly and orders her to drive to Philadelphia. Suddenly, she recognizes her captor from six years back—Cole.

In spite of her fear, Railly indulges Cole's desire for fresh air and Fats Domino on her radio—rare treats for him. The radio relates the sad story of a young boy trapped in a well, but Cole knows it's a hoax. Police are notified of the doctor's disappearance, while Railly and Cole hide out in a small hotel. Like several times before, Cole dreams of being a child, watching someone getting shot in an airport. Although looking some-what different, Railly is in the dream as well.

Continuing the trip to Philly, Cole explains his mission to Dr. Railly. He's been sent into the past to find the Army of the Twelve Monkeys, the group responsible for the virus that killed everyone. If he can return with the original germ strain, scientists may be able to find a cure and allow the survivors to come out from underground.

Bruce Willis in *12 Monkeys*.

In the City of Brotherly Love, Cole jumps from the car to inspect graffiti that includes the logo of the Army of Twelve Monkeys. Railly knows she could now pull away to safety but doesn't. A street derelict reminds Cole that he's being tracked—the voice sounds just like the inmate from the cell next to his, long into the future.

They duck into a dilapidated theater, where two men attack Railly. Cole's intense and sudden rage easily subdues them. He grabs a gun from one of the lifeless bodies and leaves with Railly.

The pair enter a storefront for the FAA—Freedom for Animals Association, where Cole demands to find the Army of the Twelve Monkeys. At first, the workers plead ignorance, but at gunpoint, they admit they know Jeffrey Goines.

The son of a Nobel Prize–winning virologist, Goines organized an underground group of twelve guerrilla activists for animal rights. He championed the cause with stunts like releasing a hundred snakes on the floor of the Senate. Railly begins to see that Cole isn't the crazed lunatic she though he was.

Suddenly, Goines made an about-face, publicly claiming that animal experiments were necessary for society and he would personally supervise all lab activity. Cole finds a Rolodex, and he leaves with Dr. Railly in a stolen car.

Cole's leg bleeds from the World War I gunshot wound, an injury he doesn't really recall. Railly treats the wound and places the bullet in her pocket. Cole grabs the doctor.

At a formal dinner in the mansion of Dr. Goines, Cole finds Jeffrey and pleads with him for the original virus. When Secret Service agents intervene, Cole is forced to run, while a television reports that police have found the strangled body of a woman believed to be Railly and continues its coverage of the boy trapped in a well.

Cole runs through the woods and comes to the stolen car, where Railly—very much alive—has been locked in the trunk. Angered at first with the confinement, the doctor sees Cole bleeding and calms herself. Yet she insists Cole's claims of a mass viral genocide is a delusion, and she urges the man to surrender. As the authorities close in on the pair, Cole vanishes.

Police try to piece together the strange events with Railly's help, and then she returns to her home in Baltimore. The doctor is stunned when a TV reports the boy trapped in a well was all a hoax—just as Cole insisted.

Cole wakes in a hospital bed, as the panel of doctors from his future welcomes him by singing a discordant version of "Blueberry Hill." They congratulate him for delivering important information on the Army of the Twelve Monkeys. But Cole just laughs, thinking it's all an illusion and he really is crazy.

Police inform Dr. Railly that, according to the ballistics report, the bullet she pulled from Cole's leg was an antique from before 1920. Shocked, she consults the World War I picture of Jose she used in her lecture and clearly sees Cole in the image.

Railly places a call to Dr. Goines, warning him that his son may be planning to steal a virus, but Dr. Goines claims to know nothing of any "Monkey army." Hanging up, he mentions the conversation to his associate—Dr. Peters—the same man who met Railly at the lecture. To be safe, Goines suggests increasing security measures in the lab.

The panel of scientists drills the events of the 1996 viral disaster with Cole, in preparation for returning him once more to the past.

Dr. Railly pounds on the door of the FAA storefront, while Jeffrey Goines and the clerks prepare for something illegal inside. She spray paints a warning on the side of the building: Is there a virus? Is this the source? Seeking Cole, Railly finds him in a crowd, and they hurry away as watchful police move toward them.

Hiding out in a sleazy hotel, Cole now readily admits he's insane and wants to stay in 1996, where Railly can cure him. In a reversal of roles, she knows the truth and needs his help to prevent the oncoming disaster.

Suddenly, Wallace—the local pimp—bursts into the room, not happy with Railly's apparent infringement on his territory. He punches the woman, and Cole's rage once more brings the conflict to a quick resolution. Just in case he isn't insane, Cole painfully removes several of his teeth—the means with which the future tracks their travelers.

Escaping into the city, Railly recalls that James had a phone number in 1990 that could leave a message for his scientists in his present. The doctor seems relieved when her phone call reaches a carpet company, figuring both she and Cole are crazy. But James confirms that the message she left was indeed the one his scientists will receive.

Jeffrey and his cohorts ride in the FAA van. They have kidnapped his father, and the senior Goines lies bagged, on the floor. He admits now that Jeffrey is insane, but he has taken steps to secure his labs.

Hitchcock's *Vertigo* plays in a darkened movie theater, and Dr. Railly disguises Cole with items purchased in a department store. If only a few weeks remain until the apocalypse begins, she intends on spending them, happy, with James.

Cole wakes from a nap in the theater and finds Dr. Railly in the lobby, with her hair now blonde. The image strikes him—she is the woman in his recurring dream. They embrace in a romantic hug.

It is sunrise and animals now run free in the streets. Graffiti from the Army of the Twelve Monkeys exclaims, "We did it!" Kathryn and James ride a cab to the airport, suddenly aware of the traffic snarl created by former inhabitants of the zoo, where Jeffrey let them out and locked his father in.

At the airport, police remain vigilant for any sign of Railly or Cole. Still in disguise, James realizes his dream was real—he was there with his family as a boy. In a desperate attempt, Cole leaves another phone message—telling the scientists that the Army of the Twelve Monkeys was only a bunch of animal activists, and, having done his job, he intends on staying in 1996.

In the terminal, Jose arrives from the future, with news of a pardon for Cole as a reward for his phone call. But when Jose tries to pass a pistol into James' hands, he refuses. Orders from the future insist that Railly be killed—if Cole doesn't do it, Jose will.

At the newsstand, Kathryn recognizes Dr. Peters and realizes he is the source of the deadly virus. Security stops Peters at the gate, insisting on inspecting his samples, and he opens one of the vials. The officers quickly move him along.

Railly and Cole argue with other security guards, desperately trying to reach Peters. James breaks through the gate and runs after Peters as he boards the plane. Just like his dream, nine-year-old James watches as officers shoot and kill his adult self. Railly spots the boy in the crowd and smiles.

Breathless, Peters sits in the first-class cabin. He meets a woman who introduces herself as Ms. Jones, in the insurance business. But the woman has been seen before—a member of Cole's panel of doctors.

Nine-year-old James watches as Peters' plane rises in the sky.

Afterwords

Director Terry Gilliam was known to many as the only American member of Monty Python's Flying Circus, the popular British comedy troupe. Moving from making small and odd animated clips for Python, he quickly established a reputation for making quirky but effective feature films, like 1977's *Jabberwocky*, 1981's *Time Bandits*, and 1985's *Brazil*, among others.

Intrigued with the notion of remaking the 1962 French sci-fi short *La Jetée*, Hollywood producer Robert Kosberg—known as "Mr. Pitch"—brought the project to Universal Studios. David Peoples, who had cowritten the screenplay for 1982's *Blade Runner*, teamed with his wife Janet to pen the script for the film, now titled *12 Monkeys*.

Universal passed on casting Nick Nolte and Jeff Bridges in the leads, and Gilliam instead chose Bruce Willis and an upcoming star named Brad Pitt (by the time *12 Monkeys* was released, Pitt's *Interview with the Vampire* and *Se7en* had come out, quickly establishing him as a major star).

Gilliam was given a production budget of $29 million, quite a low figure for a sci-fi film. Saddled with such a restricting figure, the director relied heavily on using real locations in Philadelphia and Baltimore instead of building elaborate sets. Shuttered old power stations gave the film a sense of abandoned technology, perfect for Gilliam's vision of the future.

However, the director's judgment might have been less than perfection in suggesting the appearance of a set used for the interrogation room where Bruce Willis' Cole spends several uncomfortable sessions. Seated in a chair attached to the wall by a rail, Cole is locked in and raised to an awkward height, with an ominous sphere suspended in front of him.

It was a very cool design—except the device's design was liberally (or literally) taken from a 1987 architectural illustration called "Neomechanical Tower (Upper) Chamber" by Lebbeus Woods. The architect saw *12 Monkeys* and wasn't particularly flattered by the imitation.

He sued Universal for copyright infringement, as the original work had been published in several books prior to making *12 Monkeys*. The court agreed with Woods and ruled the studio must pull the film from all theaters, having only been in release for less than a month. It could be rereleased, the court said, only after all scenes with the chair had been removed—a tedious and costly process.

Fortunately, cooler heads (and lighter wallets) prevailed, as Woods agreed to a cash settlement of more than half a million dollars, as well as an end credit that acknowledged the architect's inspiration for the Interrogation Room set.

The settlement was money well spent, as *12 Monkeys* went on to gross more than $57 million in the US, with double that figure overseas. The total of more than $168 million put the film in the Top Twenty–grossing films around the world for 1995.

The Fifth Element

Synopsis

- 1997—French/Gaumont/Columbia—125 min./color
- Director: Luc Besson
- Original music: Eric Serra
- Film editing: Sylvie Landra
- Production eesign: Dan Weil

Cast

- Bruce Willis (Korben Dallas)
- Gary Oldman (Jean-Baptiste Emanuel Zorg)

- Ian Holm (Father Vito Cornelius)
- Milla Jovovich (Leeloo)
- Chris Tucker (Ruby Rhod)
- Brion James (General Munro)
- Tommy "Tiny" Lister Jr. (President Lindberg)
- Charlie Creed-Miles (David)
- Tricky (Right Arm)
- Maïwenn Le Besco (Diva Plavalaguna)
- Richard Leaf (Neighbor)
- Julie T. Wallace (Major Iceborg)

In an ancient temple in 1914 Egypt, wall carvings tell a story of a Great Evil that descends upon Earth every five thousand years. To combat it, four elements—water, fire, earth, and air—must be strategically arranged around a fifth element—something human, a perfect being.

A strange spaceship lands in the desert next to the temple, and, to the amazement of the archaeologist and his assistant inside, large robotic aliens—called Mondoshawans—waddle into the site. They open a secret panel and recover four stones, representing the four elements, along with a sarcophagus containing the fifth.

The aliens have entrusted a priest to maintain their mission—taking care of the elements until they can use them to defend against the Great Evil. Billy, the professor's young assistant, fires a machine pistol out of fear for the aliens, and the secret panel closes. The alien commander is trapped inside, but the elements are on the ship, and it quickly takes off.

Three-hundred-plus years later, in 2263, a space cruiser tracks an unknown disturbance and reports to Lindberg, the President of the Federated Territories in New York City. Father Vito Cornelius addresses the council, believing the phenomenon to be a great evil and suggesting that attacking it would only strengthen it. Still, the space cruiser fires a massive salvo of missiles into the mass—it only grows larger and engulfs the spaceship.

Ex–war hero Korben Dallas wakes in his tiny apartment, deftly disarms a mugger waiting outside, and starts his job as a flying taxi cab driver. Meanwhile, Father Cornelius advises Lindberg there are only forty-eight hours before the evil will wipe everything out. The only things that can stop it are the five elements and the Mondoshawans.

The Mondoshawan spaceship makes its approach toward Earth, but two Mangalore fighters attack without warning. The Mondoshawan ship crashes in a ball of flames into Mars. General Munro of Lindberg's staff reports only one survivor.

In the Nucleolab, the survivor turns out to be only an arm of the Supreme Being—more than enough to recreate the entire being. Robotic arms begin to knit new bones and tissues at a rapid pace, with skin as the final addition. The result is a perfect and beautiful female form, albeit with bright orange hair.

Speaking a strange, unknown language, the woman breaks out from her enclosure and escapes into the ventilation system. Reaching the outside ledge of the building, hundreds of feet in the air, she leaps into the void and crashes into the back seat of Dallas' taxi.

Police arrive on the scene quickly and attempt to apprehend the woman. With tears in her eyes, she conveys a need for help to Dallas. While he knows it can only mean trouble, he throws the cab into gear and speeds off. The cops follow and soon, several squad cars open fire on the runaway taxi. But the cabbie's superior driving skills allow the pair to escape.

The woman weakly directs Dallas to find Father Cornelius. When he realizes he has the Fifth Element in his apartment, the priest faints dead away. When Dallas tries to steal a kiss from the beautiful woman, she quickly pulls his own gun on him, and he backs off. She does reveal her name is Leeloo. And Korben is smitten.

Leeloo flies through pages of an encyclopedia on a computer screen, boning up on the last five thousand years of mankind's history. But when Father Cornelius inquires about the whereabouts of the case with the four element stones, it has been stolen.

The case is being held by Agnot, leader of the Mangalores. An evil and well-to-do businessman named Jean-Baptiste Emanuel Zorg stands before the Mangalores in an enormous warehouse. He demonstrates the latest in handheld weapons—rifle, missiles, darts, flamethrower, capture net, even a freezing ice spray. The Mangalores are impressed, as they prepare to take delivery of dozens of them in exchange for the case. But it's empty.

Leeloo laughs, explaining the stones were too valuable to entrust to just humans, and she must meet someone in a hotel somewhere on planet Fhloston in the Angel constellation. In a rage, Zorg calls the deal off and departs, deciding to leave a single crate of weapons as consolation. Out of curiosity, one of the Mangalores presses an innocent red button on one of the guns—and the resulting explosion kills them all.

Zorg summons Cornelius to his offices. He demands the stones, not for himself but an interested customer. The priest refuses to reveal anything. While explaining his business, Zorg begins to choke on a cherry. Father Cornelius waits, but eventually slaps the man on the back and saves him. Tit for tat, Zorg agrees to spare the priest's life.

Using a remote-controlled cockroach equipped with an antenna, Zorg's aide—named Right Arm—listens in to a discussion between Lindberg and Munro. An opera diva named Plavalaguna has the stones and is scheduled to sing at the Fhloston hotel in a few hours. The president orders a single-man, covert operation to recover the stones.

General Munro informs Dallas that he will be going to the planet Fhloston, with the massive female Major Iceborg as his wife. The government has rigged a radio contest, with a trip to Fhloston as the prize and Dallas as the winner. His mission will be to recover the four stones and save the world. Somewhat reluctantly, Korben agrees.

Hearing Dallas announced as the winner on the radio, Cornelius and Leeloo make their way into his apartment at gunpoint. They demand his travel tickets, as they have an important mission: to save the world.

Gary Oldman in *The Fifth Element.*

Police arrive to apprehend Dallas, but they nab his neighbor by mistake. The arrest was orchestrated by Zorg, with Right Arm planning on taking Dallas' place on the trip to Fhloston. But the Mangalores double-cross Zorg by intercepting the police and taking the prisoner bag—which they believe holds Dallas—planning on retrieving the stones themselves and negotiating with Zorg.

The chance to steal the tickets presents itself, and Father Cornelius, crossing himself, grabs them and knocks Dallas out with one of his military awards. At the airport, he hands passports to Leeloo and his assistant, David. But Dallas shows up and takes his place at the boarding gate.

Two Mangalores, morphed into the guise of the arrested neighbor and a punky girlfriend, reach the gate and claim to be Dallas. The flight attendant quickly tags them as aliens, and the pair excuse themselves. They pull weapons and open fire on a police patrol.

As the radio prizewinner, Korben is pulled aside for a live interview with flamboyant DJ Ruby Rhod. With the super-hyped jock running his mouth at a mile a minute, Dallas barely gets in two words. Meanwhile, Right Arm tries to check in at the gate as Korben Dallas, but with two Dallases already showing up, three's a crowd and Right Arm is turned away.

Zorg, understandably disappointed to hear the news, blows up his aide via remote control, while the spaceship lifts off for Fhloston. The villain then speaks on the phone with his client, Mr. Shadow, calling from the dark mass that is the Great Evil. Shadow will soon arrive for the stones.

Landing at the flying Paradise cruise ship on the planet of Fhloston, Leeloo and Korben are welcomed by tropical music and hula dancers. But somehow, Cornelius has stowed away and made the trip as well.

Dallas joins Ruby Rhod for the gala performance of Diva Plavalaguna, as the Mangalores wait in the shadows. Blue-skinned, with a bulbous head and large hoses running down her side, the Diva begins singing a beautiful aria.

While she sings—shifting to a funk-based rhythm, Mangalores break into her suite and find the case of stones. But Leeloo, seething with rage, bursts in and dispatches the goons with swift martial arts skills.

Zorg has traveled to the Paradise, and he intercepts Leeloo as she leaves with the stones. She escapes by tossing the case to Zorg and bolting out through a ceiling air vent. Using his high-tech weapon, Zorg blasts at the woman as she tries to get away. Meanwhile, Mangalores invade the concert hall and wheelhouse, taking over the ship.

Plavalaguna is fatally wounded in the fray, as Zorg sets a time bomb on board and quickly flees in his spaceship with the case. Once again, it is empty.

As the Diva dies, Dallas recovers the stones that she hid inside her body. He leaves them with Ruby Rhod for safekeeping and comes out blasting at the Mangalores. Under heavy fire, Dallas relies on his old military training and gets out with Rhod and the stones.

They reach the control room, where the Mangalore leader holds Cornelius as a hostage. Intending to negotiate, Dallas walks in, immediately shoots the leader between the eyes, and the negotiations are over. The Mangalores have been defeated.

Korben finds Leeloo, injured and nearly unconscious, while Rhod and Cornelius find Zorg's time bomb with only a few minutes to go. The villain returns to the Paradise as guests begin to leave in dozens of lifeboat shuttles. He disarms his bomb, not realizing Dallas, Leeloo, Rhod, and Cornelius have just left in his spaceship.

As they depart the cruise ship, a dying Mangalore sets off another explosive device, destroying the Paradise and Zorg. President Lindberg is relieved to hear everyone is safe and heading directly to the temple in Egypt.

The celebration is short-lived, as the Great Evil has accelerated and is heading directly for Earth at a high rate of speed. Lindberg informs Dallas of the crisis, and Korben will get back to the president in a bit.

Leeloo quickly educates herself on the history of war and is saddened at what she learns. When the group reaches the temple, the four stones are set in place and activated. But Leeloo, tired and discouraged about mankind's behavior, can't act as the Fifth Element. With only seconds left, Korben shows her that love and other good things make living worthwhile.

They kiss and a brilliant light streams from Leeloo, shooting into space and destroying the Great Evil. The remaining mass becomes a second moon, orbiting Earth. Everyone rejoices, and, at the Nucleolab, the president wishes to congratulate Korben and Leeloo. However, they are preoccupied with each other.

Afterwords

As is frequently noted in this book, it often takes many years for a sci-fi film to see the light of the projector. In the case of *The Fifth Element*, the project was part of director and cowriter Luc Besson for more than twenty years.

As a teen living outside of Paris in 1975, Besson was often bored and began writing the film with the influence of French comic books that he often read. By

1990, his script had reached an unusable four hundred pages in length. With the help of Bronx-born screenwriter Robert Mark Kamen, the story was revised to a reasonable 125 pages or so.

Next, Besson returned to the original influence for *The Fifth Element*, calling on comic book illustrators from France and other countries to create more than eight thousand storyboard drawings to visualize the scenes. He wound up with a big-budget project, requiring FX that might not even be possible.

The Frenchman tapped into Digital Domain, the California-based visual effects shop started by James Cameron and Stan Winston, to realize his vision. Supervised by Mark Stetson, Digital combined miniatures, computer graphics, motion-controlled cameras, and advanced compositing to help make Besson's dream come true.

In one example, New York City in the twenty-third century saw the iconic Statue of Liberty no longer on an island but part of the sprawling landmass. According to Besson's backstory, the exportation of Earth water in order to colonize other planets had dropped the sea levels by three hundred feet. To expand skyscrapers, construction crews built downward into the new land, not toward the sky.

Models in various scales were employed in abundance. Many of the twenty-five Manhattan buildings were built with a ratio where one inch equaled two feet (known as 1:24 scale). Bruce Willis' antigravity taxi was larger, just the right size for a Barbie doll. Where larger expanses of landscape were needed, the popular model train scale of HO was used.

The result of cowriter/director Besson's efforts was a very entertaining film, combining lots of action, slick (and not-so-slick) humor, and a basic "save the world" story. Knowing the effects couldn't be second-rate, he devoted a large amount of the production budget toward them.

With that in mind, Besson originally thought a big star like Willis would be out of the movie's price bracket. The actor, however, assured the director, "if I like it, we'll find a way." He was right, agreeing to pass on a guaranteed paycheck and taking a percentage of the film's gross.

Smart guy, that Willis. Shot with an estimated budget of $90 million, *The Fifth Element* did poorly in the States, tallying only $63 million. But it grossed $200 million overseas, for a total of well over $260 million. It also won the BAFTA Film Award (Britain's Oscar) for Best Special Effects and earned seven César Awards (France's Oscar), winning three, including Best Director for Luc Besson.

The Matrix

Synopsis

- 1999—American/Warner Brothers—136 min./color
- Directors: Andy Wachowski & Larry (Now Lana) Wachowski

- Original music: Don Davis
- Film editing: Zach Staenberg
- Production design: Owen Paterson

Cast

- Keanu Reeves (Thomas Anderson/Neo)
- Lawrence Fishburne (Morpheus)
- Carrie-Anne Moss (Trinity)
- Hugo Weaving (Agent Smith)
- Gloria Foster (The Oracle)
- Joe Pantoliano (Cipher)
- Marcus Chong (Tank)
- Julian Arahanga (Apoc)
- Matt Doran (Mouse)
- Belinda Mcclory (Switch)
- Ray Anthony Parker (Dozer)
- Paul Goddard (Agent Brown)
- Robert Taylor (Agent Jones)

In a rundown hotel, police corner a beautiful girl named Trinity. But she quickly subdues them with an astounding demonstration of martial arts and athletic powers. Sunglass-wearing special agents take over the chase, and Trinity barely escapes by being downloaded through a telephone booth phone line.

Computer hacker Thomas Anderson meets Trinity in a bar. She strangely calls him Neo and warns him of imminent danger. The special agents apprehend Neo, despite the help of a FedEx'ed cell phone and a man named Morpheus. The agents try to solicit Neo's aid in combating Morpheus, whom they label a terrorist. When he refuses, they inexplicably seal his mouth and implant a bio-electronic bug through his navel.

Suddenly, Neo awakes from this nightmare, safe in his bed. Or is he? A phone call from Morpheus convinces Neo this is no dream, and he meets Morpheus and Trinity. They painfully extract the squirmy bug from Neo. Morpheus offers Neo the chance to learn what the Matrix is—he offers the truth about the real world. All Neo has to do is chose a red pill or blue pill—blue will return Neo to his old life. Choosing the red will take Neo deep into the Matrix. Neo takes the red pill.

Neo is reborn into an incubation pod, surrounded by thousands just like it. A spiderlike machine unplugs Neo from the womb, and he joins a group of rebels lead by Morpheus. They believe Neo is special—he is The One.

The real world is actually 2200 A.D., where Morpheus commands a pirate hovercraft, called the Nebuchadnezzar, to infiltrate the Matrix. His crew includes Trinity, as well as Apoc, Switch, Cipher, Tank and his brother Dozer, and Mouse. Neo finds the Matrix is a virtual world—a computer simulation that masks the bleak, bombed-out reality of the twenty-third century.

Keanu Reeves in *The Matrix.*

When intelligent machines took over the world in the twenty-first century, they developed a system to grow and harvest humans as an endless energy source, complete with a computer port in the back of their skulls. The Matrix merely keeps humans under control in a virtual world. Neo can't accept the truth and passes out.

When he comes to, he finds that he has been chosen as The One, the only person who can destroy the Matrix and free humanity from slavery. He is quickly educated, as hundreds of software programs are loaded into his brain. He shares a martial arts sparring program with Morpheus—Trinity's previous skills and agility are now explained. Morpheus and Neo spin, tumble, and literally fly through the air in a virtual dojo, while the crew watches Neo's uploading body flinch in a reclining chair.

A jump program allows Neo and Morpheus to span great distances across virtual city rooftops. Squid-like devices are searching for the Nebuchadnezzar, but they quickly evade the menacing machines. Meanwhile, Cipher has grown tired of the rebel life and makes a deal with the agents to turn over Morpheus.

The crew travel into the Matrix to meet the Oracle. A longtime member of the rebels, the Oracle is a cookie-baking, chain-smoking lady who does not believe that Neo is The One. As the crew prepares to leave the Matrix, they're ambushed by armed police. Mouse is killed in a hail of bullets, and his real-world body bleeds and expires.

Lead Agent Smith captures Morpheus while Cipher makes his way back to the ship before the others. He shoots Dozer and Tank with a fiery laser blast and begins to unplug the rest of the crew, killing them. As he prepares to kill Neo, the wounded Tank blasts Cipher into eternity.

The agents have Morpheus tied up in a high-rise office building, while Neo continues to insist to Trinity that he is not The One. They devise a plan to rescue Morpheus by using guns—lots of guns. A software program produces an endless array of assault weapons, rifles, pistols, and munitions. Agent Smith confesses that he must escape the Matrix, and Morpheus is the key for his escape.

Trinity and Neo blast their way past building security with two-fisted fire-power and an agile display of hand-to-hand combat against armed soldiers. They take the battle to the rooftop, dodging bullets with lighting speed. Trinity hijacks a helicopter, and Neo rakes the office where Morpheus is being held with thousands of bullet rounds from an air-powered mini gun.

Morpheus breaks his bonds and jumps out the window. Neo grabs him in mid-air, and the two dangle dangerously from the chopper. But gunfire disables the helicopter, and Neo, amazingly, saves Trinity and Morpheus—indeed, he is The One.

Morpheus and Trinity upload back to the Nebuchadnezzar, but Neo is left alone to face off against Agent Smith. They brutally beat each other with martial art moves. Neo finally wins the battle as Smith is struck and carried away by a subway train.

Sentinel robots have been dispatched to destroy the Nebuchadnezzar. Agents continue to pursue Neo through the city's streets and into tenement apartments. Sentinels attach themselves to Morpheus' ship and begin to burn through the hull with lasers.

Neo comes face-to-face with the regenerated Agent Smith, who pumps round after round of gunfire into him and kills Neo's virtual self. Trinity professes her love to the now-still real-world body of Neo—his virtual form rises and stops Smith's gunfire in mid-air, inspecting the bullets as they hang, then fall harmlessly to the hallway floor. He realizes that he is The One and sees the Matrix for the first time as it really is—digital data that glows green, without the mask of the false world.

The enraged Smith attacks Neo, who defends with only one hand—Neo destroys Smith, blasting him into binary bits. Neo returns to the ship with seconds to spare, as the Sentinels breach the inner hull. But a blast from an electromagnetic field system renders the machines useless, as Neo and Trinity embrace. Neo now carries on the mission to destroy the Matrix.

Afterwords

The first of three *Matrix* films, it bore more than a passing resemblance to a 1973 German made-for-TV film called *World on a Wire* (*Welt am Draht*) by Rainer Werner Fassbinder. That entry was based on a 1964 sci-fi novel by Daniel F. Galouye called *Simulacron 3* (also published as *Counterfeit World*). Films like 1998's *Dark City* and 1999's *The Thirteenth Floor* (another adaptation of Galouye's book) also tapped heavily into the concept of a virtual world for the masses.

Much was made about the visual effects in this flick (enough to win an Oscar, along with awards for Editing, Sound Mixing, and Sound Design). New ground was broken with the introduction of a refined version of bullet-time cinematography, a startling combination of slow-motion action and three-dimensional camera movement. The process merged high-speed motion picture photography with the images from more than one hundred still cameras, arranged in an arc around the performance. Once united with the aid of a computer, the mesmerizing effect altered motion and time in viewing gunfights and fistfights.

The martial arts in *The Matrix* were heavily influenced by the Hong Kong–based fight films of the seventies and eighties. It's no coincidence that the Wachowskis enlisted master kung fu trainer and stunt specialist Yuen Wo-Ping, director of several Jackie Chan action flicks, to work with the cast. They spent long months of daily, diligent practice—October 1997 to March 1998—to learn the martial art. The acting principles were also trained in how to cope with wires that suspended them during the stunts that allowed them to walk up walls and fly through the air.

It may be difficult to imagine just what is needed to produce the FX for a film like *The Matrix*. A small special-effects group known as Manex Visual Effects, led by John Gaeta, headed up the production of nearly four hundred visual effects shots. They were created by sixty-five computer graphics artists, along with two small Australian-based FX houses. In some cases, software programs needed to be written from scratch to handle computer effects that had never before been accomplished. Part of the CGI artists' jobs included creating simulations of the live-action martial arts fights. With angles, times, and distances carefully planned, the real shots were much easier to create and then combine with visual enhancements.

Even though the film was shot in Sydney, Australia, Chicago street names are used predominantly. It's no accident, as the Wachowskis are from the Windy City. The siblings' background in the comic book world was evident in the six hundred pages of detailed, comic-panel-like storyboards that were prepared for the film. And, like the proverbial kids-in-the-candy-store, *The Matrix* allowed the Wachowskis to indulge their love of comics, Asian kung-fu films, and Japanese anime.

As with many films, the final cast of *The Matrix* were not necessarily the first choices for the producers and Wachowskis. Imagine Nicolas Cage, Ewan McGregor, or Will Smith as Neo, or Janet Jackson as Trinity, or perhaps Jean Reno as Agent Smith, or even Val Kilmer as Morpheus. While those possibilities are fine performers, most viewers would agree the right choices won out in the end.

The Matrix cost $63 million to make and grossed more than $175 million domestically. It was successful enough to spawn two sequels, *The Matrix Reloaded* and *The Matrix Revolutions*. They were shot almost simultaneously and were released in May and November 2003, respectively. When overseas grosses are added in, *The Matrix* trilogy brought in a total of more than $1.6 billion.

A.I. Artificial Intelligence

Synopsis

- 2001—American/Warner Brothers—145 min./color
- Director: Steven Spielberg
- Original music: John Williams
- Film editing: Michael Kahn
- Production design: Rick Carter
- Based on the 1969 short story "Super-Toys Last All Summer Long," by Brian Aldiss

Cast
- Haley Joel Osment (DAVID)
- Jude Law (Gigolo Joe)
- Frances O'Connor (Monica Swinton)
- Sam Robards (Henry Swinton)
- Jake Thomas (Martin Swinton)
- William Hurt (Professor Allen Hobby)
- Jack Angel (Voice of Teddy)

Somewhere in the future, greenhouse gases have melted the polar ice caps, destroying many of the world's coastal cities and creating great hardships. Many countries have licensed pregnancy to limit the population and developed robots (called "mechas") to handle many of the world's tasks.

The next step for the people at a company called Cybertronics is to create a child android capable of loving and being loved. In less than two years, the company selects one of their employees and his wife, Henry and Monica, to have the first prototype of the child robot, a young boy named David. Their selection is a fitting one, as their own son Martin is in a coma and has little chance of recovery.

David's new pseudo-mother is cold, distant, and uncomfortable, even refusing to help him dress for bedtime. She eventually warms to her new pseudo-son, telling Henry that David is a gift. She even gives him a special supertoy that belonged to Martin, an animated and articulate stuffed bear named Teddy. Against all odds, Martin recovers and returns home. He thinks of David as just another supertoy. He provokes David into eating spinach (mechas don't eat, since they don't need to), requiring a thorough internal cleaning from Cybertronics technicians.

In a plot fueled by jealousy, Martin convinces David to cut a lock of Monica's hair while she sleeps. She wakes to find David with scissors in his hand, and Henry believes that David is dangerous. The taunting from Martin's friends cause David to pull Martin into a swimming pool for protection and Martin nearly drowns. His parents fear David, and Monica tearfully abandons him in the woods.

Joe is a handsome mecha-gigolo. He discovers one of his clients murdered and has to run for fear of being accused of the killing. David dreams of becoming a real boy like Pinocchio, a story Monica used to read to him. David and Joe, along with other discarded and damaged mechas, are hunted and captured by Lord Johnson-Johnson, who runs a Flesh Fair. These are carnival-like festivals of mecha torture and destruction. The audience mistakenly believes that David and Joe are real people and insist on their release.

The freed duo travels to Rouge City, where David wants to find the Blue Fairy from *Pinocchio*, who can turn him into a real boy. They find the holographic Dr. Know, who advises them to travel to the partially sunken city of Manhattan and find David's creator, Professor Allan Hobby. The boy comes face-to-face with a carbon copy of himself and destroys it, believing himself to be unique and the only David. He meets Professor Hobby, but is desperate to find his mother.

Ashley Scott and Jude Law in *A.I. Artificial Intelligence.*

Despondent, he dives into the watery streets of Manhattan. Joe pulls him from the water in an amphibicopter (a helicopter that is also a submarine) and bids goodbye to David. Diving underwater, David comes upon the Coney Island amusement park. He finds the Pinocchio exhibit and a statue of the Blue Fairy. David pleads with her to make him a real boy.

A corroded Ferris wheel tumbles onto the amphibicopter, trapping David and Teddy for two thousand years. Telepathic aliens excavate the now-frozen waters of the area, finding David and releasing him. Realizing he is the last remaining connection to long-extinct humans, the aliens wish to make David comfortable and happy. They read his mind and recreate his house and his image of the Blue Fairy. He again pleads with her to make him a real boy.

Teddy has saved a lock of Monica's hair when David cut it, so the aliens are able to recreate David's mom—but only for one day. When morning comes, David spends the greatest, happiest day of his existence—no Henry, no Martin, just David and his mommy. They play games and even have a birthday cake with candles. As night falls, Monica falls asleep and, for the first time—so does David. He goes to the place where dreams are born.

Afterwords

Director Stanley Kubrick had invested many years in preproduction planning for *A.I. Artificial Intelligence*, including cooking a Thanksgiving dinner to entice potential FX supervisor Dennis Muren and having an amazing fifteen hundred illustrations prepared to reflect his concept of the *Pinocchio*-influenced flick. He eventually began discussing the project with Steven Spielberg, who shared Kubrick's enthusiasm for the story.

Kubrick eventually anointed Spielberg to direct, while he would produce the film. But after the British director died in 1999, Kubrick's wife asked Spielberg to complete the project, fearing it would never be finished without Spielberg at the helm. The director agreed, completing the sci-fi vision of Stanley Kubrick as a tribute to the fallen creator, as well as seeing the concept as an excellent story to tell.

Thirteen-year-old Haley Joel Osment, nominated for a Best Supporting Actor Oscar for 1999's *The Sixth Sense*, took the difficult lead role of David. Makeup designer Ve Neill used a subtle approach to suggest David's youthful robot exterior. She shaved Osment's face (despite no evidence of a five o'clock shadow) to create a smooth, albeit artificial skin appearance. She also had a fake dental insert created to give the robot boy a perfect gum line.

Neill gave Jude Law's Gigolo Joe a more stylized look by airbrushing in a solid hairline and adding a small prosthetic jaw appliance. The cast also included honored actors like Robin Williams, Ben Kingsley, Chris Rock, and Meryl Streep, who provided voices for Dr. Know and several of the robots on the run.

Dozens of mechas are seen throughout the film, created both as physical and CG effects. Stan Winston Studios—experienced in fashioning memorable mechanicals like the Terminator—used R/C animatronics, rod and cable–controlled puppets, and even full-face prosthetics to achieve the wide variety of robots needed in *A.I.*

One mecha in particular, the Insecurity Guard seen in the junkyard, was made from a facial life cast of Stan Winston himself. It took six operators to manipulate the cables and rods in order for the character to move. The work of Stan Winston Studios, as well as that of Industrial Light and Magic, was nominated for an Academy Award for Best Visual Effects.

Despite its amazing visuals, *A.I. Artificial Intelligence* might have been too vague in its reimagining of *Pinocchio* for the average filmgoer. It brought in just under $80 million domestically, on a production budget of $100 million. It did reasonably well overseas, collecting nearly $160 million at the box office, for a total worldwide gross of almost $236 million.

Minority Report

Synopsis

- 2002—American/Twentieth Century-Fox—145 min./color
- Director: Steven Spielberg
- Original music: John Williams
- Film editing: Michael Kahn
- Production design: Alex McDowell
- Based on the 1956 Philip K. Dick short story "The Minority Report"

Cast

- Tom Cruise (Chief John Anderton)
- Max Von Sydow (Director Lamar Burgess)
- Colin Farrell (Danny Witwer)
- Steve Harris (Jad)
- Neal McDonough (Fletcher)
- Patrick Kilpatrick (Knott)
- Samantha Morton (Agatha)
- Daniel London (Wally)
- Lois Smith (Dr. Iris Hineman)
- Tim Blake Nelson (Gideon)
- Kathryn Morris (Lara)
- Arye Gross (Howard Marks)
- Ashley Crow (Sarah Marks)
- Mike Binder (Leo Crow)
- Jessica Harper (Anne Lively)
- Jason Antoon (Rufus T. Riley)
- Peter Stormare (Dr. Solomon Eddie)
- David Stifel (Lycon)

In 2054, John Anderton heads up the Department of Precrime in Washington, D.C. Floating in a small pool of a thick fluid, three mutant humans have the unique skill of precognition—they are able to envision serious crimes before they are committed. The names of victims and perpetrators are inscribed in wooden balls. Like an orchestra conductor, Anderton reviews a future murder scene in holographic detail, searching for clues—he needs the address.

Anderton and his team gear up, hurrying to catch the perp, Howard Marks, as the time clicks down. He correctly suspects his wife, Sarah, is having an affair. Marks hides in the family bedroom while Sarah and her paramour tease each other.

Police rappel from a snail-shaped hovership into the park across from Marks' home. With only seconds to spare, Anderton and his team burst in and stop Marks from murdering the two people on the bed. Police apprehend him, charging Marks with future murder. They place the Halo on his head—an electronic device that renders its wearer comatose.

A television commercial praises the success of the police and their precogs, having reduced the crime rate in D.C. to zero within one year. Legislation is pending to use the precogs across the country. Danny Witwer, from the U.S, Department of Justice, evaluates the effectiveness of Precrime firsthand in Anderton's handling of the Marks case.

Chief Anderton reveals a dark side—his addiction to a hallucinogenic inhalant called Neuroin. In a dark alley, Anderton makes his purchase from an eyeless dealer named Lycon. At home, Anderton misses his ex-wife, Lara, and his boy, Sean—missing for the last six years.

At Precrime HQ, Director Lamar Burgess warns Anderton to be wary of Witwer as he skeptically reviews the program. Armed with a warrant from the attorney general, Witwer arranges an unprecedented direct meeting with the precogs, named Agatha, Arthur, and Dashiell. Police monitor their clairvoyance through an electrical hookup.

Left alone in what is known as "The Temple," Agatha startles John when she springs from her pool and grabs him. She wonders if he can see what she does—a woman's frightened face. Agatha sinks back into the fluid and John leaves, shaken.

Tom Cruise in *Minority Report.*

Anderton pays a visit to the Department of Containment, where a guard named Gideon watches over hundreds of comatose prisoners. They find the man who drowned the woman in Agatha's vision, named Anne Lively, but the future killer is an unknown. Even stranger is the fact that Agatha's vision file is missing from the files.

Anderton shares his visit with Burgess, who is more concerned with losing control of Precrime if it goes national. He is also uneasy with rumors that John has been seen in the seedier parts of the city, something that Witwer could use against the department.

Witwer quietly inspects John's apartment, finding Neuroin canisters and videos of Lara and Sean. It is clear that Witwer has Anderton in his sights.

Agatha sees the premeditated murder of a man named Leo Crow. Reviewing the scene, Anderton is stunned to see the future killer is himself. He grabs the incriminating ball before his partner Jad can see it and tries to make sense of what is supposed to happen in thirty-six hours. Wally, the precogs' caretaker, gives the chief two minutes to escape before setting off an alarm.

Leaving in an elevator, Anderton is confronted by Witwer. He shares his findings from John's apartment, although he is unaware of the future murder. Anderton believes Witwer has set him up and shares his fears with Burgess while escaping in a maglev car. John doesn't even know a Leo Crow.

He jumps from the speeding car, landing in the midst of a classroom of contortionists. Meanwhile, in Burgess' office, Witwer presses the director for his reasons to protect Anderton, accusing him of conspiracy.

Customized billboards call out to Anderton by name as he makes his way to a mass transit line. Eye-scan recognition tips off Witwer and the police to his location. Cornered by ground and airborne officers, who wait with Halo in hand, Anderton leads his own team on a wild chase through the alleys. Gaining the upper hand in a fistfight with Witwer in an automatic car assembly plant, the chief gets free and drives away in a vehicle built around him.

He makes his way to the secluded house of Dr. Iris Hineman, an eccentric scientist who stumbled upon precrime while studying precogs years ago. She can't help Anderton, but reveals the precogs don't always agree in their visions. Should one of the three disagree in what they see, a Minority Report is created.

The chief, wracked with the guilt of having possibly incarcerated innocent people, knew nothing of this until now, but Burgess did. Insisting he will not kill Crow, Anderton needs the redeeming Minority Report, but they are all immediately destroyed. However, Hineman admits the original report always stays within the precog. All that is needed is a download. John must get Agatha.

Fearing detection by eye scan, John seeks the assistance of Dr. Solomon Eddie, a back alley surgeon who can replace his eyeballs. The doctor happens to be an old case of the chief's, sent away for treating burn victims by setting them on fire. He places an evil-looking device over John's head and begins the replacement procedure.

Witwer interviews Lara, who knows nothing of John's whereabouts. The Justice agent questions her reasoning for divorcing her husband, and she admits the memories of their lost son were just too great to bear.

John's face must remain bandaged for twelve hours, and the doctor leaves him alone, with an inhaler of Neuroin to keep him calm. Anderton dreams of Sean's disappearance from the public pool years back.

Teams of officers file out of a hovership, canvassing the poorer parts of the city. Officers Fletcher and Knott make their way into the dilapidated building where Anderton is recovering. They deploy small and spindly robotic eye-scanning spiders to help their search.

Knowing he'll be found, John immerses himself under ice water in a bath-tub. One lone bubble from his nose floats to the surface, and the spiders find him. Despite the doctor's questionable methods, their eye scan comes up negative—the operation was a success.

Dressed in an overcoat and stocking cap, Anderton injects his face with a paralyzing device Dr. Eddie left with him. John no longer resembles John but a wrinkled old man. He uses one of his old eyeballs to scan his way into police headquarters through a back entrance. Slipping into the temple, Anderton convinces Wally to help him.

Danny Witwer continues to review the holographic files of the Leo Crow future murder. A faint image in a mirror puzzles the agent, and he struggles to adjust the quality of it. Suddenly, the picture becomes clear—it is Agatha's face in the mirror. Witwer knows John's coming to get her.

He hurries to the temple too late, watching as Anderton grabs Agatha and flushes them both away in the pool. Wally is hysterical—without Agatha, the other two precogs won't see with any accuracy. With less than one hour remaining, Witwer and the police must find the room where the murder will take place.

Frozen with fear, Agatha rides with John as they flee—she is tired of seeing the future. At HQ, Witwer figures Anderton intends on proving his innocence. But he will need technical assistance in downloading the Minority Report from Agatha. The agent finds a hidden name—Rufus T. Riley.

Riley runs an uninhibited cyber-parlor where the wildest of fantasies are fulfilled. Anderton needs his help, but when he exposes Agatha as a precog, Riley falls to his knees in reverence. He hooks electrodes to her scalp, and images pour out onto a giant screen, including John shooting Leo Crow.

There is no Minority Report for John, but a convulsing Agatha reveals the image of someone drowning Anne Lively. The precog wants John to see the killer, but the images suddenly stop. Police march into Riley's place, and John pulls Agatha out into the mall. The precog perfectly directs Anderton in their escape out of the market.

John and Agatha locate the building where Crow lives, and parts of the pre-cog's precrime vision start to come true. With just five minutes to go, Anderton enters Crow's apartment, strewn with hundreds of children's photos—among them is Sean's. The realization strikes Anderton—there is no Minority Report, because he really is going to kill Leo Crow.

In a rage, John grabs Crow as he enters the room. Agatha is terrorized as Anderton manhandles Crow for kidnapping Sean, among the other children. He admits killing the boy, and John's fury continues to rain blows down upon Crow. Anderton pulls his gun on the beaten man.

Agatha pleads with the chief that he still has a choice of killing or not killing Crow. As seconds tick down to zero, John lowers his weapon and begins to read the Miranda rights to Crow.

The man begins a strange confession, disappointed that Anderton didn't shoot him. Someone promised Crow that his family would be paid handsomely if he pretended to murder Sean, prompting John to kill him. But he doesn't know who made the offer that would set Anderton up for murder.

Knowing his family gets nothing if John doesn't kill him, Crow grabs the chief's hand, places the gun to his own chest, and pulls the trigger. Anderton and Agatha quickly leave.

Witwer and Fletcher review the murder scene, and the Justice agent now knows this was a setup, with Anderton as the target. He calls Burgess and arranges a meeting to discuss the findings. In reviewing the separate precogs' visions of the Anne Lively murder, Witwer notes they differ—the murder happened at two separate times.

According to Witwer, someone found a way to cheat the system. When the Precrime crew stopped the killing of Anne Lively, somebody waited a few minutes and committed it exactly the same way—someone with access to the Precrime system. Caught as the villain and knowing the precogs are not active, Burgess shoots Witwer dead with Anderton's gun.

John and Agatha pull in to Lara's house, while she calls Burgess and asks for his help to clear her ex-husband. The director will be there shortly. Sitting in Sean's bedroom, Agatha tells John and Lara of his future, a successful life—Sean is alive, somewhere. Then John realizes that Anne Lively was Agatha's mother.

Hoverships surround the house, and officers charge John with the murders of Crow and Witwer. They place the Halo on his head, and Agatha returns to the temple, with Arthur and Dashiell.

Gideon locks Anderton away in the Department of Containment, as Burgess welcomes Lara to his house. He dresses in preparation for a banquet being held in his honor as the new National Director of Precrime. Lara mentions Anne Lively, a name that clearly shakes Burgess, but he claims ignorance. But when he offers to review the records for any drowning, Lara notes she never mentioned a drowning. Burgess insists on discussing it later.

At gunpoint, Lara forces Gideon to release her husband, while Burgess receives accolades at his banquet. Anderton calls Burgess with the facts about the Lively killing. At Lara's request, Jad plays Agatha's vision of her mother's murder, and it appears on the large screen in the banquet hall.

Lively was a junkie who gave her daughter, Agatha, up for adoption. When she cleaned up, she wanted Agatha back, but Burgess and Hineman had already turned her into a precog. Without Agatha, Precrime would have never worked. So, Anne Lively had to be eliminated.

Understanding the system, Burgess hired a John Doe to kill Anne—a murder the precogs saw and Doe was captured. Shortly after, Burgess drowned Lively in the very manner the precogs had originally seen. That second vision was considered to be a useless echo, allowing Burgess to get away with murder.

Burgess moves into the kitchen to escape, while Anderton's voice stays in his ear. At Precrime HQ, a victim ball drops, with John's name on it. The perp's ball reveals Burgess' name. The precogs see Anderton shot by Lamar, and hoverships are dispatched.

Burgess' dilemma is twofold: If he doesn't kill John, then Precrime is a failure and Lamar is out; if he does kill John, he goes away for murder, but Precrime and the precogs work. But Anderton also reminds Burgess that, since he knows his future, he has the option to change it.

Seeking forgiveness from John, Burgess makes his choice and shoots himself in the chest. As a result, the Precrime program is abandoned. Sara, now pregnant, hugs her husband, John. In some unknown and secluded location, the precogs live in peace.

Afterwords

With the success of 1982's *Blade Runner*, Hollywood reacted as if sci-fi author Philip K. Dick had just started writing (even though he died just a few months before the release of *Blade Runner*). In reality, Dick had been writing for more than three decades. In the years that followed the Ridley Scott film, producers began to tap into many of the author's unique works.

With 1990's *Total Recall* being a hit, the possibility of a sequel was considered, with Dick's "Minority Report" short story—written way back in 1956—being the basis of it. Arnold Schwarzenegger's Quaid would be in charge of mutants who could prevent crimes by looking into the future. But, like many Hollywood ventures, it stalled.

Twentieth Century-Fox and potential director Jan De Bont got ahold of the project, taking out all references to *Total Recall*. When De Bont stumbled in directing less-than-successful films like 1997's *Speed 2: Cruise Control* and 1998's *The Haunting*, Fox dropped the whole thing like a hot precog. In came Steven Spielberg, with intentions of casting Tom Cruise as the lead.

Even though he was making a sci-fi film set in the unseen future of 2054, Spielberg wanted the world of *Minority Report* set in as much foreseeable reality as possible. To do that, the director assembled more than one dozen futur-ists—architects, scientists, computer specialists, and artists—for a three-day think-tank summit in sunny Santa Monica, California. Their collective thoughts and opinions helped to shape the film's visuals with a true sense of predicted authenticity.

In the film, one of the high-tech tools used for future crime fighting were the robotic spiders. The spindly devices crawled around with a seek-find-identify agenda, keying in on a human's body heat. To avoid them, Cruise's character hid in a tub of ice water and almost got away with it. One little bubble of air gave him away.

Instead of relying on a computer-generated image, Cruise figured he could control his nostrils enough to release a single bubble on cue (it's a good thing the actor didn't have beans before shooting the scene). He popped a single bubble when needed, and Spielberg got the shot he wanted.

Another scene involved Anderton's meeting with a drug dealer whose eyes had been long ago torn from his head. Spielberg wanted the effect to be extremely graphic. Fortunately, ILM art director Alex Laurant had chicken for dinner that night. (Huh? I'll explain.) Examining the raw poultry skin, Laurant noticed its texture and realized it was perfect for the sickly remnants of the dealer's misfortune.

The art director sculpted eye sockets out of clay, then sutured in the chicken skin with a needle and thread. The ghastly result was photographed and composited onto footage of actor David Stifel's face. ILM took to kiddingly calling the character Chicken Man.

The Spielberg-Cruise team created an exciting future film noir, with the director making sure the audience left the theater with a happy ending. But the real happy ending was the success of *Minority Report*.

The budget of just over $100 million returned a domestic gross of more than $132 million for the summer release. Overseas, it took in over $226 million.

The total take of more than $358 million put *Minority Report* in the Top Ten–grossing films of 2002. Not a bad showing, considering it shared the year with blockbuster film franchises like *Lord of the Rings*, *Harry Potter*, *Spider-Man*, *Star Wars*, *Men in Black*, and James Bond.

Elysium

Synopsis

- 2013—American/Tri-Star Pictures—109 min./color
- Director: Neill Blomkamp
- Original music: Ryan Amon
- Film editing: Julian Clarke, Lee Smith
- Production design: Philip Ivey

Cast

- Matt Damon (Max Da Costa)
- Jodie Foster (Delacourt)
- Sharlto Copley (Kruger)

- Alice Braga (Frey)
- Diego Luna (Julio)
- Wagner Moura (Spider)
- William Fitchner (John Carlyle)
- Emma Tremblay (Matilda)
- Faran Tahir (President Patel)

In the latter part of the 2000s, Earth found itself dense with population, diseased, and devastated by pollution. Its cities were decayed. The rich, however, left the planet to continue their opulent lifestyles on a Torus, an orbiting space colony called Elysium. Sickness and injuries on the Torus are cured with the life-giving Med-Bay—available only on Elysium.

Poor and homeless children, like orphan Max Da Costa, could only dream of a world like Elysium. In 2154, Max is now an adult, an ex-con in the broken metropolis of Los Angeles. A robot police force patrols the city, and Da Costa finds they have not been programmed with tolerance or a sense of humor.

They break Max's arm during a routine search, and he runs into Frey, his childhood girlfriend, at the hospital where she is a nurse. A meeting with his mechanized parole officer doesn't go much better, and Max makes his way to his job at Armadyne, where he assembles the very police robots that abused him. The company's founder, John Carlyle, struggles to maintain its profitability.

A high-tech smuggler named Spider tries to sneak three shuttle ships, filled with sick and injured Earth dwellers, up to Elysium. Against executive orders, Secretary of Defense Delacourt orders them shot down by a scruffy government agent named Kruger. Two are destroyed, but a third ship lands on Elysium. Robot security either kills or deports all of its passengers.

A jammed door forces Max to inspect an assembly chamber, even though he knows it's dangerous. When the jam clears itself, Max is caught inside and becomes exposed to deadly radiation. The incident leaves him with only five days to live, and Carlyle shows no concern at all.

Delacourt's insubordinate action earns her a meeting with President Patel and his cabinet. She arrogantly defends her actions as necessary to maintain the security of Elysium, but Patel doesn't accept it. He reprimands her and orders Kruger discharged for his role in the incident.

Dying from radiation poisoning, Max knows he must find a way to Elysium and a Med-Bay. Meanwhile, Frey's daughter, Matilda, is stricken with leukemia but unable to stay at her mother's hospital.

Da Costa begs Spider for an ID and a ticket to Elysium, but the lawbreaker insists on making a deal with Max. Using a small implantable device, Max must steal information from John Carlyle's brain—the data would be worth billions of dollars to Spider. To help Da Costa's weakened condition, Spider attaches a powerful exoskeleton to his arms, back, and spine.

Secretly, Delacourt meets with Carlyle. In collusion, he will design a program to override the computer system of Elysium, which will make Delacourt president. In return, Armadyne will enjoy a generous defense contract with the

The exoskeleton side of Matt Damon in *Elysium.*

new head of state. Carlyle empties the entire reboot system for Elysium into his head, then sets a lethal protection protocol.

With friend Julio as his wheelman, Max intercepts Carlyle's shuttle as it lifts off for Elysium. Guard robots are destroyed, and Max grabs the data from the head of a fatally wounded Carlyle.

Delacourt receives word of the attack and calls in Kruger, with his reinstatement as payment for his help. The villain flies in aboard an assault ship and kills everyone but Max, who is badly wounded. He escapes in the confusion, with Delacourt ordering Da Costa's capture at all costs and a lockdown of the entire LA airspace.

Max seeks medical help from his friend Frey at the hospital. She takes Da Costa and her daughter home, where she tends to her friend. In the morning, Kruger's flying camera finds Da Costa on the run, but he downs it with a rock.

Kruger takes a terrified Frey and her daughter as prisoners in the ship, while Spider reviews the data from Max's head and realizes that, if they could reboot Elysium, everyone on Earth could become citizens of the Torus. All Da Costa wants is to get there for a chance to live.

He challenges Kruger to come and get him. When the ship lands, Max threatens to blow his own head—and all the data—to kingdom come with a live grenade, if Kruger doesn't take him to Elysium. The slimy agent eagerly agrees, and Max boards the ship. As it lifts off, Da Costa is stunned to find Frey and her daughter there.

To allow Kruger access to Elysium, Delacourt cancels the no-fly order, which also gives Spider and some of his gang the chance to fly there in his own shuttle.

Approaching Elysium, Max fights with Kruger and loses his grip on the grenade. It explodes, tearing most of the villain's face to shreds and disabling the craft. It crashes in flames in a lush garden on the Torus.

Using the crash as an "act of war" excuse, Delacourt begins her coup and has the president arrested. Frey and Matilda flee the ship and are quickly captured, along with Max. Delacourt supervises their confinement with intentions of downloading the data from Max's head, despite the fact that it will kill him.

Spider and his men slip onto Elysium, while the still-living Kruger has his face rebuilt in an advanced robotic and computerized process. Max's exoskeleton gives him the strength to break free of his bonds before the data dump can begin.

Delacourt admonishes Kruger for allowing the security breach on Elysium, and the thug responds by stabbing her to death. He then initiates his own coup by dismantling the president's administration and throwing the secretary in with Frey and Matilda. Despite her medical skills, Frey cannot save Delacourt.

Max rescues Frey and her daughter from the Armory, while Kruger has himself fitted with a powerful exoskeleton. Spider and his men find Da Costa, but Kruger finds them all. High on a catwalk, Max and the crazed Kruger engage in a vicious fight. Max disables Kruger's exoskeleton and tosses him off the catwalk to his death.

Frey finds a home with a Med-Bay for Matilda, while Max and Spider reach Elysium's computer core. Mortally wounded in the fight with Kruger, Max initiates the download that will kill him. He calls Frey to say goodbye and dies.

The Elysium computer reboots, and with it, all Earth inhabitants become citizens. Medical shuttles are dispatched to the planet, with aid and Med-Bays for all who are suffering. Recalled as children, Max and Frey run free once more.

Afterwords

Neill Blomkamp's sci-fi film debut, 2009's *District 9*, left everyone wondering what the South African director would do for an encore. While the first film stood on its own merits, it didn't hurt to have legendary filmmaker Peter Jackson producing. Blomkamp took on his next project without his mentor's assistance.

While *District 9's* underlying themes addressed the issue of apartheid, *Elysium* looked at the age-old disparity between the rich and poor in society. But the director wanted to avoid making a film with a message, making sure he delivered an entertaining summer film.

Working on the story, Blomkamp remembered a picture he had seen years back. In the mid-1970s, NASA and Stanford University conducted a study on how man might live in space on a large-scale basis. One of the possibilities was called the Stanford Torus—a ring-shaped space station. Hollywood had been ahead of the curve for years, using a similar spaceship design in films like 1955's *Conquest of Space* and 1968's *2001: A Space Odyssey*.

In the future, the director imagined the separation of classes might be achieved by putting the wealthy and their mansions on the space station, while the have-nots remained on the beaten and ravaged planet of Earth.

Relying on his South African roots, Blomkamp first approached local rapper from Die Antwoord, Ninja, to star in *Elysium*. The hip-hopper was a huge fan of Blomkamp and *District 9*, but didn't want to enter the film world through the portal of a big-budget blockbuster from Hollywood.

Staying in the world of music, the director next turned to rapper and star of 2002's *8 Mile* Eminem to play Max Da Costa. The music star was keen on the idea, but insisted the film be shot in the city where he lives—Detroit. Blomkamp was unable to agree to that and turned to award-winning Matt Damon to star.

The director also tapped his old friend and star of *District 9*, Sharlto Copley, to play the villainous Kruger. Just like in *District 9*, Copley's character underwent some terrific—and gruesome—makeup effects, although the actor's part started and ended with a making a full head cast of him.

When a grenade carried by Da Costa explodes onboard the Raven shuttle, Kruger's face is blown off. The nasty effect was accomplished by using a wax skull and silicone skin likeness of Copley, filled with fake brains and blood inside. With a high-speed camera rolling, a powerful air cannon was fired directly at the face, blasting much of it away. For added realism, actual footage of the actor's eyes was composited into the shot.

Even more amazing was the scene of Kruger's face being rebuilt. Multiple exposures were combined, starting with a highly detailed mannequin of the disfigured face and torso. Then an image of Copley's normal face was added, with additional images of real medical and forensic textures, as well as smoke elements, to complete the effect.

Hoping to maximize the impact of the film, Sony Pictures first moved the scheduled release from late 2012 to March of 2013. The move was intended to take advantage of the many moviegoers on spring break and the Easter holiday. Then it was decided to reformat *Elysium* for the enormous IMAX screen, along with standard theaters.

With an actual release in August of 2013, *Elysium* thrilled audiences around the world. Made on a production budget of $115 million (nearly four times the budget of *District 9*), it drew a disappointing $93 million in the US. But overseas ticket sales were more than double that at $193 million, for a total of over $280 million

3

I Don't Think This Is Kansas Anymore

Alternate Worlds

Hmmm . . . It's Not on the Map . . .

Often a welcome playground for sci-fi literature and films alike, the concept of an "alternate world" can assume various forms. Many times, the alternate world is what is often referred to as a parallel universe. Or it can be a revised version of what is known as historical fact. The story may occasionally include the notion of time travel as an influence on the existing "alternate world" (see chapter 4 and the idea surrounding "The Butterfly Effect").

In the world of fantasy, the 1939 film of *The Wizard of Oz*—based on the 1900 L. Frank Baum novel—demonstrated a fine example of what might be considered a parallel universe. The protagonist Dorothy Gale, comfy in the farmlands of Kansas, finds things are wholly different in the Land of Oz. Even though it exists in the same time frame as Kansas, Oz has its own flora (talking apple trees) and fauna (flying monkeys), as well as talking animals, scarecrows, and tin men.

Similar to the impact of the Butterfly Effect (chapter 4, remember?) are the results of a change to known historical fact. On a grand scale, Philip K. Dick's 1962 novel *The Man in the High Castle*, looked at the world as it were if the Nazis and Axis powers had won the Second World War (rumored to eventually become a BBC television miniseries, the story has never made it to the big screen). The same sort of speculation abounds when one considers the possibility of the South having won the American Civil War.

On a much smaller scale, Frank Capra's 1947 film classic *It's a Wonderful Life*, dramatically showed how the lack of one person could impact the lives of so many people. Without George Bailey, the quaint town of Bedford Falls became a crime-ridden cesspool of few morals (think of a Detroit city council meeting). In all cases considered, a single difference can create an alternate world with variations of exponential proportion.

The all-too familiar locale of dystopia can become a standard in the alternate world. In 1979's *Mad Max*, the depletion of natural resources (aka oil) has turned the world as we knew it into a fuel-starved land of biker gangs and a police force struggling to maintain some sort of order. Of course, dystopian futures often overlap from alternate worlds to pure stories of time travel and all sorts of sci-fi subgenres.

A flick like *Sky Captain and the World of Tomorrow* simply offers a look at a different time in history without any causal explanation. New York City in the 1930s looks a lot like we've seen it in movies and pictures, except there are ray guns, planes that flap their wings like bats, and ninety-foot menacing robots to go along with the Empire State Building and the pigeons in Central Park.

Sci-fi films that embrace alternate worlds can be downright refreshing. To borrow a lyric from a Steely Dan classic: Any world that I'm welcome to is better than the one I come from.

Mad Max

Synopsis

- 1979—Australia/Roadshow Entertainment—93 min./color
- Director: George Miller
- Original music: Brian May
- Film editing: Cliff Hayes, Tony Paterson
- Art direction: Jon Dowding

Cast

- Mel Gibson (Max)
- Joanne Samuel (Jessie)
- Roger Ward (Chief Fifi)
- Hugh Keays-Byrne (Toecutter)
- Steve Bisley (Jim Goose)
- Tim Burns (Johnny the Boy)
- Geoff Parry (Bubba)
- Vince Gil (Nightrider)

In the near future, the outback of Australia is desolate and overrun by gangs of thugs. Main Force Patrol—MFP—is the undermanned and overworked police department that struggles to keep the peace.

Several MFP cars, and an MFP motorcycle driven by Jim Goose, engage a pair of scruffy delinquents, one of whom is the wacko known as Nightrider, in a high-speed chase. Barely avoiding a young boy in the road, the cars and bike crash and are unable to continue. Picking up the chase is Officer Max Rockatansky, who pursues the Nightrider until the villain and his girlfriend die in a fiery crash.

Max enjoys downtime with Jennie, his sax-playing wife, and their infant son, before he leaves for work. At the Hall of Justice garage, a mechanic excitedly shows off a supercharged black police interceptor for Max and his friend

Mel Gibson is *Mad Max*.

Goose—sporting a broken leg from the motorcycle accident. Chief Fifi has word that Nightrider's biker gang is targeting Max for elimination as revenge for causing the villain's death.

The gang pulls into a quiet rural town to retrieve Nightrider's body. Soon, they are terrorizing the town and its people. The gang assaults a young couple, destroying their car and leaving them on the road. With them in a stupor is the drug-crazed Johnny the Boy, a favorite of gang leader Toecutter. Max and Goose drag the kid to the rundown jail.

But no one shows up to testify against the kid, so he has to be set free, amid the angry protests of Goose. Johnny the Boy threatens Goose with revenge as he leaves with Bubba, another gang member. Toecutter declares war against the Bronze—the MFP. While Goose enjoys himself at the Sugartown Cabaret, Johnny the Boy sabotages his motorcycle.

The next day, Goose's bike locks up during a high-speed run, throwing the officer and the bike into the tall brush. Dazed but in one piece, Goose summons a pickup truck to take his bike back to town. On the way, Johnny the Boy recklessly throws a brake drum through the truck's windshield, causing it to turn over. Soaked in leaking gas, the vehicle and Goose are set ablaze by Johnny the Boy, at the urging of Toecutter.

Max finds his badly burned friend at the hospital. Enraged, the cop can find no sense in the brutality, and, fearing insanity, he resigns the MFP. The chief convinces him to take a few weeks to consider his decision. Max packs Jennie and his child, setting out on a well-earned vacation.

Max's wife and child come across Toecutter and his gang, who harass them while buying ice cream. Jennie escapes with her son, and, with Max, they speed away to safety. At a secluded vacation spot, the gang catches up with the family, and when Max heads into the woods, Jennie and her boy frantically drive away.

The car breaks down. Jennie takes off on foot down the road with her child in her arms, until Toecutter and his gang run them down with their bikes. Max arrives on the scene too late to save them.

Seething with rage, Max dons his leather police uniform and takes the black police interceptor from the Hall of Justice garage. Methodically, he begins to track down Toecutter and his gang.

First, Max wins a game of chicken between his pursuit car and a group of cyclists, who are struck and left strewn across the road. Next, Max is ambushed by the gang, as they shoot him in the leg and run over his arm with a bike. He is still able to take out one of the bikers with a shotgun blast.

Johnny the Boy escapes into the fields, as Max makes it back to his car and takes off after Toecutter. The biker is too focused on Max giving chase, enough so that he doesn't notice the semi bearing down on him before it's too late, and Toecutter rams head-on into the rig.

Max drives through the night, catching up to Johnny the Boy as he pulls the boots from a dead car accident victim. Max handcuffs the boy's ankle to the damaged vehicle as it leaks fuel. Fashioning a crude timing fuse to ignite the fuel, Max leaves Johnny a hacksaw. He suggests the handcuffs will take ten minutes to cut through; Johnny's ankle will take only five minutes.

Max drives away as the vehicle explodes behind him in the distance.

Afterwords

The making of 1979's *Mad Max* answered the age-old question: Is there a doctor in the house? Why, yes—there was. He was located firmly in the director's chair.

Even while completing med school in New South Wales, Australian George Miller indulged his love of filmmaking by shooting and submitting a one-minute flick to a student competition. It won, and Miller gladly accepted the prize: a college film workshop. In the years that followed, he was an emergency room doctor on weekends and a filmmaker during the week.

Miller's medical exposure to the results of gruesome car and motorcycle accidents left him troubled and prompted the young filmmaker to conceive an action film of unique qualities. With partner Byron Kennedy, Miller revised a script originally written by James McCauseland. It would be a film of "pure cinema," as Miller once put it. He would make a silent movie—with sound. It was *Mad Max*.

Mel Gibson attended auditions for the film, only to accompany his friend Steve Bisley. Although he was a struggling young actor himself, Gibson was in no shape to perform, having been savagely beaten in a bar brawl a few days before. Still, casting folks told him to come back when his face healed. When he did, Gibson was cast as Max Rockatansky (Bisley also earned a part as Goose).

Much of the action in *Mad Max* was courtesy of the featured high-performance autos. Using cars native to Australia, the film proved there were swift muscle cars with names other than Ford Mustang, Chevy Camaro, the Olds 442, and the Pontiac GTO. The most talked-about was Max's black Pursuit Special.

The auto began its life as a 1973 Ford Falcon XB GT (Ford of Australia, having nothing in common with the cars made in Detroit). Powered by an eight-cylinder, 351-cubic-inch engine, the Interceptor was modified for the film by car customizers at Melbourne-based Graf-X International.

Mechanic Murray Smith helped install the imposing-looking supercharger in the hood of the Interceptor, but it was completely cosmetic. A small twelve-volt electric motor inside actually turned the pulley on the blower, with beefy engine rumble sound effects added in postproduction.

When shooting for *Mad Max* was finished, the Pursuit Special was put up for sale. Surprisingly, there were no takers—which turned out to be a good thing. The success of *Mad Max* prompted a sequel, *Mad Max 2: The Road Warrior*, in 1981. The car was put back into service for the second film and changed hands several times among private collectors across twenty-five years. Today, the Mad Max Interceptor is part of the Dezer Auto Collection and Museum in Miami.

A curious and simple bit of movie magic is used in the death of Toecutter. As Max's black Interceptor forces the villain and his bike into the path of a semi truck, it's obvious that a large metal shield has been painted to resemble the front of the truck cab. Mounted under the windshield, the slab prevented any real damage to the rig as it struck and then ran over the motorcycle and the dummy of Toecutter.

As indicated, *Mad Max* became a worldwide hit. Produced for a mere $350,000 Australian (equal to about $400,000 in 1979 American dollars), the film grossed nearly $9 million in America and nearly $100 million worldwide. The 1981 sequel and 1985's *Mad Max Beyond Thunderdome* took in $24 million and $36 million, respectively, in the US. (Worldwide numbers for those two movies are not available.)

As is often the case, the filmgoing public just can't get enough of a good thing, so a fourth Mad Max film—*Mad Max: Fury Road*—is slated for release in 2015. Fearing that Mel Gibson's Mad Max might have turned in his Interceptor for a wheelchair thirty-five years after the original, the lead character will be played by Tom Hardy, with a bald-headed Charlize Theron included.

Pitch Black

Synopsis

- 2000—American/USA Films/Gramercy Pictures—109 min./color
- Director: David Twohy
- Original music: Graeme Revell
- Film editing: Rick Shaine
- Production design: Grace Walker

Cast
- Vin Diesel (Richard B. Riddick)
- Radha Mitchell (Carolyn Fry)
- Cole Hauser (William J. Johns)
- Keith David (Abu "Imam" Al-Walid)
- Lewis Fitz-Gerald (Paris Oglivie)
- Rhianna Griffith (Jack)
- John Moore (Zeke Ezekiel)
- Claudia Black (Sharon Montgomery)

In deep space, the transport Hunter-Gratzner carries forty passengers toward the Tangier system, all of them in cryogenic sleep. But the debris from the tail of a comet pierces the ship's hull, killing the captain. Pilot Carolyn Fry and navigator Greg Owens awaken, only to find the Hunter-Gratzner reentering the atmosphere of an unknown planet. In a freefall, Fry ejects portions of the craft to slow their descent. To save herself, Carolyn tries to jettison passenger compartments, but that fails and the ship crash-lands on the planet.

Owens dies, along with many of the other passengers. Survivor William Johns is escorting convict Richard B. Riddick back to prison, and the tough Riddick immediately tries to overpower his captor, with no success. Imam Abu al-Walid, as well as three followers on their hajj to New Mecca, survives, as do young Jack, a stowaway; foppish collectibles dealer Paris Oglivie; and couple Zeke Ezekiel and Sharon Montgomery.

They find the sandy planet is hot and barren beneath three suns that keep it in almost perpetual sunlight. Wearing strange dark goggles, Riddick breaks free and escapes, and the rest of the group arms itself for protection against him. Spotting trees as a possible sign of water, the survivors actually find dozens of enormous skeletons of strange creatures—one of which secretly contains the hiding Riddick.

The group comes upon an abandoned settlement and a small spacecraft—evidence that humans once lived in the area. Back at the Hunter-Gratzner, another survivor appears, but Zeke shoots him dead, mistaking the poor fellow for Riddick.

Zeke adds the corpse to the rest of the dead to be buried, but becomes a bloody victim himself to some unknown monster that drags him underground. Riddick is at the scene, but is not involved with the murder and quickly walks away. Once more, Johns subdues him, this time by tearing his goggles off and leaving him blinded by the bright sunlight. Sharon accuses the convict of killing her partner.

Confined in the ship, Riddick suggests he is no longer the scariest thing on the planet and reveals his shiny, light-sensitive eyes to Fry and Jack. He insists that something else killed Zeke. Fry enters the spot where Zeke disappeared and finds unpleasant pieces of the survivor. Held by a tether, Fry is threatened by spindly aliens and has to be pulled to safety by the group.

Johns offers freedom to Riddick, in exchange for his assistance in surviving the harsh and unknown elements of the planet. Soon, water is being collected, and solar generators create power for the settlement, but there's no sign of what happened to the original inhabitants. Evidence points to their being geologists.

Flying creatures attack one of the Imam's young followers in the coring room, tearing him to pieces. The group arrives too late to save him and watch as the bat-like vermin escape down an underground chute, filled with the bones of the settlers. Noting the geologists' last work was performed twenty-two years back, Fry determines the planet experiences a triple solar eclipse at the start of that time period and puts it into pitch black.

The spacecraft found in camp is flight ready, but Johns warns Fry not to load the power cells until the very last minute. Along with being an escape artist and dangerous prisoner, Riddick is also a pilot. Considering the deal that was made, Fry trusts Riddick, but Johns doesn't.

Alone with Fry, Riddick shares a few secrets, including the fact that Johns is not law enforcement but a bounty hunter out to make a buck (or more) by capturing Riddick. Also, Johns is a drug addict, even resorting to depleting the spaceship's medical supplies for his own needs.

The suns begin to set quickly, and as the group loads the power cells onto a solar-powered truck, the eclipse stalls the vehicle. The darkness summons the deadly flying creatures by the thousands into the sky, and they tear Sharon apart as the rest of the group takes cover in the ship.

Vin Diesel in *Pitch Black*.

Seemingly safe inside, the creatures attack another follower of the Imam and the group shines every available light to blind them. They find that light actually kills the flying creatures and burns their flesh.

Armed with torches and lights, the survivors move out in the darkness, with Riddick's sensitive eyes leading the way to the downed Hunter-Gratzner. They strip it of all light sources and flammable liquids and drag the power cells to the shuttlecraft.

Jack loses a light, and the creatures begin to circle for an attack. Ogilvie begins crawling in a panic, which unplugs many of the lights and leaves him surrounded by the deadly creatures. Riddick watches as they kill Ogilvie.

The group nears a canyon, and they are surprised to find that Jack is actually a girl, posing as a boy in an effort to get by without causing any trouble. Arguments erupt, and Johns angrily reveals Fry's original attempt to dump the passenger compartments. The six survivors press on, despite the danger in the canyon.

Johns quietly urges Riddick to kill Jack as bait to draw the alien monsters away from the group. The suggestion angers Riddick, and he goes hand to hand with Johns. The bounty hunter is wounded, and as his torch goes out, the creatures attack him.

Riddick inspects the skeleton of a creature and discovers their weakness—a blind spot. The group runs through the canyon, with Riddick pulling the power cells. Hoards of creatures begin to cannibalize each other as they surround the survivors.

A creature grabs the last remaining follower of the Imam, injuring his leg, and another knocks Jack to the ground. The powerfully built Riddick wrestles with the beast and finally kills it with his bare hands.

Rain begins to fall, threatening the remaining fires that keep the group protected. A creature pulls the Imam's last follower to his death, and Riddick forces the survivors into the safety of a cave. He rolls a boulder over the entrance for protection and pulls the power cells to the settlement.

The others think Riddick has abandoned them, but they find the walls of the cave covered with fluorescent slugs that provide the lifesaving light needed to reach the ship. Riddick prepares to take off as Carolyn slips out of the cave and reaches the shuttle. He urges her to abandon the others and leave with him, but she won't do it.

They return to the cave and open it for Jack and the Imam. Creatures block their path, and, keeping low, the group moves past them toward the shuttle. A final beast blocks Riddick, then others surround him. Carolyn runs to save Riddick and finds him bleeding but alive. As she struggles to help him to the ship, a creature grabs Fry and carries her away.

Riddick preps the ship for takeoff, then abruptly stops. Wanting to give the creatures a proper farewell, Riddick waits for dozens of them to gather at the ship's engines. He then quickly throttles up and roasts them alive, crushing many more as the ship leaves the planet.

Jack wonders what should be said when the authorities begin to ask questions, and Riddick merely suggests telling them the convict died on the planet.

Afterwords

For every one superstar in Hollywood, there are perhaps twenty or more normal, working-class people who make their living in the motion picture business. The brothers Wheat—Jim and Ken—are two of those folks.

In the late 1990s, they pitched an idea for a sci-fi film about people forced to be together on a spaceship and crash on a planet filled with terrible creatures. Their inspiration was the classic western *Stagecoach* (pick your version: 1986 TV, 1966, or—the best—1939, with John Wayne).

Writer/director David Twohy picked up the idea and rewrote parts of the script. With a lean budget of $23 million, Twohy was determined to make the best of what amounted to a B picture.

Someone gave him a picture of actor Vin Diesel, and the director liked his mysterious look, along with a beefy build—perfect for the prisoner called Riddick But Twohy was disappointed with Diesel's audition and was ready to keep looking. When pressed to see him again, this time with several actresses vying for the Fry role, Twohy felt the actor fit the part perfectly.

Diesel had made his mark in Steven Spielberg's raw 1998 war epic *Saving Private Ryan*, and then followed up—and surprised many fans—by voicing the robot in the 1999 animated story *The Iron Giant*. While he relished playing the role of a bad-guy-gone-good, Diesel wasn't very happy with the custom-made contact lenses he had to wear. Calling them "pure torture," he compared them to the hubcaps from a 1960 Plymouth.

With computer-generated FX in full swing by 2000, the director still chose to use model work for much of the film. Los Angeles–based Hunter-Gratzner Industries built the main cargo ship (which, not coincidentally in the film, bore the name of the company that created it). Fashioned from a steel frame, the spacecraft also had brass fittings, a fiberglass body, with portions covered with aluminum tape. The model was nine feet long and weighed more than 250 pounds.

As a low-budget film, *Pitch Black* was a pleasant box-office surprise for everyone concerned. Domestically, it brought in nearly $40 million, with another $14 million overseas. More than doubling the production budget, the film prompted a 2004 sequel, *Chronicles of Riddick*. Now highly-budgeted at $105 million, the follow-up was disappointing, grossing only $57 million in the US and about the same overseas.

That didn't stop the thundering Diesel from teaming with Twohy once more in 2013 for another sequel, simply called *Riddick*. Made for $38 million, it was more successful, as it pulled in $42 million in America and another $56 million overseas. Totaling nearly $100 million, *Riddick* has prompted the actor and Universal to announce a fourth film in the series is underway.

Sky Captain and the World of Tomorrow

Synopsis

- 2004—American/Paramount—106 min./color
- Director: Kerry Conran
- Original music: Ed Shearmur
- Film editing: Sabrina Plisco
- Production design: Kevin Conran

Cast

- Jude Law (Captain Joe Sullivan)
- Gwyneth Paltrow (Polly Perkins)
- Giovanni Ribisi (Dex Dearborn)
- Michael Gambon (Editor Paley)
- Bai Ling (Mysterious Woman)
- Angelina Jolie (Commander Franky Cook)
- Laurence Olivier (Doctor Totenkopf)
- Kaji (Omid Djalili)

In 1939, the dirigible *Hindenburg III* moors at the top of the Empire State Building in New York City amid falling snow and searchlight beams. White-haired Doctor Jorge Vargas, fearing for his safety, insists that a parcel with two mysterious vials be delivered to Doctor Walter Jennings immediately.

Bright and ambitious Polly Perkins, a reporter for the *Chronicle* newspaper, wonders why Vargas and five other top German scientists have vanished. Despite the concerns of Paley, her editor, Perkins arranges a clandestine meeting at Radio City Music Hall. It's with Dr. Jennings, who, as the last of the group of German scientists, knows he will be the next to go missing at the bidding of Dr. Totenkopf.

Warning sirens startle the citizens on the streets, as giant flying robots swoop down on Manhattan. Cars and buildings are crushed under the feet of the mechanical men as they march down the avenues. Police weapons are useless against them.

An emergency call goes out for Sky Captain Joe Sullivan, who soars in, flying a P-40 Warhawk, and opens fire on the robots. He deploys a bomb that disables one of the machines, and the others stop in their tracks. They remove power generators and oil refineries before launching themselves into the sky. Similar stories of chaos are reported around the world.

Sullivan lands at his air base with the remains of the downed robot. Gum-chewing tech genius Dex Dearborn is thrilled to examine the machine. Joe soothes an upset stomach with milk of magnesia in his office, only to be surprised by Polly—his ex-girlfriend.

The two agree to put away their differences in order to investigate the origin of the robots and the whereabouts of Jennings. One thing is certain—both are tied to the mysterious Dr. Totenkopf, who directed a scientific project called Unit Eleven before World War I.

Sullivan and Perkins arrive at the lab of Dr. Jennings, where the scientist is barely alive. A mysterious woman in black, gifted with martial arts skills and a nasty ray gun, ransacks the place and escapes before Joe can grab her. As Jennings dies, he quietly slips the two vials into Polly's hand. Totenkopf must not get ahold of these vials. If he does, it's the end of the world.

Once more, warning sirens pierce the air, as dozens of batwinged planes attack Sullivan's base. He takes to the skies, with Polly as his copilot, to retaliate. Dex warns him not to shoot the flying wings, however, as one of them is the source of the control signal for the robots.

Weaving through the man-made canyons of Manhattan, Sky Captain leads a number of flying wings to collisions, while Dex tries to pinpoint the location of the control signal. He finds it, but is taken hostage by whip-armed robots and the mysterious woman in black, before he can tell Sullivan. Sky Captain evades the rest of the wings by converting his P-40 into a submarine and ducking into the ocean.

Joe and Polly return to what remains of the air base, now in ruins from the robot attack. Fortunately, Dex has left an important clue for Joe—a scrap of a map that points to the country of Nepal in the Himalayan Mountains.

Joe and Polly land at a snow-covered camp, greeted by the native Kaji. Reviewing Dex's map, the source of the radio signal is centered in a forbidden area that many know as Shangri-La. Reluctantly, Kaji agrees to take Joe and Polly there.

In an abandoned uranium mine, several of Kaji's men demand the vials. While Joe has no knowledge of them, Polly gives them up, as the pair is locked away in a vault loaded with dynamite. Kaji frees them at the last minute, and they are knocked unconscious by the blast.

The trio find themselves in a well-appointed bedroom, where an Asian monk agrees to help them find Totenkopf. The evil doctor has forced the locals to work in the deadly radioactive mines, and only one survivor remains. In exchange for an ornate staff that will lead them to Totenkopf, the survivor asks for the gift of life-ending peace.

With Sullivan's plane running out of fuel, he contacts Franky Cook. Another old girlfriend, she is beautiful—even with a pirate's eye patch. Cook commands a British airborne mobile airstrip in the skies. She leads the Sky Captain and other amphibious pilots to Totenkopf's hidden island lair.

Underwater, they find the entrance guarded by crab-like robots, but a salvo of torpedoes clears the way for Sullivan and Perkins. Once inside, they find a jungle setting with strange prehistoric creatures—more of Totenkopf's work.

Joe and Polly reach a launch site, where caged animals are being loaded onto an enormous rocket—a Noah's Ark targeted for outer space. Flying robots attack the duo, but they are rescued by Dex, who is piloting a hovering freight craft. With him are a number of the previously missing Unit Eleven scientists.

Jude Law and Gwyneth Paltrow in *Sky Captain and the World of Tomorrow.*

Totenkopf's plan has been to create a new world—the World of Tomorrow—using creatures from Earth and the contents of the two vials—genetic samples to make a new Adam and Eve. With the launch of the rocket, the Earth will be incinerated. And it will blast off in less than ten minutes.

The group destroys two robot guards, but a flash of electricity kills one of the scientists, and a holographic image of Totenkopt's head appears. Seeing the world abused and scarred by hatred, the doctor has decided that a fresh start is the only solution.

In Totenkopf's private office, his long-dead body is found, along with a handwritten note asking forgiveness. To stop the launch, Sullivan must board the rocket and cut the terminal for the booster engine. But he'll have no way of escaping and bids Polly and Dex goodbye.

Sky Captain is stopped in his attempt to reach the rocket by the mysterious woman in black, who happens to be a robot. As it prepares to push Joe to his death, Polly shows up and smashes the robot with a pipe.

Joe and Polly slip into the rocket as it takes off, where Perkins presses an emergency release button that jettisons the ship's living cargo to safety. The two try to disable the main booster before it's too late, and at the last second, they cause the missile to malfunction and explode.

Cook's fleet of airborne airstrips deploys planes to recover the parachuting recovery pods that hold the animals from the rocket's cargo as they splash into the sea. Sullivan and Perkins watch the glorious sight as Polly snaps a prizewinning picture of the scene.

Joe points out one problem—lens cap.

Afterwords

The story behind *Sky Captain and the World of Tomorrow* is one of resourcefulness, innovation, and planning. And for many fans, it's also one of wonder: wondering why there haven't been more adventures from Sky Captain Joe Sullivan.

Writer and creator Kerry Conran imagined a film that reflected the excitement of the great sci-fi serials like *Flash Gordon* from the 1940s, along with the equally great Max Fleischer *Superman* cartoons from the same time period.

Conran's world of 1939 would be one of marching robots and zeppelins unloading passengers at the top of the Empire State Building (while that real concept was originally considered when it was built, the strong and swirling winds up there made it strictly sci-fi). Around 1995, Conran looked to the mighty Mac computer to achieve his vision.

He spent four years in his apartment, shooting and editing a six-minute teaser—a virtual blueprint for the film's eventual opening scenes. It featured the mooring of the dirigible in New York and introduced the characters of Dr. Vargas, journalist Polly Perkins, and hero Sky Captain, as well as the marching mechanical men. (Find it on YouTube—it's magnificent in its simplicity and style.)

Conran worked very closely with his brother Kevin, a talented illustrator in his own right, to design the retro-tinged, Art Deco-influenced look of the film. Everything, from sets, robots, airships, costumes, layouts, props—you name it—came from Kevin's sketchbook, following discussions with Kerry.

As often happens in Hollywood, Kerry Conran was able to show the teaser to the right people. One of them was producer Jon Avnet (1983's *Risky Business*, 1992's *The Mighty Ducks*, 1997's *George of the Jungle*, and 2010's *Black Swan*, among many other films and TV series). Avnet immediately knew he could help Conran make the film he envisioned.

Realizing that big names can help a first-time director, Avnet showed the Conran short to Jude Law—fresh from his role as Gigolo Joe in Spielberg's *A.I. Artificial Intelligence*. Like Avnet, Law was blown away by what he saw and signed on, as actor and producer. Oscar-winning actress Gwyneth Paltrow was similarly enticed to join the cast.

Despite Conran's adventurous intentions to shoot the entire film in front of a blue screen—without the use of real sets—the actors trusted his clear vision and found the process very workable. The real work began once the live action was completed. More than a dozen visual effects houses were brought in to begin cranking out more than two thousand FX shots, combining the actors with CGI sets, robots, and special effects.

One very interesting special effect was using a dead actor as the villain. Sir Laurence Olivier, having passed away in 1989, was suggested by Jude Law as a possible foil for the Sky Captain. With usage rights approved by CMG Worldwide, footage of a young Olivier was combined with a voice actor who inserted Totenkopf's scripted lines.

The results of the efforts in making *Sky Captain and the World of Tomorrow* were mixed. Many film critics, like famed print and TV reviewer Roger Ebert, found the film top-notch, in both form and content. But filmgoers were not as convinced.

With a budget of $70 million (the producer suggested it would have been as much as $50 million higher if it had been shot conventionally), *Sky Captain* only grossed $37 million domestically. Another $20 million overseas totaled less than $60 million worldwide.

No matter, *Sky Captain* opened a door for sci-fi cinema that more filmmakers would go through for the enjoyment of many, many fans.

Children of Men

Synopsis

- 2006—American/Universal—109 min./color
- Director: Alfonso Cuarón
- Original music: John Tavener
- Film editing: Alfonso Cuarón, Alex Rodriguez
- Production design: Jim Clay, Geoffery Kirkland
- Based on the 1992 novel by P. D. James

Cast

- Clive Owen (Theo Faron)
- Michael Caine (Jasper Palmer)
- Julianne Moore (Julian Taylor)
- Clare-Hope Ashitey (Kee)
- Danny Huston (Nigel)
- Chiwetel Ejiofor (Luke)
- Peter Mullan (Syd)
- Phillipa Urquhart (Janice)

In the year 2027, the world remains in crisis, as infertility has curtailed all births since 2009. Anarchy around the world prevails, with Great Britain remaining as the last existing government. In London, the media reports the sad news that the world's youngest person has died at the age of eighteen.

Former political activist Theo Faron narrowly escapes a terrorist explosion as he picks up his morning coffee. Faron is shaken from the blast and takes the day off from his job with the Ministry of Energy, meeting his old friend Jasper. With long, gray hair, Jasper affects the appearance of an aging hippie.

Jasper's wife, Janice, sits in catatonic quiet, the result of suspected government torture. A retired political cartoonist, Jasper now spends his time cultivating—and using—high-quality marijuana. He and Faron discuss the supposed Human Project, a scientific attempt to cure the fertility issues of the world.

Theo is kidnapped by a terrorist group known as the Fishes, who seek to have Britain recognize all illegal immigrants. They are led by Julian, an American woman who happens to be Faron's ex-wife. Their infant son, Dylan, died in a flu epidemic nearly twenty years previous.

Julian needs Theo to acquire transit papers for a special refugee named Kee. The Fishes will pay for the favor, so Theo reluctantly agrees. His cousin Nigel, a government minister, arranges to get the papers after Theo relates a false story about a nonexistent girlfriend. But the papers are for joint travel only, so Faron must accompany Kee.

Julian and Theo, along with a Fish named Luke, Kee, and a lady named Miriam, drive toward the southern coast of the country. They're ambushed in a remote forest area, and Julian is mortally wounded. When police pull the car over, Luke shoots the officers dead, and the survivors pull away. Miriam holds a brief funeral for Julian, and Theo is overcome with grief.

Luke steals a car, and the group makes their way to a farm compound in an isolated area where they will be safe. Alone in the barn, Faron finds a miracle—Kee is pregnant. Julian had assured the young woman that Theo would help Kee to reach the *Tomorrow*, a boat operated by the Human Project.

The folks in the commune debate Theo's presence and whether Kee's future baby should be used as a political icon. Faron simply believes the child should be made public, but since Kee is an immigrant, the government would never allow that for the first birth in eighteen years. After some argument, Kee decides she will have her baby at the farm, then find a way to the *Tomorrow* ship.

Theo quietly finds that Luke and the Fishes were secretly behind the ambush that killed Julian, with intentions of now killing Faron and using Kee's child as a tool for their ongoing cause. He rouses Miriam and Kee from their sleep, and they slip away in a stolen car.

Michael Caine in *Children of Men*.

The trio hides at Jasper's home, where the old man suggests Syd, a military acquaintance who could help get Kee into the refugee camp in Bexhill. From there, she could go on to the *Tomorrow* vessel that operates out of the Azores, a group of islands more than eight hundred miles west of Portugal.

The Fishes invade Jasper's property. He sends Theo, Kee, and Miriam off in his car, promising to keep the marauders occupied. Jasper kills his wife out of mercy, and then Luke savagely kills the old man.

Miriam, a midwife, recalls the rash of miscarriages that began years back. Syd picks up the trio, and Kee begins to go into labor in the back of his truck. They arrive at the dispatch area for Bexhill, where they are ferried into buses.

Reaching the Bexhill Refugee Camp, Miriam pretends to be a religious zealot to draw attention away from Kee. The midwife is taken away, and Theo and Kee find their contact, a woman named Marichka, in a bizarre, shantytown-like area.

Marichka takes Theo and Kee to a nasty hovel of an apartment building. She leaves and, by the light of a single lamp, Kee gives birth to a baby girl. Crying and healthy, the child lays with her mother.

Syd and Marichka burst in the next morning, stunned at the sight of Kee's child. Syd has heard that Theo is wanted for the deadly attack in the woods and plans on collecting a big reward for his surrender. But the mean-spirited Syd antagonizes Marichka one too many times, and she attacks him, beating him with a pipe.

Marichka's family and friends welcome Theo, Kee, and her baby, and they locate a small boat that will take them to the Human Project. But the Fishes find them first in an attack on Bexhill. Kee spits in Luke's face in contempt. Still, he takes Kee and the baby away, while the other Fishes prepare to shoot Theo.

A counterattack by the military allows Faron and Marichka to escape. Theo finds Kee and her child in a building under a massive attack. An injured Luke is holding them at gunpoint, and he wounds Theo when they scramble away to freedom.

The baby's cries amaze those in the building, including stunned soldiers who immediately cease their firing. Some genuflect in reverence, but the cease-fire is short-lived as Theo, Kee, and her child make their way to the rowboat waiting for them.

Theo rows to the rendezvous point for the *Tomorrow* ship. Kee finds blood in bottom of the boat, seeing that Theo has been fatally wounded by Luke's gunfire. Kee will call her child Dylan, the same as Theo and Julian's child.

Faron dies as the *Tomorrow* appears out of the fog. Soon, the laughter of many children fills the air.

Afterwords

Director Alfonso Cuarón, having made his directorial impact with films like 2001's *Y Tu Mamá También* and *Harry Potter and the Prisoner of Azkaban* in 2004, brought a documentary feel to *Children of Men*. He shot the entire film with handheld cameras and used long single takes in order to focus on the story and not the characters.

Cuarón really didn't want to do *Children of Men* at first, but the premise of the story stuck in his head and was compelling enough to convince him to do the film. He avoided referencing the novel by P. D. James—although co-screenwriter Tim Sexton did read it—and was happy when the author saw the finished product. While it veered a bit from her original story, James did enjoy the film and was proud to be associated with the production.

The director/writer tapped actor Clive Owen early in preproduction to provide input, not only for his character but for the entire script. He spent several weeks with Cuarón sitting in a hotel room, discussing and forming many of the script elements for the film. While uncredited, Owen became as much a writer on *Children of Men* as Cuarón or Sexton.

In writing the role of Jasper, Cuarón and Sexton always referred to him as "the Michael Caine" character. Obviously, then, it made sense to get the actor himself. Caine imagined the aging hippie to be much like late Beatle—and good friend—John Lennon. The actor affected his nasal voice and even wore similar round-lens glasses to create Jasper in the image of Lennon.

Another critical character to the story is the child born to Kee—the first on Earth in eighteen years. Cuarón turned to Framestore, a London-based FX company, to create a fully believable newborn baby with computer graphics. The task was complicated enough, but the bar for a realistic scene was raised by Cuarón's aforementioned handheld cameras and a three-and-a-half-minute single take.

A limbless model was used first (having no arms or legs reduced the need for painting them out later for CG replacement). The artists digitally painted away the model, replacing it with a computer-based newborn. Additional elements of animation, lighting, and shadows were added, making for a highly powerful and authentic scene.

Everyone's efforts were awarded with three nominations for Oscars, in categories of adapted screenplay, cinematography, and film editing. *Children of Men* was produced on a budget of $76 million. Despite showing up on many critics' lists for top films in 2006, audiences didn't flock to the theaters. The film drew only $35 million domestically, with about the same overseas, for a total just short of $70 million.

Avatar

Synopsis

- 2009—American/Twentieth Century-Fox—162 min./color
- Director: James Cameron
- Original music: James Horner

- Film editing: James Cameron, John Refoua, Stephen Rivkin
- Production design: Rick Carter, Robert Stromberg

Cast

- Sam Worthington (Jake Sully)
- Zoe Saldana (Neytiri)
- Sigourney Weaver (Dr. Grace Augustine)
- Stephen Lang (Colonel Miles Quaritch)
- Michelle Rodriguez (Trudy Chacon)
- Giovanni Ribisi (Parker Selfridge)
- Cch Pounder (Mo'at)
- Wes Studi (Eytukan)
- Laz Alonso (Tsu'tey)
- Dileep Rao (Max)

Sometime in the future, Jake Sully, a wheelchair-bound Marine combat war veteran, doesn't consider his condition a handicap. In a rowdy bar, he watches a drunken lug slap a woman and immediately takes the jerk down to the floor in a fight. The chivalry earns Sully a quick exit out the back door and on his face.

Jake's identical twin brother, a scientist named Tommy, winds up murdered in a robbery, and Jake accepts an offer to take over his brother's contact with the Avatar Program. Sully wakes from five years in cryosleep on an interstellar spaceship bound for Pandora, a well-known planet far from Earth.

A shuttle brings Sully and others down to the surface of Pandora, where a huge military mining operation is in full swing. The natives, humanoids known as Na'vi, are dangerous, and Colonel Miles Quaritch, head of security, warns the new arrivals of the risks outside the fences of the facility.

Avatars are remote-controlled figures, cultured from a mix of human DNA and Na'vi DNA. People like Jake actually drive the Avatars, linked by their own DNA—the reason he could take over his brother's assignment. The hope of using Avatars is they will help to ease tensions and build trust between the Na'vi and humans.

Sully's boss is Dr. Grace Augustine, head of the Avatar Program and somewhat resentful of having to accept Jake. Unlike his brother, Jake has no education, no training, no experience—she doesn't need someone who looks like Tommy, she needs Tommy.

Receiving little sympathy, Augustine complains to Parker Selfridge, the local executive for RDA—Resources Development Administration—the organization that runs the mining operation on Pandora. Despite the hardships on Pandora, Selfridge insists there is much value in the ore they mine. Unobtainium, a mineral with amazing antimagnetic properties, fetches twenty million dollars per kilogram.

Avatar operators lie in a link pod, while technicians monitor their brain activity. Jake closes his eyes and he is a Na'vi. Nearly ten feet tall, blue-skinned, with long black hair and a thin tail, Sully finds himself thrilled to be mobile once more. He runs outside, through a playground and into a garden, where Grace's Avatar welcomes him. Sully's eyes open, and he is again in human form as he pulls himself out of the link pod.

He rolls past a line of combat helicopters, while pilot Trudy Chacon gives Jake the tour. Col. Quaritch swaps battle stories with Sully, then switches into military mode by asking the ex-Marine to collect intelligence while in his role as an Avatar. On paper, Jake's still part of Augustine, but his mission will be for the colonel. The deal is this: Jake brings back useful info, and Quaritch will arrange for a procedure to get the ex-Marine's legs back in working order.

Jake's Avatar mans a gun as armed guard in Chacon's tilt-rotor chopper as it flies over the forests, alongside blue-hued dragon-like creatures. Unique, saurian water animals wade in the river beneath the helicopter.

They set down in a clearing, with Grace's Avatar taking the lead. Sully aims at a huge, advancing, hammer-headed beast, but Grace convinces him to hold fast. Distracted by the beast, Jake doesn't notice a fierce black, tiger-like creature known as a Thanator approaching from behind. Sully runs for his life, turning to fire his automatic weapon until the snarling animal pulls away with its jaws snapping.

It grabs Sully by his backpack, and he quickly unclips it and runs, diving off the ledge of a waterfall and reaching bottom. He comes up for air and makes it to the far shore. Soaked and alone, Jake fashions a spear while a young Na'vi woman stalks him from a high branch and then disappears into the treetops.

Trudy and Grace hunt for Sully from the airborne chopper, but the oncoming dusk forces them to put off the search until morning. Alone in the night, Jake lights a torch to keep a pack of predatory wolf-like animals at bay. When they finally attack, he fights a number of them off, until the Na'vi woman swoops in with a bow and arrow to help.

Despite their differences in language, Jake tries to thank the woman. Surprisingly, she speaks English and chides him for causing the animals' deaths. She thinks all of the humans, who the Na'vi refer to as Sky People, are ignorant.

Dozens of fluttering dandelion-like seeds begin to drop around Jake, and he instinctively swats at them, which doesn't please the woman. They dance around Sully, illuminating his head and torso, then fly away.

Jake follows the woman until many Na'vi hunters surround him, on horse and on foot. They take him to their village—the Hometree—inside a gigantic tree, many times larger than a Sequoia. Sully stands before the clan leader and his wife, Eytukan and Mo'at, father and mother to the woman who saved him, asking only to learn the ways of the Na'vi people. Jake will learn, at the hands of Neytiri—the young woman's name. They call him Jakesully.

Grace wakes Jake from the link pod, and he is able to assure both Augustine and Quaritch that his Avatar is safe and getting the job done. Selfridge is more direct—all he wants is the huge unobtainium deposit that sits beneath the Na'vi's village. Jake has three months to convince the clan to move, or Selfridge will have them permanently removed.

Zoe Saldana in *Avatar*.

Back in the link pod, Jake works with the indigenous animals with Neytiri's guidance. Tsu'tey, the young warrior in line to be next clan leader, has no patience or love for Jakesully. Back at the operations center, Jake describes the layout of the village to Quaritch, using a large holographic map of the area.

Afraid of RDA interference, Grace takes her team to a remote lab in the Hallelujah Mountains, a legendary floating geographic site on Pandora. At the camp, Jake hops into a link pod, and his Avatar is climbing through the trees with Neytiri.

She beckons a wide-winged flying reptile called a Banshee to her side, where she climbs on its back. As with all the animals, Na'vi can lace nerve endings in their tails with similar tendrils on the creatures, allowing the two organisms to work as one. Jake watches as they soar away in flight.

As time passes, Sully slowly learns the Na'vi language, their skills with a bow and arrow, riding the native animals, and begins to understand their emphasis on being able to "see"—not just with the eyes but deep into the soul, as well.

Grace fears that Jake's hard work as an Avatar is affecting his health, as he seems drawn and tired. She also relates a story about a school in the forest where she tried to teach the Na'vi children. One day, Neytiri watched as soldiers gunned down her older sister in the classroom. Grace got most of the other children out safely, but the experience left an indelible mark in her memory.

With other young warriors, Jakesully makes the treacherous climb up floating unobtainium rocks and long vines to choose their own Banshee to ride.
Looking one of the flying reptiles right in the eye, Jake jumps on its back. It
throws him, nearly to his death off the cliffs, but he tries again. This time, as it
calms down, he connects with the creature's antenna and they fly.

With Neytiri still as his guide, Jakesully learns to hunt from his Banshee. The
pair is attacked by a larger flying creature called a Leonopteryx, and only their
skills as riders—plus a mass of confining vines—save them from becoming a
snack for the biggest beast in the forest. The Na'vi call it Toruk, and only a few
have ever tamed it and earned the title of Toruk Macto.

Waking in the link pod, it suddenly hits Jake—the Na'vi are now his true
world and the lab is the dream.

Col. Quaritch thinks it's time to end Jake's intel project, and, having been
successful, plans have been made for Sully to get his legs back into use once
more. But he defers, insisting that there's more work to be done, with relocation
of the Na'vi still a possibility. Losing patience, Quaritch wants it done ASAP.

Painted in white, Jakesully stands before Eytukan and the Na'vi tribe. They
all place their hands on him, and he has become a full member of their people.
Even Grace's Avatar smiles in approval.

As a member and warrior of the Na'vi, Jakesully can make his own bow, and,
more, he can choose a woman. But his choice is already made, with him and
Neytiri becoming mates forever.

The next morning, Neytiri is suddenly awakened by the sounds of dozers
tearing into the forests. But with Jake out of his link pod, his Avatar lies motionless in the grass. Neytiri struggles to pull him out of the path of the oncoming
massive machines, and he reenters his pod just in time.

Jakesully attempts to stop the movement, as Selfridge watches on a video
monitor. He coldly refuses to halt the dozers, knowing the Na'vi will get out of
the way. Armed guards open fire on Jakesully and Neytiri as they run for safety.

Quaritch looks at a video replay, angrily recognizing Jake's Avatar as his
mole. Eytukan and Tsu'tey ready their warriors to respond with warfare. Neytiri
and Jakesully try to stop them, but Quaritch enters the lab and shuts down the
link pods. Grace and Jake collapse instantly.

In the ops center, tempers run high, as Jake has betrayed Quaritch, while
Grace tries to convince Selfridge that the Na'vi's connection with their environ-
ment is a rare biological situation that deserves respect and understanding. The
RDA exec scoffs at the idea, while Quaritch knows that the Na'vi won't relocate.
That leaves the warhawk with a simple solution.

But the natives strike first, burning the bulldozers and killing many of the
soldiers. Quaritch and Selfridge plan to retaliate with gunships, but Jake gets
one hour in an attempt to convince the Na'vi to evacuate their village.

Neytiri is devastated to hear Jake was part of a plan to gain her people's trust
so they would leave. They all feel betrayed, and Tsu'tey orders Jakesully and

Grace to be bound for execution as dozens of gunships surround the Na'vi's Hometree.

Quaritch fills the tree interior with tear gas, driving the natives out into the open. He then launches incendiary rockets, setting the land on fire. Mo'at cuts Grace and Jakesully free, pleading for their help.

The gunships fire high-explosive missiles at the base of the Hometree, although Chacon pulls her chopper out of the attack without shooting. Smoke billows into sky, and the Hometree tumbles slowly to the ground, as Quaritch surveys the scene with a cup of coffee in his hand. Neytiri finds her father mortally wounded, and as he dies, he passes his warrior's bow into her hands.

From the ops center, Selfridge pulls the plug on the Avatar Program. Jakesully falls to the ground, while children pull at Grace's motionless body. The link pod is opened, and soldiers remove Jake and Grace, placing them in confinement.

Chacon breaks them out with the help of lab tech Max, and they take off in her twin-rotor copter. Quaritch tries in vain to shoot them down. But Grace has been shot in the abdomen during the escape. Trudy hooks up the chopper to a link module and slowly lifts it into the air.

They head for the Tree of Souls, a special spot in the center of the forest and the home of Eywa, the Na'vi deity. The native survivors from the massacre gather around the base of the white willow as Chacon sets the copter down.

Jake climbs into the pod, and his Avatar rises amid the destruction of the Hometree. He mounts his Banshee and soars into the sky, where he finds the Leonopteryx called Toruk. While the natives sing, Jakesully rides the Toruk and lands among them. He has tamed the beast, hoping to earn back the respect of the Na'vi and the title of Toruk Macto.

Neytiri welcomes him back, and Jakesully implores Tsu'tey to ride with him. The great warrior agrees, and Jake's Avatar must ask for the Na'vi's help to save Grace. Mo'at receives the injured woman, and her Avatar at the foot of the Tree of Souls.

Despite the matriarch's efforts, Grace dies. Filled with sadness and rage, Jakesully calls for all the clans to come together and rise up against the Sky People. The land belongs to the Na'vi—so says Toruk Macto.

Quaritch briefs his troops on the pending Na'vi attack, and they quickly mobilize in an effort to strike first. From the inside, Max tips off Jake and the others about the colonel's plan. Jakesully kneels at the Tree of Souls and prays to Eywa for help in repelling the Sky People.

Quaritch's gunships take off, with the Toruk Macto leading an enormous flock of Banshees. The gunships land near the Hallelujah Mountains, with troops exiting on foot and in large mechanized one-man units called ampsuits.

Tsu'tey leads scores of ground warriors on horse-like animals, while Jakesully drops down on the Sky People from above. The battle is on.

Powerfully drawn arrows pierce the cockpits of the helicopters, as Jakesully commands the Toruk to grab another and fling it into a mountain wall. Ampsuit guns take down cavalry warriors and drive their forces back. Chacon joins the attack, keeping Quaritch's ship occupied.

Neytiri's Banshee is shot down as she watches the carnage around her. Tsu'tey flies into the cargo hold of a gunship, downing soldiers with arrows and his size and strength. One shooter guns the warrior down, and he tumbles out of the hatch. Quaritch fires a missile, taking out Chacon in a fiery blast.

Neytiri is pinned down by ground fire as the colonel prepares to destroy the Tree of Souls with a pallet of explosives. She fixes an arrow for one final suicide assault when, suddenly, the ground thunders with the approaching hammerheads. Dozens of the beasts trample soldiers and ampsuits alike, while hundreds of wild Banshees attack the gunships.

Nervously, Quaritch readies the gunship to drop the explosives, but Jakesully jumps atop the craft and tosses a grenade into an engine vent. The blast rocks the ship forward, and the pallet of explosives rolls back into the cargo bay.

Next, Jake's Avatar prepares to do the same thing to Quaritch's craft, but a quick maneuver tosses the Na'vi to one side. Jake hangs by one hand as one of the grenades goes off, but the ship stays in flight.

The colonel blows a hatch and fires a pistol at Jake, missing but forcing the Avatar into the sky below. Using a technique taught by Neytiri, Jake breaks his fall by sliding from tree branch to tree branch safely.

Quaritch escapes in an ampsuit, just as his ship crashes to the ground. Finding the link module, he takes aim with his weapon but Neytiri rides in on a fierce Thanator. It attacks, but Quaritch kills it with a huge knife, and Neytiri is trapped under the beast.

Jakesully jumps in and parries the colonel's knife thrusts with a heavy rifle. The knife breaks, and Quaritch turns the ampsuit toward the link module. He smashes windows, looking for Jake's pod. With his attention turned back to Jake's Avatar, Quaritch grabs the warrior by his hair and holds him high. He readies a knife at Jake's throat, but Neytiri slips from under the Thanator, grabs her bow and lets fly a huge arrow.

It strikes the colonel in his chest, and Neytiri repeats the attack with a second arrow. The ampsuit tumbles over, with Quaritch dead inside. Jake springs from his pod, unable to breathe in the deadly forest atmosphere.

Neytiri jumps into the module, grabs an emergency breathing mask, and saves the man, cradling him like a baby in her arms. Jake's Avatar finds Tsu'tey, fatally injured in the battle. As he dies, Tsu'tey urges Jakesully to be the leader the Na'vi need to survive.

Under the eyes of Neytiri, Jakesully, and other Na'vi, the rest of the humans leave Pandora for good, except for Max and a few of the other lab workers. Jake releases the Toruk, and, at a grand ceremony, the human Jake passes away. But his Avatar lives on.

Afterwords

If this film were Peter Jackson's *King Kong*, it would clearly be the eight-hundred-pound gorilla in the room. Perhaps, then, *Avatar* can be considered as the eight-hundred-pound Na'vi in the room. Writer/producer/director/editor James Cameron set out to reinvent sci-fi filmmaking with *Avatar*, and he did it.

Like many of the cinematic success stories, *Avatar* was a long time in its creation. Cameron wrote his first eighty-page treatment of the story in 1994, three years before his titanic success with . . . uh, *Titanic*. His original intention was to make *Avatar* right after completing *Titanic*, aiming for a release date of 1999. But he felt the film technology needed to make his vision a reality just wasn't ready yet.

Plus, there can be no doubt that the enormous commercial success of *Titanic* provided Cameron with the leverage and resources to develop those processes necessary to make *Avatar* come true. If *Titanic* had sunk at the box office, *Avatar* might never have flown.

By 2005, Cameron was satisfied with the motion-capture software and cameras that allowed the specific and accurate acquisition of actors' emoting. Having seen believable photo-realistic, live-into-CG performances like Gollum in the *Lord of the Rings* films, Peter Jackson's *King Kong*, and Davy Jones in *Pirates of the Caribbean: Dead Man's Chest*, Cameron was convinced the time was right to move forward.

Essentially, he felt it was necessary to direct motion-capture performances in the same way a normal performance was directed—the actor or actress, in their proper movie setting, with proper lighting. It took until 2005 for CG technology to incorporate those digital elements in a satisfactory, real-time application. Additionally, Cameron was intent on making *Avatar* in 3-D.

Cameron's story was inspired by many, if not all, of the sci-fi books he read as a kid, including the *Tarzan* and *John Carter of Mars* series by Edgar Rice Burroughs. *Avatar* would tap into Cameron's varied interests, such as biology, the tech world, and responsible treatment of the environment. At the same time, he wanted an exciting adventure film that audiences around the world would enjoy.

Among the many challenges in making *Avatar* was the need to invent a separate language indigenous to the Na'vi society. Cameron called on Dr. Paul Frommer, the head of the linguistics department at the University of Southern California. The professor spent a year building sounds, syntax, and a vocabulary for the Na'vi, bearing in mind that the language had to be pleasing to the ear and appealing to moviegoers. He borrowed grammar and phonics from Polynesian, Maori, and African languages, among others.

Twentieth Century-Fox ponied up nearly $200 million for *Avatar's* production costs and were a bit nervous when Cameron revealed that the cast would essentially be unknowns. Sam Worthington came to the production with some television and film credits, and costarred with Christian Bale in *Terminator*

Salvation, earlier in 2009. Zoe Saldana offered a similar resume of smaller parts, being featured as Uhura in J. J. Abrams' reboot of *Star Trek*, also earlier in 2009. Of course, Sigourney Weaver was an old favorite of Cameron's.

The director took his cast to Hawaii to rehearse before production began on *Avatar*. Worthington, Saldana, and other performers were dressed in their skimpy outfits and acted out scenes as Cameron captured the rehearsals on a small handheld camera. When a bystander asked Worthington what was going on, the actor told him James Cameron was making a movie. Seeing the costumes and tiny camera, the pedestrian sadly observed, "Geez, he's gone a long way down since *Titanic*."

The comment couldn't have been further from the truth, as *Avatar* opened to incredible success when it was released for the 2009 holiday season. The film hit more than fourteen thousand movie screens around the world, including more than thirty-six hundred in 3-D and over two hundred in the large-screen IMAX 3D format.

In addition, *Avatar* brought home three Academy Awards, out of nine nominations. The film was recognized for Best Achievements in Cinematography, Art Direction, and Visual Effects. The other nominations included major items like Best Picture, Best Director, and Best Original Score.

Within six weeks, *Avatar* became the highest-grossing film in history and the first film ever to gross more than $2 billion around the world. The success prompted Cameron to announce an unprecedented three *Avatar* sequels, with intentions for release in 2016, 2017, and 2018.

King of the world, indeed.

4

How Fast Can I Get to the Year 2412?

The Wonders of Time Travel

Don't Step on That Ant—It Might Be Your Future Uncle

The dream and theory of time travel have spanned the worlds of science and art, as physicists have tried to prove it might be possible—and writers and filmmakers have found ways to make it possible. However, since the theme of this book is science *fiction*, we all must agree that—for the present moment—time travel does not exist.

Certainly, that condition doesn't have to stop one from considering the possibilities of forward or backward motion in the fourth dimension. The purpose of a trip through time could be great or small.

One might desire to take a firsthand look at the age of dinosaurs, or the grandeur of Napoleon's rule, or the signing of the Declaration of Independence. Or one might merely wish to know her great-great-grandmother's secret for country gravy, or be witness to the wedding of Mom and Dad, or reexperience his first kiss.

Sadly, a red flag or two immediately flies in the wind to break our bubble, spoil our party, and order everyone out of the pool. Perhaps the reddest flag is what many refer to as the Butterfly Effect—so called in reference to a wonderful 1952 sci-fi short story by Ray Bradbury titled "A Sound of Thunder."

Also known as the Cause and Effect Paradox, the inference is that, while traveling back in time, one must be very, very careful about how one interacts with the environment. If, as suggested by Bradbury's story, one were to step on a butterfly during the Cretaceous Period, it would have a profound effect on how the world develops from that point forward. The result might be slight—like subtle changes in plant life colors—or major—like everyone being born with their underwear permanently attached.

Either way, the Butterfly Effect, and time travel in general, have been tapped by Hollywood for everything from *The Simpsons* TV show to the ultra-successful *Back to the Future* trilogy. And while time travel might not be possible (yet), it sure has been fun to dream.

Slaughterhouse-Five

Synopsis

- 1972—American/Universal—103 min./color
- Director: George Roy Hill
- Original music: Glenn Gould
- Film editing: Dede Allen
- Art direction: Alexander Golitzen, George Webb
- Based on the 1969 novel by Kurt Vonnegut Jr.

Cast

- Michael Sacks (Billy Pilgrim)
- Ron Leibman (Paul Lazzaro)
- Eugene Roche (Edgar Derby)
- Sharon Gans (Valencia Merble Pilgrim)
- Valerie Perrine (Montana Wildhack)
- Perry King (Robert Pilgrim)
- Kevin Conway (Roland Weary)
- Roberts Blossom (Wild Bob Cody)
- Richard Schaal (Howard Campbell)

Billy Pilgrim types a letter to the editor of the local paper in an attempt to clarify a previous missive. The man has become unstuck in time, moving back and forth—randomly—within his life. Middle-aged as he writes, Pilgrim suddenly finds himself as a young soldier in a snowy field during World War II, dodging Nazi troops.

A chaplain's assistant, Pilgrim works hard to convince other American troops—including the impulsive and belligerent Paul Lazzaro and dim-witted Roland Weary—that he's not a German spy. Then, in a blink, Pilgrim—now a senior citizen—finds himself on the distant planet of Tralfamadore, lovingly tended to by the vivacious Montana Wildhack. She knows Billy's troubles with time-tripping are vexing. The manic Lazzaro attacks Pilgrim, but it all comes to a sudden stop as German troops take the soldiers prisoner.

Billy honeymoons with his Rubenesque wife, Valencia, who promises to lose weight for her young husband. The Nazis have taken Weary's boots, and, while the soldiers march through the mud of Belgian streets, Billy accidentally steps on his feet. In reaction, the protective Lazzaro threatens Billy. When a German photographer pulls Pilgrim away for a posed propaganda picture, the soldier jumps forward to a photo-op with his family as the new Pilgrim Building is dedicated.

The shell-shocked and haggard Colonel "Wild Bob" Cody embraces the soldiers as they board boxcars for transport to a prison camp near Dresden. Along the way, a freezing Weary dies in the arms of Paul Lazzaro, and Lazzaro vows revenge against Pilgrim, whom he blames for his friend's death.

In a hospital bed, the young Billy hides from his mom and undergoes shock treatment for a nervous breakdown attributed to his prisoner-of-war experience. Arriving at Dresden—a safe city devoid of military targets—the soldiers disembark, leaving the dead bodies of Weary and Wild Bob behind. Nazi soldiers taunt Billy, giving him a ratty woman's coat to wear against the cold. Lazzaro threatens Billy again, and a fatherly soldier, Edgar Derby, takes Pilgrim under his protective wing.

As the troops enter the showers, Billy jumps to his childhood, where his dad throws him into a swimming pool to sink or swim—he sinks. Back in prison camp, British troops merrily welcome the Yanks, singing and backslapping the stunned soldiers. Exhausted, Billy passes out and falls face-first into his bowl of soup.

He wakes in the backyard of his new home as a puppy licks his face. As the years pass, Billy teaches tricks to his dog, Spot, while Valencia seems to endlessly cook pies and cakes. The couple welcome their first child, and Spot celebrates by lifting his leg on the new mother. Escaping her wrath by slipping into the moonlit night, Billy is awed by a glowing light that emerges from the sky, then quickly vanishes.

In prison camp, Lazzaro is up to his old threatening ways, but Derby comes to Billy's aid. A diamond in the pocket of Billy's coat jumps him to a party at home, where he's had it set in a ring for Valencia. Billy slips away and comes across his son Robert with a men's magazine. Dad admonishes the teen and confiscates it. He stops to admire the centerfold, who happens to be Montana Wildhack.

Bouncing back to World War II, Derby is selected as troop leader, defeating a surly Paul Lazzaro. The election throws Pilgrim back and forth, between the war and his reception as president of the local Lions Club. A quick jump puts Pilgrim with his family at the drive-in theater, where the lovely Montana Wildhack graces the screen. As Valencia protests the actress' nudity, Billy is whisked back to a cattle car with Derby and Lazzaro.

Edgar beams about his son back home, and Billy jumps to a night when Robert was caught vandalizing a cemetery. In Dresden, an elderly German officer and teenage Nazi soldiers receive the troops. One young German soldier has eyes for a pretty local girl, who blows him a kiss from her balcony.

With his father-in-law at his side, Billy boards a plane for an optometrists' convention in Montreal. As the plane prepares to take off, Pilgrim envisions a terrible crash and tries to warn everyone. His efforts are laughed off, until the plane really does go down—just as he said it would.

The American troops are taken to Schlachthof-Fünf—Slaughterhouse-Five—where they will be housed. Bleeding, Billy is found in a snowdrift near the plane crash site by a ski-bound team of rescuers. Semiconscious, he is mumbling "Schlachthof-Fünf"—the address he was urged to remember during the war.

A hysterical Valencia roars down the street, causing accidents and rushing to be with Billy in the hospital. As she trashes her Cadillac, Billy jumps to the day

Michael Sacks (center) and Eugene Roche in *Slaughterhouse-Five*.

he gave her the car as a birthday present. The battered car reaches the hospital, while Billy undergoes brain surgery and returns to Dresden.

Billy comes through the operation, but Valencia has died from carbon monoxide poisoning—her accidents have damaged the Cadillac's exhaust system. Coincidentally, Pilgrim recovers in a hospital room next to a professor and author of military history. Mumbling that he was in Dresden, Billy is admonished by the gruff scholar to write his own book on the famous city.

Back in Dresden, Billy joins other troops for a dinner break while Howard Campbell—an American Nazi—tries to recruit the POWs to fight the Communist Russians. His pitch is interrupted by the wail of air raid sirens—everyone rushes to the bomb shelters. The bombing of Dresden begins.

Pilgrim returns home after his surgery, despite the protesting of his daughter to stay with her family. He takes his crippled old dog Spot and bids his daughter "Good night." A lit candle breaks the dark of the bomb shelter in Dresden, and the survivors emerge to survey the carnage. The once-beautiful city of culture is now a smoldering ruin. The once-cocky Nazi lad runs to find his admiring girlfriend is dead.

The previously troublesome Robert has joined the Green Berets, visiting his convalescing dad and apologizing for being a problem as a teen. Robert leaves his dad alone, and the glowing light appears once again, taking Billy and Spot to a domed habitat on Tralfamadore. Its inhabitants, living in the fourth dimension, are invisible to Billy.

Amid the wreckage of Dresden, the American troops are assigned to recover bodies and admonished that looters will be shot immediately. Dozens of bodies are burned, as the Tralfamadorians encourage Pilgrim to embrace their philosophy—ignore the bad times and concentrate on the good ones.

The Tralfamadorians may be invisible, but they can see everything—including a nude and screaming Montana Wildhack, who has also been brought to the dome. Always the gentleman, Billy offers Ms. Wildhack something to wear. The alien hosts seem preoccupied with seeing Billy and Montana mate, but Pilgrim refuses. He insists at least on getting to know her first.

In Dresden, Derby marvels at a perfect Dresden porcelain doll that survived the bombing. Innocently, he puts it in his coat pocket to show to some German officers. Without hesitation, Derby is executed for looting, as one of the Nazis tosses the china doll away. With Montana, Billy admires her new wardrobe as they cuddle on the couch.

At his home on Earth, Billy refuses psychiatric help, as suggested by his daughter and son-in-law. They simply don't believe his stories about traveling to and from Tralfamadore. Pilgrim has even witnessed his own death in the future, while lecturing in Philadelphia about life on Tralfamadore. From the crowds, an angry and aged Paul Lazzaro shoots Billy down, keeping his promise to avenge Weary's death.

Jumping to Dresden, Lazzaro tries to loot a grandfather's clock, but when Russian troops approach, he takes off and leaves Billy pinned under the timepiece. On Tralfamadore, Montana gives birth to Billy's child and the Tralfamadorians applaud, lighting the skies with a salvo of fireworks.

Afterwords

It may come as a surprise to know that famed author, Kurt Vonnegut Jr. believed that George Roy Hill's 1972 cinematic version of *Slaughterhouse-Five* was actually better than his own book. And, unlike other time-travel films, *Slaughterhouse-Five* does not focus specifically on a direction of movement—it bucks wildly between past, present, and future (as can be seen in the previous synopsis). The result is a film that centers on the traveler himself, rather than his purpose for traveling.

One of the beauties of Hill's film is that it does not concern itself with the mechanics of time travel—there is no machine, there isn't even an alien ship to whisk Billy and Montana (yes, and Spot, too) away to Tralfamadore. The director indulges in the experience—the wonder—of time travel, rather than the technicalities of it.

Much of the movie's appeal comes from a talented but largely unknown (at the time) cast. Michael Sacks gave Billy Pilgrim the innocence and gentle demeanor that allowed the character to embrace and enjoy his unique ability to jump around in time. Interestingly, Sacks retired from acting in the mid-1980s and became an expert executive in technology and software for the financial world.

Eugene Roche—who spent years on TV as a dishwasher in commercials for Ajax detergent—was the kind and fatherly Edgar Derby, a fine portrayal that made his sudden execution in the film even more shocking. Valerie Perrine, a former Las Vegas showgirl, handled the difficult task of playing most of her role as a nude Montana Wildhack with comfort and humor. Finally, Ron Leibman gave Paul Lazzaro a pure sense of paranoia and hatred of the world around him. Leibman has since performed on stage, screen, and television, winning an Emmy and Tony Award.

Despite receiving a top award at the Cannes Film Festival, *Slaughterhouse-Five*, with its budget of more than $3 million, was considered a flop at the box office.

Sleeper

Synopsis

- 1973—American/Universal—89 min./color
- Director: Woody Allen
- Original music: Woody Allen
- Film editing: Ralph Rosenbaum
- Production design: Dale Hennesy

Cast:

- Woody Allen (Miles Monroe)
- Diane Keaton (Luna Schlosser)
- John Beck (Erno Windt)
- Bartlett Robinson (Dr. Orva)
- Mary Gregory (Dr. Melik)
- Don Keefer (Dr. Tryon)

In the year 2173, a cryogenic capsule is discovered by scientists, and, against the government's rules, the man inside is revived. Like a giant Salisbury steak, he is unwrapped from his foil container and slowly brought up to temperature.

He is Miles Monroe, who lived in 1973 and operated a health food restaurant in New York City. Hospitalized for a minor peptic ulcer, complications arose, and he was frozen for two hundred years.

Slight of frame, Miles has wispy red hair and black-rimmed glasses. As he begins to respond to the doctors, an alarm sounds, signaling the presence of an unauthorized person—Monroe. Doctors Melik and Orva pass him off to security as a colleague and smuggle him away to a house in the woods.

When Miles is finally informed of where—and when—he is, the reaction is not a good one, and he faints dead away. Revived, he is agitated, concerned about his overdue rent and long-departed friends. A nuclear war has destroyed the country as he once knew it, and the United Federation is now governed with an iron hand by the Great Leader. On a positive note, Miles bought Polaroid stock at a low price and figures it must be worth millions of dollars by now.

He discovers much has changed while he was gone—tobacco and fatty foods have been discovered to be very healthy, the opposite of what was believed in his day. When the scientists seek his interpretation of historic artifacts and photos that they know nothing about, he describes: former French president Charles DeGaulle as a famous TV chef; evangelist Billy Graham, who used to double-date with God; and sportscaster Howard Cosell, whose viewing was used as a punishment for crimes, among others.

The future has also developed humanoid robots as domestic help, cooking, cleaning, and handling many jobs formerly performed by real people. Miles immediately asks if female robots have been developed, as the possibilities could be limitless. But there's no time for that, as he must be moved out to the Western District. Once there, he can join the underground movement that seeks to overthrow the Leader. As a person with no identity to the present government, Miles can help the revolutionaries know more about the sinister Aires Project that threatens to wipe them out.

As a security team takes the doctors away, Miles attempts to escape in a shoulder-harness helicopter. He then hides in a service truck for domestic robots, and, using spare parts, he disguises himself as one of the humanoids.

Monroe is delivered to the home of pretty Luna Schlosser, a poet and artist who is hosting a party for friends. Left alone in the kitchen, he quickly learns that instant pudding can have a mind of its own when adding too much water. It grows to the size of an end table, and Miles beats the menacing blob of dessert into submission with a broom.

The bohemian guests arrive, and Miles discovers the intoxicating magic of the Orb and the satisfying effects of the phone booth–sized Orgasmatron. He also discovers that Luna is quite happy as a benign member of the Federation and wants to know nothing about her friend's talk of the Aires Project.

Later, Luna takes Miles to the robot repair center, wanting his head changed for something better looking. Since the first step involves the wrenching off a robot's head, he wants no part of it and escapes. Revealing himself as a real person, he takes Luna as an unwilling hostage, and they travel deep into the wilderness.

Hungry, Miles finds genetically altered food at a farm, where bananas are the size of bathtubs and celery stalks grow as big as trees. He needs a vehicle, so he and Luna pose as a stranded couple, stopping at a home to borrow one. Luna slips away to the bathroom, where she contacts security to save her from Monroe. The duo borrows a car and a Hydro-Vac suit, an inflatable garment usually worn in space. Luna tricks him into putting the suit on, and, at the edge of a lake,

Diane Keaton and Woody Allen in *Sleeper*.

she inflates it to detain Monroe as security approaches. But the police figure Luna's contact with Miles has contaminated her, and they prepare to eliminate her. Miles comes to her rescue, and they escape by jetting across the lake in the rapidly-deflating Hydro-Vac suit.

Safe in a cave, they find a two-hundred year-old Volkswagen Beetle, which immediately starts on its first crank. Driving away, they wind up at the house where Miles was first taken. The journey has drawn the couple together, as Luna wants a reluctant Miles to join her in the Orgasmatron. Suddenly, security arrives, and Miles sends Luna into the Western District to find the Aires Project, while he stays behind. But he makes the mistake of trying to hide in the Orgasmatron and emerges, slightly toasted, into the hands of the waiting authorities.

Reprogrammed as a member of society, Miles is given a new suit of clothes (courtesy of two bickering Jewish robot tailors), a job loading an enormous machine with magnetic tape, and an apartment with a robot dog named Rags.

Meanwhile, Luna learns to live off the land and joins the underground. When she returns to get Miles, he doesn't remember her. Against his will, he is abducted by Luna and the underground. With the help of the handsome underground leader Erno, Miles is deprogrammed and becomes part of the revolutionaries. The plan is for Luna and Miles to slip into the city center, posing as doctors, to find the Aires Project.

The Aires Project turns out to be a rescue mission—the Leader was the victim of an assassination attempt by bombing. All that remains is his nose. The purpose of the top-secret project is to clone the Leader, using his nose as the starting point. Miles and Luna are mistaken for medical experts who will lead the cloning. Miles' plan is to steal the nose during the process, which will be assisted by a computer—Bio-Central 2100, Series G.

Despite their bickering, Miles and Luna begin the procedure—intending to clone the Leader directly into his suit. Miles slips the Leader's nose under his surgical mask, and the 2100 immediately notes the irregularity. Holding the nose at gunpoint, the duo make their escape. They toss the proboscis under a steamroller, where it's flattened to a grotesque shape.

Escaping in a vehicle, Luna chides Miles for being jealous of Erno, while she holds great hope for Erno as the new leader. Miles observes that they'll be stealing Erno's nose in six months—politics is something he doesn't believe in. As they kiss, Miles admits to only believing in sex and death—but at least after death, one isn't nauseous.

Afterwords

In the sixties and early seventies, Woody Allen painted his comedy movies with a broad brush of verbal and visual jokes. Films like *Take the Money and Run, Everything You Always Wanted to Know About Sex (But Were Afraid to Ask)*, and

Bananas were more concerned with getting big laughs than telling a complete story.

Sleeper was a transition for Allen, as he began to move toward making more complex films with fully developed characters. The laughs still flew fast and frequently, but his next films—*Love and Death* and *Annie Hall*—established Allen as a legitimate writer and director.

Still, *Sleeper* was one of the few films to combine humor with sci-fi. His take on present and future technology riffed on the then-nascent concept of cryogenics and freezing and thawing people, but basically made the process as simple as turning someone into a giant TV dinner. Robot pets, just now becoming reality, were a concern in *Sleeper*, lest they leave droppings of batteries on the carpet.

Allen showed great futuristic foresight, as *Sleeper* also featured video communications that mirror today's Skype, scientifically enhanced farming, the medical concept of cloning, fingerprint scanning for security access, and other concepts that may have seemed far-fetched in the early 1970s. It should be no surprise that the writer/director consulted with no less than sci-fi author Isaac Asimov, discussing the script and film at a lunch meeting. Asimov was impressed with Allen's sci-fi instincts, although the filmmaker claimed a complete ignorance of the topic.

The futuristic house where Miles Monroe hides out is a real home located west of Denver, Colorado. Known as "The Sculptured House," it was designed and built high atop Genesee Mountain by architect Charles Deaton in 1963. Featured prominently in *Sleeper*, the home's interior was never completed. Bought and sold twice in the 1990s, it eventually wound up in a foreclosure auction in 2010, selling for $1.5 million.

The voice of computer Bio-Center 2100, Series G might sound familiar to viewers—it's that of Canadian actor Douglas Rain, who voiced another film computer named Hal 9000 in 1968's *2001: A Space Odyssey*.

Shot with a production budget of $2 million, *Sleeper* grossed more than $18 million domestically, putting it on the list of Top Twenty films in 1973.

Back to the Future

Synopsis

- 1985—American/Universal—116 min./color
- Director: Robert Zemeckis
- Original music: Alan Silvestri
- Film editing: Harry Keramidas, Arthur Schmidt
- Art direction: Todd Hallowell

Cast

- Michael J. Fox (Marty Mcfly)
- Christopher Lloyd (Dr. Emmett Brown)
- Crispin Glover (George Mcfly)

- Lea Thompson (Lorraine Baines Mcfly)
- Thomas F. Wilson (Biff Tannien)
- James Tolkan (Mr. Strickland)
- Claudia Wells (Jennifer Parker)

One morning in 1985, teenage Marty McFly drops by the house of Doc Brown, a brilliant but eccentric inventor. A budding guitarist, the boy plugs into a gigantic amplifier the doc has built. One power chord and Marty is blown across the room. Apparently, the doc hasn't quite fixed it.

Late for school, he's tagged a "slacker" by hall monitor Mr. Strickland, just like Marty's father was when he went to Hill Valley High School. Later, Marty's rock group, the Pinheads, lose an audition for the school dance. One teacher tells them, "You're just too darn loud."

Marty and his girlfriend Jennifer engage in a romantic embrace in the town square, but are interrupted by a volunteer's request to donate to the "Save the Clock Tower" fund. Thirty years back, lightning struck the clock tower in the town square, and it hasn't worked since.

At home, it's clear that Marty's family is a bunch of losers. His milquetoast father, George, is bullied by his boss, Biff. His mom is a dumpy drunk, and his brother and sister are dorky nonentities. Later that night, Marty meets Doc Brown at the Twin Pines Mall, where he shows off his latest experiment. It's a snazzy DeLorean sports car fitted with his special invention—a "flux capacitor" that runs on plutonium fuel. When the car reaches eighty-eight miles per hour, it becomes a time machine.

But Brown has duped a group of terrorists out of some stolen plutonium, and now they want it back. They shoot the doc and chase after Marty in the DeLorean. He hits eighty-eight miles per hour and is whisked back in time by thirty years, where he ends up on the Peabody farm that once stood where the mall was built. The startled family thinks Marty's a spaceman from the planet Pluto. He leaves in a hurry, knocking down one of the twin pines on the property.

Seeing his familiar neighborhood as farmland just being developed into suburban housing, Marty realizes he's become a time traveler. Fresh out of plutonium fuel, he hides the car and heads for town, where the only sugar-free drink is coffee and "Mr. Sandman" by the Chordettes is a hit tune.

In the local diner, Marty sits down next to his own future *father*. George McFly is a pitiful high school nerd, harassed by the town bully, Biff. Marty follows his dad to a side street, where George climbs a tree and watches his future wife get dressed in her bedroom. He falls, and Marty pushes him out of the way of an oncoming car. George runs away, and Marty is knocked unconscious.

He wakes up in his future *mother's* bedroom. Lorraine is a cute high school girl who calls Marty "Calvin Klein," since that was the name she saw on his underwear. She is obviously smitten with him.

Finding Doc Brown's house, Marty convinces the doc that he's come from the future, and they devise a way to restart the time machine. Since they know

Michael J. Fox and Christopher Lloyd in *Back to the Future.*

when lightning will strike the clock tower—according to the "Save the Clock Tower" flyer—they plan on harnessing the power from the storm and funneling it into the DeLorean, sending Marty back to 1985.

Looking at a picture of Marty's brother and sister, Brown realizes that their images are slowly fading away. This means that Marty's trip back has somehow interfered with his mom and dad getting together. Marty and the Doc must make sure they do get together, or the siblings will disappear forever.

Biff harasses Lorraine in the school lunchroom, and Marty intervenes, coming to her rescue. It takes some effort, but Marty convinces George to ask Lorraine to the upcoming school dance. Miffed at having his fun broken up in the lunchroom, Biff chases Marty around the town square, but ends up crashing into a truck, neck-deep in manure.

Later, Lorraine asks Marty to go to the dance. Marty's plan is to go to the dance with her, but George will save the day when Marty tries to get fresh with her. Saturday night comes, and Doc and Marty prepare the wiring at the clock tower. Marty writes a letter to the doc, telling him he'll be shot on that October night in 1985 in the Twin Pines Mall. He slips the letter into his coat pocket.

At the dance, Biff pulls Marty out of the car and begins to harass Lorraine once again. George, following the plan, pulls someone out of the car, but is shocked to see that it is Biff. Nevertheless, George gathers the courage and strength to knock the bully out cold, and George and Lorraine embrace.

Marty joins the band onstage for a lively version of "Johnny B. Goode" and makes sure his parents kiss. They do, and everyone in Marty's picture returns. He bids Lorraine and George goodbye, assuring them that they'll see him again.

At the town square, the lightning strikes, and Marty returns to 1985 as planned, following some quick thinking by Doc Brown. Marty arrives at what is now Lone Pine Mall, just in time to see the doc being shot by the terrorists. He also watches himself being chased in the DeLorean, disappearing into the past.

But the doc isn't dead—he couldn't resist his curiosity and wore a bullet-proof vest after reading Marty's thirty-year-old letter. Marty says goodbye to Doc Brown, who plans on going into the future.

Back home, Marty sees that his family has changed, drastically for the better. His dad is a suave, famous science fiction writer, with Biff relegated to polishing the family BMW. His sister and brother are sharp and successful. His mom is a svelte, modern woman. Marty's trip into the past seems to have had a positive effect on the present. He embraces Jennifer, and, suddenly, Doc Brown arrives back from the future. He's worried about Marty and Jennifer's kids—something has to be done about them.

Afterwords

Visiting his parents' home in St. Louis in 1980, *BTTF* writer and producer Bob Gale found his dad's high school yearbook and wondered if they'd gone to school together back then, would they be friends? This was the genesis for the script that would become *Back to the Future*.

Director Robert Zemeckis, friends with Gale since they were both students at the School of Cinematic Arts at USC, worked with his partner to revise the script for *BTTF*—seeing it rejected more than forty times in the three years that followed its first drafting. Most studios panned it for not being edgy or sexy enough, while the folks at Disney regarded the budding relationship between Marty and his 1955 mom as incest. Fortunately, Zemeckis had forged a professional relationship with Steven Spielberg, and, once Universal Studios agreed to make *Back to the Future*, Spielberg agreed to executive produce the film.

That association came in handy when the president of Universal issued a memo stating he hated the title of *Back to the Future* and suggested the unbelievable *Spaceman from Pluto* instead. Everyone associated with the film knew that title would be a big-time loser, but no one wanted to stand up to the head of the studio. Spielberg came to the rescue by responding with his own note, thanking the president for a most humorous memo, offering that everyone loved the joke, and to keep them coming. Crisis . . . averted.

Michael J. Fox was cast to play Marty McFly, but his role in the hit TV series *Family Ties*, forced him to drop out. Once again, the president of Universal stepped in, insisting on actor Eric Stoltz. After six weeks of shooting were completed, Zemeckis and Spielberg realized that Stoltz, despite being a great actor, was not delivering the comedy needed for the film. As fate had it, the producers of *Family Ties* arranged for Fox to become available, and he was finally able to accept the part. The downside was that Fox shot his scenes for the TV show during the day and filmed *BTTF* at night—sleep became nonexistent for the young actor.

The actual time-travel device was originally supposed to be a refrigerator, with the film's climax occurring with an atomic bomb at a Nevada test site. Fortunately, cooler heads prevailed, and, after passing over the expensive Mercedes-Benz 300SL, the aluminum-hulled, gull-wing-doored DeLorean sports car was chosen, partly because it resembled an alien spaceship and allowed for the spaceman from Pluto gag at the 1955 Peabody farm.

The DeLorean time machine was designed by illustrators Ron Cobb and Andrew Probert, with construction of three film cars provided by Filmtrix and additional modifications from Mike Fink (including the flux capacitor) and Michael Scheffe. Conversion on the DeLoreans took ten weeks, at a cost of $150,000. Four additional DeLoreans were built for use on the two *BTTF* sequels.

Huey Lewis and the News, a popular 1980s band and a favorite of director Zemeckis, provided several songs for the film, including "Power of Love" (nominated for a Best Original Song Oscar) and "Back in Time." Lead singer Lewis also had a cameo appearance as the geeky teacher who gave Marty's band, the Pinheads, the thumb for being too loud.

Two sequels were spawned from this time-travel saga. In 1989, *Back to the Future Part II* took Marty and the Doc ahead to the twenty-first century, while *BTTF Part III* the following year found them in the middle of the 1880s Wild West. *Back to the Future: The Ride*, a motion simulation amusement ride featuring Doc Brown chasing Biff Tannen, was opened at Universal Studios theme parks in Hollywood and Orlando in 1991. The ride was also opened at Universal Studios Japan in 2001, while the American rides were closed in 2007.

The three *Back to the Future* films combined to gross more than $416 million at the box office in the US, with nearly $1 billion worldwide. A film series that combined the genres of sci-fi, comedy, buddy film, action-adventure, and romance, it also was responsible for adding phrases and words like "back to the future" and "slacker" to the modern-day lexicon.

Bill and Ted's Excellent Adventure

- 1989—American/Orion—90 min./color
- Director: Stephen Herek
- Original music: David Newman
- Film editing: Larry Bock, Patrick Rand
- Art direction: Gordon White

Cast

- Keanu Reeves (Ted Logan)
- Alex Winter (Bill S. Preston, Esq.)
- George Carlin (Rufus)
- Terry Camilleri (Napoleon)
- Dan Shor (Billy the Kid)
- Tony Steedman (Socrates)
- Bernie Casey (Mr. Ryan)

It's the year 2688 in San Dimas, California, and the world seems to be in fine shape—the air is clean, the water is clean, even bowling scores are up. According to Rufus, a bearded occupant of the future, this is all due to the two Great Ones—who almost didn't get things done. Fortunately, Rufus was able travel back in time to help them out.

Teenage Bill S. Preston (Esquire) and Ted "Theodore" Logan have a garage rock band called the Wyld Stallyns in 1988. But they do have a few problems— they really can't play guitar (although they do excel at air guitar), so they need to add Eddie Van Halen to the band. But to get him, they need to produce an excellent video.

In their high school history class, it's clear Bill and Ted aren't the brightest tubes in the Marshall amplifier. Bill refers to the emperor Napoleon as a "short, dead dude," while Ted believes Joan of Arc was Noah's wife. Their teacher, Mr. Ryan, lays it on the line for them—if they don't score an "A+" on their oral final exam, Bill and Ted will flunk.

Rufus arrives in 1988 via a telephone booth time machine to find Bill and Ted outside a Circle K convenience store. Suddenly, a second phone booth arrives, with another set of Bill and Ted inside. They urge themselves to pay attention to Rufus and leave.

Joining Rufus in his phone booth, Bill and Ted are transported to Austria in 1805, where Napoleon is waging war. A stray bomb blast hurls the emperor into the vortex of the time machine as it departs. Back in 1988, Rufus leaves the pair with their own time-traveling phone booth—and a very puzzled Napoleon.

The mishap gives Bill and Ted an idea—they will travel back in time to collect other historical figures and will be certain to pass their history exam. Ted's little brother is charged to stay with Napoleon while Bill and Ted are gone.

They dial up the Old West in 1879, where they find Billy the Kid in a saloon. They pull the outlaw out of a bar brawl and escape to Athens, Greece, in 410 BC. The great thinker Socrates gives a speech, and Bill and Ted make a weak attempt to exchange philosophic ideas with him. Into the booth they go, and it's off to fifteenth-century England and the castle of King Henry.

Bill and Ted spy the lovely princesses Elizabeth and Joanna and are immediately smitten. But the king will have none of it, even though the time travelers try to pass themselves off as the Earl of Preston and the Duke of Ted. Believed to be sorcerers, Bill and Ted are to be executed. At the last minute, Billy the Kid and Socrates, who have disguised themselves as the executioners, save the pair.

They all escape, traveling ahead in time to 2688, appearing before the Three Most Important People in the World and others. They all salute Bill and Ted with a symbolic strum of an air guitar, patterned after the duo's own signature tic. Meanwhile, Ted's brother has taken Napoleon to an ice cream parlor, where the emperor helps to polish off a huge bowl of frozen treats and earns a sticker as a "Ziggy Piggy."

Bill, Ted, Billy the Kid, and Socrates end up in 1901 Vienna, where they find noted psychoanalyst Sigmund Freud and decide to build up some extra credit.

They grab him, along with Ludwig van Beethoven, Joan of Arc, Genghis Khan (temped with a Twinkie), and Abraham Lincoln.

With a phone booth full of historic figures, Bill and Ted find the machine's antenna is broken and has to be fixed. Meanwhile, Ted's brother has taken Napoleon to a bowling alley. The emperor may have been a great military mastermind, but he turns out to be a rotten bowler and is thrown out of the alley, alone.

Alex Winter and Keanu Reeves in *Bill and Ted's Excellent Adventure.*

Stuck in prehistoric times, Bill fixes the phone booth with gum, chewed and generously donated by some of the world's greatest people. They arrive at the Circle K, where they first confronted themselves. Rufus advises them on how to get back to San Dimas in time for their final exam.

The booth winds up in Bill's backyard, where his mom is introduced to Beethoven, Socrates, and the others. With chores to be done, Bill enlists the group to pitch in—Freud vacuums and Lincoln irons shirts, while Beethoven washes windows and Genghis Khan cleans the toilet bowl.

Next, Bill and Ted visit the mall with their famous group, where the duo has shown some smarts by enlisting the "buddy system" among the time travelers. Bill and Ted have to find the missing Napoleon, and leave the group with a tray full of Slurpees to keep them occupied.

Napoleon is found at, where else? Waterloo Water Park. Back at the mall, Joan of Arc joins an aerobic class, while Beethoven is amused by music synthesizers, and Socrates and Billy the Kid try to work up the courage to hit on a cute couple of women. Sadly, Freud shows up to scare them off. Genghis Khan finds an aluminum baseball bat makes an effective weapon and Lincoln sits to have his picture taken.

Unfortunately, everyone is nabbed by mall security and booked at the police station. Fortunately, Ted's father is a captain at the lockup. Bill and Ted find keys to unlock the jail cells—by time traveling about, forward and backward, in order to take the captain's keys and hide them to be found. Similarly, Ted records himself calling out to his father, as a ploy to distract him while the boys release their historic friends from the hoosegow. Bill's mom helps drive everyone to the high school auditorium.

In a gala presentation, Bill and Ted introduce the group to the students and teachers. What's more, it seems the duo have learned quite a bit about history from their journey, as their friends present themselves to the crowd. Wrapping up, Lincoln encourages everyone to "Be excellent to each other" and "Party on, dude!" Needless to say, Bill and Ted have nailed their final exam.

Everyone is returned to their rightful time and place, and it occurs to Bill and Ted that perhaps they should actually learn to play guitar, rather than hatch a plot to get Eddie Van Halen. Rufus returns with the lovely princesses for Bill and Ted. What's more, in the future, the music of the Wyld Stallyns has become the basis of society.

Yet, as Rufus and the ladies join Bill and Ted for a jam session, it sounds like the Wyld Stallyns still need a lot of work. No worries, as Rufus assures everyone that "they DO get better."

Afterwords

The genesis of this (once again) sci-fi/comedy marriage came from the world of improv and skit humor. Screenwriters Chris Matheson (yes, son of sci-fi author Richard) and Ed Solomon, students at UCLA, found themselves in a workshop for improvisational comedy in 1983. The seed of thought was three dim-witted teens trying to study, talking about world affairs, and having absolutely no clue as to what they're talking about. (Doesn't that describe just about every high school study group?) The result was three dudes whose response to everything was to exclaim either "bogus" or "excellent."

A year later, the writing duo had fashioned a sci-fi script where the two protagonists traveled back in time with the help of a twenty-eight-year-old high school sophomore named Rufus. His 1969 Chevy van just happened to be a time machine, and with it, the trio was able to collect famous folks from history to attend the high school prom for the film's conclusion.

With the script in the hands of an agent, *Bill and Ted* became something every studio in Hollywood was considering. Warner Bros. liked it, but felt the time-traveling van was a bit too much like the DeLorean in *Back to the Future*. But like all the others, the studio passed on the project.

Director Stephen Herek, having just made an impression with the 1986 horror-comedy *Critters*, became attached to the script and convinced Dino De Laurentiis' company to produce the film. One of Herek's first moves was to turn the time-travel van into a phone booth (despite the fact that BBC sci-fi fave *Doctor Who* used the same device to span the decades).

After auditioning dozens and dozens of young actors, twenty-five-year-old Keanu Reeves and twenty-four-year-old Alex Winter were cast as Bill and Ted, respectively. But everyone felt that their roles should be reversed, including the actors themselves. Immediately, the concept of nerds changed to cool dudes.

The part of Rufus was changed from an over-the-hill high school student to a hip time traveler from the future after producer Scott Kroopf saw stand-up comic George Carlin at a Comic Relief performance. Herek wanted the rock band ZZ Top to be the Three Most Important People, but they declined. Still, the casting of Martha Davis, lead singer from the New Wave band the Motels; Fee Waybill, lead singer from eighties rock band the Tubes; and Clarence Clemons, sax player extraordinaire with Bruce Springsteen and the E Street Band, in those roles, as well as Go-Gos' singer and guitar player Jane Wiedlin as Joan of Arc, was a definite nod to the current music culture.

Made for an estimated $10 million, *Bill and Ted's Excellent Adventure* was a big splash at the domestic box office, grossing more than $40 million. The film's success resulted in a 1991 sequel, *Bill and Ted's Bogus Journey*, as well as short-lived animated and live-action TV shows in the early 1990s. In 2013, talk swirled about a script and director for a third film, but talk like that in Hollywood is often just that—talk.

Hot Tub Time Machine

Synopsis

- 2010—American/Metro-Goldwyn-Mayer—101 min./color
- Director: Steve Pink
- Original music: Christophe Beck
- Film editing: George Folsey Jr., James Thomas
- Art direction: Kelvin Humenny, Jeremy Stanbridge

Cast

- John Cusack (Adam)
- Rob Corddry (Lou)
- Craig Robinson (Nick)
- Clark Duke (Jacob)
- Crispin Glover (Phil)
- Lizzy Caplan (April)
- Sebastian Stan (Blaine)
- Chevy Chase (Repairman)
- Lyndsy Fonseca (Jenny)
- Collette Wolfe (Kelly)
- Kellee Stewart (Courtney)
- Jessica Paré (Tara)

Nick Webber has a thankless and less than glamorous job at a dog salon called "'Sup Dawg?" Adam Yates comes home to find another girlfriend has dumped him. Jacob, a dweeb couch potato, is Adam's nephew and lives in his uncle's basement. Hard-drinking and hard-driving Lou Dorchen pulls his Pontiac Trans-Am into his garage and, too inebriated to know better, fills it with noxious carbon monoxide fumes. Nick and Adam fear their friend Lou's drunken mistake was a suicide attempt.

Craig Robinson, Rob Corddry, John Cusack, and Clark Duke (L-R) in *Hot Tub Time Machine.*

All four get together for a nostalgic trip to Kodiak Valley Ski Resort, the site of their greatest partying days in the 1980s. But like the men themselves, Kodiak (K-Val) is showing its age. Now known as Silver Peaks Lodge, it features a surly, one-armed bellman named Phil.

Lou is hot to relive his wild past, but the rest aren't really up for it. The one redeeming factor of their hotel room—the hot tub on the balcony—invites the foursome with its warm and bubbling glow. Once immersed, the men party hard and accidentally dump a can of Chernobly, a banned energy drink from Russia that Lou brought along, onto the hot tub's controls.

In the morning, the foursome hit the slopes with a renewed vigor, and it's easy to see why: they have somehow been taken back in time by twenty-five years or so. Clues in people's clothing, hairstyles, television shows—all point to the fact that Nick, Adam, Lou, and Jacob are firmly embedded in the 1980s. As further proof, they find that Phil the bellman has two perfectly good arms. Obviously, the hot tub is a time machine.

The four are stunned to see their reflection in the bathroom mirror—it shows them as they looked in 1986—although Jacob, not yet born at that time—is a flickering version of his present self. Lou is scared; Nick is stunned; Adam hated the decade; Jacob has the time traveling all figured out.

A strange hotel repairman notes the hot tub is a very special model and warns the group not to change anything—a clear reference to the Butterfly Effect. This man obviously knows what has happened to them. The guys are now gravely concerned about repeating their actions from 1986, while Jacob is concerned that he'll never even be born.

Adam's girlfriend from the time, Jenny, pops in, excited to see Adam and looking forward to the Poison concert scheduled for later that day. But Adam knows he broke up with her during that concert, where she nearly stabbed him in the eye with a fork.

In the lobby, the guys see Kelly, Adam's sister, and Jacob immediately recognizes her as his mom, although she just thinks he's a geek. Outside, Phil entertains the crowd by making an ice sculpture with a chain saw. But he slips and falls, and Lou thinks he's severed his arm. Surprisingly, both arms are still attached.

Adam nervously visits with Jenny, while Lou relives a rough run-in he had with Blaine, a bullying ski patrol guard, and Nick haltingly gets together with a lovely lady named Tara in a hot tub—feeling that he is cheating on his wife, whom he hasn't even met yet in the future. And Blaine has unknowingly taken the Chernobly when he steals Lou's backpack.

At the Poison concert, Adam meets April, a rock journalist traveling with the band, but he refrains from interacting with her, fearing he might really goof up the future. Lou and Jacob narrowly avoid having an awkward three-way tryst back at the hot tub; the group chide Adam for not yet dumping Jenny and decide if he's not committed to following the events of the past, they won't either.

Nick and Lou watch passively as Phil twice escapes having his arm cut off in a faulty elevator. Blaine riffles through Lou's pack, figuring that items like an iPhone and the Chernobly are evidence that the Lou and the guys are Russian spies.

In an odd turnabout, Jenny breaks up with Adam, stabbing him in the forehead with a fork. Jacob finds the forlorn ex-boyfriend, high and writing terrible poetry. The repairman returns, noting that the tub must be fixed by dawn—or else. And they need the Chernobly to make it work.

Adam messes with Phil, insisting the bellman is destined to lose his arm. Lou and Nick see a football game on TV and, since Lou knows the outcome, he makes a killing by betting everyone on the score. But a final bet with a man named Rick—with unsavory sexual treats as the stakes—somehow turns out wrong, and Lou loses almost everything.

Adam and April meet up once more, and they find much in common. Nick shares a secret with Lou—he knows his wife Courtney has been cheating. Lou encourages his friend to reclaim his musical dream by performing a smoking version of "Jessie's Girl," then wowing everyone in the bar with a hit from the future, "Let's Get It Started."

Lou faces off against Blaine and his gang, and once more, just like the first time, Adam, Nick, and Jacob fail to show up for support. They find Lou, drunk and beaten, atop Chimney Point. When he chastises them for never being there for him, they turn the tables and admit that they didn't want to be dragged down into his loser world of self-pity.

Angered, Lou swings wildly at Adam but loses his footing and slides toward a fatal fall from the rooftop. The guys quickly grab Lou, but they can't hold on—it looks like everyone is doomed. Suddenly, Phil pulls everyone to safety with his two strong arms. With a renewed outlook on life, the guys set out to reclaim the Chernobly from Blaine and get back home.

But Adam has to choose between a departing April and his friends—he stays with the guys as April catches the Poison tour bus. As Adam and Jacob ransack Blaine's room, Lou and Kelly seduce each other, while Nick calls Courtney to confront her indiscretions. Unfortunately, she's only nine years old at this point, so it seems the effort is lost.

Nick, Adam, and Jacob come upon Lou and Kelly having sex, and Jacob suddenly vanishes. It's now clear to Lou that he is Jacob's father, who reappears as quickly as he vanished. In a showdown between Lou and Blaine, Lou finds something deep inside and beats Blaine bloody. Nick grabs the Chernobly, and the group leaves in a truck driven by Phil, who finally loses his arm in a grisly way being sideswiped by a snow plow.

Back at the hot tub, the group douses the controls with Chernobly, and the time warp opens. Lou suddenly decides to stay behind, vowing to be a good father to Jacob and tossing Adam in with the rest as the vortex collapses.

Adam, Nick, and Jacob arrive back in 2010, where they see what Lou has done to change the past. With knowledge of future sports results and business successes, he has married Kelly and become a very wealthy man with a massive yacht. In fact, Google is now known as Lougle.

Phil arrives with instructions for the guys on how they will get home. Once again, he has two arms, since Blaine and the ski patrol saved his severed arm on the night of the accident. The guys think they know the way home, but they're mistaken.

Adam is happily married to April. Nick Webber has become a famous music producer and head of Webber Studios. When he confronts wife Courtney about her philandering, she assures him that a strange phone call when she was nine years old has always kept her on a loyal path. Lou, Kelly, and Jacob are a happy family, following Lou's successful run as the lead singer in the rock band Mötley Lüe.

Everyone toasts their lasting friendship and good fortunes by celebrating around a festive dinner table.

Afterwords

If one were to take a raunchy men-into-boys film like 2009's *The Hangover* and ram it head-on into a time-travel film like *Back to the Future*, the result might just be *Hot Tub Time Machine*. Thanks can go to screenwriter Josh Heald, who indulged his nostalgic whims (and poor hearing) by penning the script.

During a conversation about the possibility of someone remaking the 1980s sex and ski farce *Hot Dog—The Movie*, Heald mistakenly heard the title as "Hot Tub" and was intrigued by the concept. Wanting to set his story in the eighties, he used the device of a time machine to combine the two seemingly unlike ideas.

But a film needs to be more than just a title (although many are just that), so Heald drew up a detailed outline and found MGM willing to commit to it in May 2008. Three months later, the script was near completion, a cast and director had been chosen, and *Hot Tub Time Machine* was on its way.

Like *Bill and Ted's Excellent Adventure*, *Hot Tub Time Machine* owed more than a tip of the cinematic hat to *Back to the Future*. For one, Jacob's sporadic flickering existence in the past was very similar to Marty McFly's gradually fading picture of his siblings. Also, the casting of Crispin Glover—who played Marty's father in the first *BTTF* flick—was no accident. Too, like *Bill and Ted*, the sci-fi mechanics of time travel are somewhat glossed over, being simply attributed to an SNL "Pepsi Syndrome" sort of accident. (If you don't get it, Google it.)

There's also a general nod to the eighties, with a heavy dose of period music from bands like Poison (of course), the aforementioned "Jessie's Girl" by Rick Springfield, the Talking Heads' *Once in a Lifetime*, among many others. Bill Zabka, well known as a teen villain in '80s films like 1984's *The Karate Kid*, makes a cameo appearance as Lou's betting opponent, Rick.

Produced on a moderately low budget of $36 million, *Hot Tub Time Machine* found its audience with nearly $65 million in worldwide box-office sales. The success of the film was enough to green-light a sequel, with production taking place in New Orleans in mid-2013. Most of the main cast (except for John Cusack), as well as writer Heald and director Pink, returned. According to actor Rod Corddry, the tub and its occupants will travel into the future this time.

Looper

Synopsis

- 2012—American/Sony Pictures/Tri-Star—119 min./color
- Director: Rian Johnson
- Original music: Nathan Johnson
- Film editing: Bob Ducsay
- Production design: Ed Verreaux

Cast

- Joseph Gordon-Levitt (Joe)
- Bruce Willis (Old Joe)
- Emily Blunt (Sara)
- Paul Dano (Seth)
- Noah Segan (Kid Blue)
- Piper Perabo (Suzie)
- Jeff Daniels (Abe)
- Pierce Gagnon (Cid)
- Garret Dillahunt (Jesse)
- Frank Brennan (Old Seth)

In 2044, Joe is a "looper," a young, freelance hitman for the mobs. He wields a noisy, blunderbuss shotgun in the remote farm fields of Kansas. His job is methodically to remove selected targets from thirty years in the future, where time travel has been invented, and quickly outlawed. When the targets are sent back for killing, they are bound, their heads are bagged, and they have payment in silver attached to their soon-to-be lifeless bodies. Since everyone is tagged in the future, it's difficult to eliminate people—which is why they're sent back in time for loopers to do their jobs.

In a rough and dangerous Kansas City, Joe grabs his best friend and fellow looper, Seth, for an evening on the town. Like 10 percent of the world's population, Seth has the gift of telekinetic power. The friends dance, carouse, and enjoy copious amounts of illegal drugs.

Since time travel is illegal, retired loopers are sent back in time as targets for themselves—a process known as "closing the loop." This payoff is in gold and a termination of contract. Refusing to do this can end up in their death (by someone else).

The bodies and silver bars pile up for Joe. One night, Seth bursts in, having refused to close his own loop. When his future self appeared for execution, Seth discovered a new crime lord in 2074—called the Rainmaker—had decided to close the loops on all loopers. Seth let his future self run away, and now he needs to hide at Joe's.

Joe is summoned to a meeting with Abe—a future crime boss sent back in time to manage the loopers and run his own racket on the side with the help of young gunners called "gat men." One gunsel is named Kid Blue. Abe forces Joe to choose between giving up his friend or half the silver he's accrued. Joe chooses Seth.

Old Seth runs and finds an address carved into his forearm, while his fingers begin to disappear from his hand. His face becomes deformed, and his limbs continue to disappear. He arrives at the address, where Kid Blue kills him and young Seth's dismembered body is disposed of.

Joe spends time with his showgirl friend, Suzie, then heads out to his next job. When the victim shows up, it's himself from the future, unbound. Joe fires his blunderbuss, but the blast hits the gold bars strapped to old Joe's back. The elder hitman subdues the younger Joe and escapes.

Young Joe comes to, with a note from his future self to run for his life. Back at his apartment, he finds Kid Blue has been helping himself to his silver bars. Joe runs to escape out a window but slips, falls, and passes out.

The scenario plays out once more, except this time, Joe shoots his future self dead and, finding gold strapped to the corpse, has closed his own loop. He takes his savings from his apartment and travels to Shanghai. The years pass, as Joe lives it up, spends his money, and commits all sorts of crimes.

Twenty-five years later, Joe has settled down, marrying a lovely Asian woman. But in the thirtieth year, gunmen abduct Joe, kill his wife, burn his home, and prepare to send him back in the time machine that will end his life. But he slips his bonds, overpowers the men, and escapes in the time machine, arriving at the original confrontation with his younger self.

Old Joe takes the younger Joe's truck, stopping to buy bandages and medical supplies in the city. He watches as his younger self falls from his apartment window, and he takes the unconscious Joe away. When Joe comes to, he runs.

Old Joe breaks into a library to decipher a strange set of digits written on his hand, finding three names on a map that match the number. Curiously, the name of Beatrix has appeared on his forearm, much like the address that showed up on old Seth.

The Joes meet up at a small diner out in the fields, where Beatrix is a waitress. The young Joe used his own arm to contact old Joe. They quarrel, as young Joe still intends on closing the loop and old Joe dares him to do it, then informs him that—in the future—his wife was killed when the Rainmaker's men abducted him. To save her, old Joe will find the Rainmaker in the present and kill him. Young Joe knows he must close this loop.

As they continue to argue, Kid Blue and the gat men arrive, and young Joe grabs a piece of the map in a struggle. Old Joe shoots it out with the gunmen—and himself—then escapes into the sugarcane fields. Young Joe realizes he's standing amid the gat men. He steals a jet-powered hover bike and, injured, makes his own escape into the fields.

Joe comes to the place on the piece of the map he grabbed. It's the farm of a young woman, Sara, and her young boy, Cid. Suspicious of Joe, Sara holds him at gunpoint before he explains about time travel, loopers, and old Joe. When Sara sees the number on the map, she realizes it's the date of birth and hospital code for Cid, as well as two other children born that same day. One of them must be the Rainmaker, so old Joe has plans to kill all three.

Old Joe shoots the first boy, but he's not the Rainmaker-to-be. Finding the second, he's stunned to find the boy belongs to his old girlfriend, Suzie. He does nothing but watch her apartment.

Sara slowly begins to accept young Joe, but insists on keeping Cid away from him. Cid takes to Joe anyway, sharing useful electronic toys and showing what a bright boy he is. It turns out that Sara isn't Cid's real mother—she was Sara's sister, who was killed.

One of the gat men, Jesse, comes looking for the Joes, but Sara claims to know nothing of them. Cid helps Joe to hide until Jesse leaves. But he returns, holding Sara at gunpoint in front of young Joe. Cid is startled and stumbles down the staircase. In a telekinetic rage, he destroys Jesse.

Joe realizes that with those powers, Cid will become the Rainmaker, although Sara promises to raise him right to prevent that from happening. Joe and Sara find Cid hiding in the cane fields. Knowing more gat men will come for them, Joe sends Sara and Cid away.

Kid Blue captures old Joe at Suzie's apartment and brings him to Abe. Old Joe breaks loose, shoots Kid Blue, and goes on a rampage, killing dozens of gat men and Abe as well. Wounded, Kid Blue heads out to Sara's farm.

Bruce Willis and Joseph Gordon-Levitt in *Looper*.

Old Joe brings a van loaded with gold to young Joe, urging him to go and live a good life. But that means old Joe will have to kill Cid, and young Joe won't let that happen. Kid Blue zooms in on a jet bike, but young Joe quickly eliminates him.

Old Joe reaches the escaping Sara and Cid, shooting and wounding the boy in the jaw. Enraged, he sends out a massive telekinetic wave blast, but Sara calms him. Old Joe prepares to shoot again, and young Joe, arriving at the scene, sees the future play out—Sara is killed, Cid escapes on a train, and will become the Rainmaker. In a flash, young Joe changes the scenario by killing himself with a blast to the chest. Old Joe vanishes, while Sara and her boy return to the farm. Joe's gold bars will provide a good life for them.

Afterwords

Director Rian Johnson, known for taking a film genre and putting his own spin on it, originally wrote *Looper* as a short film, influenced by the sci-fi writings of Philip K. Dick. As in many films about time travel, issues such as the Butterfly Effect and other technical matters can bog the story down. Johnson dealt with it by emphasizing the characters and deemphasizing the rules and intricacies of moving back and forth through time.

The director relied on people he'd worked with before in order to create a consistent film and comfortable atmosphere. Cinematographer Steve Yedlin was Johnson's best friend, dating back to their time spent together at USC Film School. Cousin Nathan Johnson had written music for the director's films since their preteen days. Star Joseph Gordon-Levitt worked with Johnson in his 2005 drama *Brick*.

The crux of the *Looper* story is based on Joe, played by Joseph Gordon-Levitt, who is charged with killing his older self, played by Bruce Willis. While Gordon-Levitt originally campaigned to play both parts, Johnson knew an older actor would convey the experience needed to be convincing. And to make that idea work, makeup effects would be required to turn Gordon-Levitt into a younger version of Willis.

Makeup artist Kazuhiro Tsuji, known as Kaz and a protégé of makeup wizard Rick Baker, was approached to make the transformation happen. With side-by-side pictures of the two actors, Kaz saw an impossible task—they looked nothing alike, and he turned down the challenging offer. But Johnson and Gordon-Levitt eventually convinced Kaz to take on the job of designing the makeup, with artist Jamie Kelman doing the day-to-day application.

Kaz's design relied on foam prosthetics for the nose, as well as upper and lower lips (fifty pairs in total for the shooting schedule), along with pulling Gordon-Levitt's ears back, adding eyebrows and contact lenses. The arduous task of application took anywhere from three to four hours every day.

Along with the physical transformation, Gordon-Levitt studied Willis' movies and listened to iPod recordings of Willis' voice. He also gained a lot of insight into the elder actor's mannerisms by having discussions during dinners (although there's no account of who picked up the tabs).

Film critics and the public as well found *Looper* to their liking, considering it to be an intelligent and fresh look at an old sci-fi genre. Made for a modest $30 million, *Looper* grossed more than $66 million across America. It did even better overseas, pulling in $110 million, for a total of over $176 million.

5

Bang! Zoom! To the Moon . . . and Beyond

Outer Space Travels

Art Imitating Life (Who's Art?)

By 1970, the dream of setting foot on the lunar surface was no longer a dream. The blueprint, as laid out by President John F. Kennedy and one of his legacies following his assassination in 1963, called for an American astronaut to land on the moon and return safely to Earth before the end of the sixties. With six months to spare, Apollo 11 turned sci-fi into sci-fact by pulling off what JFK had challenged.

Into the seventies, the Apollo program completed five more lunar landings (along with one breathtaking rescue mission for the seemingly cursed crew of the crippled Apollo 13—worthy of an Oscar-winning feature film in 1995, starring Tom Hanks and directed by Ron Howard). American astronauts broke borscht with Soviet cosmonauts in space during the Apollo-Soyuz Test Program in 1975.

What led into the eighties (and beyond), was the Space Shuttle program, with dozens of launches featuring a fleet of reusable space trucks—and, sadly, America's first spaceflight casualties during the Challenger and Columbia missions. The thrill and excitement of spaceflight became a very real and serious danger to those who flew—a danger never encountered on the Hollywood set of a sci-fi movie.

With the extended missions of America's Skylab, the Russian MIR, and International Space Station, living in space became reality. By the twenty-first century, talk turned toward eventual manned landings on an asteroid and, some day in the coming twenty or thirty years, on Mars.

Since Apollo 11, each new media report about spaceflight upped the ante for filmmakers to reach where they had never gone before. The challenge was, somehow, to come up with a new and fresh concept for a sci-fi film that didn't merely copy what was showing up on the evening TV news.

Getting It All Down (or Up in the Skies) on Film

The initial response from Hollywood in the early seventies was to shy away from putting anything into outer space, figuring they just couldn't compete with real images of NASA spaceflights. Of the few major sci-fi space films that did hit the screens, most relied on 1968's *2001: A Space Odyssey* as inspiration.

Doug Trumbull's *Silent Running* in 1972 and John Carpenter's *Dark Star* in 1974 both featured spacecraft that no longer resembled long, smooth cones with little fins at their bases. If nothing else, *2001* had broken the paradigm of old-school spacecraft design. If real spaceflight taught movie FX designers anything, it was the fact that aerodynamics ceased to matter once man escaped the Earth's atmosphere.

Regardless, American cinema stayed clear of outer space themes for more than the first half of the decade of the seventies.

And then came . . .

Star Wars

Synopsis

- 1977—American/20th Century-Fox—121 min./color
- Director: George Lucas
- Original music: John Williams
- Film editing: Richard Chew, Paul Hirsch, Marcia Lucas
- Art direction: Leslie Dilley, Norman Reynolds

Cast

- Mark Hamill (Luke Skywalker)
- Harrison Ford (Han Solo)
- Carrie Fisher (Princess Leia Organa)
- Peter Cushing (Grand Moff Tarkin)
- Alec Guinness (Ben (Obi-Wan) Kenobi)
- Anthony Daniels (C-3PO)
- Kenny Baker (R2-D2)
- Peter Mayhew (Chewbacca)
- David Prowse (Lord Darth Vader)
- James Earl Jones (Voice of Darth Vader)

A long time ago in a galaxy far, far away, the evil Galactic Empire wages war against the universe. Rebel starfighters fight back, and, with the aid of the lovely and brave Princess Leia, they acquire the plans to the Empire's newest and deadliest weapon, the Death Star. The artificial moon has enough firepower to destroy an entire planet.

A rebel fighter is hotly pursued by an enormous Imperial Cruiser. Two robots, the golden anthropomorphic C-3PO and fire hydrant–sized R2-D2,

are captured by Empire storm troopers as the masked and black-cloaked Lord
Darth Vader boards the craft. Leia hides the vital plans by loading them into
R2-D2's memory before she also is captured. R2-D2 and C-3PO escape to the
twin-sunned desert planet of Tatooine, where the droids are immediately seized
by the hooded scavenger dwarfs known as Jawas.

Young Luke Skywalker lives with his aunt and uncle, and they purchase the
two droids to help with their farming. Cleaning the droids up, Luke accidentally
releases a holographic image of Leia asking for help from someone named
"Obi-Wan Kenobi." Luke knows an old hermit named Ben Kenobi. Could they
be that same person?

Indeed, Ben was known as Obi-Wan and was once a revered Jedi Knight, like
Luke's long-gone father. He gives Luke a light saber, the weapon of the Jedi, and
speaks reverently of "the Force," the binding energy of the universe that gives
the Jedi his powers. Luke and Ben watch Leia's message that implores Kenobi
to deliver R2-D2, loaded with the vital secrets, to the rebel forces on her home
planet of Alderaan. Kenobi must tutor Luke in the ways of a Jedi.

Evil Grand Moff Tarkin, aided by Darth Vader, governs the Death Star.
Meanwhile, Luke's guardians are murdered by Empire troops, and the young
man wants revenge. Ben and Luke travel to town, where Kenobi demonstrates
the power of the Force by mentally overpowering some inquisitive Empire storm
troopers.

Ben and Luke enter a rough cantina bar, loaded with ugly and unsavory
characters. They engage the handsome and roguish mercenary Han Solo,
accompanied by the tall and furry Wookie named Chewbacca, to pilot them in
the *Millennium Falcon* pirate ship to Alderaan. The group makes a hasty takeoff,
followed by a cluster of Imperial Cruisers.

Meanwhile, Tarkin persuades Leia to talk by using the Death Star's power to
destroy her home planet of Alderaan. The *Millennium Falcon* arrives at the point
in space where Alderaan used to be, and the ship is quickly caught in the Death
Star's tractor beam. Once there, Kenobi goes to shut down the tractor beam
while Luke and Han discover Leia is a prisoner on board. Disguised as storm
troopers, they find her and flee, becoming trapped in a garbage compactor.
C-3PO is contacted, and R2-D2 remotely shuts the system down, saving them.

Ben turns off the tractor beam as everyone makes their way to the *Falcon*.
Kenobi squares off against Darth Vader in a daring duel of flashing light sabers.
Ben sacrifices himself, with Vader vaporizing him as the *Falcon* takes off. Now a
part of the Force, Obi-Wan's voice guides Luke.

In space, Luke and Han fight off a group of attacking TIE fighter ships. But
Tarkin and Vader have planted a homing bug on the *Falcon* and are tracking its
movement. It lands on a distant moon, where the rebels retrieve the Death Star
plans and locate its weakness. A small fighter ship could navigate the treacherous trench of the space station and fire a torpedo into an unprotected exhaust
port. A precise hit could destroy the Death Star.

German lobby card—*Star Wars*.

Han and Chewie load their reward loot and selfishly leave as Luke prepares to join a squadron of X-Wing fighters in the assault on the Death Star. Vader leads a group of TIE fighters in defense, and a wild dogfight begins. Pursued by the fighter ships, Luke enters the trench as Kenobi's voice encourages, "Use the Force, Luke." Vader zeroes in on young Skywalker, but Han Solo shows up to give the diversion that Luke needs. On instincts alone, he fires a pair of proton torpedoes and scores a direct hit. The Death Star explodes into a million points of light, and Vader's ship is thrown wildly into deep space.

Victorious, Solo and Skywalker return to the rebel base, where Princess Leia grandly decorates them for saving the universe.

Afterwords

This film, subtitled *A New Hope*, almost single-handedly rewrote the general public's expectations for believable special effects in a sci-fi movie. The idea for the film was conceived by George Lucas and producer Gary Kurtz in 1972 during the filming of 1973's *American Graffiti*. Lucas lamented the fact that there wasn't really a good adventure-fantasy film playing somewhere close that they could go see.

Although made first, *Star Wars* was actually the fourth episode of a nine-part series that the director had originally planned to make. While he reported in 1997 that his prequel trilogy would be the end of *Star Wars* with only six films, the sale of Lucas' company to Disney revived a new hope for last three movies.

Even though the old Saturday afternoon serials of *Flash Gordon* were the original inspiration for *Star Wars*, Lucas assembled a very specific blueprint for the dogfights in space by editing old black-and-white Hollywood air-war movie footage together. Overall, Lucas covered the world in his desire to create other worlds. Live action was shot with thirty sets on sound stages at Elstree Studios in England, while the visual and miniature effects were produced in Van Nuys, California. The Sahara Desert in Tunisia played the part of the make-believe world of Tatooine, with additional desert footage shot in Death Valley. Jungle scenes were shot at the Mayan ruins in Guatemala.

Sound designer Ben Burtt created the sound of a laser pistol blast by recording and enhancing the tapping of a hammer on the guy-wire of a radio tower. Knowing that sound would be just as important to the film's success as the visuals, Lucas and Kurtz quickly connected with noise reduction and audio specialists at Dolby Laboratories. The team made sure the soundtrack—dialogue, music, and sound effects—was tops in quality, during both the recording and postproduction mixing. Just as important was equipping many theaters with Dolby sound systems, designed to accurately and faithfully reproduce the audio of *Star Wars*.

Actor David Prowse was not pleased to find his Darth Vader voice was later replaced by that of James Earl Jones. But the complex costume for Darth Vader had its problems, not least of which was the fiberglass mask that made the villain's dialogue—all of which was learned and delivered by Prowse during the film's shooting—totally unusable. Additionally, slight movements in the outfit caused a lot of collateral noise, which made rerecording necessary. With postproduction in California and Prowse in his native England, the economic decision was made to use the distinctive and expressive (and local) voice of Jones for the final soundtrack.

Filmgoers greeted two sequels to *Star Wars* with plenty of enthusiasm—*The Empire Strikes Back* in 1980 grossed $223 million, while *The Return of the Jedi* in 1983 brought in $263 million. Members of the Academy of Motion Picture Arts and Science seemed to agree with the public, awarding ten Oscars to the first three films, including awards for Editing, Original Music Score, Art Direction, Costume Design, Sound, Visual Effects, plus Special Achievements in Sound Effects and Visual Effects. In total, all six films received twenty-five Oscar nominations.

All three films in the first series were rereleased in early 1997 with digital enhancements and added footage. While some critics and fans questioned the need and validity for Lucas to alter the original films, the trilogy grossed another quarter-billion dollars from a new generation of moviegoers. The reissue of *Star Wars* catapulted it into first place as the highest-grossing film of all time, with more than $460 million at the box office, before being eclipsed by 1998's *Titanic*.

The long-awaited first trilogy, beginning with 1999's *Star Wars: Episode I—The Phantom Menace*, continued to propel the franchise like a juggernaut. The film grossed $474 million domestically, in spite of the irritating, almost universally despised character of Jar-Jar Binks. *Episode II*, known as *Attack of the Clones*, opened to record-breaking crowds in May 2002 and brought in over $310 million in America. The final chapter to the prequel, *Star Wars: Episode III: Revenge of the Sith*, thrilled audiences in 2005, grossing $380 million in the US.

Overseas moviegoers watched all six films in the series for a total foreign gross of more than $2 billion. Combined with the US gross, the *Star Wars* films have earned more than $4.3 billion since 1977. Of course, that doesn't count VHS, DVD, and Blu-Ray rentals and sales, plus merchandising that included books, magazines, comics, action figures, model kits, pajamas, breakfast cereals, and, last, but certainly not least, the Jar-Jar Binks Tongue Sucker (seriously).

Lucas' sale of his company (and the *Star Wars* franchise) to Disney Studios in 2012 for perhaps a not-so-coincidental price of more than $4 billion offered a promise of more *Star Wars* sagas throughout the decade of the 2010s. *Star Wars: Episode VII*, directed by sci-fi specialist J. J. Abrams and written by the director and Lawrence Kasdan (who has also penned two previous *Star Wars* episodes, along with a quaint little film called *Raiders of the Lost Ark*), is slated to hit the screens in time for Christmas 2015.

Alien

Synopsis

- 1979—American/20th Century-Fox—116 min./color
- Director: Ridley Scott
- Original music: Jerry Goldsmith
- Film editing: Terry Rawlings, Peter Weatherley
- Art direction: Roger Christian, Leslie Dilley
- Alien design: H. R. Giger

Cast

- Tom Skerritt (DALLas)
- Sigourney Weaver (Ripley)
- Veronica Cartwright (Lambert)
- John Hurt (Kane)
- Ian Holm (Ash)
- Yaphet Kotto (Parker)
- Harry Dean Stanton (Brett)
- Bolaji Badejo (The Alien)

The *Nostromo* is a deep-space barge carrying twenty million tons of ore and seven crew members back to Earth. Halfway home, they receive a strange radio transmission and land on a distant planet called LV-426 in response to it. The landing is rough and the ship is damaged; engineers Brett and Parker figure it will take at least a day to fix.

Dallas, the commander, leads navigator Lambert and mission specialist Kane out into the harsh atmosphere to locate the source of the transmission, while First Officer Ripley and Science Officer Ash stay on board. The expedition discovers an unknown derelict ship, along with the fossilized remains of a long-dead alien pilot—a Space Jockey. Kane is lowered into a vast cavern, where he finds hundreds of watermelon-sized pods. He gets too close to one of them, and a face-hugging creature smashes through his faceplate and latches onto his head.

Ripley is hesitant to allow the ship to be contaminated by bringing the wounded Kane back aboard, but he'll die otherwise, and Ash insists he be tended to. The bony, crab-like creature is firmly fixed to Kane's face, and Dallas and Ash are unable to remove it. Cutting one of the "face-hugger's" digits releases an acid so powerful that it threatens to eat right through the ship's hull. The creature finally detaches itself from Kane and disappears somewhere on the ship. It drops onto Ripley, frightening her, but it's now dead.

Even though all repairs aren't complete, Dallas decides to take off for Earth. Kane comes out of his coma and seems none the worse for wear. He joins the crew for one more meal before they return to sleep for the ten-month trip home. But at the table, Kane begins to gag and convulse. Suddenly, a newborn alien bursts from his chest and scurries away before the shocked eyes of the crew. They quickly arm themselves and prepare to hunt the beast.

Jones, a pet cat on board the *Nostromo*, gets loose, and Brett sets out to retrieve it. Instead, he finds a seven-foot alien. Armored and bony in form, its huge phallic head has inner and outer jaws filled with chrome-like teeth. While Jones watches in the shadows, the alien's jaws lash out and grab Brett by the head.

The crew tracks the alien in the ship's air shafts, and Dallas, armed with a flamethrower, goes after it. He finds it, and the crew hears nothing as Dallas becomes the second victim of the alien.

Now in command, Ripley consults the ship's computer, called Mother, for guidance. She finds that Ash has reprogrammed it, establishing the preservation of the alien life form as the prime priority, even at the crew's expense. Ash finds Ripley and begins to throw her around, beating her up. Lambert and Parker come to her aid, smashing Ash in the skull with an oxygen tank. To everyone's surprise, his head comes off and they discover Ash is an android. The robot has been programmed by the "company" to retrieve and preserve alien life forms at all cost. The crew destroys Ash, but not before learning more about the alien—it's a "perfect hostile organism, a survivor."

Ripley decides to take the shuttle with Lambert and Parker, leaving the ship and the alien to be blown up. Lambert and Parker load supplies into the shuttle, but the alien viciously attacks and kills them both. Ripley is now left alone to fight the alien, and she sets the ship's self-destruct system to go off in ten minutes. She makes her way into the shuttle with just seconds to spare, as a blinding flash destroys the *Nostromo*.

Ripley prepares her sleep chamber for the long trip home, only to have the alien's claw lash out at her—it obviously has stowed away on the shuttle. Ripley slowly works her way into a spacesuit and purges the air from the shuttle. She blows the outer hatch, but the alien hangs on by a tether. Ripley hits the engines, and the exhaust vents hurl the alien into deep space.

Afterwords

As exciting and fun as *Star Wars* was, *Alien* delivered a different kind of entertainment: scary and blood-chilling. Quite simply, *Alien* was a haunted house in outer space. Still, many factors contributed to the impact and success of the film, as it raked in nearly $60 million in domestic box-office receipts. *Alien* also won an Oscar for Best Visual Effects and the creature's mechanical head, fabricated by Carlo Rambaldi.

Much of the visual look of the creatures and desolate landscapes was designed by Swiss artist Hans Rudi (H. R.) Giger, who had impressed the public in 1973 with his album cover art for Emerson, Lake and Palmer's *Brain Salad Surgery*. His art style, which he called "biomechanics," combined living organic beings with structured technological forms into truly frightening creatures and scenes. Early in preproduction for *Alien*, director Ridley Scott received a copy of Giger's book of illustrations *Necronomicon*. Like many who had seen it, Scott was stunned and amazed by the otherworldly images the artist had conceived. Although Giger wanted to design the film's alien from scratch, Scott insisted that the artist base the creature on those seen in *Necronomicon*.

Many people saw a more than passing resemblance between the plot and story of *Alien* and the 1958 B movie, *It! The Terror from Beyond Space*. Original screenwriter Dan O'Bannon claimed it was merely a coincidence, as his initial script was called *Star Beast*. *It!* writer Jerome Bixby admitted he noted the derivative nature of *Alien*, but he also thoroughly enjoyed the 1979 film. Both films also resembled several short stories by sci-fi writer A. E. Van Vogt, including 1939's "Black Destroyer" and "Discord in Scarlet." While Van Vogt let *It!* slide, he sued Twentieth-Century-Fox over *Alien* and won an out-of-court settlement.

Influenced by Giger's haunting design, Scott knew he needed a unique performer to fit inside the Alien costume. After interviewing several basketball players, and Peter Mayhew—Chewbacca from *Star Wars*—with no success, Scott came across a young graphic arts student from Nigeria by the name of Bolaji Badejo. Amazingly thin and six-feet ten-inches in height, he was exactly what the director wanted. Badejo took instruction in mime and split his time inside the suit with a stuntman. Even so, much of Badejo's footage as the alien didn't work out, although his chilling scene of the alien cornering a cowering Veronica Cartwright as Lambert was a keeper.

Among the many scenes that caused audiences to jump from their seats, most recall what became known as "the Chestburster" sequence. Getting the

Bolaji Badejo and Veronica Cartwright in *Alien*.

right reaction from the actors on film took a little doing, but it was worth the effort.

Actor John Hurt was set up on a reclining table, with just his head, shoulders, and arms showing, while a false body was laid over him. The rest of the cast was kept away from the set, even though they had read the script and knew something was going to happen to Kane. The crew filled the empty chest cavity with animal organs from a butcher shop, along with several pressurized hoses to spray stage blood when the time was right.

The cast finally entered the set, wondering why the crew were wearing plastic face guards and rain suits. When the infant alien burst from Kane's chest, the cast now understood why the protective gear. Ridley Scott's covert planning achieved the pure reaction of real horror from the actors that he was looking for. No one expected the gory assault of fake blood and smelly pig parts—Yaphet Kotto and Veronica Cartwright were particularly traumatized, along with film fans around the world.

Three sequels were spawned from this sci-fi shocker: *Aliens*, directed by James Cameron, in 1986; *Alien³* in 1992; and *Alien: Resurrection* in 1997. In all four films, Sigourney Weaver portrayed the tough and resourceful survivor named Ripley (although she became a cyborg in the fourth). A fourth "sequel" of sorts was released in 2004, pitting the alien against another extraterrestrial—the predator—in *AVP: Alien vs. Predator*. A return match, called *Alien vs. Predator—Requiem*, was released in 2007. In 2012, Ridley Scott directed *Prometheus* (profiled elsewhere in this chapter), which he admits shared many threads with the original *Alien* film.

In total, the seven films in the *Alien* franchise have grossed more than half a billion dollars in America and an astounding $1.2 billion around the world.

Star Trek: The Motion Picture

Synopsis

- 1979—American/Paramount—132 min./color
- Director: Robert Wise
- Original music: Jerry Goldsmith
- Film editing: Todd Ramsay
- Production design: Harold Michelson

Cast

- William Shatner (Admiral James T. Kirk)
- Leonard Nimoy (Spock)
- Deforest Kelley (Dr. Leonard "Bones" Mc Coy)
- James Doohan (Montgomery "Scotty" Scott)
- George Takei (Hikaru Sulu)
- Majel Barrett (Dr. Christine Chapel)
- Walter Koenig (Pavel Chekov)
- Nichelle Nichols (Nyota Uhura)
- Persis Khambatta (Ilia)
- Stephen Collins (Captain Willard Decker)
- Jon Rashad Kamal (Science Officer Sonak)

Somewhere in deep space, three Klingon heavy battle cruisers fire photon torpedoes into an ominous cloud mass, seemingly with no effect. Epsilon Nine, a monitor station with Starfleet, watches remotely as the ships disappear from retaliatory blasts. What's more, the cloud is heading for Earth.

On the planet of Vulcan, a long-haired and weary Spock faces three Vulcan Masters. Nearly finished with a ritual that will purge all emotions, Spock must stop—something from far away troubles him.

At Starfleet headquarters, a shuttle lands with Admiral James T. Kirk aboard. He orders new Vulcan science officer Sonak to meet him on the starship *Enterprise* in one hour. Kirk transports to the orbiting dry dock, where Engineering Officer Scotty believes more time is needed to test the refitted *Enterprise*. With the unidentified cloud mass heading toward Earth, the *Enterprise* is the only starship in the area—it must be ready to leave within twelve hours.

Kirk marvels at the majesty of the *Enterprise*, where he has been reassigned as captain of the vessel. On the bridge, the admiral reconnects with his old friends—Uhura, Sulu, and Chekov. He finds Captain Decker—until now, the captain of the *Enterprise*—and breaks the news of his replacement with Kirk. Decker's reaction is chilly and petulant.

Faulty transporters fail to deliver Sonak and another crew member completely to the *Enterprise*, and they arrive back at Starfleet dead. Until another Vulcan science officer can be found, Decker will have to fill in.

Addressing the crew of the *Enterprise*, Kirk reveals only two days remain before the cloud reaches Earth. Their mission is to intercept it and do whatever is needed to protect the planet. A report from Epsilon Nine indicates the mass is a gigantic power field, and then, just like the Klingon ships, the monitor station disappears from the skies.

The beautiful and bald Deltan navigator Lt. Ilia boards the starship, and it appears she has a romantic history with Decker. In the transporter room, Medical Officer Bones McCoy successfully comes aboard, but resents being drafted back into service.

The *Enterprise* slowly pulls out of dock and warps into service. But they encounter a debilitating wormhole, with an asteroid ahead that threatens to destroy the ship. Kirk requests phasers, but Decker suddenly takes control and orders Sulu to fire photon torpedoes. The asteroid is blasted apart at the last second, and the ship returns to a stable condition.

In his quarters, Kirk demands an explanation from Decker for his countering the original order. His response points out that using phasers would have disabled the new engine system. The commander's knowledge of the new *Enterprise* saved the ship and crew. With reluctance, Kirk will appreciate Decker's assistance.

A shuttle docks with the ship, and out steps a trimmed and ready Spock, the new science officer. Kirk and the rest of the crew are thrilled to see him, but the Vulcan's only concern is for the new engine system. Spock corrects the engine design problems, and warp speed is at full power.

In a private meeting, Kirk and McCoy question Spock about his motives for breaking his training to join the *Enterprise* crew. The Vulcan sensed a great disturbance, perhaps from the cloud that now threatens Earth.

As the starship nears the cloud field, a red alert puts everyone at the ready for conflict. Spock believes a solid object may be at the cloud's center. All attempts to transmit friendly greeting from the *Enterprise* have been ignored. Kirk disregards the aggressive recommendations from Deckard, choosing to approach in a peaceful demeanor.

A bolt of energy streams from the cloud and the force field deflectors on the *Enterprise* prevent any serious damage, but the surge injures Sulu at his console. As another bolt approaches, Spock reformats the message of peace. This time it works, and the blast of energy disappears.

The *Enterprise* moves through the cloud, amid blinding flashes of lightning. At the center lies a massive alien object, many times larger than the starship. It is unlike anything the crew has seen before, but it has the appearance of an enormous spaceship. Suddenly, a brilliant beam of plasma enters the bridge—a probe from the alien vessel. A single branch of light reaches out toward Ilia, and she is gone in an instant.

A tractor beam pulls the *Enterprise* through a star-shaped opening, closing behind the ship. Ilia reappears aboard the starship, now a mechanized probe device to collect data for the alien power called V'Ger. Its mission toward Earth is to meet the Creator, where the two entities will become one.

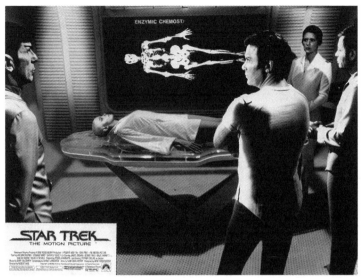

US lobby card—*Star Trek: The Motion Picture.*

With only hours before V'Ger reaches Earth, it's hoped that memories from the previous relationship between Decker and Ilia can provide some connection to the alien entity. But according to Ilia, the crew of the *Enterprise* are destined to become lifeless data units like her.

Spock dons a spacesuit and ventures into the void of space in an attempt to make direct contact with V'Ger. He reaches the inner world of the alien and attempts a mindmeld with it, but he is blasted, unconscious, back toward the *Enterprise*. Kirk has followed Spock, and he brings the Vulcan back into the ship.

Safe in sick bay, Spock has seen the living machine that is V'Ger. While it is technologically advanced, Spock found the alien to be cold and barren. Furthermore, V'Ger seeks answers to its own purpose for existing.

Nearing Earth orbit, V'Ger sends out a signal for the Creator but receives no response. The alien then launches ominous glowing spheres into a pattern surrounding the Earth, preparing to destroy it. V'Ger considers human life to be an infestation like bacteria, in need of elimination. To deal with V'Ger, Spock advises treating it like a child who seeks knowledge and answers.

Through Ilia, V'Ger demands to know why the Creator did not respond. Thinking fast, Kirk won't reveal the answer until V'Ger removes its threat to Earth. In a petulant tantrum, the alien bombards the *Enterprise* with energy bolts, and Kirk orders the bridge to be cleared.

The stalemate is finally broken—the admiral agrees to disclose the information V'Ger seeks, but only to the alien directly, not through Ilia. A tractor beam once more pulls the *Enterprise* forward toward the center of V'Ger.

With Ilia leading the way, Kirk, Spock, Decker, and McCoy step out onto the alien planet. At the center of V'Ger is a large communications dish. Kirk wipes dirt away from a placard on its side, and V'Ger turns out to be *Voyager VI*, a NASA satellite from three hundred years back that disappeared into a black hole.

When the probe emerged, the machine planet literally interpreted *Voyager's* programmed directives—collect all data and return the information to its creator. In doing so, the massive accumulation of data created a consciousness in the planet. But with three hundred years passing, the code to retrieve the satellite's data became obsolete, preventing V'Ger from completing the mission.

Searching records on Earth, Starfleet locates the ancient code and transmits it to Uhura and the crew on V'Ger, proving they are the Creator that V'Ger seeks. But V'Ger must join with the Creator to connect with the human presence in order to complete its task.

Decker volunteers himself—by sacrificing his life, he will fulfill the V'Ger's needs and restore the close relationship he once had with Ilia. Decker and Ilia are consumed in a shower of sparkling lights, while Kirk, Spock, and McCoy return to the *Enterprise*. V'Ger's journey is complete, and it vanishes into another dimension.

For the *Enterprise* and its crew, the journey has just begun.

Afterwords

The voyage of *Star Trek*, through its demise and rebirth, took creator and producer Gene Roddenberry where no Hollywood exec had gone before. On the air for three seasons—from 1966 to 1969—it was a favorite of fans but not the bigwigs at NBC television. Plus, it was hard to fan the flames of fantastic fiction when man was really landing on the moon—both seen on TV.

Syndicated reruns, a Saturday morning cartoon version, and fan conventions (see *Galaxy Quest*) kept *Star Trek* fresh in the public's minds after the cancellation of the TV series. Roddenberry started talking with Paramount Pictures about a big-screen feature film of *Star Trek* in 1973. By mid-1975, the producer took up an office at the Paramount studio to write the script—not coincidentally, the same office he kept when the TV show was on the air. The film was scheduled for release by Christmas of that same year.

But Paramount, not at all happy with Roddenberry's script, began dragging its feet. They sought other writers' input and tried giving the property to their TV division, who pretty much gave it back with no useful results. In mid-1976, a new list of writers was suggested, with big names like Francis Ford Coppola, George Lucas (!), and Robert Bloch (writer of *Psycho*). Eventually, Harold Livingston wrote the shooting script, based on a story by Alan Dean Foster.

With that settled, a director was the next to be found. Once more, suggestions like Spielberg, Lucas, and Coppola just didn't pan out, and Philip Kaufman, who had written 1976's *The Outlaw Josey Wales*, was selected. But when Paramount suddenly decided to turn *Star Trek* back into a TV series, Kaufman left to direct a remake of *Invasion of the Body Snatchers* (found elsewhere in this book).

Perhaps not surprisingly, the proposed TV series was redirected to becoming a feature film (yes, again) by the end of 1977. That decision might have been influenced by the success of another movie that had come out over the summer—a little number called *Star Wars*.

When the announcement was made in early 1978, it was major news—*Star Trek: The Motion Picture* would be a $15 million production, directed by multiple-Oscar winner Robert Wise (experienced in sci-fi by helming 1951's *The Day the Earth Stood Still* and 1971's *Andromeda Strain*).

The resulting film actually cost $35 million to make, returning more than $80 million for the Christmas season in 1979. What's more, *Star Trek: The Motion Picture* prompted nine sequels, totaling nearly three-quarters of a billion dollars in domestic ticket sales—not to mention a full reboot in 2009 and subsequent sequel that took in nearly half a billion dollars on their own. On top of all that, add in four separate TV series across nearly twenty years.

Obviously, the success of the *Star Trek* franchise—in all its varieties—was something the TV execs never envisioned back in the 1960s.

Stargate

Synopsis

- 1994—American/Metro-Goldwyn-Mayer—121 min./color
- Director: Roland Emmerich
- Original music: David Arnold
- Film editing: Derek Brechin, Michael J. Duthie
- Production design: Holger Gross

Cast

- Kurt Russell (Colonel Jack O'Neil)
- James Spader (Dr. Daniel Jackson)
- Jaye Davidson (Ra)
- Viveca Lindfors (Catherine Langford)
- Alexis Cruz (Skaara)
- Mili Avital (Sha'uri)
- John Diehl (Lt. Kawalski)
- Carlos Lauchu (Anubis)
- Erick Avari (Kasuf)
- Derek Webster (Brown)
- Erik Holland (Professor Langford)

A strange spacecraft descends into a small village in the North African desert in 8000 BC. People scatter, but one unafraid young man approaches the ship and is engulfed in a blinding shaft of light.

In Giza, Egypt, in 1928, an archaeologist, Professor Langford, and his young daughter, Catherine, make an amazing discovery. Amidst a vast dig, an enormous circle of cover stones lies in the ground. Beyond it rises a large stone ring, more than twenty feet in diameter. At its base is a fossil of a jackal's head. In Catherine's hands, she holds a gold necklace with the eye of Ra, the Egyptian Sun God.

In the present, Catherine—now an old woman—enters a symposium on Ancient Egypt. The lecturer, a linguistics professor named Daniel Jackson, makes the bold claim that the Egyptians did not build the Great Pyramids. Unfortunately, he doesn't have any idea who did, and his audience gets up and leaves, laughing. Catherine also quietly departs.

In a pouring rain, Jackson finds relief in the back of the elder woman's car, where she offers the professor a special job—translating an unusual set of ancient Egyptian hieroglyphics. Having been tossed out of his apartment and lost his grants, Daniel can hardly pass up the opportunity.

At a remote military installation in Colorado, Jackson finds the Giza cover stones waiting for his inspection. He quickly corrects a previous attempt at translation, revealing the stones were an entry point to the Stargate of the god Ra.

Retired air force colonel Jack O'Neil, despondent over the sudden loss of his young son in a shooting accident, is reactivated and has been placed in command of the Stargate project. He immediately restricts all information to military personnel only.

After several weeks of work, Jackson identifies star constellations on the cover stones. The military, however, has been holding out on the professor—not only have they recovered the cover stones, but they have the Stargate itself at the facility. And, apparently, it's functional.

Operating like some sort of gigantic combination lock, the Stargate rotates, tumblers lock into position, and a shimmering, water-like portal fills the center of the ring. Technicians send a robotic probe through the Stargate, and it arrives somewhere across the universe. The wormhole in the Stargate closes, with everyone in awe of what just occurred.

Data from the probe indicates the other side of the Stargate has different markings, but the atmosphere is the same as Earth's. However, a trip through the portal would be useless without deciphering the marks. Jackson volunteers his talents for the mission.

Packing reference books for the dangerous endeavors, Jackson receives the Ra necklace from Catherine as a good luck charm. With gear loaded, O'Neil and his troops—along with Jackson—pass through the event horizon in the Stargate. The trip is startling, frenzied, and rapid—"a rush," as one soldier observes.

The team moves ahead into what appears to be an Egyptian temple and onto a vast desert. O'Neil and Jackson stand in awe, as they regard the Great Pyramid of Giza, with three moons in the sky above it.

Raising the ring in *Stargate*.

The return trip will not be as easy as thought, since Jackson can decipher the markings on the Stargate, but he needs to find stone tablets that indicate their sequence. O'Neil orders a camp to be established at the base of the pyramid. The troops are miffed at being deserted in God-knows-where.

Inside the pyramid, O'Neil is assembling a cylindrical device when Lt. Kawalski interrupts him. Outside, Jackson spots strange animal tracks and follows them to a large buffalo-like creature called a mastadge. Wearing a harness, it has obviously been domesticated. But the animal gets spooked and bolts, with Jackson caught in the reins and dragged behind it.

O'Neil, Kawalski, and Brown catch up to them, amazed to see an enormous ancient mining operation. Hundreds of workers toil away in the heat. It's up to Jackson to somehow communicate with them.

Seeing the Ra necklace, the ancients all bow in reverence. O'Neil tries to calm a boy named Skaara by shaking hands, but the lad runs away, screaming. The people's leader, named Kasuf, returns with Skaara and invites the visitors to his city. Jackson reasons it might be the best way to get back home.

In the stone city of Nagada, the caravan reveals a large symbol of the Eye of Ra. The blare of a shofar horn sends everyone scurrying to close the doors of the city. At the soldiers' camp, a sandstorm drives the troops inside the pyramid for safety.

O'Neil fires his rifle at the crowd in an attempt to get out, but Skaara points out the approaching sandstorm, and the soldier backs off. Kasuf feeds and entertains his guests, then takes Jackson away to be washed and treated like a god.

Kasuf's daughter, Sha'uri, offers herself to Daniel, and, despite the temptation, he kindly refuses. Not wanting to insult Kasuf, Jackson keeps the young woman in his tent, but finds his attempts to communicate with her to be very difficult. Yet, to his surprise, she does recognize the symbol for Earth.

With radios useless in the sandstorm, the soldiers at the pyramid are forced to wait it out. Suddenly, an alien ship settles over their site amid crackles of lightning. The villainous Anubis strikes down several of the soldiers, showing his claw-like gloves and jackal-shaped headpiece.

O'Neil sits alone until Skaara finds him. The soldier teaches the boy about the manly art of smoking cigarettes, until a choking fit puts Skaara off it for good. O'Neil gives Skaara his Zippo lighter as a gift. When he innocently picks up O'Neil's gun, the colonel—remembering the tragedy of his own son—yells and scares Skaara off.

Skaara proudly displays his flaming treasure to his friends. O'Neil can't find Jackson, and after a frustrating attempt at asking the boys, Skaara finally gets the message. With a mastadge acting like a bloodhound, O'Neil finds Jackson and Sha'uri.

Daniel reads ancient glyphs, which tell of Ra, an alien who came to Earth thousands of years before. He took the body of a young boy in search of eternal life and proclaimed himself ruler. He brought many more aliens to Earth with the Stargate, to mine a mineral that gave Ra life everlasting. But when a rebellion erupted, the Stargate was buried.

Kawalski locates a stone with the symbols necessary to engage the Stargate, but the important seventh marker is worn down and useless. O'Neil and the others leave Nagada, with Sha'uri sad as Daniel walks into the desert. Unseen, Skaara and his pals follow.

Returning to the pyramid, the group finds the alien ship firmly planted over the site. They rush into the structure, where an alien guard immediately kills Brown with an energy blast from his staff.

O'Neil and Jackson reach the Stargate, greeted by the jackal-headed Anubis and two guards. Entering the spaceship, the two men meet Ra, dressed in fine robes and a golden mask, escorted by dozens of children. The alien has found the bomb that O'Neil left at the Stargate. Ra removes his headpiece, revealing himself to be the boy taken thousands of years ago.

O'Neil grabs a staff from one of the guards and kills him with an energy blast. In an attempt to save the soldier, Daniel takes a deadly return blast meant for O'Neil. The children immediately form a protective ring around Ra, and Anubis knocks O'Neil unconscious. Ra notes the necklace around Daniel's neck.

Anubis tosses the colonel into a water pit, joining Kawalski and other soldiers. Meanwhile, several alien fighter ships attack Nagada, killing many of the town with laser-like blasts. Skaara and his friends arrive to find the remains of the massacre, as Sha'uri wonders about Daniel.

On the ship, Daniel rises from a sarcophagus very much alive, his wound completely healed. Speaking in an ancient dialect, Ra explains he will send O'Neil's bomb back through the Stargate, enriched with the mineral being mined. He reasons that since he created Earth's civilization, he can destroy it as well.

Ra must prove his authority, ordering Jackson to kill his companions. If he doesn't, then he will be killed. The ruler tears the necklace from Daniel's neck, as there can be only one Ra.

A public execution of the soldiers will show the city of Nagada that Ra is all-powerful. Anubis hands a blaster staff to Daniel. From the crowd, Skaara uses the reflective Zippo to signal Jackson—the boy and his mates have armed themselves with the soldiers' rifles.

Daniel spins and fires wildly at the throne, while the boys fire their guns into the air. The crowd scatters, and Anubis and the guards fire their weapons. O'Neil and Daniel escape on a mastadge into a raging sandstorm.

The pair finds Skaara, the Nagadan rebels, and O'Neil's troops in a rocky cave. Shaking, the colonel explains the original plan: blow up the Stargate if any trouble arose. Daniel notes that Ra now plans to send the bomb back, enriched with the mineral that will destroy the world. O'Neil intends to stop the bomb before it goes through.

Daniel questions the colonel's attitude in accepting death so easily. Just because he lost his son, O'Neil shouldn't be so quick to condemn the soldiers and rebels who want to keep fighting. In the meantime, Ra rages over the escape of his enemies.

Skaara helps Daniel discover the seventh symbol—the key to going home. Hundreds of slaves work the mines, until the rebels uncover themselves and kill one of the guards. Kasuf now sees the gods he fears are merely human.

Ra sends the bomb to the Stargate as a caravan approaches the pyramid. Suddenly, the convoy of slaves and soldiers becomes an attack group, engaging the guards in gunfire. Alien fighters respond from the air as O'Neil, Daniel, and Sha'uri are sealed inside the temple.

At the Stargate, O'Neil arms the bomb, with only seven minutes before detonation. A guard blasts Sha'uri, and Jackson responds by killing the guard. Daniel boards the alien ship with Sha'uri in his arms and takes her to the sarcophagus where he was revived.

O'Neil and Anubis fight hand to hand, while the alien fighters continue to strafe the people outside. The colonel kills Anubis, while Daniel and an unconscious Sha'uri make their way back to the interior of the pyramid. With less than two minutes to go, O'Neil begins to dismantle the bomb.

Kawalski and the mob surrender, and the aliens land their craft. Seemingly defeated, the rebels watch as Kasuf appears on the ridge with thousands more— the alien pilots are doomed. Ra sees the defeat and starts his escape in the spaceship.

Sha'uri awakens as O'Neil and Jackson get the same idea. Unable to disarm the bomb, they use the alien ship's transport to send the device back up to the departing craft. With only a few seconds left, Ra receives an explosive parting gift and the bomb detonates, killing him.

The rebels cheer as Skaara and his friends salute O'Neil. Sha'uri and Daniel kiss. Later, the colonel and his troops return through the Stargate, while Daniel stays behind with Sha'uri. He sends the Ra necklace back with O'Neil.

Afterwords

Director Roland Emmerich and screenwriter Dean Devlin first connected on the 1992 action sci-fi flick *Universal Soldier*, which starred Jean-Claude Van Damme and Dolph Lundgren. Subsequent brainstorming sessions revealed that Emmerich was fascinated by the mystique of ancient Egypt, while Devlin imagined a film that would be like Lawrence of Arabia going into outer space.

Their resulting script was *Stargate*. While studios were interested, they figured it would cost more than $100 million to make, and no one was willing to commit that much money. Eventually, two studios—American-based Carolco and French-based Le Studio Canal+—agreed to bankroll the project, with one caveat. The studios would only pony up $55 million to budget *Stargate*.

Accepting the challenge, Emmerich knew he would have to keep a close watch on the effects in order to stay within the budget. The director picked East Coast–based Kleiser-Walczak Construction Company (don't let the name fool you, they really were an FX company) to create the needed CGI. Although they were based in Massachusetts, they set up shop in LA to be close to the action.

Despite the reliance on computer FX, practical set pieces—like the titled Stargate—were built full scale. Brit effects veteran Kit West—with credits back to Hammer's 1965 *She*; the 1968 Quatermass film, *Five Million Years to Earth*; as well as Star Wars' *Return of the Jedi* and *Raiders of the Lost Ark*—constructed a twenty-two-foot metal ring. Coated in fiberglass, it had a motorized outer ring that worked like a huge combination lock. The action inside the ring was supplied via CGI.

Patrick Tatopoulos, known to many as one of the judges on Syfy Channel's makeup competition, *Face Off*, as well as production designer on films like 1996's *Independence Day* and 2004's *I, Robot*, provided key concept designs for the film. He created the warrior characters, including Ra, by combining an Egyptian look with Japanese samurai inspiration.

Emmerich liked Tatopoulos' work so much he asked the designer to stay on and supervise the actual building of the creatures. He brought in more than forty techs and artists to get the job done, including creating the unusual mammoth-like animal known as the mastadge. Instead of opting for an entire animatronic figure or stop-motion animation, Tatopoulos built a mechanical head that fit over a real Clydesdale horse.

Stargate ended up as a film with a Jekyll and Hyde reputation. Many viewers felt the first half of it was the greatest thing since *Citizen Kane*, but the remaining half left everyone wanting—and expecting—a lot more. Even so, it was a hit at the box office, grossing more than $71 million domestically, with another $125 million overseas.

Contact

Synopsis

- 1997—American/Warner Brothers—150 min./color
- Director: Robert Zemeckis
- Original music: Alan Silvestri
- Film editing: Arthur Schmidt
- Production design: Ed Verreaux
- Based on the 1985 novel by Carl Sagan

Cast

- Jodie Foster (Eleanor Arroway)
- Matthew McConaughey (Palmer Joss)
- Tom Skerritt (David Drumlin)
- James Woods (Michael Kitz)
- Angela Bassett (Rachel Constantine)
- David Morse (Ted Arroway)
- William Fitchner (Kent Culler)
- John Hurt (S. R. Hadden)

Billions and billions of radio transmissions from Earth have traveled far beyond our galaxy of the Milky Way. With the help of her father, Ted, six-year-old Ellie Arroway tweaks a shortwave radio to talk with someone a thousand miles away. Ellie wonders if she could reach farther, talking to other planets in the solar system. Her dad believes anything is possible, but he dies before he can see his daughter's success.

As an adult, Ellie earns her doctorate in astrophysics and begins working with SETI—Search for Extra-Terrestrial Intelligence—at the one-thousand-foot Arecibo dish radio telescope facility in Puerto Rico. Her tasks include scanning deep space, examining pulsars and other cosmic phenomena for signs of life.

At a café, she meets Palmer Joss, an author, theologian, and spiritualist who seems smitten with Ellie. Former supervisor David Drumlin, recently named as scientific advisor to the president, arrives at Arecibo to review the results of SETI.

Ellie and Palmer share an intimate moment, but she is too preoccupied with her work to commit to anything serious with Joss. Unfortunately, Drumlin pulls the funding for SETI, considering it to be nonsense and a waste of time.

The SETI team begin to go their separate ways, with Ellie making a passionate pitch for funding to billionaire industrialist S. R. Haddon. He admires her commitment and vision, awarding an endowment for her research team to continue. They resume their search of the sky at the Very Large Array (VLA), a collection of twenty-seven dish telescopes on the high ground of New Mexico.

Four years later, as their efforts have yet to turn up anything substantial, Drumlin threatens to once again cut the support by refusing to renew the lease on the government-owned antennae when it expires in three months. Even Dr. Kent Culler and other members of Ellie's team are ready to admit defeat.

US one-sheet—*Contact.*

Joss uses the media to question the ethics of spending billions of dollars on science when mankind continues to grow farther and farther apart. One evening, Ellie is thrilled to discover positive contact with something far out in the cosmos, from the star Vega. Suddenly, the pulsing signal translates to a series of prime numbers—proof of intelligence.

News media jump on the story, as do the military and the government—including David Drumlin. Michael Kitz, the national security advisor, questions the potential of a security breach to America.

Kent's closer examination of the signal reveals a video component along with the audio. The transmission turns out to be an old 1936 German broadcast of Hitler's opening announcement to the Olympic Games in Berlin.

At the White House, Chief of Staff Rachel Constantine shows her concern that a zealot like the Führer turns out to be the first thing to come from outer space. Arroway explains that politics has no bearing on the received signal. President Bill Clinton acknowledges the efforts of Ellie and her team and vows to support any future activities in the same direction.

That same direction includes the discovery of tens of thousands of pages of encrypted data in the return signal. It seems, however, that Drumlin will override Arroway and her team, taking control of the decoding project on behalf of the US government.

Meanwhile, conservative spokesperson Richard Rank accuses the scientific community's research of intruding on religion, while members from both sides of the matter descend on the area around the VLA, mostly just to be part of the hoopla. Ellie is disgusted with all of it.

Breaching the security of the project, investor S. R. Hadden summons Ellie to his plane, where he outlines a plan to keep her well involved in the project at hand. As a former engineer, Hadden's review of the encoded data has led to breaking the encryption.

A high-level meeting in Washington pits the science of Dr. Arroway and Drumlin against the beliefs of Rank and Joss, as well as the paranoia of Kitz and the military. Hadden's deciphering of the signal reveals literal blueprints for constructing some sort of advanced machine. Joss acts as a voice of reason, suggesting they reach for common ground.

Unaccustomed to dressing for formal occasions, Ellie primps for a grand reception, moving past loud religious zealots, including a man named Joseph, outside the hotel. Palmer is impressed, but isn't deterred from arguing the existence of God with Ellie.

Arroway had offered her opinion that the directions might be for a human transport, and she was right. As the discoverer, Ellie's name tops a short list, which also contains Drumlin, of possible travelers, but an elite selection committee—including Palmer—will make the final choice.

Construction on the transport begins at Cape Canaveral, with a budget estimated at more than $300 billion. Many fear the mission will end in failure and death. Palmer wonders why Ellie would spend four years on her trip that, considering Einstein's theory of relativity, would actually encompass fifty years. When—and if—she came back, everyone she knew and loved would be dead. Like most scientists, Arroway believes the effort will result in answers.

Fearing Ellie's lack of faith wouldn't properly represent mankind, Joss admits he agreed with the final choice of the devout Drumlin as the traveler. Thousands flock to the launch site at the Cape, as preparations continue for a full test of the IMC, the International Machine Consortium.

Watching from Mission Control, Ellie is stunned to see Joseph, the religious fanatic, appear on the launch gantry. He detonates explosives strapped to his chest, destroying the machine and killing Drumlin, as well as many others.

Saddened, Ellie returns to New Mexico, where Hadden contacts her from the Russian Mir space station. The billionaire has traveled into space in the hope of slowing the cancer that is slowly killing him. He also reveals a second machine, secretly built by his company, in Hokkaido, Japan. Dr. Arroway is Hadden's choice to make the trip.

Although she'd rather not, Ellie accepts safety equipment and a suicide capsule from doctors as she prepares for her journey. Aboard a navy ship in the Pacific Ocean, Palmer surprises Ellie by showing up at her cabin door. He admits the real reason for not originally choosing her for the mission—he didn't want to lose her.

With a protective suit that resembles the armor of Joan of Arc, Ellie approaches the capsule. Mounted to a gantry, it sits above three concentric rings—hundreds of feet in diameter—that spin around each other. When the capsule is dropped into the center of the machine, a tremendous acceleration of matter should occur.

Bravely, Arroway straps into the cockpit, while Joss, Kitz, and Culler monitor her progress in Mission Control. Communications begin to break up, but the launch continues. The capsule drops into the core of the machine and, in a buffeting and blinding flash of light, she enters a series of wormholes.

Suddenly, Ellie floats weightless in a calm and quiet peace. The amazing sights of stars and galaxies leaves her speechless. She appears to arrive at a white, sandy beach, with clouds and a sun seemingly at arm's length. A Vega alien approaches, taking the familiar guise of her father to ease the experience.

Other civilizations—but not all—have made a similar trip, on a path that existed long before the Vega society found it. Their signal to Earth was merely a response to the radio transmissions they had received from the planet.

With that, the voyage must end. The alien advises taking small moves, and, suddenly, Ellie's capsule splashes into the water under the rings. Mission Control considers the mission as a malfunction since—for them—the capsule fell straight through the rings upon release. For Ellie, she was gone for eighteen hours. The world wants to know what really transpired.

Kitz resigns his advisor position to head an aggressive inquiry into the IMC mission, accusing Arroway of being delusional. He even suggests Hadden, recently died, could have financed the supposed trip as an elaborate hoax. Without any concrete evidence of her voyage since her telemetry recorded only static, Arroway can only ask the committee and the world to accept her story in a leap of faith.

Ellie and Palmer embrace. Privately, Kitz and Constantine realize that Arroway's video telemetry actually recorded eighteen hours of static.

Eighteen months later, Ellie continues her work at the VLA, encouraging a group of touring children to never stop searching for answers.

Afterwords

Many sci-fi films come from brilliant minds. On the other hand, *Contact* came from a brilliant mind that also happened to be a world-renowned astrophysicist.

As such, the film found its roots firmly based in science and reality. Even with those credentials, it was a project that took nearly twenty years to reach the screen.

Sagan, involved with SETI—the Search for Extra-Terrestrial Intelligence, a not-for-profit organization—used his experience to pose the question: What if searching deep space for alien life resulted in a reply? Sagan and wife Ann Druyan, along with film exec Lynda Obst, wrote a movie treatment based on that very premise in 1979.

The project bounced around Hollywood for ten years while, in the meantime, Sagan decided to just turn his original idea into a best-selling novel in 1985. Finally, *Contact* got approval for production in 1993, but ran into more issues. One errant story idea that surfaced found the pope (!) involved as a major plot point (no word if his Boss would have given him time off from the Vatican).

Mad Max creator George Miller was originally tapped to direct, with two-time Oscar-winning actress Jodie Foster cast in the lead. But production delays and script-doctoring resulted in Miller getting the boot (however, Foster remained). *Back to the Future* franchise and 1994's *Forrest Gump* director Robert Zemeckis came in to take over (having already turned the job down before Miller).

It's a sure thing that any film about deep space exploration is bound to involve dazzling visual effects, and *Contact* was no exception. Ken Ralston, longtime special FX collaborator with Zemeckis, headed the team to produce them through Sony Pictures Imageworks. Other FX houses to work on *Contact* included Peter Jackson's Weta Ltd., ILM, and Warner Digital Studios.

While the pope idea was shelved (fortunately), Zemeckis still found a way to include a major cameo appearance by the president of the United States—although Bill Clinton, the sitting exec in 1996, never set foot inside a sound stage.

A conference at the White House press room showed the president addressing the real possibility of intelligent communications from deep space. Using a process that Zemeckis and Ralston first employed in *Forrest Gump* to combine actors with historic footage, they first took a 1996 address Clinton had made in the Rose Garden about exploring the chances of life on Mars.

Some of the prez's comments on exploration and discovery were spot-on to adapting for the film. Clinton was digitally removed from the Rose Garden (something the Grand Old Party would like to have seen on a permanent basis) and composited with a press room background. The result gave a rare sense of realism to the sci-fi story.

Of course, it is said that "it's not nice to fool Mother Nature." One may want to paraphrase that into "it's not nice to fool an astrophysicist and his wife," at least as far as *Contact* was concerned. Sagan and wife Ann penned a very proper, but pointed, letter to Warner Bros. producers in 1995 objecting to many of the scientific inaccuracies that appeared in a draft of the shooting script. It's impossible to say if Sagan would have approved of the final release, as he passed away nearly eight months before the film came out.

As a 1997 summer blockbuster, *Contact* really wasn't. The film cost $90 million to produce and barely grossed that in the US with $100 million. Overseas, it drew another $70 million. But in a year that saw films like *Titanic*, *Men in Black*, and *Lost World: Jurassic Park*, *Contact* was just a drop in the ocean of space.

Starship Troopers

Synopsis

- 1997—American/Tristar Pictures—129 min./color
- Director: Paul Verhoeven
- Original music: Basil Poledouris
- Film editing: Mark Goldblatt, Caroline Ross
- Art direction: Bruce Robert Hill, Steve Wolff
- Based on the 1959 novel by Robert A. Heinlein

Cast
- Casper Van Dien (Johnny Rico)
- Dina Meyer (Dizzy Flores)
- Denise Richards (Carmen Ibanez)
- Jake Busey (Ace Levy)
- Neil Patrick Harris (Carl Jenkins)
- Clancy Brown (Sgt. Zim)
- Seth Gilliam (Sugar Watkins)
- Patrick Muldoon (Zander Barcalow)
- Michael Ironside (Jean Rasczak)
- Eric Bruskotter (Breckinridge)
- Anthony Ruivivar (Shujumi)

Somewhere in the future, a TV promo on the Federal Network encourages civilians to sign up for military service. As a member of the Mobile Infantry (M.I.), a civilian can become a "citizen" and help save the world. The Earth is in fierce battle with giant bugs that inhabit the Klendathu planet system in deep space. A live broadcast from one of the planets shows a battle heavy with casualties, even taking the on-the-scene reporter.

Only a year before, in Buenos Aires, the young and handsome Johnny Rico is distracted from Mr. Jean Rasczak's high school history and ethics class by the beauty of his girlfriend, Carmen Ibanez. She dreams of being a starship fleet pilot. Just as well, as the biology class dissection of a huge bug reveals Carmen's weak stomach for blood and guts. Classmate Carl Jenkins is a brilliant student with psychic powers.

Johnny scores the winning touchdown in a game resembling arena football called "jumpball," the pass thrown with pinpoint accuracy by the Tigers' fine

Bagging a brain bug—*Starship Troopers.*

female QB, Dizzy Flores. His catch beats defender Zander Barcalow, who also has eyes for Carmen and is headed for Fleet Academy.

Johnny's parents are dead-set against his desire to enter Federal service. At the graduation dance, Diz makes a play for Johnny, but he's stuck on Carmen. Johnny angrily leaves his parents for M.I. boot camp, while Carl heads for Military Intelligence and Carmen is off to Fleet Academy, where Zander just happens to be an assistant instructor.

Johnny quickly learns the road to citizenship is not an easy one. In camp, the tough drill instructor, Sgt. Zim, quickly sets the tone by breaking the arm of recruit Breckenridge and roughly subduing the recently transferred Diz in a hand-to-hand combat exercise. The cocky and toothy Ace Levy aspires to be squad commander and becomes friends with Johnny.

Carmen proves to be a crazy but cocksure cadet, steering the huge starship *Roger Young* with reckless accuracy. Johnny's enthusiasm earns him the role of squad commander, but his conquest is short-lived, as Carmen sends him a "Dear Johnny" letter—actually a mini CD disc. Carmen is committed to a career in spaceflight, and there's no room for Johnny in that life. Ironically, Johnny admits he joined Federal service only because Carmen was signing up.

His luck continues to go sour, as his negligence gets Breckenridge killed in a live-ammo exercise. Johnny is sentenced to a public lashing, and he resigns in disgrace. He calls his folks by videophone, and all is forgiven. Unfortunately, some unknown disturbance cuts the conversation short. Rico heads dejectedly down "Washout Lane," but war is suddenly declared against the bugs. An enormous plasma-powered meteor has leveled Buenos Aires, and he decides to stay with Federal service.

On the eve of the big invasion, Johnny runs into Carmen, but mutual jealousy between Johnny and Zander leads to blows. They're quickly separated, and it's off to war. M.I. is dropped onto Klendathu by starships, as deadly plasma streaks into the skies from the abdomens of immense beetles. Nuclear bazooka shells destroy the creatures, but hundreds of crab-like arachnid warriors swarm to counter the attack. As big as bulldozers, they quickly overcome the infantry, with Ace unable to handle the command of his squad. Soldier Shujumi is torn apart by the bugs, while another soldier is dragged deep into the bug's lair. Retreat is sounded, but Johnny is mortally wounded by the pincers of a bug.

The Federation is reeling from the defeat. A new sky marshal is appointed, and the fleet must now be prepared for bugs that can think. Carmen finds that Johnny is dead, but modern medicine repairs his wounds and revives him. Ace, Johnny, and Diz are assigned to a new unit, the "Roughnecks"—Rasczak's Roughnecks, led by Johnny's former instructor.

Their first assignment is to mop up for a Fleet attack of an outer Klendathu planet. While the infantry can handle the stray arachnids, a huge fire-breathing beetle may do everyone in. But Rico's courage puts him piggyback on the beast, where he destroys it with a grenade. A nighttime celebration finds Rasczak appreciative of his troops' efforts, and Diz finally gets together with Johnny.

Rasczak's Roughnecks find a deserted and devastated Federal outpost on Planet P. They engage in a fierce battle with thousands of arachnids and airplane-sized dragonflies. Rasczak is torn in half by some unseen bug, and Rico does the noble thing by putting him out of his misery. Carmen and Zander lead a rescue retrieval mission, but Diz is killed as she calls on her quarterback skills to hurl a grenade into the mouth of a fire-spewing bug.

Carl has become a colonel in Military Intelligence. The massacre on Planet P was a trap, set by some sort of "brain bug." The plan now is to return to P to capture it. Rico is now commanding lieutenant of the troops—called "Rico's Roughnecks."

Starship *Roger Young* is destroyed by a stream of plasma, but not before Zander and Carmen escape in a small landing craft. It crashes deep inside Planet P. They are surrounded and subdued by arachnids. A huge bulbous slug slowly slithers toward Zander. This is the "brain bug." Using a long pointed probe, it pierces Zander's skull and sucks his brains out. As it advances on Carmen, she severs the probe with a concealed knife. Johnny comes to the rescue, threatening the bugs with a nuclear device. Soldier Sugar Watkins sacrifices himself by detonating the bomb, as the rescue party grabs Carmen and makes a hasty exit.

The brain bug does likewise, avoiding the deadly blast. But it's soon captured by Zim, now a private in Federal service. Netted and tied down, the bug is psychically probed by Carl, who discovers the bug's fear. It was Carl's telepathic powers that led Johnny to Carmen's rescue. With a brain bug in captivity, the bugs will finally be defeated by the starship troopers.

Afterwords

Director Paul Verhoeven took a tremendous amount of heat from critics and fans who viewed *Starship Troopers* as an endorsement of a society controlled by a fascist military, appearing to some as embracing neo-Nazism—a criticism that also dogged Heinlein's original novel. Those folks failed to see the director's use of fascist imagery—including storm trooper–style costume design and recruitment plugs within the film that mirror those produced by German film-maker Leni Riefenstahl for Nazi Germany in the 1930s—to actually question the validity and point out the dangers of such a government.

Verhoeven was originally cool to the prospect of directing *Starship Troopers*, thinking a film with giant bugs was "silly." On second thought, he considered the project to be intriguing, and it offered another chance to work with FX master Phil Tippett, who had collaborated with the director on *RoboCop*. Tippett was anxious to improve the digital animation techniques he had created for *Jurassic Park*. The film's budget of nearly $100 million was evident, as it relied on more than 550 visual effects shots. By comparison, *Lost World: Jurassic Park* had only 170 visual effects shots.

Most of the "planetary" sequences were shot near Casper, Wyoming, in an area with the attractive name of Hell's Half-Acre. The geography was so desolate and remote, producers worked with local officials to build access roads to the site. Verhoeven put his young cast into the military spirit by holding his own twelve-day boot camp at Hell's Half-Acre, complete with tents, snows, and raging winds, all under the watchful eye of a retired captain from the US Marines.

One might think that a futuristic, military government—capable of design-ing and building massive battle ships for deep space travel—would equip their fighting soldiers with weapons formidable enough to swat the threat of interstellar bugs. And while they did have mobile nuclear tactical weapons, their main ordnance was merely a rifle with a shotgun and a machine gun strapped together (many of today's SWAT teams are better equipped than the starship troopers).

The mythical Morita MK 1 rifle was designed to be a futuristic shell that incorporated two real weapons—a Ruger AC556 assault rifle on top, capable of single-fire, three-burst, or full-automatic use—and the twelve-gauge, pump-action Ithaca Model 37 Stakeout shotgun underneath. Several dozen fully functional Morita MK 1 rifles were built for *Starship Troopers*, with hundreds of rubber replicas made for use by extras. A total of more than 300,000 rounds of blank ammo were fired during the shooting of the film—enough for every man, woman, and child in the towns of Abilene and Amarillo, Texas.

Part of the future military makeup in *Starship Troopers* was based on racial and gender equality, which led to the well-watched coed shower scene. Verhoeven had featured a similar scene, although smaller scale, in *RoboCop*, where future law enforcement officers saved water by sharing locker facilities. For *Starship Troopers*, the director closed the set on the day of shooting and didn't rush his performers in stripping down to their birthday suits. Once everyone was ready, actress Dina Meyer wondered why only the performers were naked. Not wanting to carry a double-standard, Verhoeven and Director of Photography Jost Vacano immediately disrobed, creating a level playing field (perhaps).

In the end, *Starship Troopers* didn't do as well as anticipated, pulling in $55 million in domestic receipts, with another $65 million from overseas tickets. Yet the film had enough appeal to warrant three (albeit inferior) direct-to-video sequels: *Starship Troopers 2: Hero of the Federation* in 2004, *Starship Troopers 3: Marauder* (with Casper Van Dien returning to the role of Johnny Rico), and the completely computer-generated *Starship Troopers: Invasion* in 2012, which resembles watching a feature-length video game.

Prometheus

Synopsis

- 2012— American/Twentieth Century-Fox—124 min./color)
- Director: Ridley Scott
- Original music: Marc Streitenfeld
- Film editing: Pietro Scalia
- Production design: Arthur Max

Cast
- Noomi Rapace (Elizabeth Shaw)
- Michael Fassbender (David)
- Charlize Theron (Meredith Vickers)
- Idris Elba (Janek)
- Guy Pearce (Peter Weyland)
- Logan Marshall-Green (Charlie Holloway)
- Sean Harris (Fifield)
- Rafe Spall (Millburn)
- Kate Dickie (Ford)

Long, long ago, at the edge of a thundering waterfall, a strange being called an Engineer—humanoid, pale like a piece of porcelain, tall and powerfully built—watches as a large disk-shaped spacecraft rises into the sky. He drinks from a metal dish and is immediately stricken by something terrible. It begins to eat away at his body, even down to his very DNA. Dead, he tumbles into the rushing waters and disintegrates. With this action, the seeds of human life on Earth are sown.

In 2089, a team of archaeologists works at a site in the Isle of Skye, Scotland. Pretty Dr. Elizabeth Shaw and her boyfriend, Charlie Holloway, discover ancient cave paintings that clearly depict a star map—more pointedly, a set of directions.

Four years later, the *Prometheus*—a scientific exploration spacecraft—travels into deep space. Among the crew, all deep in hypersleep, are Shaw and

Holloway. David, a very humanlike android, monitors their condition. Alone and roaming the ship, he amuses himself by playing basketball and watching films like *Lawrence of Arabia.*

The *Prometheus* nears its destination, and David awakens the crew, including Meredith Vickers, the beautiful but cold mission director. At an orientation meeting, elderly Peter Weyland addresses the group via a video recording made two years before. He is the founder of the Weyland Corporation, which has underwritten the mission at nearly $1 trillion.

Shaw and Holloway note that archaeological finds from all over the world feature the same image as the one found in Scotland. They show a large being, pointing to a specific star cluster many light years from Earth. The doctors consider it as an invitation to visit the destination they have just reached.

Shaw and Holloway consider these beings as the creators of human life on Earth, which is why they refer to them as Engineers. The crew laughs in skeptical disbelief as the *Prometheus* prepares to land.

Vickers summons Shaw and Holloway to her opulent quarters, also a self-contained module. It contains a grand piano, antique furniture, and its own Med-Pod—a chamber capable of almost any medical remedy. The director makes it clear that she thinks little of the project—and the doctors' work—asserting that they are merely employees under her supervision.

The *Prometheus* sets down on the planet known as LV-223, with the crew donning bubble-helmeted spacesuits. They roll across the planet's surface in an eight-wheeled personnel carrier and two rovers, heading toward a massive but decayed conical structure—obviously built by someone.

Inside, the crew deploys a series of flying probes that scan the layout with lasers, relaying the data back to the ship as a three-dimensional map. Despite warnings, the group find the air breathable and remove their helmets as they move through the caves.

David locates a panel of controls in a stone wall and presses them, producing wispy holographic images of space-suited aliens running through the corridors. The team investigates further and finds the decapitated body of a large and long-dead alien. Two scientists, Millburn and Fifield, have seen enough, and they nervously head back for the ship.

Engaging another panel opens a door, with the alien's severed head on the other side. The walls of the cavernous room are covered with a beautiful mural, and many metallic canisters are neatly arranged on the floor. David notes they are organic, as one begins to melt like black wax on a candle.

Shaw and Holloway place the alien head in a specimen bag, while David flash-freezes one of the canisters. Everyone has to return to the *Prometheus* in a hurry as a violent storm quickly approaches. But Millburn and Fifield, lost somewhere in the caves, are forced to ride out the storm before they can be located.

In the ship's lab, Shaw, David, and crew member Ford examine the Engineer's skull and find the exterior is actually a helmet. The head underneath

Charlize Theron, Noomi Rapace, and Michael Fassbender (L-R) in *Prometheus*.

is humanoid and seemingly comes to life when a probe is inserted. Quickly moved into a containment case, the head explodes into a messy mass of goo.

Shaw and Ford discover the DNA from the Engineer matches that of humans, while David removes the alien canister from the deep freeze. He takes a small amount of black fluid from the container onto his finger and places it into a glass of champagne. Charlie, already half in the bag, drinks it on David's offer of good health.

Millburn and Fifield continue their aimless movement inside the pyramid, looking for some way back to the *Prometheus*. They discover a mound of dead Engineers, all in their space suits, but each seems to have had something burst from its torso.

On the ship, Captain Janek informs the pair that some form of life is showing up on his map of the caves, but then disappears. Janek dismisses it as a glitch, but Millburn and Fifield aren't so sure.

Shaw and Holloway share an intimate moment. So do Janek and Vickers, after the captain challenges the mission director to prove she isn't a robot like David. But with no one in the radio room at the *Prometheus*, there's no one to respond to Millburn and Fifield's call. The pair have encountered an alien snake emerging from black seepage on the ground.

At first, it seems harmless, but then it coils itself around Millburn's arm with lightning speed. The snake constricts itself, breaking the scientist's arm, and when Fifield cuts it in half with a knife, he's sprayed with acid. The snake regenerates a new head, enters the tear in Millburn's suit, and forces itself down his throat. Fifield falls face-first into the muck, where his helmet melts onto his face.

Holloway finds himself not feeling very well, but he still joins Shaw, Janek, and others who head out in a search mission for Millburn and Fifield. On his own, David enters a secret chamber, where thousands and thousands of canisters are stored. Video of his journey is fed back to Vickers, who watches with great interest.

Moving further into another chamber, the android suddenly cuts the video feed back to Vickers. Meanwhile, the search team finds the dead bodies of Millburn and Fifield, and, on closer inspection, the alien snake scurries out of Millburn's mouth and away in the muck. Holloway's condition worsens, and he collapses. The team helps him to his feet, and, returning to the *Prometheus*, Shaw requests medical assistance from Vickers, but the director wants nothing that could infect the ship and its crew.

David stands on a platform as an amazing holographic display unfolds before him. An Engineer seats itself in a cockpit and opens a three-dimensional map of vast solar systems, including the one that contains Earth. And in an instant, the display collapses to nothing. Noticing four glass coffin-like pods, the android puts his ear close to one and smiles.

The search team rushes back to the ship, but Holloway's condition continues to fail as large, dark lesions begin to open on his face. Vickers blocks their entrance to the *Prometheus*, holding a flamethrower to prove her resolve. Holloway knows there's no hope for his survival and moves toward Vickers. She triggers the flamethrower and burns Holloway to death, as Shaw screams.

David examines Elizabeth for any contamination and notes that she is three months pregnant. Shaw is stunned; being intimate within the last day hardly results in an embryo finishing its first trimester. David admits the fetus on the video screen is not normal.

Now in great pain, Shaw realizes she needs an abortion and makes her way to Vickers' Med-Pod. She programs emergency abdominal surgery and lies down in the machine as her stomach throbs and bulges. Soaked in sweat, Shaw endures the incision and watches in shock as the device pulls something vile and squid-like from her midsection. It squirms and wriggles its tentacles, as Shaw is sutured and she slips out from under the creature.

Janek notes that Fifield's video camera has just come back online, and it's right outside the ship. Several crew members check it out and find the scientist has mutated into a monstrous creature. It tosses them around like dolls, and, even with Janek igniting the flamethrower and others pumping shell after shell into it, the thing is finally killed when someone runs it over with the personnel carrier.

Covered in blood, Shaw comes upon David and others, who are tending to a still-alive but very aged Peter Weyland. Apparently, Shaw and Holloway's discovery convinced the old man that those who created humans should be able to save them—or at least Weyland—from dying. Shaw admits that what she did was wrong and they should leave the planet right away.

Janek discovers that LV-223 was a military base for the Engineers, where they developed dangerous biological weapons—the contents of the canisters. But the deadly organisms got out of control and left the planet in ruins. The captain is committed to keeping the Earth safe from those weapons, no matter what.

Wearing robotic supports, Weyland prepares to join the rest of the crew on their excursion back to the pyramid. Vickers tries to convince the man—her father—to stay behind and that even a king's reign has to end.

Undeterred, Weyland ventures into the caverns with the rest of the team. On the *Prometheus*, Janek erases the pyramid from the holographic map and discovers the caverns are actually a horseshoe-shaped spacecraft.

David takes the team to the chamber where he viewed the amazing display. He awakens an enormous Engineer from one of the pods, speaking to it in its native tongue. Its reaction is to attack the group, decapitating David and killing Weyland and Ford. Shaw runs for her life.

Vickers seems pleased with the events and announces that it's time to go home, while the Engineer activates a pilot's cockpit that rises from the floor. He climbs in, and, wearing an elephantine-nosed biosuit, the Engineer resembles a Space Jockey.

Shaw barely escapes as the horseshoe-shaped craft begins to lift off from LV-223, headed for Earth with its deadly cargo. She pleads with Janek to stop the alien ship, but Vickers separates from the *Prometheus* in her escape module, landing safely on the planet. Janek and his two crewmen fly the *Prometheus* into the alien ship, destroying it. The debris lands on Vickers, killing her instantly.

Shaw takes an axe and returns to Vickers' module, intent on killing the thing to which she gave birth. Incredibly, it has grown to gigantic proportions, and what's more, the Engineer has made its way onto the module as well. It attacks Shaw, but, thinking quickly, she activates the doors to Vickers' quarters and the creature pulls the Engineer in with its huge tentacles. She escapes as the monster forces a slimy tendril down the Engineer's throat.

David's head is still functioning, and he contacts Shaw, convincing her that once they find another alien ship, he can fly her away from LV-223. She recovers the android, not wanting to return to Earth but to fly to where the Engineers came from. Shaw needs to know why they created humans and then wanted to kill them. They find a ship, and the pair lifts off from LV-233.

Back in Vickers' module, the Engineer thrashes on the floor. Its chest bursts open, and an alien rises from the body. Bony in form, its huge phallic head has inner and outer jaws filled with chrome-like teeth.

Afterwords

For *Prometheus*, Ridley Scott found that he needed to be not so much a director as an acrobat. The balancing act in which he found himself tasked Scott with creating a prequel to the successful franchise that *Alien* had invented in 1979 while introducing new and unique ideas to allow the present film to stand on its own.

One recurring concept from *Alien* was the mysterious Space Jockey found on the distant planet LV-426. Many filmgoers thought the derelict form was a creature with an elephantine snout. But as originally conceived by artist H. R.

Giger, the fossilized remains were from a biosuit, a combination of pilot and its cockpit as one unit. The supposed elephant trunk was actually an air hose.

The Space Jockey/Pilot Chair in *Prometheus*, however, is not the precursor of *Alien* (remembering that the 2012 film actually takes place in 2089 to 2093, while the original is set about thirty years ahead of that period). The crew in *Prometheus* lands on LV-223, an entirely different planet. But the Space Jockey/Engineer is from the same race of ETs in both films—equally appropriate as a host for the evil chest-bursting alien as Kane was in the 1979 film (that movie's Space Jockey showed evidence of alien gestation and birth as well).

One new concept in *Prometheus* was the alien race of Engineers. Resembling living statues from ancient Rome and Greece, they were largely the product of concept artist Neville Page. Since Ridley Scott wanted as many real actors as possible throughout the film, seven-foot-one-inch actor and former basketball player Ian Whyte was cast as one of the statuesque Engineers.

Daniel James was another actor portraying an Engineer, becoming a sacrifice in the film's opening scenes. It was decided to combine practical effects with CGI added later. James wore a full-body silicone prosthetic that weighed fifty-five pounds. After taking a fatal drink, the Engineer began to decay as the liquid pulsed through his circulatory system. Weta Digital in New Zealand detailed the motion and deterioration via computer imagery composited over the actor's performance.

If Scott's *Prometheus* answered some of the questions raised in *Alien* (he admits that none of the other flicks in the *Alien* franchise had any real relationship to his 2012 entry), just as many new questions were introduced—with definite intent. The director and Twentieth Century-Fox were betting on a successful enough film to merit a sequel to the prequel.

Made on a budget of $130 million, *Prometheus* didn't quite gross that much domestically. However, the overseas take was much better—more than $276 million. Given this total of $400 million worldwide, *Prometheus 2* has been written, although Scott has a number of projects in the pipeline that will keep the sequel's completion a few years in the future.

6

Can't We All Just Get Along?

Keep Your Friends Close, but Your Aliens Closer

Many sci-fi films draw from the premise that the Earth and its inhabitants are weak, stupid, and incapable of behaving in a civil manner. Unable to properly coexist in the universal community, our world is viewed by some other planet's race as requiring celestial supervision. The invaders often regard us as one big day-care center in need of a diaper change.

Other times, outer spaceniks look at Earth as one big produce section, just ripe for the picking, in the solar system supermarket. Sometimes, the Earthlings are a valuable commodity; often, we're just in the way, as the aliens only want our real estate and resources. The idea of living in peaceful harmony is as foreign as the aliens themselves.

Into our atmosphere they soar, where the wrongdoers first encounter the military, believing our puny weapons to be no match for their superior intellect and armaments. The alien invaders figure their conquest of the world will be a cakewalk—by the final reel, they find otherwise.

Invariably, the world's top scientists must find a way out, but often it's an everyday person or the simplest of solutions that saves the day (see John Nada in *They Live* or the yodeling of Slim Whitman in *Mars Attacks!*). Occasionally, the military buddies up with the scientists, having finally gotten over their macho versus Mensa differences. They work together to defeat the onslaught of bug-eyed intruders (although they sometimes look just like us, as in *Invasion of the Body Snatchers*).

One variation on the theme of an otherworldly invasion involves the introduction of some sort of natural disaster that threatens all of Earth. Films like *Deep Impact* or *Armageddon* (take your pick, they're basically the same) involve a celestial body hurtling on a crash course with Earth. Once more, science and government must combine their resources to avert the catastrophe. (Is such a calamity possible? Perhaps . . . just as my winning the lottery and getting to hang out with Cameron Diaz is possible—hence the fiction part of sci-fi.)

Capable filmmakers know that audiences like these action and thrilling flicks, with the threat and danger of aliens capturing our world and compromising our ways of life. We pay to see them because we know, regardless of the danger on-screen, we leave safe and sound when the lights go up.

Unless, of course, we're driving home. Then all bets are off.

Invasion of the Body Snatchers

Synopsis

- 1978—American/United Artists—115 min./color
- Director: Philip Kaufman
- Original music: Denny Zeitlin
- Film editing: Douglas Stewart
- Production design: Charles Rosen
- Based on the 1955 novel *The Body Snatchers*, by Jack Finney

Cast
- Donald Sutherland (Matthew Bennell)
- Brooke Adams (Elizabeth Driscoll)
- Jeff Goldblum (Jack Bellicec)
- Veronica Cartwright (Nancy Bellicec)
- Leonard Nimoy (Dr. David Kibner)
- Art Hindle (Dr. Geoffery Howell, DDS)
- Joe Bellan (Harry)
- Kevin McCarthy (Hysterical Man in Street)
- Don Sigel (Taxi Driver)
- Robert Duvall (Priest)

From some distant world, shapeless creatures travel toward Earth and begin to land amid the falling rain. They start to multiply and branch out, spreading in the water runoff. With small seed pods, they sprout pink flowers. At a local park in San Francisco, children play and an expressionless priest sways on the swing set.

Elizabeth Driscoll picks one of the unusual flowers and brings it home with her. She notes the plant's rarity to her live-in boyfriend, Geoffrey, but he is not interested.

Matthew Bennell, an inspector from the Department of Health, pays a visit to the kitchen of an upscale eatery. He is not pleased with what he finds in the entrees and even less pleased to find the windshield on his car broken upon leaving the restaurant, courtesy of the disgruntled help.

Elizabeth, a coworker with Matthew at the Health Department, discovers that Geoffrey has suddenly become cold and distant, seemingly overnight. At her office, she and Matthew seem oblivious to the folks who stare blankly at them in hallways and from behind doors.

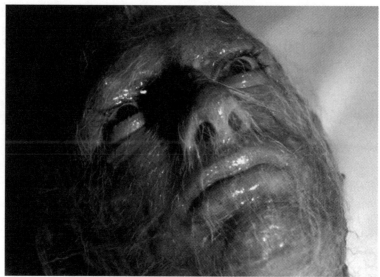

A furry clone of Jeff Goldblum in *Invasion of the Body Snatchers*.

At Matthew's home, Elizabeth shares her conclusion that Geoffrey is just not Geoffrey. Her colleague suggests a meeting with Dr. David Kibner, a friend who's a well-known psychiatrist as someone who could ease some of her concerns.

Matthew drops off some shirts at the local Chinese laundry, where the shop owner not-so-coincidentally notes his wife is not acting like his wife any more. The comment is not lost on Bennell, who stops to greet Harry, a banjo-playing street musician, and his boxer dog, on his way back to the office.

Elizabeth follows Geoffrey one day, watching as he congregates with strangers who carry unknown bundles with them. She tells Matthew about the experience while they drive to meet Kibner. In the middle of their drive, a hysterical man pounds on their car and warns of something unknown coming. "You're next!" he cries as he runs away, only to be struck and killed by another driver. When Bennell calls police to follow up on the accident, they have no record of it.

At Kibner's book release party, Elizabeth empathetically watches while another woman tearfully tells the doctor about her husband not acting like her husband. He smoothly calms her fears, asking for trust. Privately, Kibner admits to Matthew and Elizabeth that he's been hearing the same story more frequently, but he passes it off as people looking for ways to avoid commitment in their relationships.

Another friend of Bennell's, a highly strung fellow named Jack Bellicec, runs a mud bath business with his wife, Nancy. Jack decides to take a dip to relax. Closing up for the night, Nancy thinks her husband is resting on a table. But when she removes the sheet, it's really a featureless humanoid form, and Jack, in the flesh, is standing behind her.

Matthew arrives to find that the body, still devoid of features and even fingerprints, may actually be the not-yet-completed clone of Jack. Extremely tired, Bellicec takes a nap, and when he does, the clone opens its eyes. A startled Nancy wakes her husband, and the replicant's eyes close. What's more, Jack's bloody nose has now appeared on the duplicate.

Rushing to Elizabeth's home, Matthew sneaks in the back entrance and finds a clone of Elizabeth nearly complete, while the real woman sleeps nearby. Matthew takes the unconscious Elizabeth to his car and drives off.

Kibner arrives at the Bellicecs' mud baths, but there is no body to be found anywhere. Matthew and Elizabeth get there, where Nancy takes the now-awakened Elizabeth to Bennell's apartment. Accompanied by Bellicec and Kibner, Matthew summons the police to investigate Geoffrey and his home, but the body of Elizabeth is also gone. Kibner calms everyone, while the authorities and Geoffrey seem unconcerned about the entire situation.

The Bellicecs, along with Matthew and Elizabeth, try to make sense of everything, with Kibner at the lead. The only conclusion that can be reached is people are being duplicated while they are sleeping, but if that's true, Kibner wonders what can be done about it. The doctor agrees to connect Bennell with the city's mayor, who happens to be a patient of Kibner's. Unseen, the doctor leaves with Geoffrey.

The group concludes that the strange flowers that seem to be appearing everywhere are the source of the human reproductions, but Elizabeth is rebuffed when she tries to have them tested at her lab. When the mayor's office agrees to see Bennell, they insist on complete secrecy. Matthew gets the runaround wherever he calls. Even the Chinese laundry owner admits his wife is "all better now," and the woman who was so upset at the bookstore admits her husband is fine as well.

Kibner gives Elizabeth a sleeping pill and leaves Matthew's, while the others doze off. Fuzzy tendrils stretch from a pod and wrap around Matthew's hand as he sleeps. An enormous flower blooms, and from it, a clone of Bennell begins to grow. The same happens with Elizabeth, Nancy, and Jack.

Nancy, now up, screams and wakes Matthew, and she rouses Elizabeth and Jack. Bennell tries to notify the police, but they already know who is calling, and he just hangs up. As a crowd of replicants begins to surround the house, Nancy, Jack, and Elizabeth flee. Matthew stays back long enough to destroy the nearly completed clones with a garden hoe. The alien crowd emits shrill shrieks as they spot Bennell and the others.

The four escape into the streets, with pod people close behind. Jack and Nancy run to draw their attention away from Matthew and Elizabeth, who grab a taxi to the airport. But a roadblock keeps them from leaving the area, and they take off on foot, seeking refuge at their office. They watch from a window as dozens of people on the street carry pods to continue the reproduction. To stay awake, Matthew and Elizabeth take methamphetamines.

Jack and Kibner show up at the office—emotionless, they're pod people now. They promise new lives for the couple, but Matthew overpowers Jack and kills him, with Kibner locked in a lab freezer.

In a stairwell, Elizabeth and Matthew meet Nancy, who has found that she can walk undetected among the aliens by completely hiding her emotions. On the street, they join a line receiving pods but their cover is blown when Elizabeth is shocked to see Harry's boxer dog—now hideously cloned with his owner's human face.

Aliens screech as Matthew and Elizabeth run off, but Nancy keeps her calm and emotionless expression. The couple hops in the back of a passing truck and escape the mob. They arrive at a warehouse, where thousands of pods are being grown and loaded onto trucks.

Running for safety, Elizabeth sprains her ankle and is unable to continue. Matthew leaves her to investigate some distant music, only to find it's a broadcast as boatloads of pods head out around the world.

Returning to Elizabeth, Matthew finds her asleep, and as he hugs her, her body crumbles to bits. A nude clone of Elizabeth stands, coldly assuring Matthew that the metamorphosis is painless and beckons him to fall asleep. He flees and begins to sabotage the pod-growing facility, setting it on fire. Running into the night, Matthew escapes the pod people who chase after him.

Days pass and Matthew returns to his job at the Health Department, acting out the charade of emotionless alien life. Even he and Elizabeth do not share glances. On the street, Nancy calls to him, believing they're still among the few remaining humans.

But the shrill scream from Matthew's mouth proves otherwise.

Afterwords

America's postwar fear of a Communist takeover in the 1950s was rampant, so it's no wonder that Jack Finney's 1955 book about humans being replaced by alien spores was seen as an allegory for the loss of individual freedom. The 1956 film of *Invasion of the Body Snatchers*, by director Don Siegel and starring Kevin McCarthy, did nothing to dispel that theory.

While many folks consider the 1978 film to be a remake of the 1956 version, actress Veronica Cartwright claimed it was a continuation of the story. That would explain how McCarthy was still running in the streets after more than twenty years (must have cost him a fortune in footwear). Not coincidentally, Siegel made a cameo appearance as the taxi driver in the 1978 version.

Screenwriter W. D. Richter, having written only a few comedy scripts like 1973's *Slither* and 1976's *Nickelodeon*, wrote a first draft of *Invasion of the Body Snatchers* at the request of Warner Bros. It was supposed to be a low-budget remake, and the only thing the studio wanted from Richter was a rewrite of the original.

Warners then passed on it, so United Artists picked it up, with young Philip Kaufman as director. The setting for the story was switched from a small town to San Francisco, considering how the focus on American lifestyles had turned toward bustling metropolises since the 1956 version. Maybe alien pods could capture the lives of a little burg back then, but taking over a major city in the 1970s would be a much more impressive and frightening feat.

Much of the fright was courtesy of makeup effects artists Tom Burman and Eduoard Henriques. One scene showed Donald Sutherland's character asleep while a seed pod created his clone. It first emerged as a slimy infant, devoid of distinct features, which was accomplished with a simple puppet-like maquette. Then little person Joe Gieb was made up with foam latex appliances to show the creature as it grew. The final version, now looking something like Sutherland, was a full-sized silicone figure covered with fine nylon fibers that resembled corn silk.

Another startling scene revealed a dog with the face of its homeless owner. Burman made a life cast of actor Joe Bellan, along with a separate cast of a boxer dog named Misty. The makeup artist attached a face-hugging foam latex mask of Bellan onto Misty's head, giving her a face only the dog's owner could love.

An interesting cameo by Robert Duvall—a major actor in films like 1971's *THX 1138*, 1972's *Godfather*, and 1976's *Network*, among many others—showed a priest silently staring and swinging in a playground at the film's start. A friend of Kaufman, Duvall happened to be in town during the shoot and did the scene for free. The director later revealed that the priest represented the first seed-pod clone.

Invasion of the Body Snatchers was a big hit for the Christmas holiday season in 1978. Budgeted at $3.5 million, it brought in nearly $25 million at the domestic box office.

Predator

Synopsis

- 1987—American/Twentieth Century-Fox—107 min./color
- Director: John McTiernan
- Original music: Alan Silvestri
- Film editing: Mark Helfrich, John F. Link
- Production design: John Vallone

Cast

- Arnold Schwarzenegger (Dutch)
- Carl Weathers (Dillon)
- Elipidia Carillo (Anna)
- Bill Duke (Mac)
- Jesse Ventura (Blaine)
- Sonny Landham (Billy)
- Shane Black (Hawkins)

- Richard Chaves (Poncho)
- R. G. Armstrong (Gen. Phillips)
- Kevin Peter Hall (Predator)

An alien spacecraft soars through space. As it nears Earth, something is jettisoned and enters the atmosphere.

A team of mercenaries, led by an ex-military man named Dutch, lands by chopper in a desolate tropical area. Assisted by CIA agent Dillon, their mission is to rescue a lost cabinet member, feared captured by guerrillas. US General Phillips has brought in Dutch and his men because they are the best at this kind of operation.

The covert team of seven is dropped into the jungle, where they locate the stripped remains of a helicopter. A Native American tracker named Billy finds evidence of guerrilla activity, and the team takes off on their trail.

Suddenly, they're startled to find three human bodies, hung upside-down and skinned like a hunter's prey. Their dog tags reveal them to be Green Beret soldiers, but Dillon knows nothing about them or why they were there.

While the men move quietly through the jungle, someone or something watches from above, seeing their forms as thermal images. They come to the guerrillas' camp, where Dutch watches as a hostage is shot dead.

The men quickly pick off the sentries guarding the camp. The muscular Dutch places an explosive charge in the back of a pickup truck and then lifts it off its blocks, sending it rolling into the middle of the camp. He detonates the charge by remote, and his team attacks the guerrillas. Tobacco-chewing Blaine wields a handheld GE minigun, spraying the area with hundreds of bullets in seconds.

The body count is high as Dutch and his team efficiently move through the camp. Dutch knocks a guerrilla woman cold, and Mac reports that all the hostages are dead. It seems the important cabinet member was really CIA, and Dillon admits he lied to get Dutch and his men to swiftly end the threat of a messy rebellion.

With plenty of guerrilla soldiers still in the area, Dutch and his men leave quickly, taking the woman—named Anna—with them. As they depart, something unseen is still tracking them—something with huge claws.

The group enters a dangerous valley—the only way across the border to their pickup zone. Anna breaks free and runs, only to be stopped by Hawkins. But before the others reach them, the invisible predator swoops in, slays the mercenary, and drags his bloody body away.

Dutch and his men find only traces of Hawkins, and Anna can only explain that she saw the jungle come alive and attack him. The team looks for the rest of Hawkins, but the predator has hung his remains high in the trees—just like the three Green Berets.

Blaine is killed by the predator, and Mac, seeing something, grabs the dead soldier's minigun and unloads a hail of bullets. Soon, everyone is cutting

Kevin Peter Hall is the *Predator*.

down the forest with a deafening din of gunfire. Eventually out of ammo, Mac continues to hold the trigger, and the gun's carriage whistles as it spins uselessly.

The soldiers believe their barrage hit nothing, but something left a splotch of fluorescent green goo on a nearby leaf. Mac rigs trip wires and flares for protection as the team beds down for the night. Meanwhile, the predator appears briefly, revealing a cloaking system that allows it to be seen or unseen as needed. Tending to its leg wound, it cries out in pain—a startling sound the soldiers hear. Even the fearless Billy is scared.

Mac is on watch when something trips the flares, and he stabs at it with his knife, but it's just a wild boar. During the commotion, Blaine's body disappears. Dutch finally concludes that his team is being hunted, one by one, from out of the treetops. Against Dillon's orders, Dutch is determined to find and kill whatever is tracking and killing the group—before no one is left.

Everyone, including Anna, sets traps and snares to catch whatever is after them. Soon, one of the traps captures the predator in its net, but it quickly blasts its way out. Pancho is seriously injured by an enormous log. Mac runs after a vague image of the hunter, and Dillon runs after Mac.

Dutch, Anna, Billy, and the wounded Pancho slowly make their way toward the pickup zone. Mac and Dillon spot a blurred image of the predator on a tree limb, but it kills Mac with a blast from its weapon. Dillon quickly meets a similar fate.

Billy tosses his rifle away, preparing to meet the hunter with only a long-bladed knife. Dutch, Anna, and Pancho keep moving, only to hear Billy's scream of death. A laser blast kills Pancho, and Dutch fires into the trees. Anna runs as Dutch is wounded by the predator's blast.

Now the conflict has become a one-on-one battle between prey and the predator. Dutch tumbles into a river and swims to shore, with the alien close behind. By a stroke of luck, Dutch has become covered in mud, which masks his thermal image to the predator. Despite being nearly on top of the human, the hunter does not see him, and it walks off.

Dutch rigs deadly traps of spikes, trip wires, and pendulous logs, and fashions explosive arrows, as the hunted has now become the hunter. Under the light of a full moon, Dutch ignites a torch and utters his war cry—summoning the predator for battle.

Hiding high in the trees, Dutch waits for his prey. He shoots an arrow at the approaching predator, and it explodes at its feet. Not seeing Dutch, the predator fires in all directions, and the fight is on.

Dutch tumbles from the trees and clings to the underside of a log as the alien walks across it. Traces of glowing green blood show the predator is wounded, and it leaves a trail for Dutch to follow. He spots the alien and dives into the river, only to be pulled from the water by the creature.

Pinned against a rock, Dutch is surprised when the much-bigger predator releases him and walks a few paces away. The creature removes its weapons, armor, and protective face plate, revealing a monstrous lizard-like face with twin mandibles. The predator would prefer hand-to-hand combat with his opponent.

The creature pummels the ex-soldier with blows to the head and body. Dutch crawls, hoping to lure the predator into one of his traps. But the creature senses something is wrong and moves at Dutch from another direction. But it still comes directly under a massive log, which Dutch is able to dislodge and drop onto the creature.

It is mortally wounded, but Dutch decides not to finish it off with a large stone. As it dies, the predator triggers a device strapped to its forearm, laughing. Dutch runs as a nuclear explosion rocks the land.

From a helicopter in the air, the rescued Anna watches the rising mushroom cloud with General Phillips. Amid the smoke, Dutch stands tall as the chopper lands to pick him up.

Afterwords

It's difficult to say if there has ever been a sci-fi film with more testosterone per on-screen minute than *Predator*. It was a band of military guerrillas, played by some of the biggest dudes in Hollywood, facing off against an alien who has come to Earth for sport, played by an even bigger dude.

Brothers Jim and John Thomas, babes in Hollywood's writing community, had fashioned their first-ever script around the idea of alien hunters who chose Earth as their hunting grounds, with humans as their prey. Called *Hunter*, the script miraculously made its way—without representation—into the hands of producer Joel Silver at Twentieth Century-Fox.

The idea was eventually whittled down to just one alien hunter, and the prey would be the aforementioned big and brutish military men. The Predator was designed as a skinny, big-headed, lizard-looking beast with (hold on to your Belgian waffles) martial artist and actor Jean-Claude Van Damme hired to be inside the suit. It was thought his agile skills as a warrior would translate to a spirited performance.

It didn't. After just two days, the Muscles from Brussels bolted, claiming the suit was hot (it was) and no one would know who was inside (they wouldn't). Director John McTiernan, with only the low-budgeted 1986 horror flick *Nomads* under his belt, called on Kevin Peter Hall—all seven-foot two-inches of him—to get inside a totally redesigned Predator costume.

Who else but Stan Winston would come to the rescue, doing in only six weeks what normally would have been a yearlong job. Winston took his creature inspiration from an image of a Rastafarian warrior that hung on Silver's office wall. Add to that a suggestion from James Cameron (yes, *Terminator, Titanic, Avatar*—that James Cameron) to add flapping mandibles to the face. Predator became one mean-looking MF (Monster/Fighter . . . what were you thinking?).

Heading up the team of macho men was former Mr. Olympia, Arnold Schwarzenegger, at six-foot-two and 260 pounds. Next was pro wrestler (and former Navy Seal) Jesse "The Body" Ventura, at six-foot-four and 265. Ex-pro footballer Carl Weathers was six-foot-two and 220 pounds. Bill Duke was over six-foot-four and 230, while Sonny Landham was six-foot-three-inches. (That much beef is usually found in the back room of a butcher shop.)

Predator's filmmakers were still unsure about the soundness of the script, so they slyly decided to add a bit of insurance to the cast. Shane Black, having successfully written *Lethal Weapon* and *Monster Squad* in 1987, was given the on-screen role of radio operator Hawkins. With shooting located deep in the jungles of Mexico, it was figured he could punch up the script when it was needed (in reality, it wasn't).

The end result was the first of several popular films in the *Predator* series. With a $15 million budget, the 1987 film grossed nearly $60 million in the States, with another $38 million overseas. *Predator 2* in 1990 and *Predators* in 2010 brought in more than $82 million to the domestic franchise. Two crossover films with *Alien—Alien vs. Predator* in 2004 and *Aliens vs. Predator—Requiem* in 2007—added more than $120 million to the kitty. All together, *Predator* films have grossed more than a quarter-billion dollars in the US.

Alien Nation

Synopsis

- 1988—American/Twentieth Century-Fox—91 min./color
- Director: Graham Baker
- Original music: Curt Sobel

- Film editing: Kent Beyda
- Production design: Jack T. Collis

Cast

- James Caan (Detective Sergeant Matthew Sykes)
- Mandy Patinkin (Detective Samuel "George" Francisco)
- Terence Stamp (William Harcourt)
- Kevin Major Howard (Rudyard Kipling)
- Roger Aaron Brown (Detective Bill Tuggle)
- Jeff Kober (Joshua Strader)
- Leslie Bevis (Cassandra)
- Brian Thompson (Porter)

Los Angeles, in 1991, has become the landing site for a spaceship of working-class aliens—called Newcomers—who can't return to their planet. Formerly slaves, they are now free on Earth. But Earthlings resent their arrival and fear integration with them—at work, at school, everywhere. Although nearly humanoid in appearance, the aliens have bald, speckled heads; inset ears; and a penchant for sour milk, which is like liquor to them.

Like many on Earth, LA detective Matt Sykes has little use for the Newcomers. People derogatorily call them slags, and their neighborhoods are slagtowns. Out on street patrol, Sykes and partner Bill Tuggle interrupt a convenience store holdup. Two Newcomers kill the alien storekeeper, along with Tuggle.

Sykes chases the shooters into a tunnel, but one drinks an unknown liquid from a small vial and runs at full speed toward Sykes. He empties his weapon at the alien, who finally falls dead. The other jumps and throttles the cop, until police sirens scare the thug away. One of the responding officers is a Newcomer, and Sykes wants none of his help.

The next day, the same Newcomer—named Samuel Francisco—is selected to be the first alien promoted to detective, and, despite his personal feelings toward the aliens, Sykes volunteers to team up with him. They will investigate the Warren Hubley case, a homicide with similarities to the previous night's shooting. Refusing to introduce his new partner as "Sam Francisco," Sykes is happy to call him George. Although George attempts to be cordial with his new partner, Matt is all business.

Realizing the Newcomers are not easily stopped by normal gunfire, Sykes picks up a revolver that fires the massive four-five-four Casull cartridge—larger than the deadly .45 Magnum. Detective Sykes dislikes Francisco and the other Newcomers, but thinks their being partners will help him to apprehend the aliens that killed Hubley and possibly Tuggle.

At the morgue, the detectives find that both Hubley and one of the slags killed the night before worked at a local methane refinery—a gas the Newcomers find harmless. But some sort of unknown liquid is also being refined at the plant.

James Caan and Mandy Patinkin in *Alien Nation*.

The detectives find William Harcourt, a successful Newcomer businessman and associate of Hubley's, at a swanky dinner held in his honor. They also meet his aide, Rudyard Kipling. But neither can give any insight into the killing of their colleague.

Sykes and Francisco next hit a Newcomer bar to locate a tough slag named Porter, the son of the slain shopkeeper. After a rough introduction, he points the cops toward a club called Encounters and a Newcomer named Joshua Strader, who was also connected to Hubley.

But Strader is being held by thugs working for Harcourt, who is operating a massive and illegal narcotics business. He wants Strader to push *jabroka*, a drug native to the Newcomers. But Joshua refuses, and he is tossed into the ocean, where the saltwater is like acid to the aliens.

At Encounters, the cops find Strader's girlfriend, a Newcomer stripper named Cassandra, but she seems more interested in Sykes. He doesn't feel particularly daring and quickly excuses himself from the lady's dressing room.

At Matt's place, the duo begin to unwind—Sykes with vodka and George with spoiled milk. The relationship may be thawing a bit, as Matt shares family photos with his partner. But Sykes' bawdy humor is lost on George, while they become a bit tipsy. The next morning, someone tries to wire a C4 bomb to Sykes' car. But George is passed out in the back from the night before, and he scares the thug away.

Strader's remains are found on the beach, but Francisco won't go close to the ocean. Sykes lets his partner out before investigating, and several fellow detectives taunt him about working with a Newcomer. Matt surprises himself by sticking up for George and bloodying one cop's nose for good measure.

Lab tests on the alien Sykes killed revealed a presence of jabroka in the blood, but George refuses to tell Matt about it. When pressured, the alien insists that humans must never know about the drug and how it affects Newcomers, or it will seriously jeopardize their existence on Earth. The question is: how and where did the alien get the jabroka?

An alien database shows that all the Newcomers involved in the recent events were quarantined together when first arriving on Earth. With them was William Harcourt. Sykes and Francisco now realize Harcourt is the mastermind behind the narcotics ring.

They find the manufacturing facility, but the drug has been taken somewhere else. Enraged, George begins to destroy the gear single-handedly and then turns his attention on the lone worker there. Sykes and the alien play "good cop, bad cop," surprisingly with George as the out-of-control police officer. The persuasion results in locating the jabroka at the Encounters club.

An incensed George interrupts Harcourt's meeting with his minions, threatening to detonate the C4 bomb if Harcourt doesn't turn over the drugs and himself. Gunfire breaks out, with Harcourt and Kipling escaping—carrying the jabroka—in the confusion by stealing a police car. Sykes and Francisco follow in a high-speed chase.

The two cars wind up in a deathly race of chicken—and neither driver gives in. Kipling is killed in the crash, and George is unconscious. Sykes corners Harcourt, but the alien ODs on jabroka, choosing death rather than be apprehended.

Harcourt's body is taken away by ambulance, with Sykes and Francisco in another car. The overdose of jabroka has actually turned Harcourt into a stronger and more violent creature and he breaks out of the ambulance.

The two detectives track Harcourt to the docks, where Sykes empties his revolver into the villain. The slugs don't stop him; he runs along a pier and onto a fishing trawler, with Sykes coming aboard as well. George jumps into a police copter and watches as the boat heads out of the harbor.

Matt tackles Harcourt, and the pair tumble into the ocean. The saltwater sends the Newcomer to a watery grave, and, despite the painful and corrosive effects to George's hand and arm, the alien pulls Matt to safety.

Despite having some earlier doubts, Matt walks his daughter down the aisle at her wedding, with his permanent partner—George Francisco—in attendance.

Afterwords

Borrowing heavily from 1967's *In the Heat of the Night*, *Alien Nation* was a film that combined action with issues like discrimination and immigration (similar to *District 9* more than twenty years later). *In the Heat of the Night* tensely teamed Rod Steiger's racist sheriff with Sidney Poitier's black detective in the Deep South. In fact, the working title for the sci-fi film was *Outer Heat*, tipping its cinematic hat to the previous drama.

Mandy Patinkin, fresh from the popular 1987 fantasy film *The Princess Bride*, took the pivotal role of alien Newcomer cop Sam Francisco. Curiously, the part was originally named George Jetson, after the futuristic cartoon character from the 1960s. When producers Hanna-Barbera refused permission to use the name (at the last minute, by the way), filmmakers were forced to rename Patinkin's role.

Patinkin wanted to know more about the life of a police officer—even a nonalien cop, so the actor spent two weeks with the finest of New York City. He attended the police basic training course, rode along on patrols, worked on his aim at the firing range, and spent time at the local precinct, chatting up the officers.

The actor also found the extensive four-hour alien makeup job to be understandably uncomfortable. Designed by Alec Gillis, Shane Mahan, John Rosengrant, and Tom Woodruff Jr. at Stan Winston Studios, the entire production required an amazing ninety sets of thin latex appliances for the actor. Add to that the hundreds of additional full head masks required for the background performers, and it's easy to see how difficult creating an alien race can be.

Another makeup challenge involved the death of Newcomer Harcourt. With the aliens being deathly reactive to saltwater, the villain tumbled into the ocean with Detective Sykes. To create the acidic corrosive effect on Harcourt, the makeup crew carved out sections of the foam latex head and filled the holes with Bromo Seltzer—used to relieve heartburn, it came in a powder that foamed up when it came in contact with water. The whole appliance was covered with gelatin. Off-camera techs filled the headpiece with hot water from a syringe, and when that hit the makeup, everything bubbled up and melted away—rather disgustingly.

James Caan, playing Sam Francisco's Earthling counterpart, found the experience of *Alien Nation* to be less than satisfying. While he enjoyed working with Patinkin quite a lot, Caan wasn't totally thrilled with director Graham Baker. Nevertheless, Caan was a total professional and worked his way through the picture (after all, he did get paid handsomely for the job).

Produced on a budget of approximately $16 million, *Alien Nation* grossed over $25 million domestically, with another $7 million overseas. The total take of $32 million prompted one season of a Fox Network TV series with the same name the following year, as well as six made-for-TV movie sequels throughout the 1990s.

They Live

Synopsis

- 1988—American/Universal—93 min./color
- Director: John Carpenter
- Original music: John Carpenter, Alan Howarth
- Film editing: Gibb Jaffe, Frank E. Jimenez

- Art direction: William J. Durrell Jr., Daniel Lomino
- Based on the 1963 short story "Eight O'Clock in the Morning," by Ray Nelson

Cast

- Roddy Piper (Nada)
- Keith David (Frank)
- Meg Foster (Holly)
- George "Buck" Flower (Drifter)
- Peter Jason (Gilbert)

John Nada is homeless, a brawny drifter looking for work in Los Angeles. A blind street preacher rants about the evils of greed and those who control the masses, but Nada pays little attention. He eventually finds work on a construction crew, where he's befriended by a coworker named Frank.

The pair settle in at a shantytown, where a resident named Gilbert welcomes Nada's handyman skills. Frank misses his family back in Detroit and cynically disdains the plight of the hard-working poor people in the world. Nada believes in patience and the good of America.

One evening, Nada notes a television program being hacked by a signal that warns of a scientific plot underway to control the public through oppression. The plan keeps the masses sedated and unconcerned about the world around them. The broadcast, interrupting cable channel 54, gives viewers unusual headaches.

Nada is curious about odd around-the-clock activity at a nearby church, but Gilbert, a member, just brushes it off. When John peeks into the building, he finds the singing choir is only a tape recording. The church looks more like a warehouse, holding hundreds of cartons and lab equipment. The preacher discovers Nada, but he slips away. He shares his discovery with Frank, who wants nothing to do with it.

That night, police clear the church and tear down the shantytown. Most of the residents escape, but several—including the preacher—are beaten to death. Later, Nada comes back to the church, where he opens one of the cartons, only to find dozens of sunglasses. He keeps a pair, then stashes the rest in a garbage can.

Curiously, when he dons the shades, they reveal messages hidden all over the city. A billboard for computers actually reads "OBEY" when seen with the sunglasses. Others urge "MARRY AND REPRODUCE," "NO INDEPENDENT THOUGHT," "CONFORM," "SUBMIT," "STAY ASLEEP," and "CONSUME." A newsstand reveals magazines that offer the same messages of control.

Even more startling is the face of a man next to Nada. Seen with the sunglasses, the man is a living ghoul—skull-like, with rotting flesh and silver eyes. Without, he looks just like another businessman buying a newspaper. The money he spends reads "THIS IS YOUR GOD."

Nada is dazed at the discovery—all over the city, many people of all sorts have the same frightening appearance, although without the special glasses, everyone looks normal. When Nada confronts one of the strange-looking people, she flags him as "one who can see." Using a wrist-radio, she notifies others of the discovery, and Nada slips away.

Two police officers—not of this Earth—try to subdue Nada, but he kills them. Grabbing a pistol and shotgun, John enters a bank. He boldly states, "I have come here to chew bubble gum and kick ass ... and I'm all out of bubble gum." He kills several of the aliens, but, setting his sights on another, Nada is amazed to see him simply vanish.

He escapes out the back into an alley, where he finds a human police officer. Seeing the difference,

US one-sheet—*They Live.*

Nada doesn't shoot but safely sends the cop away. In a parking garage, John forces an Earth woman named Holly into her car, and they drive away.

At her apartment, Nada starts raving about what he's seen. Of course, Holly thinks he's a wacko. Nada makes small talk, trying to show Holly he's not off his rocker. It turns out that she is the assistant program director at cable station 54. Catching him off-guard, Holly kicks Nada through a window and calls the police.

John returns to his construction site, where he tries to convince Frank of what he's found. But Nada is now a wanted killer, so Frank wants nothing to do with him. Having left the sunglasses at Holly's, John goes back to the alley to get another pair. But the can has been emptied, and Nada has to climb through a garbage truck to retrieve the box.

Frank has followed John, wanting to at least give him his paycheck. When Nada tries once more to convince Frank of the situation—this time, with the sunglasses as proof—a brutal fistfight ensues between the two. When both are totally exhausted, Nada forces the glasses onto Frank—who now sees the truth. Sore and swollen, the pair take a room in a flophouse.

Gilbert finds them and brings them to a secret meeting of "seers." The sunglasses are replaced by contact lenses, which are more effective. Gilbert reveals that the plot revolves around aliens who wish to use the Earth and its inhabitants as a source of resource development—sort of a "third world" plan. Once the planet is depleted of its useful supplies, the aliens will move on, leaving it empty and dead. What's worse, they have developed clandestine relationships with certain groups of humans, who have become part of the plan . . . and very rich from it.

Assembling a guerrilla assault unit, the group has to find the source of the controlling signal. Surprisingly, Holly shows up at the meeting, proving to John that she finally tried the sunglasses. As she offers an apology, an explosion rocks the building, and police swarm in with guns blazing. Gilbert and many others are killed, but Nada, Frank, and Holly flee to the street.

With a wrist-radio taken from an alien, Frank opens a portal through which he and Nada escape. Searching through a maze of corridors, the pair find themselves at a grand banquet, where the elite humans celebrate their success with the aliens.

John and Frank are surprised to find one of the drifters from the shantytown has become one of the collaborators. Thinking they're now part of the team, the drifter shows them around, including an incredible space portal. They arrive at the nerve center, where the controlling signal originates. It happens to be the studios of cable channel 54.

The former drifter vanishes as John and Frank shoot their way into the newsroom and head toward the roof, where the transmitting antenna is located. With alien soldiers in pursuit, they find Holly. When Nada moves ahead of the group, Holly—a collaborator—shoots Frank in the head.

On the roof, Holly holds John at gunpoint as a police helicopter hovers overhead. Nada is able to shoot Holly dead before destroying the antenna with gunfire. A sniper shoots Nada down, and, as a parting gesture of defiance, displays a finger not normally used to wear a ring.

With the transmitter in ruins, the aliens and their plans are now revealed to the world.

Afterwords

Up until 1988, director John Carpenter's filmography was filled with horror films like 1978's *Halloween*, Stephen King thrillers like 1983's *Christine*, and action-adventure films like 1986's *Big Trouble in Little China*, among others. All were great vehicles for entertainment, but nothing that resembled cynical criticism of politics and advertising in 1980s America.

Then came *They Live*.

Carpenter had become dissatisfied with the political landscape in America. He was also disillusioned with the sly and persuasive practice of subliminal messaging in the media, so much that he was moved to do something about it, even though it was not a new concept.

Much has been written over the years about the placement of hidden messages in print ads, TV commercials, and movie theaters in order to influence the buying habits of the public. Way back in 1957, an experiment in a New Jersey cinema inserted single frame images into the movie *Picnic*, encouraging the audience to eat popcorn and buy soda pop (by the way, the ploy didn't work).

No matter, the insertion of hidden gimmicks and images (nowadays called Easter eggs) in our everyday lives supposedly can move us to crave food, drink, cars, and the all-important s-e-x. Moviemakers are well known to use the device to enhance the experience for the filmgoer, one of the more famous examples being found in the 1973 shocker *The Exorcist*.

At several points in the flick, director William Friedkin inserted images of a ghoulish face known as Captain Howdy, appearing for only fractions of a second. Despite the brevity of exposure, audience members (including yours truly) found themselves duly scared—to the extent of having no more bejesus within their bodies.

With that idea firmly established, *They Live* dove head-first into the idea that our daily existence was being externally directed by subliminal messages, courtesy of some not-so-friendly aliens. Hero John Nada (Spanish for "nothing') waged a one-man war to expose the plot to control our world.

A strong character required a strong performer, and Carpenter could have found none more appropriate than Roderick Toombs—known to millions of pro-wrestling fans as "Rowdy" Roddy Piper. Having just started the transition from the wrestling ring (one kind of acting) to the big screen (another kind of acting), Piper handled a major role in a major sci-fi film quite well.

The original short story by Ray Nelson, "Eight O'Clock in the Morning," was first published in 1963 in an issue of *The Magazine of Fantasy and Science Fiction*. Nelson collaborated with artist Bill Wray (cartoonist for *Mad* magazine and *The Ren and Stimpy* cartoons, as well as painter of beautiful urban landscapes) in 1986 to produce a comic book story called "Nada" in *Alien Encounters*.

Carpenter drew from Nelson's short story to write the screenplay. But since his girlfriend Sandy King and Roddy Piper helped with much of the dialogue, the director was compelled to credit Frank Armitage—a pseudonym—as the screenwriter.

Makeup artist Francisco X. Perez—credited as Frank Carissosa—created the decayed cadaver-like makeup for the aliens, based on Carpenter's vision of zombiesque villains. Abandoning the idea of designing a high-tech alien, the creatures in *They Live* were decomposed and, as such, in need of whatever the Earth's population had to offer.

The fight scene to end all fight scenes—inspired by the John Wayne–Victor McLaglen epic dustup in 1952's *The Quiet Man*—between Piper and Keith David lasted more than five minutes. Despite its spontaneous look, the tussle was rehearsed for a month and a half between Piper (a natural, considering his wrestling and boxing backgrounds), David, and stunt coordinator Jeff Imada. The shooting of the scene took three days, with very few of the punches being pulled.

They Live was produced on a budget of $3 million and opened at the number one spot in American theaters, grossing double that amount the first week. The film fell off the domestic charts quickly (worldwide box office numbers are not available), but still totaled more than $13 million in US ticket sales for Carpenter's movie with a message.

Species

Synopsis

- 1995—American/Metro-Goldwyn-Mayer—108 min./color
- Director: Roger Donaldson
- Original music: Christopher Young
- Film editing: Conrad Buff
- Production design: John Muto

Cast

- Ben Kingsley (Xavier Fitch)
- Michael Madsen (Preston Lennox)
- Alfred Molina (Dr. Stephen Arden)
- Forest Whitaker (Dan Smithson)
- Marg Helgenberger (Dr. Laura Baker)
- Natasha Henstridge (Sil)
- Michelle Williams (Young Sil)
- Whip Hubley (John Carey)

An American government program, known as "SETI"—Search for Extra Terrestrial Intelligence, has been in operation for thirty years. In a government lab in Utah, lab technicians prepare to terminate a young girl in a glass cage who's been under their study. She crashes through the glass and escapes by hopping onto a freight train, showing she certainly is no ordinary girl. She effortlessly flings a lecherous hobo across the boxcar, killing him. The girl steals a suitcase and changes trains, heading toward Los Angeles.

The head of the government project, Xavier Fitch, assembles a crack team to track her down. Preston Lennox is a freelance assassin, brought in whenever the government needs "a problem solved." Dan Smithson is an empath—a "seer" who can read the emotions and rationale of someone's actions. Dr. Laura Baker is a top biologist, and Dr. Stephen Arden is a professor of anthropology and behavior.

Alone on the train, the young girl dreams of being chased by a fearsome, spike-laden Ghost Train and is startled to find dozens of slithering tentacles bursting from her body. She has turned into a huge cocoon, transforming into a beautiful young woman. She kills a train conductor and takes her uniform.

Fitch addresses his search team, revealing that "SIL" (as she is called) is the result of alien DNA (received in a galactic communication) combined with a human egg. SIL has the ability to mature at a very rapid rate. The team is assigned to "search and destroy" the alien.

SIL arrives in LA, with the team not far behind. They attempt to create a pure alien from the DNA, in the hopes of learning its behavior. But the experiment goes awry, as Laura and Preston are trapped in the test chamber with the rapidly growing creature. Fitch refuses to let them out, citing it's against procedural protocol. He yields at the last moment, and the creature is incinerated in the chamber.

The alien girl goes to a nightclub, where she picks up a man. She goes home with him, but decides he's not her type and kills him. The team discovers the body, and they deduce that SIL is attempting to mate. On the run, SIL is struck

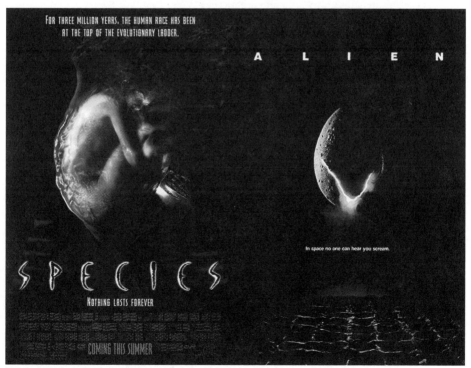

US one-sheet—*Species* and US advance one-sheet—*Alien*.

by a hit-and-run driver and ends up in the hospital. The ER doctor is astonished to watch her broken shoulder repair itself in mere seconds.

SIL leaves with John Carey, the handsome Good Samaritan who brought her in. At his home, SIL tries to mate with John, but kills him in his hot tub. The team arrives as she escapes, stealing a car and some clothes. She invades a home, tying up the female owner. SIL cuts her own thumb off, which, amazingly, regenerates, them removes the thumb of her captive.

The team cases the nightclub where SIL had been the night before. She shows up, and the team takes off after her in a car chase. But the cunning SIL has brought the homeowner along as a hostage and has loaded the auto with gasoline. She jumps just before the car explodes in a fiery ball. The team finds SIL's severed thumb and believes the case is closed.

But SIL has dyed and cut her hair and is not stalking the team. Pres and Laura have fallen for each other, while SIL seduces Professor Arden. She kills him after mating, transforming into a horrifying creature—part lizard, part gargoyle, part machine. The team breaks out the heavy artillery, and they go after SIL with flamethrowers.

Moving through the sewers of LA, SIL grabs Fitch and kills him. The pregnant SIL rapidly comes to full term and gives birth. The toddler-sized newborn feeds on a rat, catching it with a long, darting tongue. Dan burns the infant creature in self-defense but slips, nearly falling into a blazing river of oil.

Laura becomes stuck while SIL chokes Lennox with her long tentacles. He cuts himself free and empties his automatic weapon into SIL. She falls into the inferno as Pres frees Laura and they pull Dan to safety. But SIL isn't done yet, grabbing Dan in a deadly tug-of-war. Pres fires a huge shotgun charge into the beast, killing SIL.

Afterwords

Many filmgoers noted the similarities in the appearance of SIL with the creature from 1979's *Alien*. It's no surprise, as Swiss artist and designer H. R. Giger brought his distinctive biomechanic style to both creatures. Once again, Giger's book of illustrations *Necronomicon*, was the only influence needed to convince producers that he was the right person to create SIL. It would be the rare chance to combine something scary with something sensual.

But in the end, Giger was disappointed, feeling MGM was too reliant on the previous success of *Alien* to let his work on *Species* stand on its own. For example, one advance poster for *Species* featured SIL curled into a fetal position against a black background—closely resembling the *Alien* poster with the face-hugger egg.

Citing costs, MGM was hesitant to shoot the dream sequence where SIL imagines the Ghost Train bearing down on her. Giger, who had also designed the spike and skull-laden train, paid $100,000 out of his own pocket to cover the shoot (although only a small portion of it was included in the final cut). Add in extensive legal wrangling over unused promotional materials, and one can understand why the studio does not receive a holiday card from Giger.

Canadian model Natasha Henstridge was only twenty years old when she won the role of the alien SIL, allowing her to make the move from a career in modeling to the world of films (she would reprise the role in two of the *Species* sequels). With much of the alien effects performed with CGI by Boss Film Studios, and a full-sized animatronic figure built by Steve Johnson and XFX Inc., Henstridge was spared the discomfort usually associated with playing an otherworldly being.

The actress did have the unique honor of cutting off her own thumb—with some help from makeup wizard Johnson. With her real thumb folded under, a latex prosthetic thumb was attached in its place. She then cut it off, with CGI from Boss allowing it to grow back.

Other members of the cast included Michael Madsen, who has stated he was very proud of *Species*, but felt the first sequel—where he reprised his character—was not very good at all. Marg Helgenberger recalled the sewer scenes as looking very cool, but the cave scene "really, really sucked." Alfred Molina noted that despite the fact the cast came from a wide variety of backgrounds, they quickly gelled into a unit that "got on really well."

Species brought in $60 million in domestic box office gross, with another $53 million overseas. Totaling more than $110 million around the world, the film had enough legs to prompt a sequel. But *Species II* in 1998 was unable to break past the $20 million line, despite a production budget of $35 million.

No matter, the franchise was kept alive with Sci-Fi Channel's *Species III* in 2004 (followed by a release to the video market) and a fourth entry, the direct-to-video *Species—The Awakening* in 2007. By then, there was nothing remotely associated with the original 1995 film, other than having *Species* in the title.

Independence Day

Synopsis

- 1996—American/Twentieth Century-Fox—142 min./color
- Director: Roland Emmerich
- Original music: David Arnold
- Film editing: David Brenner
- Production design: Oliver Scholl, Patrick Tatopoulos

Cast

- Will Smith (Captain Steven Hiller)
- Bill Pullman (President Thomas J. Whitmore)
- Jeff Goldblum (David Levinson)
- Mary McDonnell (Marilyn Whitmore)
- Judd Hirsch (Julius Levinson)
- Margaret Colin (Constance Spano)

- Randy Quaid (Russell Casse)
- Robert Loggia (General William Grey)
- James Rebhorn (Defense Secretary James Nimziki)
- Harvey Fierstein (Marty Gilbert)
- Vivica A. Fox (Jasmine Dubrow)
- James Duval (Miguel Casse)
- Guiseppe Andrews (Troy Casse)
- Lisa Jakub (Alicia Casse)
- Ross Bagley (Dylan)
- Mae Whitman (Patricia Whitman)
- Brent Spiner (Doctor Brakish Okun)
- Harry Connick Jr. (Captain Jimmy Walker)
- Adam Baldwin (Major Mitchell)

July 2nd—The dark, lonely solitude of the moon is broken as a vast spacecraft passing by sends the lunar dust into tremors. A deadly shadow engulfs the moon, with the Earth on its horizon. A remote tracking post in New Mexico intercepts the ominous drone of the alien's radio signal.

At the Pentagon in Washington, D.C., General Grey of Space Command hurriedly notifies Defense Secretary Nimziki and President Whitmore of the impending arrival of an unknown visitor from space. A veteran combat pilot from the Persian Gulf War, Whitmore is blasted by the media as a wimp. White House Director of Communications Connie Spano has her hands full trying to preserve his honor and image.

In New York City, David Levinson beats his father Julius in a chess game in Central Park. The young Levinson heads off to his job as a broadcast satellite technician for Compact Cable. With his boss Marty, he finds the approaching spacecraft has interrupted satellite transmissions.

In Imperial Valley, California, crop duster Russell Casse, in a drunken stupor, dusts the wrong crops. The president and his staff are informed that more than thirty smaller craft (although they each are fifteen miles in diameter!) have broken off from the mother ship and are expected to arrive in less than thirty minutes. The whole world is threatened by these approaching craft, as Russia beams live TV pictures of the billowing clouds that precede the warships' arrival.

The president listens in horror as an AWACS tracking plane is engulfed in a fiery ball created by the alien craft. He takes a firm stand by staying at the White House, while ordering the government's leaders into a safe area. Whitman and Grey fear hostilities from these unknown visitors.

Casse, trying to soothe his hangover in a local diner, is tormented by some local yahoos. They remind him of his claim that he was once kidnapped by aliens in a UFO. But their scourge is broken by tremors as an alien craft blankets the sky.

Across America, the icons of freedom and democracy are covered by the dim shadows of the huge alien spaceships. David discovers the alien signal is a coordinating countdown for the craft that blanket the world. In six hours, time will be up. His ex-wife happens to be Connie, and David convinces his dad to drive to D.C. Once there, he hopes to persuade the president, with whom he once had a fistfight, of his theory.

In Southern California, Marine Captain Steven Hiller leaves for El Toro Air Base, although his girlfriend Jasmine would prefer he stay. Elsewhere in California, the president's wife is pressed to leave quickly. David makes his way to the White House, and Whitmore reluctantly accepts his theory.

When a military helicopter's attempts to communicate with the aliens are met with total destruction, Whitmore decides to evacuate Washington. As Air Force One streaks for the sky, the countdown concludes—time's up. Powerful blasts of energy burst from the spaceships, and landmarks like the Empire State Building and the White House are obliterated. The aliens wage their attack, and millions perish in explosions and fire. Jasmine and her son Dylan barely escape by diving into a tunnel stairwell.

July 3rd—The president and his entourage are safe in the sky, but there's no word of his wife. Hiller and his hotdog buddy Jimmy Walker join a squadron of Marine jet fighters who engage hundreds of alien fighter ships. Their efforts to damage the warships are thwarted by an invisible force field. The aliens inflict heavy casualties on the brave fighter pilots, and Jimmy is killed during a dangerous maneuver.

The fight is now a personal one for Hiller, and he engages a lone alien fighter in a fierce game of cat and mouse. He ejects from his plane, and the alien crashes in the desert. Hiller taunts the damaged craft, yelling, "*Who's* the man? *Who's* the man?" When a spindly alien creature suddenly emerges, Hiller slugs it, saying, "Welcome to Earth!"

On Air Force One, Nimziki advocates a full nuclear strike against the aliens, and David interferes by objecting to the use of atomic weaponry. The argument is stilled by David's father, who reminds everyone that it was David who saved the lives he did by breaking the countdown code. Julius contends the government's known about alien encounters ever since the Roswell UFO of the 1950s. When the president assures him that there is no Area 51, Nimziki sheepishly responds, "That's not entirely accurate."

Meanwhile, Jasmine finds the president's wife, who's been seriously injured in a helicopter crash. The president lands at Area 51, finding a huge operation of covert research. Major Mitchell and the quirky Dr. Okun welcome the president. Everyone stares in awe and disbelief at a captured UFO and aliens, kept like museum exhibits. Okun calls it "The Freak Show."

The president challenges David to decipher the aliens' technology. Hiller, along with Casse and an array of mobile vans, arrives at Area 51 with the unconscious alien in tow. Okun heads a team to examine the alien, but it wakes and takes Okun hostage. Whitmore offers a truce, but the alien telepathically reveals its plans—death to Earthlings. The alien is killed in a hail of military gunfire.

Inside Area 51 in *Independence Day*.

The president orders a nuclear strike, while David and Connie realize they still love each other. Hiller hijacks a chopper and finds Jasmine and the president's wife. Houston is the first nuclear target, but the atomic blast has no effect on the alien craft.

The president's wife is brought to a hospital, but it's too late. She quietly passes, leaving the president and his little girl Patricia alone.

July 4th—David, in a drunken rampage, suggests that everyone continue to ecologically mess up the planet so the aliens won't want it. His father consoles him, believing that everyone can lose faith. He helps his son up from the cold concrete floor, so he won't catch cold.

David is suddenly struck by this brilliantly simple idea—give the aliens a "cold," in the form of a computer virus. Placing a virus in the mother ship should disable the shields on all the spacecraft, making them vulnerable. Nimziki jeers at the idea, and the president fires the defense secretary.

Through low-tech Morse code, the world is notified of the planned counterstrike during the virus attack. Every available pilot, able-bodied or not, is recruited for the mission. Casse and Whitman join in as well. Hiller marries Jasmine in an impromptu ceremony.

With Steve to pilot the Roswell alien craft, David will get the ultimate ecological chance to save the world. In a stirring speech to the pilots, the president proclaims, "Today—we celebrate our Independence Day!"

Hiller and Levinson soar off into space as the fighter pilots wait to attack. The pair make their way through the vast and spindly interior of the mother ship. They dock, where the virus is uploaded into the alien's computers.

In the skies, an initial missile is still blocked by the invisible shield, but Whitmore insists on a second shot. The virus has now taken effect—the missiles penetrate and strike the ship with explosive force. Alien fighters are quick to respond, and a wild dogfight ensues.

On the mother ship, Hiller and Levinson become stuck and appear to be doomed. The fighter planes can't do enough damage to disable the alien ship, and it prepares to fire its devastating energy pulse into the Area 51 base.

All missiles are spent, but Casse comes to the rescue with one final weapon. He heads toward the vulnerable cone of the warship, but his missile jams and does not launch. He sacrifices himself by flying into the cone, laughing at his unseen enemies with "Hello, boys—I'm back!" The jet and its onboard missile explode, taking the huge warship down in flames.

The word is spread across the world—the aliens can be defeated. Meanwhile, Hiller and Levinson fire a disabling nuclear missile into the belly of the mother ship. The impact shakes them free, and they make a quick exit from the mother ship as it explodes in a shower of glowing debris. The heroes appear to be enveloped in the speeding and fiery remains of the ship, but a faint signal is picked up on radar.

With their ship crashed into the desert floor of Nevada, Hiller and Levinson are embraced by Jasmine and Connie. The president and General Grey offer their congratulations. Amid the exploding and burning ruins of the alien ships, the president's daughter offers a simple wish of celebration—"Happy Fourth of July, Daddy."

Afterwords

Writer/producer/director Roland Emmerich and writer/producer Dean Devlin took great pains to pay homage to the entire genre of sci-fi with 1996's *Independence Day*. Located within the 145-minute epic were no less than sixteen references, direct or indirect, to some of the greatest sci-fi films ever made.

- *When Worlds Collide* (1952)/*Kronos* (1957)—Both films provided the basis for the early scene in *ID4* where astronomers used photographic plates to illustrate a definite change in the position of celestial bodies.
- *The Thing* (1981)—John Carpenter's version of the 1951 Christian Nyby/ Howard Hawks classic featured a scene where Wilfred Brimley performed a dissection on a dog-turned-alien. *ID4* featured a scene where an almost unrecognizable Brent Spiner performed a similar dissection on the alien retrieved by Will Smith.
- *Warner Brothers/Marvin the Martian*—The huge warships had a design that was very reminiscent of the wide, flat spaceship with a vertical fin, piloted

by Bugs Bunny's extraterrestrial enemy Marvin the Martian in cartoons like *Haredevil Hare* (1948) and *Hare-way to the Stars* (1958).

- *Airplane!* (1981)—Randy Quaid mimicked Lloyd Bridges' recurring regret that "I picked the wrong day to give up . . ." by stating "I picked a helluva day to quit drinking" as he went off to battle the aliens.
- *2001: A Space Odyssey* (1968)—HAL, the computer villain, was parodied when Jeff Goldblum powered up his laptop once he was connected to the mother ship. An ominous mechanical orb appeared on his screen, as the computer blankly said, "Good morning, Dave."
- *Close Encounters of the Third Kind* (1977)—Civilized communications with the aliens were attempted by means of a sequence of flashing colored lights. A similar array of lights was presented, by helicopter, in *ID4*. The response was slightly different, however. *CE3K* answered with music and pulses of light; *ID4* answered with a deadly laser blast.
- *Jurassic Park* (1993)—Jeff Goldblum lampooned his own character in Steven Spielberg's multimillion-dollar dinosaur film. Frantically leaving the grip of the mother ship, he urged Will Smith to "Go faster . . . you must go faster!" much as he did in *Jurassic Park* from the back of the Land Rover as a snapping T. rex advanced on him.
- *Poltergeist* (1980)—The innocent observation of the late Heather O'Rourke, who peered into a TV screen and said, "They're baaack!" is similar to Randy Quaid's announcement to the aliens. Bathed in the blue glow of the death ray, he stated, "Hello, boys—I'm baaaack!"
- *Right Stuff* (1983)—Sam Shepard, as air pioneer Chuck Yeager, nearly killed himself by planting an F-104 Starfighter into the ground in Philip Kaufman's tribute to America's early days of the space program. Shepard walked toward the camera, with the wreckage smoldering in the background. *ID4* had heroes Will Smith and Jeff Goldblum show up in a similar scene, having crashed their alien craft into the desert floor after destroying the mother ship.
- *War of the Worlds* (1952)—George Pal updated H. G. Wells' 1898 Martian invasion by having the aliens succumb to germs found on Earth. *ID4* basically provided the same sort of demise for the aliens, although the "germs" in this case were a "computer" virus.
- *Stargate* (1994)—Emmerich and Devlin tipped their caps to their own previous cinematic accomplishment; during the LA holocaust, a bus crashed into a billboard that happened to be featuring *Stargate*. (This shot was removed from the final theatrical cut.)
- *Alien* (1979)—The general gangliness and appearance of the invading creatures, including the design of the exoskeleton, drew heavily from the H. R. Giger design for *Alien*.
- *Star Wars* (1977)—The opening shot of the alien ship revealed itself in the same, long overhead shot of the battle cruiser in the opening of Spielberg's blockbuster space epic. Also, President Whitmore's unsuccessful attempt

to launch a missile into the core of the alien ship was similar to Luke Skywalker's first assault on the Death Star.

- *Planet of the Apes* (1968) and *Escape from New York* (1981)—The scene of mass destruction featured a shot of a fallen and destroyed Statue of Liberty, reminiscent of the chilling final shot in *Planet of the Apes*. The broken icon of freedom also appeared as part of the fallen Big Apple in John Carpenter's *Escape from New York*.
- *The Day the Earth Stood Still* (1951)—Russell Casse's kids were watching the classic Robert Wise sci-fi film when the aliens made their first appearances in the sky.

The combination of sci-fi adventure and big-screen summer action flick resulted in a very successful payday for *Independence Day*. The writing/producing team of Dean Devlin and Roland Emmerich had shown promise with *Stargate* in 1994, but *ID4* paid off big, earning more than $300 million in the US, with over $500 million overseas.

Having a worldwide total of more than three-quarters of a billion dollars, *ID4* seemed to be begging for a sequel. Twenty years after the first invasion, Emmerich and Devlin plan to produce not one but two films to return to the story. *ID Forever Part One* has a scheduled release date of summer in 2016 (Lord knows, that could change). There's no word if any of the original cast would return.

Mars Attacks!

Synopsis

- 1996—American/Warner Brothers—106 min./color
- Director: Tim Burton
- Original music: Danny Elfman
- Film editing: Chris Lebenzon
- Production design: Wynn Thomas
- Based on the 1962 Topps Trading Cards

Cast

- Jack Nicholson (President James Dale, Art Land)
- Glenn Close (First Lady Marsha Dale)
- Annette Bening (Barbara Land)
- Pierce Brosnan (Professor Donald Kessler)
- Danny Devito (Rude Gambler)
- Martin Short (Press Secretary Jerry Ross)
- Sarah Jessica Parker (Nathalie Lake)
- Michael J. Fox (Jason Stone)
- Rod Steiger (General Decker)
- Tom Jones (Himself)

- Lukas Haas (Richie Norris)
- Natalie Portman (Taffy Dale)
- Jim Brown (Byron Williams)
- Lisa Marie (Martian Girl)
- Sylvia Sidney (Grandma Norris)
- Paul Winfield (General Casey)
- Pam Grier (Louise Williams)
- Jack Black (Billy Glenn Norris)
- Janice Rivera (Cindy)
- Joe Don Baker (Glenn Norris)
- O-Lan Jones (Sue Ann Norris)
- Christina Applegate (Sharona)
- Ray J (Cedric)
- Brandon Hammond (Neville)

Four miles outside of Lockjaw, Kentucky, the savory smell of barbecue tickles the nostrils of a local farmer. But the appetizing aroma becomes highly unappetizing as a stampeding herd of blazing cattle passes before his startled eyes.

Thousands of flying saucers are preparing to advance on the Earth. US President James Dale awaits the arrival, soliciting opinions from his staff. Press Secretary Jerry Ross thinks it's a great PR opportunity, while hawkish Army General Decker believes it's a national threat. Soft-spoken Army General Casey agrees with Professor Donald Kessler, who thinks there's no harm intended by the Martians' visit. Meanwhile, the first lady frets over what material would look best in redecorating the Roosevelt Room.

Across the country in Las Vegas, former Heavyweight Boxing Champion of the World Byron Williams calms separated wife Louise about their mischievous boys' behavior. Barbara Land is a recovering alcoholic, while her conniving husband Art has grandiose plans to open the Galaxy, the best casino in Vegas.

In New York City, vain GNN reporter Jason Stone and his trendy and vapid girlfriend, TV host Nathalie Lake, watch as the president addresses the nation. Dale confirms that visitors from Mars will soon arrive.

Out in Perkinsville, Kansas, the dysfunctional trailer-trash Norris family awaits the visit from space. Young Billy Glenn Norris thrills to the thought of pulling "Martian detail" in the army. In Washington, D.C., Louise Williams is a metro bus driver. During her route, she catches her truant sons, Cedric and Neville, deftly shooting video-game aliens in an arcade.

Nathalie interviews Professor Kessler about the Martians, and they flirt on camera, which makes Jason jealous. Suddenly, a Martian cuts into the broadcast. Dressed in flowing robes, the bare-brained, large-orbed creature barks in an unintelligible tongue. Marsha Dale refuses to "have that thing" in her house.

The president and his staff watch as Kessler demonstrates a language-translating device, which might still have a few bugs in it. At an Al-Anon meeting, Barbara believes the Martians intend on being peaceful and forging an ecologically safe existence.

The Martian ambassador adjourns Congress in *Mars Attacks!*.

Billy Glenn says goodbye to his folks and girlfriend Sharona as he leaves for military service. His soft-spoken brother Richie is considered the outcast of the family and is relegated to taking his senile grandma back to the rest home. Grandma loves the yodeling songs of Slim Whitman.

General Casey is tapped to personally welcome the Martians, to the obvious disapproval of General Decker. A crowd of thousands waits in the desert of Pahrump, Nevada, while Jason, Nathalie, and her Chihuahua, Poppy, report the event live for their respective networks.

All of a sudden, a spinning silver disc appears out of the sky and lands on six crab-like legs. A long, tongue-like ramp extends from the bottom. The Martian ambassador, wearing a flowing red robe and clear bubble helmet, descends with eight armed escorts. General Casey welcomes them, as the translating device reveals the Martians have "come in peace."

One of the crowd releases a symbolic dove, which is immediately destroyed by the Martian's ray gun. Casey is next, as live TV covers his demise. All hell breaks loose, and Billy Glenn is burned alive defending his country. Jason reaches out to save Nathalie, but she ends up holding his smoldering hand, as he has been vaporized. Nathalie and Poppy are taken aboard the departing ship.

The president is aghast at the events, but Kessler suggests the possibility of a misunderstanding. Dale issues an olive branch in a radio broadcast, but the Martians think little of his offer. They conduct fiendish experiments on their hostages, including grafting Poppy's barking head onto Nathalie's beautiful, bikini-clad body.

The Martians issue an apology to Dale, requesting the chance to address a joint session of Congress. But it's merely a dirty trick, as the meeting turns into another massacre. Grandma Norris seems amused as she watches the carnage on TV. "They blew up Congress!" she laughs, as the Martians take Kessler hostage.

General Decker insists on using nuclear weapons against the Martians, but Dale disagrees, screaming at the general to "Shut up! Shut up!" Meanwhile, Kessler and Nathalie share an intimate moment on the spaceship, considering Kessler's head now has no body and Nathalie's head is attached to Poppy's canine body.

Jerry picks up a beautiful bubble-headed blonde for a tryst in the Kennedy Room of the White House. But the mood is broken when she bites off his finger and turns out to be a Martian in disguise. Infiltrating the first family's bedroom, it takes the president hostage, only to be blown to pieces by the Secret Service.

Donning pressure suits, thousands of Martians prepare for invasion. One readies a bubble-topped mechanical robot, equipped with huge pincer grips for hands. Thousands of ships descend on Earth as the invasion begins. The Martians play a balancing act with the Washington Monument. They bowl a strike with the statues on Easter Island. They recarve Mount Rushmore into the image of Martians.

The first lady is crushed by the Nancy Reagan Chandelier. Cedric and Neville Williams, on a school tour at the White House, put their arcade skills to work. Grabbing ray guns, they blast Martians just like video targets.

In Vegas, Art Land and his schemes come to a crashing end, as the Martians topple the Galaxy Casino. Byron needs to get to his family in Washington, and Barbara Land has a plane loaded with supplies. All they need is a pilot. Singer Tom Jones has his show rudely interrupted by Martians, who prove to be better warmongers than backup singers. Jones, who just happens to be a pilot, hooks up with Byron, Barbara, a rude gambler and a casino hostess, Cindy.

A distraught Dale listens to his phone in horror as the French president is disintegrated by the Martians, as the Eiffel Tower topples in the distance. Decker finally convinces the president to use nuclear weapons, but the Martians merely suck up the explosion and inhale it like helium, complete with high-pitched voices.

Glenn and Sue Ann Norris are smashed in their trailer by the alien robot, as Richie escapes to save his grandma. The rude gambler tries to bribe a Martian with his Rolex watch, but is blasted to bits.

As Richie arrives at the rest home, the Martians wheel a huge ray gun toward Grandma Norris. Listening to Slim Whitman on headphones, she has no clue as to what's about to become of her. But she accidentally pulls her headphones from their jack, and the room is filled with the yodeling tones of "Indian Love Call." The Martians cringe; they quiver; their heads explode in a sloppy green mess. Their Achilles' heel has been found.

Decker confronts Martians in the war room, and they reduce him to the size of a bug, then squash him under an alien boot. Dale makes a heartfelt plea to the invaders for peaceful coexistence, but they trick him with a fake handshake and plant the Martian flag in him, killing the president.

While anarchy reigns in the streets, Richie and his grandma reach KWBS Radio and broadcast Slim Whitman across the land. At the Vegas airstrip, Byron diverts the Martians, taking all comers in a bare-knuckle fistfight. The rest of the group escapes in Barbara's plane. The aliens finally swarm over the champ as the plane soars overhead.

The strains of Slim Whitman continue to fell the Martians around the world. Kessler and Nathalie share a final moment together before the mother ship crashes into the sea. The military restores order, and Byron somehow has made his way back to his family in Washington.

In a mariachi-tinged tribute, Richie and his grandma receive the Congressional Medal of Honor from Taffy Dale, the first family's young daughter and only surviving member. Somewhere in the remote wilderness, Cindy and Barbara return to nature, as Tom Jones sings, "It's Not Unusual."

Afterwords

For those old enough to remember, a nickel could buy a lot of thrills in 1962. Among those five-cent gems was the Topps Chewing Gum series of trading cards called *Mars Attacks*. Originally called *Attack from Space*, the fifty-five-card set told a story of a Martian invasion. It was gory, it was sexy, it was brutal (enough so that thirteen of the cards were redrawn on the orders of Topps' president, Joel Shorin).

The bare-brained aliens were largely influenced by the Metaluna mutant from the 1955 sci-fi classic *This Island Earth*. The entire card series started after the creators saw the cover of a ten-year-old EC comic, *Weird Science*, issue sixteen. Painted by legendary comic artist Wally Wood, it depicted a scene of kids watching in amazement as ugly Martians landed on Earth.

The *Mars Attacks* cards were quite popular with kids in 1962; they weren't very popular with their parents. A flood of letters, as well as a phone call from a district attorney in Connecticut complaining about the shocking nature of the artwork, marked a swift end to the success of the cards.

As one might expect, *Mars Attacks* (or simply, Martian cards, as we in the neighborhood called them) remained the stuff of legend. Being on the market for such a short time, our discussions led to (largely hearsay) estimates of their "C of C" (coefficiency of coolness). Several attempts at reprints in the 1980s answered our by-then-adult curiosity about the cards and piqued the interest of an entirely new generation of sci-fi fans.

In the early 1990s, filmmaker Tim Burton asked his friend and associate Jonathan Gems to write a screenplay based on the scary cards Burton remembered from his childhood. With Warner Bros. acquiring the film rights on behalf of Burton, Gems' original script budgeted out at an impossible $280 million. Twelve drafts later, Burton had a script that he and Warner Bros. could agree on—still with an impressive budget of $75 million.

Borrowing from 1970s producer Irwin Allen's concept of filling a disaster film with a myriad of A-list stars, Burton wanted Warren Beatty or Paul Newman for the role of President James Dale. Jack Nicholson—no lightweight himself—took the part, as well as that of real estate developer Art Land.

Likewise, Susan Sarandon was targeted for Barbara Land before Annette Bening got the part (as close to Beatty as Burton could get). Stockard Channing, Diane Keaton, and Meryl Streep were considered for the first lady, but then Glenn Close took the role. Hugh Grant might have played Professor Donald Kessler, but Pierce Brosnan—having just started his tenure as 007 in 1995's *GoldenEye*—played the scientist instead.

It's clear that Burton had major performance firepower on the screen to face off against the Martian attack. Combined, the cast accounted for thirty past or future Oscar nominations (not to mention two additional for Burton himself), as well as five Academy Award wins.

Coincidentally, *Independence Day* opened in the same year as *Mars Attacks!* (Burton claimed to have no knowledge of the concurrent production), although *ID4* beat Burton's film to the screen by more than five months. But while *ID4* took itself seriously and featured a mostly B-list cast (Will Smith was still considered a TV star), *Mars Attacks!* went in the completely opposite direction. It featured the aforementioned big-name cast and planted its tongue firmly in alien cheek.

While the people of Earth won the war against the aliens in both films, *ID4* was the clear winner at the box office against *Mars Attacks!* With the previously noted budget of $75 million, *Mars Attacks!* struggled to bring in only half that amount in domestic box office. With overseas ticket sales taking in more than $63 million, the total barely broke $100 million.

Although Warner Bros. spent $20 million in marketing *Mars Attacks!*, many people felt they didn't have a proper handle on promoting the film in America. While Burton didn't at first notice it, he did believe European audiences got his film better than American filmgoers—even though the Europeans had never seen the Topps cards.

Deep Impact

Synopsis

- 1998—American/Paramount/Dreamworks SKG—121 min./color
- Director: Mimi Leder
- Original music: James Horner
- Film editing: Paul Cichocki, David Rosenbloom
- Production design: Leslie Dilley

Cast

- Robert Duvall (Spurgeon Tanner)
- Téa Leoni (Jenny Lerner)
- Elijah Wood (Leo Biederman)
- Vanessa Redgrave (Robin Lerner)

- Morgan Freeman (President Tom Beck)
- Maximilian Schell (Jason Lerner)
- James Cromwell (Treasury Secretary Alan Rittenhouse)
- Laura Innes (Beth Stanley)
- Leelee Sobieski (Sarah Hotchner)
- Rya Kihlstedt (Chloe)
- Charles Martin Smith (Dr. Marcus Wolf)

It's a starry night in Richmond, Virginia, and a high school class of young astronomers scans the sky with their telescopes. One young man, Leo Biederman, spots an unusual object and photographs it. He forwards it to Dr. Marcus Wolf, a preeminent astronomer in Arizona and supporter of the kids' work.

With a little investigation, the doctor determines the object is a comet—set on a collision path with Earth. He names the heavenly body Wolf-Biederman and, while driving to notify officials of the dangerous discovery, dies in a fiery accident on the highway.

One year later, US Treasury Secretary Alan Rittenhouse suddenly announces his resignation, and gossip over the reason abounds at the offices of cable news channel MSNBC. Reporter Jenny Lerner investigates and finds, apparently based on his phone conversations, the secretary was having an affair with someone named "Ellie."

Lerner confronts Rittenhouse about Ellie, and all he really admits is that he wants to spend time with his family. She leaves, only to be suddenly forced off the highway by FBI agents. Taken to an empty hotel kitchen, Jenny is stunned to find Tom Beck, the president of the United States, waiting for her. He convinces the reporter to wait two days before doing anything with her information, promising her a front-and-center position at his press conference, which will explain everything.

Ever the perceptive journalist, Jenny notes that the President mentioned E.L.E., rather than the name of Ellie. With an Internet search, Lerner finds the letters are an acronym for Extinction Level Event—the kind of occurrence that killed off all the dinosaurs on Earth.

Jenny meets up with her dad, Jason, and his new bride, Chloe—an encounter that is somewhat awkward, as Jenny is clearly preoccupied with her secret. Chloe's suggestion of having an encouraging "life goes on" attitude prompts peals of ironic laughter from Jenny.

At the White House press conference, the president explains that a massive object in space—the Wolf-Biederman comet—is bound for a collision with Earth. Russia and the United States have assembled a spacecraft named the *Messiah*, with the mission of landing on the comet and destroying it before the impact happens.

Jenny gets her question—actually several—but the most pointed question wonders if Secretary Rittenhouse's resignation was based on the probability that the world is doomed. The president calmly avers that Earth will prevail.

The Biederman comet slams into the ocean in *Deep Impact.*

Leo Biederman becomes an instant celebrity, as do the astronauts of the *Messiah.* Veteran space traveler Spurgeon Tanner finds himself an outcast among the other astronauts. They resent him since he hasn't been specifically in training for this mission and is only a familiar and reassuring face for the public to see.

A space shuttle lifts off from Cape Canaveral, carrying the crew to the orbiting launch site of *Messiah.* They transfer to the spacecraft and begin their voyage of many months to Wolf-Biederman.

As the *Messiah* approaches the comet through its tail, the crew arm the nuclear weapons that will be used to destroy the icy rock before it reaches Earth. The team don their spacesuits, and on Earth, Jenny Lerner mans the anchor desk for MSNBC and reports on the crew's progress. Tanner takes the controls to skillfully guide the craft into the comet.

Their mission is risky—they must land on Wolf-Biederman and plant the nuclear warheads into the comet while the *Messiah* is in darkness. Once it rotates toward the sun, reactive emissions of gas and ice could destroy the craft. The window of time is less than seven hours.

Tanner safely lands the craft, and tethers are deployed to stabilize it. A drilling machine called a Mole begins to auger deeply into the comet, where the weapons will eventually be detonated. But the Mole jams at only a short distance in, and the team is stranded in a crevice. The Mole restarts its mission. Tanner manually flies the *Messiah* in to save them, as the sun rises on the comet's surface.

A sudden eruption of gas blasts one of the astronauts into space, as the *Messiah* recovers the rest of the crew and leaves the surface of Wolf-Biederman. Reaching a safe distance from the comet, the warheads are detonated.

But the explosion does not destroy the comet. President Beck reports the weapons broke it into two pieces—both of which are still heading toward Earth. The remaining contingency plan has two components. One will be a last-minute effort by Russia and the US, who will focus every long-range nuclear warhead at the comets with the hope the impact will knock them off their paths.

The second part involves the random selection of eight hundred thousand people, who will join two hundred thousand leaders, scientists, doctors, artists, and others already chosen. Together, those one million people will be housed, along with plants and animals, in what's being called the Ark—a system of caves deep in the state of Missouri—for two years. The same events are going on in other countries around the world.

Jenny returns to the airwaves to announce the procedures for the lottery, including the exclusion of those over fifty years of age. At the Biederman home, a phone call informs them their family has been preselected. On board the *Messiah*, the crew decide to try and make their way back to Earth.

Leo has good news for his teenage girlfriend, Sarah. If they get married, she and her family will be allowed to move to the Ark with the other preselected folks. At the White House, the president is troubled by the rampant crime and looting that has erupted.

A military bus arrives to pick up the Biedermans and Hotchners, but Sarah's family is not on the list for some reason. She refuses to leave her folks, and the bus heads out without the Hotchners.

At MSNBC, Jenny receives word that her mother, Robin, has taken her own life. Her father finds Jenny in the rain. He is alone, as his new wife has left him, but Jenny is unmoved and leaves in a taxi.

People and animals are moved into the Ark in Missouri, including the Biedermans. But Leo turns back to join Sarah. Jason Lerner visits his daughter in an MSNBC conference room, sharing some family photos in another futile attempt to reconcile with Jenny.

Less than a day remains until the impact of the two comets and the missiles of the world are launched to divert their tracks. Once more, the president takes to the airwaves to report the grim news of failure, with no options remaining.

The smaller of the two comets—Biederman—will land in the Atlantic Ocean, close to the East Coast of the United States. The result of the impact will be tidal waves of enormous size and destruction. The second comet—Wolf—will land in Western Canada soon after, resulting in lingering clouds of dust and debris that will kill all life above ground, much like the fate of the dinosaurs.

Aboard the *Messiah*, Tanner suggests a one-way trip into Wolf to detonate the nukes that remain on the ship. The suicidal mission would blast the bigger comet apart, giving the Earth a better chance of surviving the impact of Biederman. Mission Control in Houston is notified of the crew's plan.

At MSNBC, a rescue helicopter has only enough room for six passengers, although seven production personnel remain. They draw straws and Jenny's boss, Beth, gets the short one, leaving her and her preschool daughter out of luck. Jenny rushes the little girl to the helicopter, insisting that Beth take her on the rescue chopper. She does and it takes off, leaving Jenny alone on the roof.

Leo finds Sarah's house empty and takes a motorbike through the mass of jammed traffic. He locates the Hotchners, who send Leo, Sarah, and her newborn sister away to safety. Meanwhile, Jenny spends the last moments with her father at his beach house.

The Biederman comet roars through the sky and lands in the sea with a devastating impact. Giant waves swallow Jenny and her father, New York City, and the land along the Eastern Seaboard. Leo, Sarah, and her sister climb safely to high ground as the waters wash below them.

The crew of *Messiah* bids goodbye to family members at the Houston Space Center. Tanner guides the spaceship into Wolf, and the comet explodes, with tiny bits of it harmlessly entering the atmosphere.

President Beck makes an address from the steps of the Capitol—being rebuilt—in Washington, D.C., describing the devastation and loss of life around the world, along with his gratitude for the numerous sacrifices made. Thousands upon thousands of survivors cheer as he urges everyone on to a new beginning.

Afterwords

In the world of sci-fi cinema, not all invasions of Earth are organic or robotic. Occasionally, an errant celestial body threatens to eliminate the world as we know it. And the concept is not necessarily new. In 1951, George Pal based his film *When Worlds Collide*, on a 1933 novel of the same title by Philip Wylie and Edwin Balmer.

In the mid-1970s, David Brown and Richard D. Zanuck—producers of mega-hits like 1973's *The Sting* and 1975's *Jaws*—revisited Pal's picture and drew up an outline for a new version. Although the head of Paramount Pictures loved the idea, the project wound up in the dustbin (like so many others in Hollywood).

Nearly twenty years later, the duo resurrected their outline. Bruce Joel Rubin, Oscar-winning writer of 1990's *Ghost*, and Michael Tolkin, Oscar-nominated writer for 1993's *The Player*, teamed up to pen the screenplay for *Deep Impact*. Mimi Leder, a director known for episodic TV and movies made for the tube, had one feature film under her belt before *Deep Impact*—1997's *The Peacemaker*, an action-espionage flick with George Clooney.

Special effects for the film were broken into three broad areas of focus—the comet itself, model work for the *Messiah* spacecraft, and the resulting tidal wave. Filmmakers were very conscious of keeping *Deep Impact* grounded in scientific reality. Experts like the astrogeological husband-and-wife team of Eugene and Carolyn Shoemaker where tapped to advise on the creation and CG animation of the comet.

A ten-foot model of the *Messiah* was built from steel, fiberglass, and aluminum, with fiber optic lighting. While a smaller, six-foot version was also built, the larger model provided the addition of greater details. The art department based their design on the thinking that NASA and Russian space programs would use existing space hardware for the *Messiah*.

With Steven Spielberg executive producing, it was a certainty that ILM would head up the FX work, including the wild water work resulting from the comet's impact into the Atlantic Ocean. After using real water turned into being a washout, the decision was made to model the tidal wave and destruction with computers.

Similar to the same-year/same-plot release of *Independence Day* and *Mars Attacks!* in 1996, the year of 1998 saw the release of *Deep Impact* and *Armageddon* within two months of each other. Spielberg even threatened to sue Touchstone, the studio that produced *Armageddon*, but nothing ever came of it. Both films were filled with big-name stars: Affleck, Willis, Freeman, Duvall, Redgrave, Tyler, Buscemi, and many more.

While *Armageddon* came out on top in the box office, *Deep Impact* still made a very respectable showing. With a budget of $80 million (only 60 percent of what *Armageddon* cost to make), *Deep Impact* pulled in more than $140 million domestically (compared to more than $200 million for *Armageddon*). Overseas, *Deep Impact* put nearly $210 million in its pockets (*Armageddon* grossed over $352 million).

With a total of $350 million in total ticket sales, many filmgoers around the world bought into the scientific reality of *Deep Impact*.

Galaxy Quest

Synopsis

- 1999—American/Dreamworks SKG—102 min./color
- Director: Dean Parisot
- Original music: David Newman
- Film editing: Don Zimmerman
- Production design: Linda DeScenna

Cast

- Tim Allen (Jason Nesmith)
- Sigourney Weaver (Gwen DeMarco)
- Alan Rickman (Alexander Dane)
- Tony Shalhoub (Fred Kwan)
- Sam Rockwell (Guy Fleegman)
- Daryl Mitchell (Tommy Webber)
- Enrico Colantoni (Mathesar)
- Robin Sachs (Sarris)
- Missi Pyle (Laliari)

Galaxy Quest was once a small but popular TV series about the outer space exploits of the crew of the NSEA *Protector*. Eighteen years later, it is the theme of an annual convention for geeks and dweebs who, dressed as their favorite characters, come to celebrate the long-canceled show.

Emceed by actor Guy Fleegman, a minor actor who played a nameless character in the show's final episode, the event allows former cast members to reunite. Blonde bombshell Gwen DeMarco played Lt. Tawny Madison, whose main job was to parrot whatever the ship's onboard computer would say. British actor Alexander Dane portrayed Dr. Lazarus, the alien science officer on the *Protector*, who coined the wordy catchphrase "By Grabthar's hammer, by the suns of Warvan, you shall be avenged." Dane regrets ever taking the part, recalling he was once a great thespian.

Fred Kwan was the technical officer, Sgt. Chen. Quiet and agreeable, he doesn't mind the fans' attention. Tommy Webber, a former child star who played Laredo, the ship's pilot, resents the lateness of the show's star. Self-centered Jason Nesmith, who portrayed Peter Quincy Taggart, commander of the *Protector*, is nowhere to be found.

Nesmith finally shows up, to the indifference of his loathing former coworkers. After some commotion, the cast of *Galaxy Quest* take the stage for their anxious fans. Signing autographs, it's obvious Dane would rather be anywhere else, but Nesmith enjoys the adulation of his fans. And while he holds romantic thoughts of Gwen DeMarco, the feeling isn't mutual.

Without including the others, Jason has booked a personal appearance of his own. An odd-looking group—claiming to be Thermian aliens and led by Mathesar—approaches Nesmith as Commander Taggart and ask for his help. But he brushes them off, believing them to be the fans who hired him for the private gig the next day.

During a stop in the men's room, Nesmith accidentally gets an earful, and it's not good. He realizes he's a laughing stock, as well as not respected by his former coworkers. The reality depresses Jason, and the rest of his day is a daze. He spends the evening watching *Galaxy Quest* reruns and drinking—hard.

Hung over, Nesmith is awakened the next day by Mathesar and the Thermians. Again, they plead for his help or their people will perish at the hands of the villain Sarris. Still thinking they are just a group of fans, Nesmith joins them for a limo trip and takes a nap.

When he wakes up, Jason finds himself on the command deck of a real *Protector* spacecraft. Still not realizing his old TV show has become reality, Nesmith jokes with the crew and videoconfers with Sarris, a reptilian general. The alien states his threatening demands, and Jason kiddingly responds by ordering a full weapons attack. Tiring of the whole scene, Nesmith asks to leave and is given a teleporter device to send him back. Immediately, he soars through the vastness of space back to his patio. It finally strikes him—this is no joke.

Sam Rockwell, Alan Rickman, Tim Allen, Daryl Mitchell, Sigourney Weaver, and Tony Shaloub (L-R) in *Galaxy Quest*.

The rest of the cast are hesitantly attending the grand opening of a retail store, and Nesmith, being late once more, rushes from his car in a parking garage. He accidentally bumps into a *Galaxy Quest* fan, and in the confusion, Jason's real teleporter gets exchanged with the fan's replica.

He excitedly tries to tell the cast about his extraordinary experience, and, of course, they don't believe a bit of what he says. The Thermians arrive, asking everyone to return to the ship to negotiate a truce with Sarris. Disgusted, the cast leave Nesmith, thinking he's still drunk. But fearing that they're passing up a gig, the cast reconsider and suddenly find themselves aboard the *Protector*.

The Thermians greet the cast with awe and reverence. It seems they received the broadcast signals of the old *Galaxy Quest* shows and, believing them to be true, historical documents, have based their entire society on the contents of the series. Needless to say, the cast are stunned.

The cast take their places on the command deck—it seems all their previous performances have been rehearsal for what is now the real thing. Laredo takes the *Protector* out of the spaceport, only slightly scraping it against its side.

The craft is headed to a meeting with Sarris, who wants the Omega Thirteen device. Of course, it was only mentioned once in the final episode of the show, so no one knows what it does. No matter, the Thermians built one from what they saw, and, if mishandled, it could destroy the universe.

Initial negotiations with Sarris don't go well, and he fires on the *Protector*. Nesmith orders the ship to turbospeed, and they land in the middle of a galactic minefield. The ship and the crew are roughed up a bit, but make it through.

Unfortunately, the beryllium sphere—the ship's power source—has been damaged and must be replaced.

Mathesar tries to apologize for failing Nesmith and the cast, and they reveal the truth to him—they are mere actors and *Galaxy Quest* was not historical fact, but pure fiction. The Thermians have only begun to grasp the concept of deception and don't understand.

A source of beryllium is located on a nearby planet, so Nesmith and his crew shuttle down to retrieve some. In a mining camp, they spot cute little aliens—who turn out to be vicious cannibals. Jason takes command, devising a plan to decoy the aliens, while the crew grabs a beryllium sphere.

The scheme almost works—the crew get a sphere into the shuttle, but they have to take off and leave Nesmith behind, surrounded by dozens of aliens. Despite his total lack of ability, Fred is encouraged to retrieve Jason with a digital conveyor on the *Protector*. But his aim is poor, and he transports a pig-lizard instead. It arrives on the ship, but not in its normal state—the creature is completely inside-out, and it explodes.

Jason is left to face off against a thundering beast made from rock. Fred is too scared to attempt another digital conveyance, but Nesmith encourages him to try once more. It works, just as Jason is about to be crushed by the creature. Now famously shirtless, Nesmith returns, to the relief of his coworkers.

Nesmith and his crew plan to go home, but, sadly, the Thermians have no planet to which they can return. Sarris has made his way on board, torturing Mathesar, and insisting on obtaining the Omega Thirteen. Jason admits that he and the cast are actors and the *Galaxy Quest* historical documents were just a TV show. Sarris forces him to apologetically reveal the truth to Mathesar and the Thermian is devastated at the learning the facts.

The villain sets the *Protector*'s core to overload and explode in just nine minutes, but Jason has a plan. Recalling a plot form one of the *Galaxy Quest* episodes, he leads Dane into a fake fight, allowing the pair to subdue Sarris' guards. Meanwhile, Sarris has opened an airlock and is slowly suffocating the Thermians.

Jason and Gwen need to shut the core down and neither of them knows how. Nesmith, however, recalls someone who does. Remembering his collision that exchanged communicators, Jason contacts superfan Brandon on Earth. With the Internet, the teen pulls in his knowledgeable friends to assist, while Tommy watches old shows to bone up on how to fly the ship.

Brandon leads Jason and Gwen to the center of the Omega Thirteen, which is a time machine capable of going back thirteen seconds. As Jason observes, "Time to redeem a single mistake." The pair moves ahead to the chompers—a maze of guillotine-like metal blocks. Ignoring Gwen's protests, Jason safely leads her through the contraption—prompted by Brandon.

Fred cleverly uses the digital conveyor to pull the rock creature from its planet, placing it on board in the midst of a large group of Sarris' guards. Guy and a pretty Thermian named Laliari watch the ensuing mayhem approvingly. In fact, Laliari shows her appreciation by passionately kissing Fred.

A Thermian called Quellek has always idolized Dane, who has remained quietly aloof. That changes when Quellek is mortally wounded by one of Sarris' men. Dane is sincerely moved as Quellek dies and delivers his catchphrase—for the first time with real emotion and conviction. Enraged, he tackles the assailing guard.

Jason and Gwen reach the core and, at Brandon's direction, simply press a blue button to shut the system down. But the seconds continue to tick down as it appears the button had no effect. Facing death, Jason and Gwen embrace, only to find the system safely shutting down with one second to go.

Jason and his crew reach the command deck as the Thermians keep Sarris' men under control. Tommy deftly guides the *Protector* back through the galactic minefield, and Sarris orders his spaceship to give chase. The *Protector* turns around to play a deep-space version of chicken with Sarris' ship.

The villain's arrogance blinds him to the fact that the *Protector* is now magnetically pulling a large group of mines behind it. Tommy sharply veers the *Protector*, leaving the mines directly in the path of Sarris' ship. His spacecraft is destroyed as it collides with dozens of mines.

Everyone celebrates as the *Protector* heads back to Earth, but Mathesar is sad, hoping Jason and his crew would stay on. The Thermians are in need of a commander, and Nesmith believes Mathesar is the right alien for the job.

The *Protector* makes the trip through a black hole, but Sarris has secretly come aboard. Disguised as Fred, he begins to systematically kill Jason and the crew. Seriously wounded, Jason calls for the activation of the Omega Thirteen.

Going back thirteen seconds, Jason is now able to head off the bogus Fred as he enters. As he changes to Sarris, Mathesar is able to render the villain unconscious. The Thermian boldly states the catchphrase of Commander Taggart: "Never give up, never surrender."

But Tommy is unable to slow the ship down as it approaches our planet. Jason and his crew must separate from the *Protector* and the Thermians, or everyone will die. Bidding heartfelt goodbyes, the *Galaxy Quest* cast—with Laliari joining Fred—break away in a shuttle and enter the atmosphere.

With the help of Brandon and his friends, the shuttle is able to land—albeit a bit roughly—at the convention center. Crashing through a wall, the cast emerges to the thundering applause of hundreds of *Galaxy Quest* fans.

But Sarris, still on the command deck, comes out armed and ready to confront Jason. A quick blast from the commander's ray gun eliminates the alien—all to the cheering fans, who believe everything they've seen has been staged for their pleasure. Jason and Gwen hold a romantic embrace.

Offering sincere thanks to Brandon and his friends, Jason shares the spotlight with the entire cast ensemble.

In epilogue, the *Galaxy Quest* series is revived, with the entire cast returning to their original roles. Plus, Laliari has joined the crew, and Guy is no longer a nameless extra but plays Roc Ingersol, the *Protector*'s security chief.

Afterwords

To paraphrase a quotation from the great Ernest Hemingway: "The greater the work . . . the easier the parody." If that's true, then *Galaxy Quest* must have been an awfully easy project. Taking direct aim at the iconic *Star Trek* TV series and its die-hard fans, the 1999 sci-fi comedy skewered not only the show but the rabidity and obsession that some fans of anything sci-fi demonstrate. At the same time, it paid homage to the well-known program and the cast.

Playwright-turned-screenwriter David Howard—an admitted "Trekkie once removed"—penned an original draft called *Captain Starshine* after hearing Leonard Nimoy's voice on a coming-attractions trailer. Imagining an actor trapped in a role he couldn't escape, Howard took one step further by wondering what would happen if real aliens showed up.

Turned over to screenwriter Robert Gordon for additional work, the script became *Galaxy Quest*, and Harold Ramis—writer of 1978's *Animal House*, 1984's *Ghostbusters*, as well as directing 1980's *Caddyshack* and 1993's *Groundhog Day*, among many others—signed on to direct. When he left the project to handle 1999's *Analyze This*, Dean Parisot came aboard.

Produced by Dreamworks SKG, the film had high-octane assistance from Steven Spielberg, as well as visual effects from Industrial Light and Magic and alien effects from Stan Winston Studios (a not-too-shabby group of supporters).

Kevin Kline and Alec Baldwin were originally the first and second choices to play the William Shatner–like role of Jason Nesmith, but Tim Allen eventually got the part. Sigourney Weaver, playing directly against her strong character of Ripley in the *Alien* series, wore a blonde wig as buxom babe Gwen DeMarco. Alan Rickman—pre-*Harry Potter* series—took the part of Alexander Dane, a once-proud Shakespearean actor who stoops to play a Spock-like role.

For the most part, those associated with the real *Star Trek* franchise took the spoofing of *Galaxy Quest* in good-natured stride. Patrick Stewart, playing Captain Jean-Luc Picard in the *Star Trek: The Next Generation* series, originally avoided seeing *Galaxy Quest*, fearing ridicule. Once convinced to take a look, the actor found it "brilliant . . . No one laughed louder or longer in the cinema than I did." George Takei, Sulu in the original *Star Trek* TV series, joked that *Galaxy Quest* was "a chillingly realistic documentary." William Shatner, Captain James T. Kirk on the original 1968 show—and clearly the target of parody by the character of Jason Nesmith—kiddingly admitted, "I don't know what Tim Allen was doing . . . I was trying to understand who he was imitating."

In a brilliant piece of advance promotion, a "mockumentary" was produced for the E! Entertainment network. The half-hour show presented a proposed "Twentieth Anniversary" look back at *Galaxy Quest*, supposedly reuniting the cast for the upcoming feature film. With tongue firmly in cheek, the actors—along with behind-the-scenes members like production designer Linda DeScenna and alien effects master Stan Winston—spoke about the series and their relationships. It had all the feel of those "celebrities dragged through the mud" type of shows that are abundant on cable channels like E!

Galaxy Quest was first conceived as a much darker film, as Parisot compared the plot to 1939's *Wizard of Oz*—each character in search of something necessary to complete their life. The violence was stepped up, and some salty language was featured as well. Wishing to avoid a revenue-restricting rating of PG-13 (or higher), changes were made in postproduction to tone down the intensity and keep *Galaxy Quest* in a more family-friendly mode.

The strategy worked. With a budget of $35 million, *Galaxy Quest* opened on Christmas Day of 1999 and eventually grossed more than $71 million domestically. With overseas ticket sales, the film took in over $90 million in total.

Cowboys & Aliens

Synopsis

- 2011—American/Universal—119 min./color
- Director: Jon Favreau
- Original music: Harry Gregson-Williams
- Film editing: Dan Lebental, Jim May
- Production design: Scott Chambliss
- Based on the 2006 graphic novel by Scott Mitchell Rosenberg

Cast

- Daniel Craig (Jake Lonergan)
- Harrison Ford (Woodrow Dolarhyde)
- Olivia Wilde (Ella Swenson)
- Paul Dano (Percy Dolarhyde)
- Sam Rockwell (Doc)
- Clancy Brown (Meacham)
- David Carradine (Sheriff John Taggert)
- Noah Ringer (Emmett Taggert)
- Abigail Spencer (Alice)
- Adam Beach (Nat Colorado)

In 1873, on the vast and desolate land known as the Arizona Territory, a shoeless and wounded cowboy wakes on the ground. He has a strange metal bracelet on his wrist, and, despite his attempts to remove it with a rock, it will not come off.

Three horsemen come upon the stranger and plan to take him to the nearby town of Absolution, perhaps for bounty money. He doesn't agree with their plan and quickly subdues them, taking shoes, a gun, and a horse.

Reaching Absolution, the local preacher named Meacham treats the stranger's wound and finds he has amnesia. Percy Dolarhyde, a young and drunken bully, shoots up Doc's Gold Leaf Saloon, and the proprietor is not at all amused. The stranger subdues the kid, but not before Percy wounds a bystander. Sheriff Taggert is forced to lock the kid in jail, despite a warning that the punk's rich cattleman father won't be pleased.

Out on the Dolarhyde ranch, a tremendous explosion rocks the land. Cattle are destroyed as fires burn the brush.

Taggert recognizes the stranger from a wanted poster as Jake Lonergan, a known outlaw. Over in Doc's saloon, Lonergan enjoys a drink on the house and meets Ella. The pretty woman has a particular interest in Jake's bracelet. Taggert and some deputies try to arrest Lonergan, but he overpowers them. Ella quietly comes from behind to knock Jake out.

War veteran Colonel Woodrow Dolarhyde accuses one of his ranch hands of killing his cattle and starting fires. As Taggert prepares to turn over Percy and Jake to federal marshalls, the elder Dolarhyde rides into town. It was Lonergan who stole Dolarhyde's gold from a stagecoach, so he wants both his boy and the outlaw.

The night sky glows with strange lights in the distance. As they approach, Jake's bracelet begins to flash its own lights. Suddenly, an alien craft soars overhead, blasting the town's main street with some sort of weapon. Cables swoop down from the ship, randomly grabbing people and pulling them in, including Taggert and Doc's wife, Maria.

Lonergan's bracelet becomes a weapon, blowing a hole in the carriage where he was locked up with Percy. Dolarhyde tries to drag his frightened son to safety, but the boy is pulled away by an alien cable. Jake fires his bracelet at

Strangers come to town in *Cowboys & Aliens*.

an approaching craft, and it crashes, sliding to a stop on the street. Lonergan and Dolarhyde cautiously move toward the ship, when a wounded alien sprints away into the desert.

In the morning, Lonergan leaves town on horseback. Ella follows, but he wants no part of her. Dolarhyde leads a posse, including Meacham, Doc, Ella, and Taggert's young grandson, Emmett, on the trail of the wounded alien.

Jake comes upon an abandoned cabin, where some things slowly come back to his memory. He recalls Alice, his beautiful lover, and the stolen gold. He also pictures Alice being abducted like the townsfolk.

Lonergan joins Dolarhyde's posse as they come across a deserted paddle-boat, upended and hundreds of miles from any water big enough to carry it. They take refuge inside, away from a driving rain.

Being a medical man and business owner, Doc has no knowledge of fire-arms. Meacham loans him one and shows him the basics of using a gun. In a rare act of kindness, Dolarhyde shares his apple with Emmett, along with giving the boy a knife he has been eying.

The alien attacks, quickly killing several of Dolarhyde's men. Emmett comes face-to-face with it, and Meacham draws its attention. The creature pounces on the preacher before Lonergan can drive it away with blasts from the bracelet. Mortally wounded, Meacham urges Jake to find the kidnapped townsfolk.

The next morning, Jake and Doc take the time to pray over the fallen posse members and then join Dolarhyde. The cattleman is slowly warming to Emmett, urging the young boy to "be a man" when the time comes.

Entering a valley, the remaining people are ambushed by bandits—who just happen to be Lonergan's old gang. He tries to rally them, but the men are under new leadership, and they know that Jake took Dolarhyde's gold to go away with Alice. Jake is beaten, but he kills the new boss with his bracelet.

The posse heads out as Jake's old gang follows. Four alien ships attack, and Ella is pulled away under one. Lonergan rides alongside the ship, then jumps atop it. He disables the craft as Jake and Ella fall into the river. An alien bursts from the water, attacks Ella, and Jake blasts it with his bracelet.

A weakened Jake carries Ella back to the group, but her injury has taken its toll. Chiricahua Indians take the posse, blaming them for the alien invasion, and lay Ella's body on a burning funeral pyre. Her naked form rises from the flames—she is an alien. The invaders seek gold from the Earth, and she has come to stop them. But everyone must band together to succeed.

The Chiricahuans treat Jake for his injuries, and his memories continue to return. He recalls Alice being sacrificed in alien experiments, getting the alien bracelet snapped onto his wrist, and—most importantly—where their base of operations is located.

Led by Lonergan and Dolarhyde, the Indians and posse arrive at the alien mother ship, buried deep in the desert. The creatures have set up a mining operation, pulling gold from the ground. With reinforcements recruited from Jake's old gang, the group of only a few dozen prepare to attack the aliens.

The Indians position themselves among the rocks, high above the conning tower of the mother ship. Jake and his gang approach the base and begin climbing the tower. They set off a large bundle of dynamite, and the aliens emerge to retaliate.

Dolarhyde's posse attacks the aliens from horseback, while Jake and Ella make their way underground. The Chiricahua fire from the rocks, and, although the aliens are large and quick, they begin to go down.

The Colonel is cornered by an alien, but Nat—his Apache aide—saves him. The alien turns and attacks Nat, mortally wounding him. As he dies, Nat notes that he always wanted a father like Dolarhyde. Likewise, the Colonel always wanted a son like Nat.

Jake and Ella find the abducted townsfolk, mesmerized by an alien light. She destroys it, and they slowly come out of their daze to escape. Jake guards the entrance, shooting aliens with the bracelet as they head toward him menacingly.

Emmett runs to elude an alien, taking refuge in a crevasse. The creature opens its chest, revealing a second set of arms and claws. Reaching for Emmett, the boy takes the knife that Dolarhyde gave him and bravely kills the alien.

With Ella's help, Jake is able to remove the bracelet, and they move quickly to the core of the mother ship. Ella takes the bracelet and bids goodbye to Jake. An alien grabs the cowboy and straps him into the examination table he once before occupied.

But before the experimenting can begin, Dolarhyde begins firing his pistol into the beast. Jake frees himself, and the pair finish off the alien. They escape the ship as it blasts off, with Ella still inside. She uses the bracelet as an explosive device, blowing the spacecraft apart in the sky and sacrificing her life. Those who were freed from the ship slowly begin to reconnect with their loved ones.

At Doc's saloon, the townsfolk celebrate their new riches of gold, and Percy shares a soft drink with Emmett. With the new prosperity will come growth and change. Dolarhyde and the sheriff agree to make Lonergan a free man by faking his death at the alien battle. Jake rides out of town into the distance.

Afterwords

With *Cowboys & Aliens*, the pairing of the western and sci-fi movie genres was truly unique for Hollywood. To a lesser extent, the 1999 steampunk western *Wild Wild West*, combined many facets of both film types, but nothing had ever been done like *Cowboys & Aliens*. The project took nearly fifteen years, from concept to screen, to arrive.

Scott Mitchell Rosenberg, publisher of Malibu Comics in the mid-1990s, scored a success by converting his *Men in Black* comic books into movie magic. He sought to repeat the process at his new Platinum Studios with *Cowboys & Aliens*. In 1997, Universal Studios and Dreamworks SKG teamed up to acquire the film rights to the concept.

The project bounced around in development hell for several years, while Rosenberg published the story as a graphic novel in 2006. In 2008, Robert Downey Jr., fresh from his first *Iron Man* film, signed on to star as Jake Lonergan. Two years later, Downey left the project to reprise his successful role as Sherlock Holmes in the 2010 sequel.

Not coincidentally, the director from *Iron Man* and *Iron Man 2*—Jon Favreau—was attached as director for *Cowboys & Aliens*. With Downey out, James Bond was in. Favreau picked Daniel Craig, the current 007 with two Bond films under his gun belt, to play Lonergan.

And who better to put up against Bond? How about Han Solo or Indiana Jones? We're talking action-adventure royalty, with Harrison Ford assuming the role of Colonel Woodrow Dolarhyde, a cold cattle baron. Oddly enough, when Ford found the script called for Dolarhyde to carry a whip (for those living under a rock, the weapon of choice of Indiana Jones), he quickly ran his marking pen through that idea.

Expectations were sky-high for *Cowboys & Aliens* when it was released in July 2011 as a summer blockbuster. Look at it this way. These members of the *Cowboys & Aliens* team had film track records accounting for the following box office grosses:

- Executive Producer Steven Spielberg—$4.1 billion
- Producer Ron Howard—$1.8 billion
- Director Jon Favreau—$900 million
- Actor Daniel Craig—$1.3 billion
- Actor Harrison Ford—$3.8 billion.

All totaled (give or take a few million), those five represented more than $12 billion in prior ticket sales. As such, it was believed that the chances were very good that *Cowboys & Aliens* would be a moneymaking hit.

It wasn't. Produced on a budget of over $160 million, *Cowboys & Aliens* grossed only $100 million domestically, with another $74 million. The total gross meant that, even with all the high-powered on-screen and behind-the-scenes support, the film was a flop.

In retrospect, Favreau felt the biggest problem with *Cowboys & Aliens* was the title. The odd pairing inferred a comedy; audiences found something wholly otherwise. The film's first advance trailer, seen by moviegoers more than six months earlier, invoked laughs. It was possible they expected a tongue-in-cheek action film with a lighter tone, like the *Sherlock Holmes* and *Pirates of the Caribbean* franchises.

What they got was a cool and inventive sci-fi film, but that wasn't what they paid for.

7

How Long Can You Stay?

Friends from Other Worlds

Haven't We Met Somewhere Before?

Historically speaking, sci-fi films usually focused on the thought that visitors from other worlds ultimately meant to do dastardly harm to Earthlings. As noted in the previous chapter, the little green men from Mars (or wherever), arrived at our front doors with the intentions of taking over our planet, believing this solar system wasn't big enough for the both of us. As such, cinema's normal reaction was to call out the military to eliminate the villains before they eliminated us.

Even in 1951's *The Day the Earth Stood Still*, a visit from space alien Klaatu was greeted with big fears and bigger guns. When Klaatu pulled out a present for our president, it was mistaken for a weapon—he was shot and wounded for his thoughtfulness (maybe he should have brought a Bundt cake instead).

Modern sci-fi films have been much more open to the concept of visitors from outer space possibly being friendly, hoping to forge a lasting relationship with Earth people (with the promise of perhaps exchanging intergalactic casserole recipes). The easing of interstellar paranoia in films may or may not have been consistent with the gradual easing of the Cold War tensions that had been so prevalent in the real world during the 1950s and 1960s.

The policy of détente, offered with mutual respect from American and Russian governments during the seventies and eighties, may have provided the spark for feel-good sci-fi films like *Close Encounters*, *E.T.*, *Starman*, *Cocoon*, and others. It was suggested that aliens did not necessarily want to be our masters and frequently extended a spacial delivery of goodwill and harmony.

The truth is, through thousands of years, man has disagreed with fellow man, whether it be over land, money, religion, or the fairer sex. Sometimes, cooler heads have prevailed—other times have resulted in major wars. As time goes on, there probably will always be some sort of conflict on planet Earth.

But there's no reason why that should extend to our spacely neighbors. There's no reason we shouldn't welcome extraterrestrials with open arms (and tentacles). Their visit may be nothing but a simple need to borrow a cup of galactic sugar—at least as far as Hollywood is concerned.

Close Encounters of the Third Kind

Synopsis

- 1977—American/Columbia—135 min./color
- Director: Steven Spielberg
- Original music: John Williams
- Film editing: Michael Kahn
- Production design: Joe Alves

Cast

- Richard Dreyfuss (Roy Neary)
- Teri Garr (Ronnie Neary)
- François Truffaut (Claude Lacombe)
- Melinda Dillon (Jillian Guiler)
- Bob Balaban (David Laughlin)
- Cary Guffey (Barry Guiler)

A junkyard in the Mexican Sonora Desert suddenly finds itself the home of World War II fighter planes, missing since 1945. David Laughlin, a mapmaker by trade, is the translator for Claude Lacombe, a French expert in such phenomena. An old native claims "the sun came out last night and sang to him."

Air traffic controllers in Indianapolis monitor a near-miss between a passenger plane and an UFO, but no one wishes to officially report anything. In Muncie, Indiana, four year-old Barry Guiler watches as his roomful of toys comes alive. Someone or something has been in the house, since the front door is open and the refrigerator's contents are strewn about the floor. Jillian, his mother, sees the young boy running into the field under a starry night sky.

Nearby, Roy Neary and his wife Ronnie are raising three young kids. An engineer for the power company, Roy is sent out to investigate a widespread outage. Stopping at a railroad crossing, he waves on a passing motorist, but doesn't notice as the lights behind him go straight *up* in the air. A strange disturbance tosses the contents of his truck cab around, and he looks up to see a blinding sea of light. Just as suddenly, it's gone.

Roy drives frantically through the countryside and barely misses hitting Barry and his mom on a quiet road. Along with several others, they see three brightly colored UFOs speed past them, followed by the police. Roy and the police watch as the UFOs split off and disappear into the night sky. Excitedly, Roy wakes his family and drags them out to share in the experience, but they see nothing.

The side of Roy's face appears sunburned the next morning, which he attributes to the UFO lights. Roy's night excursion gets him fired from his job.

German lobby card—*Close Encounters of the Third Kind.*

Halfway around the world, Lacombe and Laughlin find hundreds of East Indians chanting a five-note melody that they claim came from the skies. Lacombe reveals his find to a small, excited conference.

On the road where the UFOs were spotted, Roy meets Jillian and Barry, and they all seem to be obsessed with a box-like shape. As Barry builds it in the dirt, Roy says, "This means something, this is important," At Goldstone tracking station in California, a radio transmission is discovered to be map coordinates. Laughlin, the former cartographer, locates them as being somewhere in Wyoming.

Lacombe transmits the five-note phrase and receives the same in response. Meanwhile, Barry taps the same melody on his xylophone. Billowing clouds and strange lights approach Jillian's house. Frightened, she shuts the house tight. She grabs the phone to call for help, but she only hears the five-note phrase on the line. Barry slips out of the house and is gone, as Jillian yells to the disappearing lights in the sky.

The government, meanwhile, has devised a plan to evacuate the area around Devil's Tower in Wyoming so they can rendezvous with the UFOs. Roy is still obsessed with the box shape and even carves it in his mashed potatoes. He screams to the void in the sky—"What is it?" Ronnie, confused and upset, takes the children and leaves her husband.

Soon, Roy has built a huge model of Devil's Tower in his living room. A TV report about a railcar disaster near Devil's Tower provides Roy with the visual connection he's been looking for. Jillian shares the revelation, and they independently set out for Wyoming, although the military is turning everyone away from the area.

Roy and Jillian meet up at an evacuation center and decide to cut through back roads toward Devil's Tower. Detained by the military, Roy is questioned by Lacombe and Laughlin as to what he expected to find. Roy knows the toxic gas story is a put-on and wants to know what's going on, but he gets no answers. Roy and Jillian are loaded with others into a helicopter for relocation. Lacombe argues with the military that these people should not be treated like prisoners because something has invited them to this spot.

Roy and Jillian escape from the helicopter and head toward Devil's Tower. Climbing up and over, they find an installation that could only be a landing strip for the UFOs. As night falls, several brilliantly colored crafts fly into the area. There's a buzz of activity on the ground, with cameras rolling and data collection begun. The five-note phrase is repeated over a huge sound system, and the UFOs respond in kind, then speed away. Applause breaks out, and everyone thinks it's been a huge success.

But then an enormous "city of lights" emerges from out of the heavens. Bigger than Devil's Tower itself, the craft slowly settles over the landing site. Roy and Jillian venture down to mingle and get a closer look, as a musical conversation ensues between the mother ship and the scientists. The bottom of the craft opens, and hundreds of long-missing travelers, pilots, and sailors slowly walk down the ramp. Barry runs to the open arms of his mother.

Lacombe spots Neary and quickly convinces the military to consider his situation. A spindly creature steps from the craft, followed by dozens of child-sized aliens. Dressed in a red military jumpsuit, Neary joins a group of mission specialists who will be journeying into space on the mother ship. Lacombe nods to Roy as he boards the ship. A single alien approaches Lacombe, and they exchange sign-language greetings before the alien boards the craft. Barry quietly says "Bye," as the huge ship lifts into the sky.

Afterwords

Director Steven Spielberg didn't think *Close Encounters of the Third Kind*, often called *CE3K*, would break even at the box office. He was slightly off, as it raked in more than $116 million in its initial domestic release. With overseas sales of over $170 million, the total neared $300 million.

Long a believer in UFOs, Spielberg always wanted to make a film about a visit from outer space—his first film made at age seventeen, *Firelight*, basically laid the groundwork for *CE3K*. After his success with *Jaws*, the director had substantial pull with the execs at Columbia Pictures and had little problem getting the green light for *CE3K*, which he originally wanted to title *Watch the Skies*. Still, he ran a very tight ship during its production. In fact, security was so tight that Spielberg himself couldn't get on the set one day because he didn't have the right security badge.

While film locations included Wyoming, California, Mexico, and India, the expansive UFO landing site was actually built inside a dirigible hangar in

Mobile, Alabama—now known as Brookley Industrial Complex—surrounded by a beautifully painted matte. Production designer Joe Alves politely declined an offer to use the largest sound stages at Columbia, figuring an area four times as big would be needed. The hangar at Brookley was four-hundred-fifty feet long, two-hundred-fifty feet wide, and ninety feet high.

The quaint and simple Neary tract house in the film was also found in Mobile, Alabama. Alves and associate producer Clark Paylow told Columbia about the house, suggesting that the purchase price of around $35,000 was cheaper than building the numerous sets that would have been needed. When the studio refused, Alves and Paylow planned on buying the house themselves, dressing it inside and out for the film, then selling it when shooting was completed. What's more, they could rent it to Columbia for *CE3K*. Of course, the studio execs became apoplectic when they heard that plan. They relented and bought the house for the production.

At one point in *CE3K* during the mother-ship landing scene, a man with a blue jacket and goatee stepped toward it. He was Dr. J. Allen Hynek, the world's preeminent authority on UFOs at the time and the film's technical advisor.

At the time of its 1977 release, Spielberg had planned a sequel, but the closest he ever came was to assemble a "Special Edition" in 1980. It earned another $15 million at the box office and featured scenes not seen in the original theatrical release, including Roy Neary's venture inside the mother ship—scenes that the director later regretted. Spielberg felt the interior of the spaceship was something that should have remained a mystery, to be seen only in the minds of the viewers.

E.T.—The Extra-Terrestrial

Synopsis

- 1982—American/Universal—115 min./color
- Director: Steven Spielberg
- Original music: John Williams
- Film editing: Carol Littleton
- Production design: James D. Bissell

Cast

- Henry Thomas (Elliott)
- Dee Wallace (Mary)
- Peter Coyote (Keys)
- Drew Barrymore (Gertie)
- Robert MacNaughton (Michael)

Evening time in a remote area of California finds a group of squat aliens quietly completing a plant-collecting excursion on Earth. Suddenly, several cars come upon the scene, and the aliens are forced to quickly leave in their spaceship. But in their haste, one of the extraterrestrials is left behind.

In a nearby suburb, single mom Mary takes care of her three young children. Mike is in his mid-teens, blonde-haired Gertie is around eight, and Elliott is about twelve years old. When he goes out to meet the pizza delivery man, Elliott comes across something in their storage shed. The rest of the family investigates, but find nothing.

Later that night, Elliott ventures back outside and comes face-to-face with E.T., but the extraterrestrial escapes into the dark. Next evening, Elliott camps out in the backyard and E.T. shows up, proving to be a friendly, intelligent creature. Elliott hides him in his room. Meanwhile, a group of men investigate the nearby woods, looking for something.

The next morning, Elliott fakes illness so he can stay home and play with E.T. Soon, Gertie and Mike meet E.T. and agree to keep the alien a secret. He demonstrates the ability to levitate objects and revive dead plants. When he goes to school the next day, Elliott leaves E.T. at home. The alien discovers beer in the refrigerator, and, as he drinks it, due to a psychic connection between the two, Elliott mysteriously feels the intoxicating effects during biology class. He releases the frogs that are doomed for dissection and, during the uproar, kisses the prettiest girl in class. When his mom is called to bail him out of trouble, Gertie teaches E.T. to talk.

Using some electronic and household items, the alien fashions a device to contact his planet, as E.T. wishes to "phone home." All the while, a group of men are closing in on E.T. using high-tech surveillance gear. Elliott cuts his finger, and E.T. magically heals it with his own glowing finger.

Going out for Halloween, Elliott and E.T. use the transmitting machine to send a message into space but then get separated. Meanwhile, a group of men

Henry Thomas and friends in *E.T. the Extra-Terrestrial.*

swarm over Elliott's empty house, scanning and probing with sophisticated electronic equipment.

Next morning, Elliott ends up sick at home, and Mike finds E.T. in the same condition near a riverbed. Elliott shows E.T. to his mom and tells her he's dying. She's frightened of E.T., but before she can take her family away, the house is overrun by a group of men. They turn out to be government scientists and military officials who cordon off the house and turn it into a huge lab where they can study E.T.

One scientist, identified by a set of jangling keys, empathizes with Elliott. He tells him that E.T. is a miracle and he's glad that Elliot found him first. Elliott and E.T. are both laid out on surgical tables amid a mass of medical equipment. As the alien slowly dies, Elliott seems to break his mysterious connection with E.T. and recovers. The medical team unsuccessfully attempts to revive E.T.

As the alien is prepared for removal, Elliott discovers he's really still alive and that E.T.'s message home has gotten through. With the help of Mike and his friends, Elliott takes E.T. away in a hijacked truck. They grab bicycles at the playground and lead police and government officials on a wild chase. When it seems they are about to be caught, E.T. magically takes the boys' bicycles into the air and away to safety.

Arriving at the spot from where E.T. sent his message, a spaceship lands to take him home. The alien bids Elliott's family a thankful goodbye, and, heading for home, he reminds Elliott that he'll always be with him in his heart.

Afterwords

Spielberg once again showed his ability to tell a good story using children as the focus, just as he had done in *Close Encounters*, not to mention his comfort with the visitor from outer space theme. In fact, the genesis of *E.T.* sprouted from the ending of *CE3K*, as Spielberg wondered what might have happened if the lead mother-ship alien (the one he referred to as Puck) had stayed behind with Roy Neary and his family.

Spielberg had been developing a sci-fi script written by John Sayles and Ron Cobb called *Night Skies*. But the story was full of horrific aliens who terrorized a simple farm family, and that idea made no sense to Spielberg—why would extraterrestrials travel millions of miles across the galaxy just to do that? He changed direction and made E.T. an intelligent and gentle being.

Italian craftsman Carlo Rambaldi designed and built the three articulated full-size puppets of *E.T.* on a budget of $1.5 million and a six-month schedule established by the director. After abandoning the thoughts of creating a Muppet-like creature—like Yoda in *The Empire Strikes Back*—Rambaldi decided that a mechanical, cable-controlled animatronic figure was the way to go. Four E.T. heads, filled with motors, gears, and electronics, were radio-controlled for close-up work. Even the irises in the alien's eyes were built to dilate or contract by means of cable controls.

Drew Barrymore, just six when shooting started, found herself in her first major role as Gertie. Spielberg encouraged improvisation from his young cast, with Barrymore ad-libbing "I don't like his feet," among other lines. Elliott's first kiss is planted on a young Erika Eleniak, who would go on to pop out of a cake in Steven Segal's 1992 *Under Siege* and appear as Elly Mae Clampett in the 1993 film version of *The Beverly Hillbillies.*

When Elliott cleverly enticed the alien to his backyard with candies, it was a clear example of how cinematic product placement can affect business in America. The M&M/Mars Company was originally approached to create a promotional tie-in between the movie and their bite-sized chocolates, with M&Ms being used as alien bait in the film. For whatever reason, they passed on the opportunity.

The Hershey's Chocolate Company had a little-known peanut butter product called Reese's Pieces. Jack Dowd, the VP of New Product Development for Hershey's, saw the possibilities and committed $1 million of advertising funds across a six-week period. Timed to coincide with the opening of *E.T.*, Reese's saw their sales tripled in just two weeks. What's more, the candy started showing up in counters of more than six hundred movie theaters across the country, not to mention in the mouth of a certain extraterrestrial.

E.T. was one of film history's biggest box-office hits ever for the time, grossing $400 million before its twentieth anniversary rerelease in 2002, not including videotape, DVD, or Blu-Ray editions. The reissue brought in another $35 million in box-office receipts. With the overseas box office, *E.T.* totaled nearly $800 million—in the days when $100 million films were considered blockbusters.

The movie also earned nine Oscar nominations and won four gold statues for sound effects, visual effects, original music score, and sound. *E.T.* also took a Golden Globe for Best Drama, as well as a Grammy Award for best album of original music for film or television.

Starman

Synopsis

- 1984—American/Universal—115 min./color
- Director: John Carpenter
- Original music: Jack Nitzsche
- Film editing: Marion Rothman
- Production design: Daniel Lomino

Cast

- Jeff Bridges (Starman)
- Karen Allen (Jenny Hayden)
- Charles Martin Smith (Mark Shermin)
- Richard Jaeckel (George Fox)

Voyager 2, a deep-space probe, is launched from Cape Canaveral, carrying messages of welcome from Earth to anyone who might intercept the spacecraft. On Earth, a young widow named Jenny Hayden sadly watches home movies of her departed husband, Scott.

A UFO enters Earth's atmosphere, raising the fears of the US military. Fighter jets are scrambled and intercept the craft, forcing it to crash in northern Wisconsin. The director of the National Security Agency, George Fox, is notified of the event, along with a contracted SETI—Search for Extra-Terrestrial Intelligence—scientist, Mark Shermin.

An alien—simply a ball of light—emerges from the crash and makes its way to Jenny's home. Using a bit of Scott's hair kept in a scrapbook, the alien clones itself into a likeness of him, growing in seconds from an infant to full adulthood.

Jenny, stunned and terrified at seeing the metamorphosis, grabs a gun but passes out. The alien innocently turns the home movies on, absorbing how Scott talked and moved—and how he used a gun for target practice. The starman is a quick learner.

He uses a small, marble-like sphere to communicate with his home, noting that Earthlings are hostile, and a rendezvous is arranged for Landing Area One in three days' time. Jenny comes to and, against her better judgment, leaves with the starman in her car. Military helicopters fly overhead, searching for the crash site.

Using another sphere, the starman fashions a map of the United States, and Jenny IDs Arizona as his destination for the rendezvous. They drive through the night, as Shermin hovers in an army helicopter and lands at the crash site. The alien craft is dug out and recovered.

Jenny, confused and at wit's end, tries to finish the ordeal by crashing headlong into a van. The accident is avoided, and she claims she's a victim of kidnapping. The van driver tries to help, but another silver sphere in the starman's hand blows up a tree and scares the driver into fleeing the scene. Although his language skills are limited, the starman explains that he has taken the appearance of Jenny's dead husband in order to calm her.

Stopping for gas, Jenny tries to leave a message for help on a restroom mirror, but the starman pulls it before anyone can see it. Jenny fears for her life and urges the starman to just shoot her. But he releases the gun's magazine and reassures Jenny that he means her no harm.

The starman begins to drive Jenny's car and, realizing they are hungry, speeds through a yellow light and causes an accident between a hay-bale-toting semi and a sedan. If the starman doesn't make the rendezvous in Arizona in three days, he will die. Meanwhile, Director Fox finds Shermin's entire story of an alien who has landed on Earth and cloned itself into the image of a dead Wisconsin house painter difficult to believe.

Jenny and the starman reach a truck stop diner for something to eat, where Jenny tearfully explains marriage and love to the alien, along with proper eating etiquette. She starts to sneak away on a bus, but watches in amazement as the starman gives life to a hunter's dead deer and it runs away. The hunter and his pals are none too pleased with losing their trophy and beat up the starman, until Jenny gets their attention with her pistol in hand. They scatter, and she realizes she must stay with him on the trip to Arizona.

The couple pulls into a Holiday Inn for some quick rest, unaware that local police and the military are watching their activities. When Jenny and the starman leave, the cops follow and, seeing Jenny's gun in the starman's hand, fire a round at the car, fatally striking Jenny in the head.

The starman bursts through a roadblock and drives into a disabled tanker-truck as it explodes in a tremendous fire-ball. Holding one of his silver spheres, he emerges from the flames, carrying the lifeless body of Jenny. They disappear into the night, as Shermin arrives to survey the scene.

The starman and Jenny slip away from the wreckage in a

He has traveled from a galaxy far beyond our own.
He is 100,000 years ahead of us.
He has powers we cannot comprehend.
And he is about to face the one force in the universe he has yet to conquer.
Love.

JOHN CARPENTER'S

STARMAN

COLUMBIA PICTURES PRESENTS
A MICHAEL DOUGLAS — LARRY J. FRANCO PRODUCTION
JEFF BRIDGES   KAREN ALLEN
JOHN CARPENTER'S
STARMAN
CHARLES MARTIN SMITH   RICHARD JAECKEL
JACK NITZSCHE
BARRY BERNARDI   BRUCE A. EVANS & RAYNOLD GIDEON
MICHAEL DOUGLAS   LARRY J. FRANCO   JOHN CARPENTER

US one-sheet—*Starman.*

prefab mobile home under tow. As the truck rolls west, the starman tightly grips one of the metal spheres. It glows, and Jenny slowly comes back to life. But the starman is gone, having hitched a ride.

Jenny reaches Shermin by phone, insisting she hadn't been kidnapped by anyone. She hitches her own ride with a hot-rodder and heads after the starman. Everyone's travel is halted by a military roadblock, as Shermin and other troops search for the starman. The hot-rodder sets off an explosion with a gas can, creating a diversion for Jenny to grab the starman. They ride away from the scene in the back of a pickup truck.

The pair act like hobos, riding in a boxcar as it heads west. Jenny teaches the starman about making love. As the military determines that the starman's destination is Arizona, Shermin is dismayed to see their eventual plans for his capture include being strapped to a steel autopsy table.

Despite Jenny's diagnosed infertility, the starman assures her that she will have a boy from their lovemaking, the son of her husband. Although human, the child will have all the knowledge and wisdom of the starman, and, when he grows up, he will be a teacher. If Jenny does not want the baby, the starman can stop it. But there is no question that she does.

It appears that Jenny and the starman have overshot their destination, finding themselves in Las Vegas instead of Winslow, Arizona. Jenny has lost her wallet, but the starman takes her only quarter and hits the slot machines. With a little influence, he strikes it rich on a half-million-dollar jackpot, and the couple drive away in a brand-new Cadillac.

Shermin and Fox have differences about handling the alien once it's captured. Fox sees the mission as military based, ordering troops to carry live ammo. Shermin is appalled, since the Earth actually invited the alien to visit.

In a little diner outside the rendezvous spot, Shermin catches up with Jenny and the starman. The alien reveals that his world has visited Earth before, finding the inhabitants an interesting species. When things are the worst, it brings out the best in them. Shermin knows he must help the starman to make the rendezvous and go home. He tells state troopers that the two were the wrong people, and he lets them go.

The Barringer Meteorite Crater is the rendezvous point, obviously created when aliens landed eons ago. Fox leads a group of armed military helicopters and ground troops into the area, seeking to keep the alien from leaving. A salvo of warning fire doesn't stop them, and a large, spherical craft slowly drops from the skies.

A soft snow and red light surround Jenny and the starman as he prepares to leave. Jenny can't join him on the trip back, for she would die on his planet. They exchange loving goodbyes, and he gives Jenny a silver sphere as he leaves, assuring her that the baby will know what to do with it.

Afterwords

Director John Carpenter, known for creating top-notch and gritty horror films like 1978's *Halloween* and 1982's *The Thing*, and action-thrillers like 1981's *Escape from New York*, wanted to broaden his scope by helming a film that combined the genres of sci-fi and romance. The script for *Starman* bounced around for five years at Columbia Pictures, with executive producer Michael Douglas convincing the studio to develop it instead of a script that eventually became a film with a similar story known as *E.T.* (Hey, everyone makes a bad choice every once in a while.)

Starman passed through the hands of five different directors before landing in the lap of Carpenter. After Kevin Bacon and Tom Cruise were considered for the title role, Jeff Bridges was picked to play the nameless alien who fills the vacancy in Karen Allen's heart. The actress had broken into films as Katy,

Boone's girlfriend, in the 1978 megahit *Animal House*, and became a fixture in moviegoers' minds as the love interest of Indiana Jones in 1981's thrilling blockbuster *Raiders of the Lost Ark*.

The premise of an alien responding to an invitation to visit Earth was pulled directly from the headlines of the day. NASA launched the unmanned *Voyager 2* spacecraft in 1977, intending to study the outer planets of the solar system and continue on to interstellar space. Included was a twelve-inch golden record, as well as a cartridge, stylus, and instructions on how to build a device to play the contents of the record. The disc contained all sorts of musical selections, from Bach, Mozart, and Beethoven, to an Indian raga and the rockin' "Johnny B. Goode" by Chuck Berry. There were also dozens of images of life, science, and nature on planet Earth.

The disc offered greetings in fifty-five different languages, from the extinct Semitic Akkadian to the Chinese dialect of Wu. Obviously, one of them piqued the interest of (and made sense to) Jeff Bridges' alien species and prompted them to make the trip in the film. (It should be noted that more than thirty-five years after its launch, *Voyager 2* continues to function. It has traveled more than nine-and-a-half-billion miles from Earth. No signs of alien response—yet.)

While *Starman* focused on story more than FX, filmmakers brought in the "Holy Trinity of Makeup" to handle the starman transformation from newborn to adult. Dick Smith, Rick Baker, and Stan Winston handled the effects for youth-to-adult, baby, and face-stretching effects, respectively. The three, unfortunately, weren't incredibly thrilled with their results, as director Carpenter had insisted on downplaying the scene as not being something that stopped the show.

While reviews were quite favorable for *Starman* (and Jeff Bridges earned an Oscar nomination for Best Actor), the box-office results were only so-so. Made on a budget of $24 million, its domestic gross was only $28 million—making everything essentially a wash.

Cocoon

Synopsis

- 1984—American/Columbia—117 min./color
- Director: Ron Howard
- Original music: James Horner
- Film editing: Daniel Hanley, Michael Hill
- Production design: Jack T. Collis
- Based on the 1985 novel by David Saperstein

Cast

- Don Ameche (Art Selwyn)
- Wilford Brimley (Ben Luckett)

- Hume Cronyn (Joe Finley)
- Brian Dennehy (Walter)
- Jack Gilford (Bernie Lefkowitz)
- Steve Guttenberg (Jack Bonner)
- Maureen Stapleton (Mary Luckett)
- Jessica Tandy (Alma Finley)
- Gwen Verdon (Bess McCarthy)
- Herta Ware (Rosie Lefkowitz)
- Tahnee Welch (Kitty)
- Barret Oliver (David)

At the Sunny Shores Retirement Home in St. Petersburg, Florida, elderly residents retrieve their packages as gruff Ben Luckett and his wife Mary return from the grocery store. Joe and Alma Finley fill their folding cart with bags, as Bernie Lefkowitz collects his laxatives and quietly reminds his wife Rosie that she has already met Ben. Nearby, spry Bess McCarthy leads a dance class and flirts with Art Selwyn.

Like a trio of mischievous schoolboys, Ben, Joe, and Art sneak into an empty private estate with a refreshing indoor pool nearby. Meanwhile, a less-than-satisfied customer stiffs fishing guide Jack Bonner. His displeasure is short-lived, as a group of strangers—led by a man named Walter—books his boat for a month.

Ben, Joe, and Art's naughty trip to the pool is canceled when they see Walter and his group renting the property. The group then head out to sea, giving Jack a unique map by which to navigate.

Failing his vision test, Ben is forced to give up his driver's license, while Walter and his group work with torches underwater. They retrieve several large, egg-shaped objects from the sea bottom.

Feeling adventurous, Ben, Joe, and Art sneak into the swimming pool once more, now finding it partly occupied by the strange pods that Walter's group brought up. The three men splash and dive, frolicking in the water like children. They return to the home rejuvenated, with amorous intentions with their partners. Now the boys can't seem to get enough of the pool.

Walter and his group continue to pull pods from the ocean, and Jack's curiosity is piqued more than ever. Kitty, a pretty member of the group, lies when pressed to reveal the contents of the cargo. Bonner injures his foot and Kitty soothes the pain, but politely rebuffs his advances, claiming to be unlike other any women he's known.

Joe's physician is amazed at his patient's revitalized condition, with his diagnosed cancer in complete remission. The eight elderly friends hit the town for a night of dinner and dancing, although Bernie—who hasn't been in the pool—sits on the side with Rosie while his friends cavort on the dance floor.

Bonner has his hands full trying to keep his boat running and can't resist the temptation to take a peek when Kitty disrobes in her cabin. But the young woman doesn't stop at just her clothing and begins to remove her human form, revealing a brilliant and glowing alien underneath.

Wilford Brimley, Hume Cronyn, and Don Ameche (L-R) in *Cocoon*.

A frightened Jack runs topside and jumps overboard, then realizes he's too far to swim anywhere. Bonner reluctantly reboards his boat, where Walter and his crew try to calm him.

Walt explains they come from the planet Anterea. Thousands of years ago, a group of Antereans was left behind in life-saving cocoons during an expedition to Earth, as a land known as Atlantis sank. Walter and his group only wish to retrieve those cocoons and go back to Anterea. Convinced of their sincerity, Jack agrees to help with the recovery mission and keep everything secret.

Ben, Joe, and Art persuade Bernie to join them at the pool, but the cocoons keep him out of the water. Walter and his people catch the quartet spying on them as they shed their human suits, and the old men run back to the home.

The staff at Sunny Shores don't believe what the men saw, but they do contact police at their insistence. Walter charms the police, promising not to press charges as long as there's no more trespassing.

Without the pool, old age catches back up with Ben and Art, as Joe's cancer returns. Walter kindly agrees to Ben's bold request to keep using the pool, as long as they stay away from the cocoons.

Ben, Joe, and Art, along with Mary, Alma, and Bess, head off to the pool, but Bernie loudly protests the whole idea and pulls Rose with him as he walks back to the home. The sextet have their fun in the pool, joking with the aliens. Ben even recovers his faltering eyesight—and his driver's license. Art tears up a disco dance floor, dazzling everyone with an impressive break dance.

Jack and Kitty seem to be falling for each other. Instead of physical expressions, she shares glowing energy with him in the pool, and Jack experiences satisfaction like no other human ever has.

Ben and Art are afraid that the group's demonstration of vim and vigor may be too much, as they promised Walter they would keep things quiet. Joe goes too far, flirting with a lunch-counter waitress and being unfaithful to Alma. She knows of his indiscretion and leaves him to stay with Bess.

Bernie's loud condemnation of Joe's actions angers the old man, and he knocks two home attendants down with one punch each. Unfortunately, Bernie also mentions the invigorating effects of the pool, and everyone from the home invades it en masse. They splash, they play, they even bounce a cocoon like a beach ball.

The mob's irresponsible action infuriates Walter, who orders everyone out of the pool. It's too late, as the dozens of people have taken the alien life force from the water. Walter has lost two of his people and, for the first time, feels the grief of losing someone close.

Rose passes away, and, heartbroken, Bernie carries her to the pool in an effort to revive her. Sadly, Walter and the pool's waters are unable to bring her back, and an ambulance takes Rose's body away.

Ben visits Walter to apologize. The alien regrets not having enough time to return the remaining cocoons to the ocean, as the group has to leave the next day. Ben offers to get his friends to help with returning them to the water.

The old folks carry the cocoons to Bonner's boat in a driving rain and, out at sea, move them back to their original underwater places in Atlantis. Back on the boat, Walter thanks Ben and his friends for the assistance. What's more, he offers the chance for Ben and about thirty of his friends to return to Anterea with the rest of the aliens. They would never get sick, grow older, or die.

Ben and Mary bid goodbye to their daughter—who knows nothing of their plans—and their grandson David—who does. Art closes his bank account, passes out the bills to incredulous bystanders on the street, then marries Bess. Joe apologizes and reconciles with Alma. A select group of retirement residents agree to join Ben and his friends as they prepare to leave forever.

Ben's grandson spills the plan to his mother, as the boatload of seniors prepare to shove off, but Bernie can't be convinced to join them. The staff at Sunny Shores discovers many of the residents are missing and notify the police.

Jack's boat heads out, as David jumps aboard at the last minute to be with his grandparents. Coast Guard boats and a helicopter take off after the shipload of travelers. As the authorities close in, David jumps overboard to draw attention away from Jack's boat.

The Anterean spaceship appears in the night sky and, in a dense fog, pulls Jack's boat in, along with its passengers. With a pile of cash from Walter and a goodbye kiss from Kitty, Jack jumps into a lifeboat bobbing in the water.

A beachside memorial service is held for the supposed casualties of the boat lost at sea. But David looks skyward and smiles, because he knows better.

Afterwords

Cocoon was the first of a planned trilogy of novels by author David Saperstein, Unpublished, it bounced around Hollywood until Twentieth Century-Fox worked with producers Richard Zanuck and David Brown and director Robert Zemeckis to prepare it for filming. But Fox got cold feet when they screened an early cut of Zemeckis' previous film, *Romancing the Stone*. Smelling failure, they fired Zemeckis from *Cocoon*. (What did they know? *Romancing the Stone* grossed more than $80 million worldwide, and Zemeckis moved on to direct a trilogy of his own—the *Back to the Future* trio—that pulled in a total of nearly a billion dollars around the world.)

The new director for *Cocoon* was none other than Opie Taylor—or Richie Cunningham, depending on what TV channel was on in your house and when you watched it. Ron Howard, acting in *The Andy Griffith Show* in the sixties and *Happy Days* in the seventies, and fresh from helming 1982's *Night Shift* and 1984's *Splash*, stepped in to direct the sci-fi story of *Cocoon*. Only thirty-one years old, he prepared to give orders to performers ranging from their fifties to their late seventies.

Leading the veteran cast was Don Ameche, who, at seventy-seven, had spent more than fifty years in films, television, and radio, including playing half of the battling yet hilarious husband-and-wife team known as *The Bickersons*. Ameche had been recently introduced to a new generation of fans when he appeared as the conniving Mortimer Duke in 1982's *Trading Places*. His role in *Cocoon* earned him an Academy Award for Best Supporting Actor.

Other senior members of the cast were the septuagenarian husband-wife team of Hume Cronyn and Jessica Tandy, seventy-seven-year-old Jack Gilford, sixty-seven-year-old Herta Ware, Gwen Verdon and Maureen Stapleton—both relatively young in their late fifties—and Wilford Brimley who, at fifty-one, was made up to play a much older character. More youthful performers in *Cocoon* were Brian Dennehy, Steve Guttenberg, and Tahnee Welch, daughter of sexy star Raquel Welch.

With a theme that tapped into the "aliens going home" vibe, Howard kiddingly referred to *Cocoon* as *Close Encounters on Golden Pond*. While not overloaded with FX, the film still delivered great visuals, including cocoons and animatronic dolphins from Robert Short and his effects team. The rest of the special effects earned an Oscar for Ken Ralston and the folks at Industrial Light and Magic.

Given a budget of $18 million, Howard brought in a first-rate flick with sci-fi entertainment for young and old alike. *Cocoon* was one of the Top Ten–grossing films of 1985, taking in more than $76 million in the US, with a total of $87 million worldwide. The success convinced most of the cast to come back in 1988 for *Cocoon: The Return*, although the domestic box office of not even $19 million was somewhat disappointing.

Men in Black

Synopsis

* 1997—American/Columbia—98 min./color
* Director: Barry Sonnenfeld
* Original music: Danny Elfman

- Film editing: Jim Miller
- Production design: Bo Welch
- Based on the 1990 Marvel graphic comic series by Lowell Cunningham

Cast

- Tommy Lee Jones (Kay)
- Will Smith (James Edwards/Jay)
- Linda Fiorentino (Dr. Laurel Weaver/Elle)
- Vincent D'Onofrio (Edgar/Alien)
- Rip Torn (Zed)
- Tony Shalhoub (Jack Jeebs)
- Siobhan Fallon (Beatrice)
- Mike Nussbaum (Rosenberg)
- Richard Hamilton (Dee)
- John Alexander (Mikey)
- Keith Campbell (Criminal)

The night flight of a bug is interrupted by the windshield of a van. US Border Patrol officers stop the vehicle and its cargo of illegal Mexican aliens. A black Ford pulls up, and out step Agents Kay and Dee, members of the elite Division 6 of Immigration and Naturalization Service. Kay speaks fluent Spanish to the aliens, reassuring them that everything will be OK.

He stops at an odd-looking fellow who obviously has no understanding of the language. The rest are released over the protests of the Border agents, while Kay and Dee take the odd one to a remote section of the desert. This is an alien all right, but the kind of alien from another world. "Mikey" is a political refugee, who seems willing to surrender to the special agents, but a Border officer spooks him and he runs. Kay pulls an ominous chrome-plated weapon and blasts Mikey into streams of sticky blue entrails.

With a blinding flash, Kay uses a "memory neuralizer" to erase the past moments from the minds of the Border Patrol. Dee is discouraged. He had pulled his weapon on Mikey first, but couldn't pull the trigger. The elderly agent is ready to retire, and Kay erases his career in a flash.

On the streets of New York City, young NYPD officer James Edwards tracks down an elusive criminal after a grueling chase. But the thug pulls a strange weapon and escapes by running straight up a wall of the Guggenheim Museum. Cornered on the roof, the outlaw babbles something about the world coming to an end and jumps to his death.

A flying saucer crashes on a remote farm. Farmer Edgar investigates and is skinned by the saucer's alien inhabitant, who tries the farmer's hide on for size. It's a bit snug, but it will do. Beatrice, Edgar's wife, is startled for find her husband looking somewhat different as he guzzles massive amounts of sugar water.

Officer Edwards' strange chase story is not sitting well with his superiors, but beautiful Deputy Coroner Laurel Weaver believes him. Kay shows up, flashes Weaver, and takes Edwards to see Jack Jeebs, a pawnbroker. Jeebs is nervous; he

Tommy Lee Jones and Will Smith are the *Men in Black*.

knows Kay but claims to know nothing about his accusations of dealing in alien weapons. Kay threatens to blow his head off, and he does. But another grows back immediately—Jeebs is also an alien. He reveals his stash of alien weapons and admits to selling a reverberating carbonizer to another alien. It seems that someone is going to be assassinated.

Edwards is dazed and confused over the whole scene, but a flash of Kay's neuralizer makes everything a lost memory. Kay sizes up Edwards as a tough and resourceful officer and invites him to "MIB" in the morning.

The next day, Edwards finds himself at the Brooklyn Battery Tunnel, testing with the best of the brightest US military soldiers. The cocky Edwards outperforms them all and is selected to become a member of the "Men in Black." These are special agents in charge of protecting the world from dangerous extraterrestrials. But if he joins, he must give up his identity, his friends, his family—everything, forever.

After some deep thought, Edwards is in and discovers the world is full of aliens from all over the galaxy. At a huge complex and receiving center, he finds that there are more than fifteen hundred registered aliens from other worlds. Zed, the director of MIB, gives Edwards his black suit and sunglasses, along with his new identity—Jay.

Meanwhile, the new Edgar has stolen a truck and is stalking the ruler of the Arquillian Galaxy, who is masquerading on Earth as Rosenberg, the jeweler. Edgar is also having problems adjusting to his human suit—it's a bit too tight.

He catches up to Rosenberg in a restaurant, killing him and taking what he believes to be the miniature Arquillian Galaxy.

Jay takes on his first assignment, helping an alien couple deliver a "baby" in the back of a car. It's not easy, as a huge tentacle grabs Jay and bangs him repeatedly on the roof of the car. The "baby" is born; a squid that cutely regurgitates all over Jay.

Kay checks the supermarket tabloids, which are actually alien tip sheets. They lead Jay and him to Edgar's farm. Beatrice confirms that he's gone and was acting very strange before he left. Kay flashes Beatrice and tests the farm's soil. There's no doubt that they are after an alien bug, a vile and dangerous creature.

Deputy Coroner Weaver receives Rosenberg's body and discovers he's definitely not of this world—he's actually a large organic machine, run by a tiny alien creature in the head of the ruler. Dying, he cryptically offers, "The galaxy is on Orion's belt." It must be found, or intergalactic war will result. Weaver figures out who Jay and Kay are and is immediately flashed—again.

MIB Headquarters detects a mass exodus of aliens—they know something is coming soon. An Arquillian battle cruiser approaches from deep space. Edgar is ransacking Rosenberg's jewelry store and realizes that the ruler's cat is Orion. Jay tries to subdue the escaping alien with a tiny weapon called the Noisy Cricket. It may be tiny, but it blows huge holes in walls, and the recoil sends Jay flying.

Kay pays a visit to Frankie, an alien informant who happens to be masquerading as a pug dog. Kay has to get rough, as startled passers-by watch the agent throttle the small dog. But Frankie fesses up. The galaxy could be something small, like a marble. What's more, it's the best source of subatomic energy around. No wonder the bugs want it.

At the morgue, Weaver discovers the tiny galaxy around the cat's collar—Orion's belt. Jay and Kay are too late to stop Edgar from grabbing the galaxy and escaping with Weaver as a hostage. It swallows the galaxy and takes off for

Richard O'Brien in *Rocky Horror Picture Show* and Harsh Nayyar in *Men in Black*.

the site of the 1964 World's Fair in Queens. Two flying saucers that landed back then were hidden there as part of a futuristic exhibit.

The Arquillian battle cruiser issues an ultimatum—deliver the galaxy or the Earth will be destroyed. Jay realizes Edgar is going to escape in one of the flying saucers at the fair. It does, but Jay and Kay shoot it down amid a crashing cloud of dust and debris.

The alien finally sheds Edgar's skin, showing itself to be a huge cockroach. It swallows the agent's weapons, and Kay goads it into swallowing him too. The bug tries to escape in the second saucer, but Jay stops it and Kay blows the alien in two from the inside. They congratulate each other, unaware that the bug's remaining torso is about to strike. Weaver blows it to smithereens, noting, "Interesting job you guys have." The agents retrieve the galaxy, and the world is safe.

Kay's ready to retire—he hasn't been training a partner; he's been training a replacement. He hands Jay his neuralizer, saying, "See you around, Jay." His friend replies, "No, you won't."

The latest tabloids herald the return of a man after a thirty-five-year coma—it's Kay, who has rejoined his long-lost love. Weaver has become Elle, one of the Men in Black. She and Jay will defend the Earth from intergalactic threats. Perhaps the world and its galaxy are part of some vast larger universe, where strange creatures use them to play marbles with—who knows?

Afterwords

It would have been interesting to see the producers' first choice to play Agent K—Clint Eastwood. Chris O'Donnell and *Friends*' David Schwimmer were both originally approached to play James Edwards, as was John Turturro to play Edgar.

There is a character that strongly resembles the ghoulish Riff Raff from 1975's *The Rocky Horror Picture Show* in *MIB*. Silently appearing as a newsstand vendor with Frank, an alien pug dog as his partner, it is not (as many have suggested) Richard O'Brien, the original actor from the cult classic.

Makeup designer Rick Baker must have thought it was déjà vu all over again, as director Barry Sonnenfeld felt the MIB headquarters was too sterile and needed many more aliens as background characters in those scenes. It was the same sort of dilemma that had given Baker the chance to fill the cantina scene with seedy sorts in *Star Wars* twenty years previous. But with only a few weeks remaining on the production schedule, Baker was forced to farm out the additional creature creation to the ME-FX, XFX, and KNB EFX Group effects houses.

Will Smith was considered to be a real trooper in the scene where he played midwife to an alien birth. Although the newborn was as cute and cuddly as a squid-like creature could be, it did regurgitate into Agent Jay's face. As Smith cradled the animatronic figure, off-screen techs pumped a thick solution of methylcellulose and oatmeal right into his kisser. Methylcellulose is an organic compound that mixes with water to create a thick, clear, and unpleasant-looking gel. If you've seen someone get slimed in *Ghostbusters*, or the drooling creature in one of the *Alien* films, you've seen methylcellulose in action.

Sylvester Stallone, Steven Spielberg, George Lucas, Danny DeVito, Dionne Warwick, Al Roker, Anthony Robbins, and Newt Gingrich, along with director Barry Sonnenfeld and his daughter Chloe, show up as registered aliens on the MIB tracking screen.

MIB grossed more than $250 million domestically, with overseas ticket sales bringing in an additional $338 million. The total take of nearly $600 million led to two sequels: *Men in Black II* in 2002 and *Men in Black 3* in 2012. The second *MIB* film grossed more than $440 million around the world, while the latest one scored $624 million. The three flicks account for more than $1.6 billion—more than enough reason to support thoughts of an *MIB 4* in the future. While stars Smith and Jones have indicated they might be convinced to return, it's very likely the next MIB agents will have new initials.

District 9

Synopsis

- 2009—American/New Zealand/Canada/South Africa/Tri-Star Pictures—112 min./color
- Director: Neill Blomkamp
- Original music: Clinton Shorter
- Film editing: Julian Clarke
- Production design: Philip Ivey
- Based on the 2005 short film *Alive in Joberg*, by Neill Blomkamp

Cast
- Sharlto Copley (Wikus Van De Merwe)
- Jason Cope (Christopher Johnson and Grey Bradnam)
- Nathalie Boltt (Sarah Livingstone)
- David James (Colonel Koobus Venter)
- Eugene Khumbanyiwa (Obesandjo)
- Louis Minnaar (Piet Smit)
- Vanessa Haywood (Tania Van De Merwe)

In 1982, an enormous alien spaceship came to rest over the city of Johannesburg, South Africa. Its inhabitants, insect-like, scavenging creatures that walk on two legs—disparagingly called "prawns" by the locals—were in need of food and care. The South African government set up a tent city beneath the ship as a temporary location for the aliens, an area known as District 9. An independent agency called Multinational United—MNU—was brought in to manage the affairs and needs of the aliens.

Nearly thirty years later, Wikus Van De Merwe is an agent for MNU Alien Affairs. The aliens have not integrated well with the locals and, following riots and killings, must be segregated from the general population. District 9, and its population of nearly two million aliens, will be relocated away from Johannesburg. Wikus is chosen to direct the program. As a civilian, his agenda seems to conflict with one of the private military (PMC) officers named Colonel Koobus Venter.

The evictions begin, but don't go well at all, as the aliens aren't keen on being moved. Some can be enticed with cans of cat food—an item they enjoy immensely—but many refuse to be evicted. What's more, groups of Nigerians— led by the evil Obesandjo—have preyed upon the prawns, dealing in black market weapons, prostitution, and other vices.

Wikus and his team discover a shack used for breeding prawns, with dozens of eggs fed by the blood of cattle. Wikus, insensitive to the aliens' brood, has the hovel burned to the ground, amused to note how the eggs burst like popcorn.

MNU, also an enormous manufacturer of weapons, has a secondary purpose for relocating the aliens. They have their own cache of weapons that's very attractive to MNU, although they are designed to be used only by prawns, not humans. Breaking that barrier would bring a new source of revenue for the company. So, as the aliens are moved, a search for any weapons is routinely made.

Several aliens—Christopher Johnson, his son, and a friend—have scrounged and worked to collect and refine a strange fluid, which they store in a small cylinder. Wikus searches the friend's shack and finds the cylinder, then clumsily sprays himself in the face with the fluid by accident.

Led by Colonel Venter, soldiers also find a huge hoard of weapons in the friend's shack. When the friend tries to escape, the soldier coldly shoots and kills him. Johnson has quietly witnessed all of this and, when Wikus arrives at his shack, refuses to be evicted. The MNU agent threatens to take Johnson's son away to Child Services, but he leaves the two aliens alone as he finds himself feeling unwell. At his office, Wikus' nose begins to drip a black substance, and his fingernails come off.

Johnson and his son search for the missing canister, while Obesandjo obtains an enormous exoskeleton walker from the aliens in exchange for one hundred cans of cat food. The Nigerians are also feeding off the aliens, superstitiously believing they have mystic and magical powers in their flesh.

A surprise celebration at Wikus' house doesn't go well. Piet Smit, his father-in-law and the MNU executive who arranged for the promotion, chides him for too many alien deaths in the field. Also, Wikus gets sicker and sicker as the evening goes on, vomiting black goo on his cake. The party breaks up early.

At the hospital, Wikus is stunned to find his left arm, bandaged from a field injury, has transformed into an alien tentacle. In front of his tearful wife, Wikus is placed in a hazmat bag and flown away by helicopter.

In a bio-lab, it becomes apparent that Wikus is slowly assimilating the alien DNA into his own. Like other prawns, he can fire their proprietary weapons.

Sharlto Copley (center) and Jason Cope in *District 9*.

While his father-in-law looks on, the decision is made to use Wikus as a biotechnical source for all sorts of organic material. His sacrifice will make millions for MNU.

Just seconds away from vivisection, Wikus breaks free and becomes a fugitive in Johannesburg. He evades the military, but is unable to reach his wife or return to his house. With nowhere else to run, Wikus sneaks into District 9.

The military searches by helicopter, and Wikus slips into a shack, which happens to be Johnson's. He pleads with the alien to hide him, and, reluctantly, Johnson agrees. When Wikus passes out, Johnson and his boy stash him in an underground space.

Johnson knows Wikus took the cylinder, which is now in the hands of the people at MNU. The boy innocently reveals that the underground space is actually a vehicle, capable of flying back to the spaceship over Johannesburg. All that's needed is fuel—which happens to be the contents of the missing cylinder.

Wikus is thrilled to discover that Johnson could fix his alien hand on the mother ship if only they could get up there. Johnson proposes a dangerous attempt to recover the fluid from the MNU headquarters. If they get it, Wikus thinks he can go home to his wife, the aliens can get back to their ship, and everything will be just fine.

Wikus goes to Obesandjo to buy some weapons, but the villain is only interested in taking Wikus' alien arm for its magic powers. As his men prepare to cut it from Wikus, he grabs an alien blaster and holds everyone at bay, while he takes a bagful of weapons and flees.

Smit and Venter think they have traced Wikus in District 9, and a tactical team rushes Johnson's shack, only to find it empty. But a blast shakes the MNU headquarters, as Wikus and Johnson make their way inside. Workers evacuate the building, and Venter tries to find the invaders as they search for the cylinder.

Wikus and Johnson find the fluid, but Johnson sees for himself what MNU has been doing in their horrible experiments with his kind. He is frozen with shock and sorrow, while Venter catches up with the duo. Johnson snaps out of his funk in time to fashion a bomb and blow a hole in a wall, where he and Wikus escape in an MNU vehicle

Venter chases them back to District 9 by helicopter. Wikus discovers that Johnson must save his people first, so it will take three years to fix the human. That schedule angers Wikus, so he knocks the alien unconscious and climbs into the underground spaceship, where Christopher's son has been hiding.

Colonel Venter bursts into the shack, demanding to know where Wikus has gone. The boy shows Wikus how to start the ship, and it slowly rises from the ground, forcing Venter and Johnson out of the shack. A battery of PMC missiles quickly disables the spacecraft, and it crashes. Johnson watches as his chance of returning to the mother ship vanishes and he's taken away in an MNU van.

Venter drags Wikus away from the rubble, while Johnson's son watches from behind a bundle of cables. But Obesandjo's men ambush the vehicles, taking Wikus to the Nigerian bandit as Venter calls for backup.

When they arrive, a full-scale skirmish erupts between the soldiers and Obesandjo's troops. But all he wants is Wikus' alien arm—once eaten, the villain believes he will be all-powerful.

As they prepare to cleave the arm, Johnson's son—obviously a very bright boy—contacts the mother ship from the crippled shuttle. In turn, a remote signal is sent to the alien exoskeleton that Obesandjo had purchased from the aliens. It comes alive, and its offensive powers seem unlimited. As mercenaries fire their guns at it, the exoskeleton merely collects the bullets into a magnetic mass—then fires them all back at the shooters, killing them all. Obesandjo is eliminated by a well-placed explosive probe to the forehead.

Wikus climbs into the exoskeleton as the mother ship slowly begins to move from its position. Venter and his men press Johnson to reveal his plans, but he won't talk so they prepare to kill him. Wikus steps in, shooting soldiers and providing cover for Johnson to get back to his son.

Large guns begin to take their toll on the exoskeleton, so Wikus urges Johnson to take his son and go. He will keep the soldiers busy while the alien escapes. Johnson promises to come back for Wikus in three years.

Wikus maintains his one-man war against the soldiers as Johnson gets to his boy in the ship. The mother ship settles over it and slowly pulls it skyward with a beam of light. An MNU vehicle crashes into the exoskeleton, knocking it over and revealing Wikus to Colonel Venter.

Three days after exposure and Wikus is nearly half-transformed into an alien. Venter prepares to shoot Wikus at point-blank range, but other prawns intervene and tear the officer to bits.

The mother ship leaves as citizens of Johannesburg cheer. Wikus disappears, to speculation of his death or abduction by another country. MNU's illegal genetic research program is brought to light as the relocation of the aliens is completed. The area of District 9 is demolished, while the new District 10 holds more than two-and-a-half-million prawns. Tania Van De Merwe finds a small metal flower on her doorstep one day, while an alien fashions another one somewhere in District 10.

Afterwords

Wholly different from the feel-good themes of *E.T.* and *Cocoon*, *District 9* distinguished itself with its gritty documentary style, repulsive alien species, and many scenes with improvised dialogue. With support from producer Peter Jackson (following an aborted feature film project of the video game *Halo*), director Neill Blomkamp set the story in his homeland of South Africa, where the prejudiced apartheid government ruled for many years. While the story was sci-fi, the inspiration was racial segregation.

District 9 grew from a six-minute film Blomkamp, a director of TV commercials, music videos, and computer-generated FX, created in 2005. Called *Alive in Joberg* (slang for Johannesburg in South Africa), the short presented a fake documentary news story on aliens from another world forced to cohabitate with citizens of Johannesburg. Blomkamp used real interviews, which he conducted with people who answered questions about the real-life issue of Nigerian and Zimbabwean refugees living in South Africa. Intercut with impressive FX shots of hovering spaceships and vague images of aliens, *Alive in Joberg* set the tone for a great feature film four years later.

Blomkamp had a clear vision in his head as to what the aliens should look like. He saw them as being insect-like but bipeds. Without some sort of humanoid appearance, Blomkamp felt there was no chance of developing an empathy with the viewing audience. The original plan was to use fully articulated costumes and prosthetic makeup for alien actors, but the creatures were essentially digitally created in all but the closest of shots. South African actor Jason Cope wore a gray motion-capture suit and performed the actions on the sets for all the aliens seen on the screen. His performances were then matched to CGI creatures for final compositing.

The film was Blomkamp's first feature film, and with a cast of novices or actors completely unknown to audiences outside South Africa, the chances for an international hit were slim. Lead actor Sharlto Copley, a longtime friend of the director's, was a pioneer exec in the late-developing but fast-growing broadcast TV industry in South Africa. He was a producer and had a small role as a police officer in Blomkamp's *Alive in Joberg* before he accepted the challenge of *District 9*.

The success of *District 9* was unexpected. Part of it can be attributed to the clever and vague marketing ploy of Sony Pictures, who distributed the film. Long before the film's release, signs and bus cards around America offered cryptic caveats of "For Humans Only," with a website and/or phone number for more information. Based on signage seen in the film, the buzz needed to stir interest began.

Shot on a reasonably slim budget of $39 million, *District 9* grossed $115 million in America. With another $95 million around the world, the total of more than $200 million was a pleasing result for all involved. It impressed enough people to garner a nomination for a Best Picture Oscar, a rarity for sci-fi films.

Super 8

Synopsis

- 2011—American/Paramount—112 min./color
- Director: J. J. Abrams
- Original music: Michael Giacchino
- Film editing: Maryann Brandon, Mary Jo Markey
- Production design: Martin Whist

Cast

- Joel Courtney (Joe Lamb)
- Elle Fanning (Alice Dainard)
- Kyle Chandler (Jack Lamb)
- Riley Griffiths (Charles Kaznyk)
- Ryan Lee (Cary)
- Zach Mills (Preston)
- Gabriel Basso (Martin)
- Ron Eldard (Louis Dainard)
- Glynn Turman (Dr. Woodward)
- Noah Emmerich (Colonel Nelec)
- Bruce Greenwood (Cooper)

In the winter of 1979, fourteen-year-old Joe Lamb struggles to accept the death of his mother Elizabeth, in a steel plant accident. His father, Jack, deputy sheriff in the small Ohio town of Lillian, angrily detains a factory coworker—Louis Dainard—believing his careless drunken hangover forced Liz to work his shift at the factory.

Four months later, summer vacation arrives for students at Lillian Middle School, including Joe and his four pals—the hulking Charles, hyperactive Cary, nerdy Preston, and bookish Martin. Charles has written a zombie movie, *The Case*, which he's directing with his friends and plans to enter into a local film festival. Things get a bit uncomfortable when he asks Louis Dainard's pretty teen daughter Alice to play the female lead in the production.

Despite having no license, Alice picks everyone up in her father's car at midnight, and the kids set up at a darkened train station to shoot an important scene for the film. With the horn of an approaching train, the kids rush to capture it as an exciting background on film as they roll the camera.

But down the tracks, a pickup truck swerves directly into the path of the diesel engine. The train derails in a fiery crash, as freight cars smash into the station and the kids flee for their lives. Amid the carnage, no one realizes their fallen Super 8 camera is capturing the entire event.

The group pick themselves up, shaken but unharmed. Strewn about the wreckage are strange white cubes—heavy, textured, about the size of a baseball—and Joe pockets one. They find Dr. Woodward, their school's biology teacher, was the driver of the now-smashed pickup truck. Bloodied and injured, he warns the kids not to tell anyone about the accident—or an unidentified "they" will kill them and their parents. Stunned, the kids grab their camera and quickly leave as soldiers swarm the area. But an empty film package tips US Air Force Colonel Nelec that the disaster was likely caught on film by someone.

The next day, the local news reports the mysterious crash while the military investigates. Joe and Charles drop the film off for developing, which will take several days. Joe convinces a reluctant Alice to shoot some more scenes for *The Case*, but he gets thrown off the Dainard property by her angry father. And it appears that Joe has developed a crush on Alice.

The air force acts quickly to clear the scene of the train wreck, taking care to recover the hundreds of strange cubes. On behalf of his town, Deputy Lamb wants to know the contents of the train, but Colonel Nelec refuses, assuring him there was nothing of a dangerous nature. The sheriff of Lillian is unconcerned and urges Jack to take a break.

At a local service station, the sheriff's fill-up is interrupted by something that crushes the front of his car. The officer disappears, and then the unknown creature turns its attention on the station attendant, who is dragged screaming out of the building.

Strange things continue in Lillian, as the town's power surges—the power lines are disappearing, packs of family dogs run away, and dozens of autos are missing their engines. Lillian's citizens are scared, fearing an invasion by the Russians. But a ham radio operator has noticed the US military has been using a number of normally cleared frequencies. Something is heard about a project called "Operation: Walking Distance."

The kids shoot a scene in their neighborhood, while the military searches Woodward's home and files. Deputy Lamb pulls up, orders Joe into his cruiser, and then confronts Nelec about "Walking Distance." The officer suggests meeting later to further discuss what Lamb knows. Jack also prohibits his son from having any contact with Alice or her father.

Joel Courtney in *Super 8*.

At Lillian Airfield, Nelec immediately places Deputy Lamb under arrest and, unable to secure any information from the injured Dr. Woodward, has him killed by injection. Clearly, Nelec is after something living—and vows to capture whatever it is.

Alice shows up at Joe's house, and they watch old home movies of Liz when Joe was a baby. Alice reveals that her father had been drinking and was unable to work his shift the morning of the factory accident, and Joe's mom took his place. It makes Alice cry. The cube Joe took from the train wreck begins to vibrate on his desk, amazing the couple. Suddenly, it shoots off through a wall and disappears.

Alice returns home to her drunken father, who throws her out of the house. She rides away on her bike, and her dad follows in his car, trying to apologize. But he crashes into a parked car and watches in horror as a huge creature takes Alice away.

Nelec puts "Operation: Walking Distance" into action, setting brushfires to evacuate the townspeople, while Joe and Charles pick up the developed film. They watch it, stunned, seeing an alien creature escape from one of the smashed boxcars.

The air force moves busloads and truckloads of Lillian's population to military centers, claiming the fires have completely blocked off the town. Joe finds a bloodied Mr. Dainard on a cot; he's still reeling from witnessing his daughter taken by the creature. No one will believe what he saw—but Joe does.

The kids make their way out of the air base, thanks to the dope-dealing clerk who worked at the camera store and has a car. Deputy Lamb gets free and dons the uniform of a soldier, while the kids break into their school and find Dr. Woodward's files and films.

They reveal an amazing story from Woodward's days as a government researcher in the early sixties, working on a top-secret project to study an alien who crashed on Earth in 1958. The films, taken inside a remote hangar, show the creature's spacecraft breaking into thousands of cubes. A tape-recorded narration details how the creature only wanted to return home, while the government kept it confined and conducted torturous experiments. The kids realize that Woodward crashed into the train in an effort to help the creature escape. But Nelec and other soldiers burst in and recapture the kids.

On the way back to the center, the creature slams into the bus carrying the boys. It terrorizes the soldiers and kills Nelec as the kids escape out the back. Jack, still dressed as a soldier, slips Dainard out of confinement to find their children. In a speeding Jeep, the two fathers mend their feud.

In town, the kids arrive to find themselves in the middle of a battle zone, as tanks and other weapons blast away. However, the soldiers aren't doing the firing—something else is controlling the fray. Dodging the shells, Joe and Cary find an underground lair at the town cemetery.

The pair discover an elaborate device the creature has built under the town's water tower, plus dozens of people from Lillian—still alive but trussed upside-down. Alice is among them. Cary creates a distraction with his endless supply of fireworks, while Joe rescues Alice, as well as the sheriff and another young woman. But the creature quickly grabs those two for a bite, leaving Joe, Cary, and Alice at its mercy.

Somehow, as the creature grabs him in its claws, Joe reasons with the creature. Drawing on his experience of losing his mother, he convinces the alien that bad things happen, but life can go on. The alien should just go home. Joe is put down, and the creature begins to gather all sorts of metal, magnetically pulling it to the water tower.

Along with the metal come the thousands of cubes stored in military trucks. The kids and townspeople watch as the creature assembles a launch vehicle atop the water tower. Jack and Louis reconnect with their kids and embrace.

The spacecraft slowly lifts off, while Joe finally lets go of a locket—pulled by the magnetic field—given to him by his mom many years back. Joe and Alice hold hands as the spaceship disappears into the black sky of night.

During the film's closing credits, *The Case* is screened.

A detective investigates the death of someone attacked by a zombie. The detective questions the president of a chemical factory about the incident. There seems to be a connection between the plant and the outbreak of zombies. And the president is hiding something.

In building 47, the detective is attacked by a crazed zombie, and he saves himself by impaling the zombie's head on a group of nails. The detective insists on sending his wife away for her own safety, while a dangerous train wreck interrupts the sad goodbye.

The next day, the couple stand beyond the wreckage, amazed that they survived. Another zombie attacks and is killed by the detective. Two weeks pass, and the zombie threat continues. An old soldier friend passes information along to the detective about a suicide committed by someone who could no longer keep a secret.

A doctor at the chemical plant developed a compound, intended as a military weapon, that turned the people into zombies. But he has created an antidote for it. Before it can be tested on one of the zombies, the doctor is bitten and becomes a zombie himself. The detective kills both zombies and grabs the antidote.

Arriving home, he finds his wife has become a zombie and, after a struggle, injects her with the antidote. Preparing to shoot her, the detective is relieved to see it worked, and they embrace.

In an epilogue, director Charles Kaznyk addresses the viewers at the Cleveland International Super 8 Film Festival, encouraging them to select his film. Suddenly, the detective's wife—still a zombie—attacks Charles, then she lunges at the camera.

Afterwords

The anticipation for the release of *Super 8* was palpable, thanks in part to the heavyweights behind it. Producer Steven Spielberg's credentials needed no explaining, and writer/director J. J Abrams had thrilled audiences with the 2009 big screen reboot of *Star Trek*, as well as producing the hit 2008 monster movie *Cloverfield*.

Both embraced the project as a tribute to their youthful days, where they shot their first films with Super 8 home-movie cameras. In fact, Abrams intended on shooting *The Case*, his film-within-film (the one the kids are shooting) on actual Super 8 film, but the FX folks at ILM couldn't handle the graininess and low resolution of the home format when trying to add the CG effects.

In an example of art-imitating-life-imitating-art-imitating . . . oh, never mind. *The Case*, supposedly written, directed, shot, and teched by the six kids in *Super 8*, was actually written, directed, shot, and teched by the six kids in *Super 8*. J. J Abrams told them it had to be a zombie film, and that was really the only restriction he placed on the young filmmakers. They quickly collaborated and were as proud of making *The Case* as they were *Super 8*.

The key to *Super 8* is the spectacular train crash that releases the alien creature, which the kids accidentally capture on film while shooting their zombie movie. The impressive scene was accomplished with a combination of real physical effects and CGI in postproduction. Using a large, barren area at the Firestone Ranch near Los Angeles, techs built a full-scale train station and laid some train tracks. Pyrotechnicians set low-grade explosives and flash pots around the area. A large green sled was set onto the train tracks, and stunt doubles replaced the kids in the scene.

After two days of building, preparations, and rehearsals, the scene was ready—with such a massive setup, there was only a chance for one take. With Abrams calling "Action!" the sled crashed through the station (the lumber having been precut to break away), as the stunt doubles ran from the accident, while explosions lit the night. In five seconds, the shot was complete.

Later in postproduction, computer FX artists replaced the green sled with a train car, added additional track and scenery to create a perspective view, and inserted more train cars, debris, explosions, and smoke to complete the scene.

As well as great FX, Abrams felt he needed the right kids to take *Super 8* over the top. He knew they should be real prepubescents (as opposed to casting older performers who could "play" young) and held a nationwide search for the lead role of Joe Lamb. Idahoan Joel Courtney was visiting his brother in California for the summer and had hopes of maybe landing a TV commercial. His initial interview with Abrams went well, and, with a dozen callbacks, Courtney got the part.

With kids being kids, on-set pranks were inevitable. On—of all days—April Fool's Day, actor Riley Griffiths pulled the prank, breathlessly telling director Abrams that he'd accidentally left the highly top-secret script for *Super 8* in the local mall. When he went back to retrieve it, it was nowhere to be found. Needless to say, Abrams went into immediate cardiac arrest. After a few sweaty minutes, the all-clear was sounded, and everyone had a good laugh.

Super 8 obviously struck a chord with fans who enjoyed Spielberg films like *E.T.* and *Close Encounters*, as well as coming-of-age films like 1986's *Stand By Me.* Produced for a budget of $50 million, *Super 8* grossed more than $127 million in the US, with another $132 million overseas. With countries like Japan, France, and Spain leading the way, the total gross for *Super 8* was nearly $260 million around the world.

8

Are You Sure That's Safe?

Sci-Fi-entists and Their Experiments

The Mad Doctor Asked the Miniature Mutant to Be a Little Patient . . .

The relationship between a doctor and his or her patient is a sacred one. The medical profession works diligently to develop trust and respect from those who are in need of their services. The frail, sick, and wounded expect compassion and healing from those who have taken the Hippocratic Oath.

But the whole thing goes out the window when one considers Dr. Victor Frankenstein (in the many *Frankenstein* films), Dr. Gogol (in the underappreciated 1935 *Mad Love*), Dr. Henry Jekyll (and his other side, Edward Hyde), Dr. Hannibal Lecter (from 1991's *Silence of the Lambs* and its cinematic progeny), even the evil Dr. Caligari and his cabinet (from the great silent 1920 German art film).

Doctors and scientists in the film world are often driven by the need to go where no one has gone before (they must be related to Captain James T. Kirk). Something inside them longs for fame, greatness, immortality, or a pile of greenbacks.

In their quest for the not-yet-discovered, these people of science ignore the rules of provenance, prompting the inevitable closing line: "He tampered in God's domain" (the curse of Bela Lugosi's Dr. Eric Vornoff in Ed Wood's "so bad it's good" *Bride of the Monster* in 1955. There are many others like it.).

That also can lead to what is commonly known as the "Oops Factor." In 1980, *Altered States'* Eddie Jessup poked his scientific nose into isolation tanks and, not sure of where he was going, nearly killed himself and those he loved. Entrepreneur John Hammond's Jurassic Park—intended purely as an amusement attraction—proved why man and dinosaurs were never meant to play together. In 2011's *Contagion*, filmgoers hopefully learned why hand-washing is so important. (Psst! Deadly virus—Pass it on . . . .)

The attraction of sci-fi films in this subgenre for filmgoers is—most likely—the thrill and roller-coaster ride of being one of the victims, one of the participants in the on-screen crisis. It's hard to say if any of the audience sympathizes with the evildoers, unless they have serious relationship problems with their partner or boss (and, yes, that is possible).

Either way, as the lights come up in the theater at the end of the film, the audience gets to go home, safe and sound . . . unless they have a doctor's appointment.

Altered States

Synopsis

- 1980—American/Warner Brothers—102 min./color
- Director: Ken Russell
- Original music: John Corigliano
- Film editing: Eric Jenkins
- Production design: Richard McDonald
- Based on the 1978 novel by Paddy Chayefsky

Cast

- William Hurt (Eddie Jessup)
- Blair Brown (Emily Jessup)
- Bob Balaban (Arthur Rosenberg)
- Charles Haid (Dr. Mason Parrish)
- Miguel Godreau (Primal Man)

In the late 1960s, Eddie Jessup is a psychophysiology college professor who begins experiments in sensory deprivation using an isolation tank. He meets Emily, a PhD candidate in anthropology, at a party, and they quickly fall for each other.

Aided by Arthur Rosenberg, Jessup puts himself into the tank, where he has wild religious hallucinations and sees images of his dead father. Emily convinces Eddie to get married, and several years pass.

When Arthur comes east to visit, Eddie is now a full professor on the staff of Harvard Medical School. He talks of restarting his isolation tank research. Emily and Eddie separate; she goes to Nairobi, while he goes to Mexico. He experiments with native hallucinogens, seeing wild images of native rituals, Komodo dragons, and Emily's naked body turning into a sand sculpture in a dust storm.

Eddie brings the potion back to Harvard, where he witnesses Dante's Inferno and fields of crucifixions. Dr. Mason Parrish is a skeptical colleague who believes an untested drug like this is pure danger.

But his curiosity gets the best of him, and he joins Arthur as Eddie enters the school's isolation chamber. Inside, he tells of returning to the beginning of man. Hours pass, and Eddie is pulled from the chamber, bloodied and claiming the hallucinations have externalized—they've become reality. He remembers running through wild lands, hunting and feeding on goats.

A quick set of X-rays reveal that Eddie actually became a primitive man during his session in the tank. That night, he wakes to find his body convulsing and bulging, as his feet appear to belong to a gorilla. He quickly makes notes of the experience.

Jessup feels he's on the verge of a tremendous breakthrough of genetic and psychological importance. He asks Emily to watch his next session to validate the experiment. Instead, he goes alone and emerges from the tank as a vicious primal man. He attacks a janitor and a guard and escapes into the streets, seeking refuge in the Boston Zoo. He pounces on a goat.

Mason and Emily bail Eddie out of jail after he's found naked in the zoo. He doesn't remember much about the experience, and Emily believes Eddie actually did become another form of being.

Along with Mason and Arthur, Emily monitors Eddie's next trip into the tank, and they watch in amazement as he begins to change. He transcends his own being, becoming a blinding and powerful ball of protoplasm. The control room window blows out, and Arthur and Mason are knocked cold. Emily wades into a billowing sea of light and pulls an unconscious Eddie to safety.

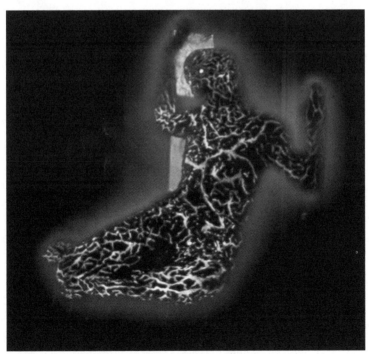

Blair Brown in *Altered States*.

They take Eddie to Emily's, where Arthur is near manic about the reality of what's happened. Mason wishes to deny it ever happened and argues with Arthur about the morality of it all.

In the morning, Eddie is full of love and appreciation for Emily, for it was she who brought him back from the "terror of the beginning of life." He's afraid to stay with her and their children, fearing the uncontrollable results of his experiments.

He suddenly becomes a writhing mass of protoplasm, and Emily reaches out to him, saying, "You made this real—you can make it unreal." As their hands touch, Emily becomes a charred and glowing ember in human form. Jessup struggles and pounds the floor, trying to reverse the metamorphosis. He finally succeeds and embraces Emily. She too returns to normal, as Eddie says, "I love you."

Afterwords

Altered States is one of those rare films that seem to have been destined for production, no matter what pitfalls it came up against (supposedly, an amazing twenty-six directors passed on making it). It started out as a Columbia picture to be directed by Arthur Penn, who gained prominence by helming *Bonnie and Clyde* in 1968 and *Little Big Man* in 1970.

Effects were to be created by John Dykstra, and the screenplay was written by Paddy Chayefsky, based on his 1978 novel. Two years later, after nearly everyone was fired or quit, it was released as a Warner Bros. film and directed by Ken Russell. Visual effects—with some wild hallucinogenic depictions—were coordinated by Bran Ferren.

The only constant was the brilliant work of makeup artist Dick Smith, who was asked to design and redesign the bizarre full-body foam latex appliances for Hurt and Blair, as well as a unique simian makeup for the primal man, played by Mexican dancer Miguel Godreau.

Smith's genius with innovation can be witnessed in the climax, where Emily appears to become a burning mass after touching Eddie. A full-latex suit covered actress Blair Brown, including her face. Smith attached ScotchLite reflective material in a branch-like pattern all over the suit. An out-of-focus image of reddish bubbling water was front projected onto the suit, with the final result appearing to be a human body turned into a glowing mass of volcanic lava.

Lead actor William Hurt was very happy performing in repertory theater, although he had appeared in a few TV shows in the late 1970s. By chance meeting, he was hooked up with Chayefsky, and, even though he repeatedly refused the role of Eddie Jessup, Hurt finally gave in.

The actor thought he would be working with Arthur Penn, but what no one knew at the time was that Paddy Chayefsky was dying of cancer. The writer feared that he would be dead before *Altered States* was finished, considering Penn's slow and deliberate directing style. Believed to be faster and more efficient, Russell was brought in to take the helm (and fight it out with Paddy).

Chayefsky was so upset at the eventual outcome that he requested his name be removed from the film (after having an honest-to-goodness, full-out fistfight with the director. He ended up credited under the pseudonym "Sidney Aaron," Chayefsky's real first and middle names.).

After all the trials of getting *Altered States* to the theaters, audiences seemed to appreciate the effort. Made on a budget of $15 million, the film grossed nearly $20 million domestically—numbers that compared well with other 1980 releases such as John Carpenter's *The Fog*, the musical *Fame*, and even Martin Scorsese's *Raging Bull*.

Ghostbusters

Synopsis

- 1984—American/Columbia—105 min./color
- Director: Ivan Reitman
- Original music: Elmer Bernstein
- Film editing: David Blewitt, Sheldon Kahn
- Production design: John Decuir

Cast

- Bill Murray (Dr. Peter Venkman)
- Dan Aykroyd (Dr. Raymond Stantz)
- Sigourney Weaver (Dana Barrett)
- Harold Ramis (Dr. Egon Spengler)
- Rick Moranis (Louis Tully)
- Annie Potts (Janine Melnitz)
- William Atherton (Walter Peck)
- Ernie Hudson (Winston Zeddemore)
- Slavitza Jovan (Gozer)
- David Margulies (New York City Mayor)

At the New York Public Library, peculiar things are happening. Someone—or something—is invisibly moving books through thin air. Cards in catalog files are flying skyward like a toaster gone mad. And something strange scares a librarian out of her wits.

In the collegiate paranormal studies office of Doctors Egon Spengler, Ray Stantz, and Peter Venkman, several students undergo psychic tests conducted by Venkman—with less than conclusive results. The work is interrupted when the trio are summoned to investigate the unusual goings-on at the library.

Armed with cameras and detecting devices, they find ectoplasmic slime as proof positive that something is out of the ordinary. They spot an apparition—an elderly woman in Victorian garb—and try to speak to it. She shushes them—standard library behavior. A second approach turns the ghost into a screaming toothy monster, and everyone quickly evacuates the building.

Spengler excites the team by suggesting a ghost could actually be captured and held. But before anything can get started, the university cuts their funding and throws them off campus. Against his better judgment, Ray takes a loan on his house, and the money puts the three scientists into business as the Ghostbusters. They rent a broken-down firehouse as their base of operations.

Pretty concert cellist Dana Barrett arrives at her upscale Central Park apartment, where nerdy accountant neighbor Louis Tully invites her to his party. Quickly brushing him off, Dana finds she has problems of the paranormal kind. A carton of eggs begins to burst and cook spontaneously, and a demon dog grows the name "Zuul" and seems to be living in her refrigerator.

Meanwhile at the Ghostbusters, Ray buys an old worn-out Cadillac ambulance for transportation, and the team have hired Janine Melnitz to be their new secretary. But business is pretty slow, until Dana comes in to report the strange occurrence at her apartment. The Ghostbusters will investigate, but Venkman's interest is in Dana, more as an attractive woman than a client. He escorts Dana back to her place, where everything seems perfectly normal. But she is not swayed by Venkman's sudden declaration of love for her and kindly asks him to leave.

That evening, a call of paranormal activity comes in to the Ghostbusters office, and the team roll out onto the streets in their white ambulance with an

Harold Ramis, Ernie Hudson, Bill Murray, and Dan Aykroyd (L-R) in *Ghostbusters*.

Ecto-One license plate. At the swanky Sedgewick Hotel, the quirky twelfth floor is becoming active after years of being calm.

Spengler, Stantz, and Venkman are each equipped with nuclear-powered proton packs and, being a bit tense on their first real case, accidentally blow a maid's service cart to smithereens when they reach the twelfth floor.

Stantz comes upon a glowing green blob of protoplasm, sloppily feeding on the remains of a room service meal. But one blast from his proton pack scares it into thin air. It reappears in front of Venkman and angrily attacks the Ghostbuster, leaving him covered in a thick slimy mess.

The team find the protoplasm in the hotel's ballroom, and they prepare to capture it with their packs. Spengler warns his partners not to cross their proton beams, as that would result in disastrous consequences. The Ghostbusters fire their beams, and, amid much destruction in the room, they finally force the green glob into a toaster-sized trap. The charge for the service is $5,000, which the hotel manager reluctantly agrees to pay.

The Ghostbusters quickly gain notoriety and success in catching phantasms. In fact, business is going so well, they have to add another member to their team—Winston Zeddemore. And Dr. Venkman still has romantic intentions with Dana Barrett, although he has found that Zuul is an ancient demigod connected with Gozer, the god of destruction. The lady finally breaks down and agrees to a date with him.

The trapped ghosts are being stored in an onsite containment device at the office. But self-important Walter Peck of the Environmental Protection Agency insists on inspecting the facility, fearing for the unknown ecological danger the kept ghosts may pose. Venkman denies access to Peck, who threatens legal action.

Spengler notes that there's a recent increase in paranormal activity in the city that could be dangerous. As he speaks, lightning is striking Dana's apartment building, and a real demon dog is breaking free from inside a gargoyle on the roof. The perilous pooch with glowing red eyes bursts into Dana's apartment, as claws erupt from her armchair and hold her captive.

Louis' party is in full swing, although his client guests are less than enthusiastic about their milquetoast host. The demon dog has found its way into Louis' bedroom and crashes its way into the soiree. It chases Louis as he runs into the street trying to escape.

Peter shows up for his date with Dana, but she is no longer the demure and soft-spoken cellist. Under the hypnotic influence of Zuul the Gatekeeper, she is a wild-haired and sexy raven. Wondering if Venkman is the Keymaster, she is awaiting the coming of Gozer the Destructor. Dana makes a beeline for her bedroom, and, despite his own desires, Peter realizes she is possessed. Barrett begins to levitate above her bed, until Venkman can sedate her.

Still in the streets, Louis is also possessed—in fact, it turns out he is Vinz Clortho the Keymaster, searching for the Gatekeeper and awaiting the arrival of Gozer. The NYPD pick Louis up and drop him off, straitjacket and all, with Spengler at the Ghostbusters office.

Ray and Winston drive in the Ecto-One and, considering all the recent paranormal activity, contemplate the chilling possibility that the end of the world is near.

The next day, Peck arrives at the trio's offices, armed with a legal writ and intending to shut down the protection grid of storage facilities. A ConEdison tech throws the switch, and all hell breaks loose. Everyone runs out of the building as a fiery hole blasts through its roof and Dana quickly awakens. The ghosts are loose, and New York City is thrown into a panic.

The Ghostbusters are placed under arrest, and Ray points out that Dana's apartment building seems to be designed as a natural attractor for the worst from the spirit world. Years ago, the architect, Ivo Shandor, built it as access to the underworld.

Louis gets back to his apartment building and finds Dana in the ruins of her living room. The Keymaster and Gatekeeper embrace, with the certainty that nothing good will come out of that union.

At city hall, the mayor and department heads are unsure of how to respond to the crisis. Even the church's cardinal seems lost. Peck blames the Ghostbusters for the disaster, but the mayor throws him out and supports whatever the Ghostbusters can do to save the city.

Police and military troops are mobilized as the streets begin to seize and buckle. Crowds cheer as the Ghostbusters enter the Central Park building. The skies above it darken, and lightning crackles around the rooftop. It travels through Dana and Louis, focusing on an outside façade before the pair turn into demon dogs.

The façade is a stairway to crystalline doors. Ray, Egon, Peter, and Winston arrive in time to see the lithe female form of Gozer ascend the steps. She blasts the quartet with bolts of lightning, perilously sending them to the edge of the building.

Climbing to safety, the Ghostbusters fire their proton packs at Gozer, but she deftly avoids the beams before disappearing completely. The top of the building begins to break apart, and the crowds below scatter.

An evil ethereal voice gives the team the option of choosing their Destructor. Peter urges everyone to completely clear their minds, but Ray inadvertently imagines the Stay-Puft Marshmallow Man. Suddenly, a gigantic marauding white marshmallow man is marching down the streets, crushing cars and buildings in its way.

Set afire with proton packs, the creature begins to climb the side of the apartment building. Despite the danger of death, the Ghostbusters make a last-ditch attempt to reverse the catastrophe by crossing the beams of their weapons. Aiming at Gozer's entrance, the flashing beams create an enormous explosion. Massive streams of sticky marshmallow cream land everywhere—including on Peck.

The four Ghostbusters are covered in a gooey white mess, but otherwise are in one piece. There's no sign of Dana or Louis, but statues of the demon dogs break apart, revealing them to be alive and no longer possessed.

As Peter and Dana embrace, the crowds cheer once more for the victorious Ghostbusters.

Afterwords

It's not a guarantee, but a quick peek in the dictionary under "cult classic" just might reveal *Ghostbusters*. Full of stars, special effects, and catchy music, the 1984 film spawned a sequel, two animated television series, and a bunch of fans who love to dress up in authentic Ghostbuster costumes at every sci-fi convention that will have them.

Dan Aykroyd, celebrated alum from the founding class of TV's *Saturday Night Live*, had long had an interest in psychic research and all things paranormal. With those themes in mind, he drafted a movie script for himself and good buddy John Belushi. When the latter out-of-control comic died in 1982, fellow *SNL* member Bill Murray was recruited.

Producer and director Ivan Reitman—producing successful films like 1978's *Animal House*, as well as directing Murray in 1979's *Meatballs*—saw the possibilities for a funny FX film. He brought in Harold Ramis—ex-Second City vet and director of the successful 1980's *Caddyshack* and 1983's *National Lampoon's Vacation*—to cowrite with Aykroyd, along with becoming the screen's third Ghostbuster.

With those creatives on board, Columbia Pictures agreed to front a $25 million budget—as long as the film was ready for release within the year (considering the expansive FX needed, that was one tall order to fill).

Berni Wrightson, an illustrator long known for his artwork in DC comics, *Creepy* and *Eerie* magazines, as well as cocreating *Swamp Thing*, brought his talents to *Ghostbusters* as conceptual artist. His style, heavily influenced by the EC horror and sci-fi comics from the 1950s, helped to formulate the unique look of the film's odd but humorous creatures.

In the film, the Ghostbusters set up their paranormal business in an old firehouse. In actuality, two separate firehouses were used for the shoot—one in NYC for the exteriors, the other in a seedy part of LA for the interiors. While the West Coast location was no longer active, the New York house was still being used for firefighting.

Curiously, no one seemed to look into the possibility of another *Ghostbusters* ever being made. Production was well underway when someone noted that former *F Troop* stars Larry Storch and Forrest Tucker had done a live-action Saturday morning kiddie show in the mid-1970s with the same title for the Filmation production studio. Longtime Hollywood horror favorite and gorilla portrayer Bob Burns showed up in full simian suit as well.

Columbia Pictures reached an agreement with Filmation over the use of the title. But when the film became such a big success, Filmation exercised their right to use the title for their own TV series of cartoons in 1986. To protect the film's identity, Columbia responded by creating *The Real Ghostbusters*, an animated series that ran for seven seasons.

Part of *Ghostbusters'* success can be attributed to the film industry's evolution in the seventies of using the summer and holidays for blockbuster entertainment. With a concept originally developed by films like Spielberg's *Close Encounters* and *E.T. the Extra-Terrestrial*, and Lucas' *Star Wars* franchise, *Ghostbusters* was the first film to combine comedy with big-budget FX to create a filmgoing experience that everyone wanted to see.

And, see it they did. With the production budget eventually hitting $30 million, *Ghostbusters* took in nearly $300 million around the world and was the second-highest-grossing film of the year. The 1989 sequel, *Ghostbusters II*, grossed more than $200 million, which put it into the Top Ten–grossing films for that year.

Talk, via interviews and innuendoes, has surrounded the making of a second *Ghostbusters* sequel for many years. Aykroyd and Reitman have maintained a strong hand in the process, although it's agreed that new and younger Ghostbusters will be needed (apparently, no one wants to see paranormal protoplasm being chased by men with walkers).

Re-Animator

Synopsis

- 1985—American/Empire Pictures—95 min./color
- Director: Stuart Gordon
- Original music: Richard Band
- Film editing: Lee Percy
- Art direction: Robert A. Burns
- Based on the 1922 short story "Herbert West—Reanimator," by H. P. Lovecraft

Cast

- Jeffery Combs (Herbert West)
- Bruce Abbott (Dan Cain)
- Barbara Crampton (Megan Halsey)
- David Gale (Dr. Carl Hill)
- Robert Sampson (Dean Alan Halsey)

Police accompany the dean of a medical school in Zurich, Switzerland, as they rush to investigate a commotion in the classroom of Dr. Gruber. They have to break in, and when they do, Dr. Gruber is found convulsing on the floor, with

Jeffery Combs gets a head in his work in *Re-Animator*.

student Herbert West crouching over him. West is pulled away, and Gruber stands up, screaming. His face is twisted and blue, and his eyes bulge until they burst. The doctor falls over, dead, but West claims he gave him life.

At Miskatonic Med School in Massachusetts, young doctor Daniel Cain works in vain to save a patient. He takes the body to the morgue, where Dean Alan Halsey introduces him to a new student, who just happens to be Herbert West. They both meet preeminent brain surgeon and instructor Dr. Carl Hill. West knows, and is contemptuous, of Hill's experiments on the will of the human mind.

Cain, who is engaged to Megan, Halsey's daughter, posts an ad looking for a roommate, and West takes him up on the offer. Herbert finds the basement is perfect for his needs, although Megan is disturbed by his chilly demeanor.

Dr. Hill demonstrates the process of removing a human brain for his class, although West is a distracting influence. Herbert accuses Hill of stealing Gruber's original theories, and the doctor threatens the young student with failure in his class.

Halsey recognizes Hill's work as genius, although he also appreciates the doctor's skill at attracting large financial grants for Miskatonic. Hill also finds Megan to be a very attractive woman.

Megan discovers Dan's pet cat, Rufus, dead in West's refrigerator. He claims the cat died from suffocation, but Megan believes West killed the cat. Cain also wonders about a curious glowing green fluid that West has chilling in the fridge.

Later, Dan is awakened by screams and finds West has revived Rufus. But the cat is vicious and running amok, attacking both men.

When they kill it (again), Herbert is amused and laughs. Revealing his green liquid reagent to Dan, he dreams of conquering death and seeks his help. He shows the skeptical Cain that reanimation of the dead is possible by reviving Rufus' broken body once more with his fluid.

Dan explains the events to Dean Halsey, who promptly expels West from school and suspends Cain. The pair sneak into the morgue, where West tests his reagent on a recent cadaver. It works, but the result is a violent beast that breaks out of the morgue. It kills Dean Halsey, who had been looking for Cain and West. Herbert finally eliminates the creature by boring through it with a bone saw.

Herbert wants to revive the dean, since his body is very fresh. It works—sort of—but the dean is in a zombie-like state. A shocked Megan finds her father, while West fabricates a story to protect Cain and himself. The dean is locked up in a straitjacket, and Dr. Hill convinces Megan to turn over her father to his care.

Dan reveals the entire truth to a sobbing Megan, while Dr. Hill pays a visit to West. The doctor demands Herbert give him the secret to revival, threatening the young man with blackmail. West reluctantly turns his notes over to the doctor and then kills Hill when he is peering through a microscope.

Herbert uses a shovel to decapitate the doctor and then places the head in a specimen tray. West injects both parts of Dr. Hill with the reagent, and, amazingly, they individually return to life but act like a single entity. Hill's body knocks West unconscious and leaves with his head in his hands, as well as West's serum.

Hill reaches his office, where the now-lobotomized Halsey is a slave to the doctor's orders. The dean must kidnap his daughter for Hill and bring her to the morgue. He knocks out Cain and delivers Megan to Hill, while West wakes Dan and they realize what has happened.

Stripped nude, the girl is strapped onto a dissecting table. Hill's body takes his head and assaults Megan, while professing his love for her. West interrupts the ugly scene and distracts Hill while Dan pulls Megan from the table.

But Dr. Hill has been experimenting with laser lobotomy and now holds power over the cadavers in the morgue. They all spring to life and attack Herbert, Dan, and Megan. Hill attempts to lobotomize West, but Megan somehow reaches her father's mind. Halsey crushes Hill's head, and the zombies stop their assault.

West injects an overdose of reagent into Hill's body, and it bursts open, with the large intestine wrapping around Herbert, trapping him. Dan and Megan nearly escape, but a zombie strangles the girl in the elevator before Cain can close the doors.

He brings her lifeless body to the emergency room, but efforts to revive her are hopeless. But as the room clears, Cain takes a vial of West's serum and injects Megan. The picture fades to black and she screams.

Afterwords

As it rarely but sometimes happens, a film comes out, makes its rounds in the theaters, then disappears into the sunset—only to develop a life of its own that seems to last forever. They can often come from the "so bad they're good" stack, but one legitimate example in the sci-fi world is 1985's *Re-Animator*.

Writer/director Stuart Gordon came from simple but important beginnings in Chicago. In 1970, he founded the Organic Theater, where he produced and directed groundbreaking plays like *Sexual Perversity in Chicago* (written by David Mamet and produced as the film *About Last Night* in 1986), and *Bleacher Bums*, among others.

Always a fan of horror writer H. P. Lovecraft, Gordon wanted to do a different take on the Frankenstein theme and drew from the sixty-year-old Lovecraft story. His first intention was to adapt it into a play, then he considered episodic TV, and, finally, he realized a movie was the way to go. Doing research at a morgue showed Gordon that those who embalm like to have a few laughs to break the solemnity—and the silence.

The result was a combo of yells and yuks, with Jeffrey Combs making the role of Herbert West entirely his to keep (reprising it in two sequels: *Bride of Re-Animator* in 1989 and *Beyond Re-Animator* in 2003). Barbara Crampton, just twenty-seven years old at the time, had made her mark with TV soap operas and a small role in Brian De Palma's *Body Double* in 1984.

Much has been made about the rather unique scene in *Re-Animator*, involving a nude Crampton on a lab table and the attention she receives from the severed but living head of David Gale. Crampton admits it's the one scene that everyone asks about, and she had no reservations in doing it.

Distributed by the small independent Empire Pictures, *Re-Animator* was shot for the low, low price of just $700,000. It returned more than $2 million in domestic box-office receipts, not to mention the ensuing VHS, DVD, and Blu-Ray rentals and sales.

The relentless success of *Re-Animator* moved Stuart Gordon to return to the stage in 2011 with *Re-Animator: The Musical* (what else?). Never one to skimp on the gore, Gordon called in the film's original FX crew to ensure the first three rows of the audience would be splashed with blood.

Jurassic Park

Synopsis

- 1993—American/Universal—126 min./color
- Director: Steven Spielberg
- Based on the 1990 novel by Michael Crichton

Cast

- Sam Neill (Dr. Alan Grant)

- Laura Dern (Dr. Ellie Sattler)
- Sir Richard Attenborough (John Hammond)
- Jeff Goldblum (Ian Malcolm)
- Bob Peck (Robert Muldoon)
- Martin Ferraro (Donald Gennaro)
- Joseph Mazello (Tim Murphy)
- Ariana Richards (Alexis Murphy)
- Wayne Knight (Dennis Nedry)
- Samuel L. Jackson (Arnold)

On Isla Nublar, an island near Costa Rica, game warden Muldoon directs work-men as they move a strange unseen creature into a holding cage. Their hard hats boast the logo for "Jurassic Park," but they look very much like big-game hunters. The gatekeeper raises the gate, but he slips and is quickly devoured by whatever is inside.

Developer John Hammond has created "Jurassic Park" as the ultimate theme park. But Gennaro, the investors' lawyer, insists on having someone with credibility sign off on the authenticity of the park. They secure the services of paleontologist Dr. Alan Grant, paleobotanist Dr. Ellie Sattler, and noted mathematician Ian Malcolm.

They are helicoptered into the island base and will take the weekend tour. If they approve, the park can then open to the public. The scientists are all skeptical but are quickly convinced, as well as stunned, when they see a live, full-grown brachiosaurus grazing on plants.

At the visitor center, they find that Hammond has "farm-raised" a park full of living dinosaurs from DNA. Taken from mosquitoes locked in amber for millions of years, the dinosaur blood provides the genetic codes for creating species of prehistoric creatures. The scientists certainly believe what they now see but question the ethics of tampering with nature.

Dennis Nedry is the designer of the software that runs the entire park, but he is unhappy with the money that Hammond has paid him. He plans to sneak out DNA samples of all the dinosaurs in exchange for receiving $1.5 million from a rival exhibition company.

As the scientists prepare to take the tour, Hammond's grandchildren, Tim and Lex, show up. Everyone boards remote-controlled tour vehicles, while Hammond remains in the control center with the chain-smoking computer expert Arnold and Nedry.

The tour starts out to be less than impressive, as the dinosaurs don't really seem to be waiting to be viewed by tourists. Soon, the test groups leave the jeeps, and Ellie has the chance to treat a sick triceratops. But a tropical storm is bearing down on the island, and the tour must return quickly.

Meanwhile, Nedry sets up a computer system diversion in order to hijack the DNA. He's obviously nervous as he heads into the embryo storage area, where he pilfers the vials and uses a fake shaving cream canister to sneak them out. He grabs a jeep and heads off to meet his connection at the boat dock. Meanwhile,

T. rex amok in *Jurassic Park*.

Arnold tries to get into the computer system that has shut down, but Nedry has locked out everyone.

In the park, the cars have stopped by the T. rex area. As a steady rain comes down, a low thunderous sound shakes the cars. From out of the darkness, a huge snarling T. rex appears, and Gennaro runs for cover in the restrooms. The kids' flashlight attracts the dinosaur's attention. It crashes through the car's roof, trying to get at the children. The T. rex turns the vehicle over, tearing at the car while Grant and Malcolm draw its attention with flares.

The T. rex buries Malcolm in the debris of the restroom, where it makes a meal out of the cowering Gennaro. Lex and Grant escape, but the T. rex pushes the car, with Tim inside, over a paddock embankment.

From the command center, Hammond asks Muldoon and Ellie to get the people out of the park. Arnold can't get Jurassic Park powered back up. Meanwhile, Nedry crashes the jeep and winds up playing hide-and-seek with a dilophosaurus. Mistakenly thinking it's harmless, Nedry goes back to the jeep, where the dinosaur spits thick venom into his face and kills him.

Grant and Lex save Tim from the tour vehicle as it comes crashing down through the trees. Ellie and Muldoon find the injured Malcolm and get him into their car. They take off just as the T. rex takes off after them. They make a terrified run for it as the T. rex follows in close pursuit. They barely escape, and Malcolm wryly wonders, "Think *that* will be on the tour?"

Grant, Tim, and Lex take refuge in a tree, where they fall asleep. Meanwhile, Hammond tells Ellie about his first exhibit, a flea circus in Scotland, and how he wanted Jurassic Park to be real and not an illusion. Ellie shows him that thinking he's in control of Jurassic Park is also an illusion.

Next morning, Grant and the kids are awakened by a brachiosaurus grazing in the treetops. Later, Grant discovers hatched dinosaur eggs, evidence that the dinosaurs have learned to breed on their own. Hammond and Arnold decide they can just reboot the entire park system and reset everything. But the main power is located in a shack at the other end of the compound, so Arnold goes to take care of it.

Meanwhile, Grant and the kids find themselves in a stampede of dinosaurs and watch as the T. rex attacks one of them. Arnold doesn't come back, so Ellie and Muldoon go to see what happened. Stalked by a pack of velociraptors, Ellie runs to the shack as Muldoon unsuccessfully takes them on.

While Ellie prepares to power up the system, Grant and the kids climb a powerless electric fence. Tim doesn't make it down as the power goes on, and the jolt throws him to the ground. A raptor has gotten Arnold and chases Ellie. Grant revives Tim, and they get back to the center.

Grant goes to find Ellie, and the kids are chased into the kitchen by a pair of raptors. They escape, and Lex, a computer hacker, starts loading the computer systems up as a raptor threatens to get into the command center.

With all systems back online, the raptors break through and Grant, Ellie, and the kids climb into the ceiling grid. Trapped by the raptors, they crawl onto a fossil skeleton display. Just as the raptors are about to strike, the T. rex appears, grabbing the smaller dinosaurs and tossing them around like hay bales.

As the group escapes the center, Grant tells Hammond, "I've decided not to endorse your park." Hammond agrees as everyone helicopters away from Jurassic Park.

Afterwords

For years, filmmakers have wrestled with the challenge of how to combine two forms of life that have been separated by nearly sixty million years—humans and dinosaurs. The earliest such films, like 1925's *The Lost World* and 1933's *King Kong*, used stop-motion animation to achieve the feat, thanks to pioneer effects wizard Willis O'Brien. Likewise, his brilliant protégé, Ray Harryhausen, delivered dinosaurs in 1966's *One Million Years B.C.* and 1969's *Valley of Gwangi* by means of animated miniatures.

The combination of a man in a hot rubber suit and hand puppets worked with mixed success. Japan and Toho Studios used them well in the original 1954 (1956 in America) *Godzilla, King of the Monsters*. The 1957 low-budget film *The Land Unknown* didn't use them well at all.

Even lower down on the budget chain were films like 1940's *One Million B.C.* (no, not the same film as above) and 1960's *The Lost World*. These films offered a poor excuse for dinosaurs, in the form of real lizards with rubber dorsal fins glued on. Not only were they totally unbelievable, the practice was downright cruel.

Michael Crichton's 1990 novel *Jurassic Park* challenged Hollywood once more as Steven Spielberg prepared to put the story on the big screen. As technology had taken saurian-sized steps across the years, the director wanted to augment top-notch stop-motion animation with full-sized animatronic dinosaurs where possible. But when FX master Dennis Muren showed a test reel of computer-generated dinosaurs to Spielberg, the decision was made to go digital.

Wanting to place the focus of the film directly on the dinosaurs, Spielberg avoided casting big-name stars for *Jurassic Park*. Although Harrison Ford was considered for Dr. Alan Grant, Sam Neill got the part. Wayne Knight, having just started his supporting role of Newman on TV's *Seinfeld*, was chosen by Spielberg without ever auditioning. Academy Award–winning director Sir Richard Attenborough was convinced to end his fourteen-year absence from acting to take the important part of John Hammond.

King Midas of the Movies, Spielberg once again struck gold with this film, as *Jurassic Park* has made more than $1 billion around the world since its release in 1993. That figure includes a 3-D version released in 2013, which pulled in more than $43 million.

Techno-author Michael Crichton penned a sequel, *Lost World*, in 1995, and the world anxiously awaited its transformation into another blockbuster film by Spielberg. When released in 1997 as *Lost World: Jurassic Park*, only Jeff Goldblum remained from the first film. Made with a massive budget of $73 million, the film grossed more than $600 million worldwide.

A second sequel, *Jurassic Park III*, opened in the summer of 2001. While Spielberg remained connected to the series as executive producer, *JPIII* was directed by Joe Johnston (having made *The Rocketeer* in 1991 and *Jumanji* in 1995, among others), with Sam Neill and Laura Dern reprising their roles. As usual, the franchise raked in the dough, to the tune of nearly $370 million around the globe.

The series has been a guaranteed money machine, as the three films have brought in nearly $2 billion—excluding VHS, DVD, Blu-Ray rentals and sales, and a very lucrative array of merchandise. With that in mind, it's no surprise to know a third sequel, tentatively titled *Jurassic World*, is scheduled for release in the summer of 2015.

I Am Legend

Synopsis

- 2007—American/Warner Brothers—101 min./color
- Director: Francis Lawrence
- Original music: James Newton Howard
- Film editing: Wayne Wahrman
- Production design: Naomi Shohan
- Based on the 1954 novel by Richard Matheson

Cast

- Will Smith (Robert Neville)
- Alice Braga (Anna)
- Charlie Tahan (Ethan)
- Salli Richardson-Whitfield (Zoe Neville)
- Dash Mihok (alpha male zombie)
- Emma Thompson (Dr. Alice Krippen)

Dr. Alice Krippen has found a miraculous cure for cancer by genetically altering the virus for measles. However, three years later finds the city of New York a barren wasteland, empty and devoid of human life—but for one person.

A single red Mustang speeds through the streets into Central Park, driven by former army officer and scientist Robert Neville. Alongside him is his German Shepard, Sam. Neville is hunting deer that roam the land. On foot, the pair stalk a fine five-pointer, until a family of lions gets to the animal first, attacking it and dragging it away.

As the sun is setting, Neville and Sam must rush from the streets to the safety of their fortified townhouse. The home is stockpiled with canned goods and prepared foods, and Neville entertains himself by watching long-ago recordings of television shows.

He recalls the dreadful night some years back when news of the virus mutating into something terrible threw the country and the world into chaos, forcing Neville to take his wife and young daughter out of New York during the

Will Smith and German shepherd Abbey in *I Am Legend.*

evacuation of the city. An expert on viruses, he believed he could find a solution to this tragedy.

Now, in 2012, Neville and Sam keep fit by running on matching treadmills. Robert continues to search for a solution in his basement laboratory, experimenting on crazed rats infected with the virus. He may be seeing some positive results, but needs a human for further tests.

In a methodic canvas of the city, Neville collects supplies from empty shops and dwellings. As amusement, Robert has placed mannequins in a video store, where he holds one-sided conversations with them. Robert broadcasts a message on AM radio, advising anyone who hears it that he will be at the South Street Seaport every day for a half-hour at noon. He is seeking any other survivors who may be out there, but his search seems futile.

Another deer hunt draws Sam into a darkened underpass. Clearly shaken, Neville follows his dog, where he comes upon a bloodthirsty zombie. It chases the pair into the daylight and freezes in pain from the bright sunlight, allowing Robert and Sam to escape.

Neville sets a trap, using his blood as bait for the zombies. In little time, he bags a specimen and returns to his lab. A young female, the zombie is strapped to a table, and Neville injects the serum into her. After initial signs of encouragement, the results are negative, and Robert dejectedly locks the zombie into a glass-walled storage room.

Curiously, Neville is immune to direct contact and airborne exposure to the virus, although dogs like Sam are only safe from the airborne type. The scientist also notes that the creatures seem to be more desperate in their search for life and have become devoid of any human social traits.

On a date that he has determined is his birthday, Robert drives the streets and is shocked for find someone—or something—has moved his mannequins. Unfortunately, Neville has fallen for the same sort of trap that he rigged for the zombies and is caught in a snare. He cuts himself free as night falls, but is wounded in the leg with his knife.

Neville drags himself to the car as snarling infected dogs attack and Sam is injured. Back in his lab, Robert injects Sam with the serum in an attempt to save his pet, but it's no good, and he's forced to put the dog down as it turns on him.

Now completely alone, an enraged Neville drives into the night, plowing into creatures as they approach his car. But they turn his vehicle over, and, as they prepare to attack, the zombies are frightened away by a brilliant light.

In a daze, Robert recalls the terrible night of the evacuation. With his wife and daughter apparently safe on a departing helicopter, he helplessly watched as it collided with another chopper in the sky.

Neville wakes up in his home, where he finds the two survivors who saved him from the zombie attack. Anna and a young boy named Ethan heard Neville's broadcasts and are now heading to Vermont, where a survivor camp supposedly exists. After an initial angry response of denial, Robert apologizes and is determined to stay. He knows he can find a solution to the virus.

Anna believes divine intervention brought them together, but Robert loudly denies the existence of God, citing the victims of the deadly and affecting virus as proof. The sound of creatures approaching the house interrupts him—they have finally found Neville.

He sets off explosive booby traps, destroying dozens of zombies. But one makes its way in through an upper window and attacks Robert. He chases it off with a barrage of gunfire and finds another creature breaking through the roof, as Anna and Ethan hide nearby. Neville stops it with more gunfire.

Hundreds of zombies continue their assault as the three humans make their way down to the lab. The creatures swarm the house, and Neville finds the female zombie in his basement has finally responded positively to the serum. Locked behind the glass walls of the storage room, he pleads with the attacking creatures that he can save them.

One zombie—the alpha male—begins to crack the glass, and Neville realizes the antidote is in the blood of the female he treated. He gives a vial of it to Anna and locks Ethan and her safely behind a wall. Robert sets off a grenade, sacrificing himself and destroying the creatures in the lab.

Days later, Anna and Ethan reach the survivor camp in Vermont, with the single vial of the antidote. It would be the salvation of civilization and make Robert Neville a legend.

Afterwords

Often heard in life, "I wouldn't (fill-in-the-blank) if you were the last man on Earth!" Richard Matheson's 1954 novella *I Am Legend* set up the premise for that arrangement—smack dab in the midst of a world of vampires—to come true. In fact, Hollywood's first cinematic foray into the story was in 1964, called (surprise!) *The Last Man on Earth*.

Starring Vincent Price, the film was originally intended as a project for England's premier studio for horror, Hammer, with a script written by the author himself. But uptight British censors balked at such a sordid subject, so the production moved to Italy, and US distribution was done through American-International Pictures. A second shot at the novel came in 1971, that one starring Charlton Heston and called *The Omega Man*. It was produced by Warner Bros.

Fast-forward twenty-six years, and Warner Bros. still held the rights to Matheson's story. Armed with a fresh script, Ridley Scott would direct the new version of *I Am Legend*, with action superstar Arnold Schwarzenegger in the lead role. Scott left the project, others came in, Ahh-nold left, and the proposed budget mushroomed to more than $100 million. To top everything, by 2002, the head of Warner Bros. admitted that he hated the story.

Austrian-born Francis Lawrence, a director of music videos and one feature film—2005's *Constantine*—was finally chosen to helm *I Am Legend*, with Oscar-nominated Will Smith cast as Robert Neville.

Lawrence originally wanted to use real actors for the zombies (replacing the original vampire villains from the novel), with makeup effects created by Christien Tinsley. However, after one week of shooting, the director felt he had a group of white-faced mime actors instead of fearsome zombies. At that point, the decision was made to deliver the zombies via computer-generated graphics. The actors would still be used, but instead of makeup, they would be wearing motion-capture suits.

In retrospect, Lawrence had regrets about not being able to spend a proper amount of time on the FX during postproduction. He felt the quality of the visual effects was very uneven. Lawrence also questioned his decision to show the zombies with such detail, feeling that keeping them in the shadows would have made the film much scarier.

No matter, *I Am Legend* was a success in spite of the second-guessing. With a robust production budget of $150 million, the film was a hit for the Christmas holiday season. Domestic ticket sales amounted to more than $256 million, with an overseas box-office take of nearly $330 million. With a total of nearly $600 million, *I Am Legend* was one of the top-grossing films for 2007.

In the subsequent 2008 release of DVDs and Blu-Ray discs, an alternative ending was included, one that wasn't as clear or satisfying for many who watched it. In it, the attacking alpha male smears the glass with an image of a butterfly and Neville notes the female zombie has a similar tattoo. Despite the apparent danger, Robert opens the glass door, apologizes, and returns the female to the creatures.

While threatening Neville, the zombies do not attack him, but take the female and leave. The next day, Neville, Anna, and Ethan travel to Vermont, while Anna continues broadcasting messages of hope to anyone who can hear them.

Inception

Synopsis

- 2010—American/Warner Brothers—148 min./color
- Director: Christopher Nolan
- Original music: Hans Zimmer
- Film editing: Lee Smith
- Production design: Guy Hendrix Dyas

Cast
- Leonardo DiCaprio (Dom Cobb)
- Joseph Gordon-Levitt (Arthur)
- Ellen Page (Ariadne)
- Tom Hardy (Eames)
- Ken Watanabe (Saito)
- Dileep Rao (Yusuf)

- Cillian Murphy (Robert Fischer)
- Tom Berenger (Browning)
- Marion Cotillard (Mal)
- Pete Postlewaite (Maurice Fischer)
- Michael Caine (Miles)
- Tai-Li Lee (Todashi)

A man washes up on the shore next to a grand Japanese castle. With him are only a handgun and a brass top. He's brought before an old Asian man, who seems to recognize the fellow and the brass top from many years back.

Dom Cobb and his associate Arthur make a sales pitch to Saito in the same dining room, but years earlier. Their service is protection from theft of thoughts and ideas. During dreams, those things are vulnerable to pilfering—called extraction—and Cobb is the best at extracting. Before he can teach the protective tricks to Saito, Cobb must have total access to the man's mind. Saito will consider the offer.

Explosions rock the streets of a rioting city while, in a dingy hotel room, Cobb, Arthur, and Saito are all asleep, attached to a portable device that administers the sleep drug called Somnacin. A man named Nash anxiously checks them as seconds tick by.

Cobb and Arthur walk the exterior of Saito's castle and fear their prospective client knows what's going on. Cobb is confident that he can get the job done. He recognizes Mal, a beautiful woman, and wonders why she's there.

In an upstairs bedroom, Cobb ties a rope to the leg of a chair where Mal sits. He tosses the rope over the side of the building and rappels down. Mal disappears and the rope slips, but Dom still makes his way through the kitchen with gun drawn.

Deftly, he shoots several guards and reaches Saito's safe. Opened in no time, it holds a single envelope, which Cobb switches with one in his waistband. Suddenly, Saito and Mal discover Cobb, and they hold Arthur at gunpoint. Saito understands they're all sleeping and demands to know the identity of Cobb's employer.

Mal shoots Arthur in the leg, and, seeing his pain, Dom swiftly shoots Arthur in the head. Arthur immediately wakes from his slumber in the hotel room, unhooking the Somnacin. An earthquake begins to destroy Saito's castle, and Cobb runs for safety. Saito opens the envelope, only to find blank paper. The castle collapses on Saito as Cobb quickly reviews the contents of the real envelope.

Cobb won't wake up in the hotel room, so Nash is forced to give him the kick—a predetermined wake-up. Nash dunks Cobb into a full bathtub, cascades of water flooding the castle. Saito wakes in the hotel room and grabs Nash. Cobb jumps from the tub and quickly subdues the Asian, pushing him to the floor.

The rioting nears the hotel, while Saito notes the carpet is the wrong color and realizes it's all a dream. He admits that everything has been an audition for Cobb—an audition that failed.

Arthur and Nash sleep on a speeding bullet train as a man named Todashi places headphones from an MP3 player on Nash—it's the sign that a kick is coming. As the music begins to play, Cobb knows his employer, Cobol Engineering, will not accept failure, so he grabs Saito and holds a gun on him.

Saito is amused and impressed—it seems that Cobb created a dream within a dream. However, it is not Saito's dream, but Nash's. Rioters break into the room—Nash's kick—and he awakens on the train. Cobb, angered that Nash got the color of the carpet wrong in the dream, unhooks everyone from the Somnacin doser—it's now everyone for themselves before Saito wakes up.

Alone in Kyoto, Cobb spins his brass top and receives a phone call from his young children. They miss their dad when he's away on business, and he has to remind them that their mother—Mal—isn't around anymore.

Dom and Arthur find a helicopter waiting on the roof, with Saito and a beaten Nash, who tried to sell out Cobb, inside. The bruised man is taken away, while Cobb and Arthur take his place on the chopper. Saito wants the men to do an inception job, the opposite of an extraction—for him. If Cobb accepts, Saito will make things right for Dom to return to America, where authorities suspect he killed Mal. Despite Arthur's skepticism, he takes the Asian up on the offer.

The job involves implanting an idea into the mind of Saito's competitor. If the target can break up the company he runs for his father, then Saito's company will profit greatly as a result. Cobb will build his team for the project.

With Nash gone, Cobb selects Ariadne as a new dream architect. The recommendation comes from Miles, Dom's father-in-law and a Paris professor who taught him what he knows about dreams.

At an alfresco café, Cobb outlines the structure of dreams to Ariadne, then demonstrates that they are in a dream at that very moment. Buildings, streets, the very landscape of their surroundings explode around the two as they sit—unharmed—in the middle of it all.

Ariadne, hooked to the Somnacin machine, wakes suddenly in an empty warehouse with Arthur and Cobb. Reentering the dream, Ariadne receives a tour from Dom as he points out the details. Getting a feel for it, the woman's mind begins to fold the city and its buildings on top of itself, with no seeming disruption of activity.

Soon, Ariadne builds entire structures from her memory, a process Cobb finds to be dangerous. If whole scenes are created from a memory, the line between reality and the dream will become blurred. Knowing she has created the dream, people in it surround Ariadne in anger as Mal—from Dom's hookup—steps from the crowd and stabs her. Shaken, the dream architect wakes immediately.

Arthur urges Ariadne to adopt a totem—some small object that acts as an immediate reality check. For example, his is a single die and Dom's is the brass top. Angered, she leaves, but Cobb knows she'll come back.

Next, Dom needs a forger and travels to Mombasa, where he recruits Eames, a top-quality forger and impersonator. He points out two men who have been

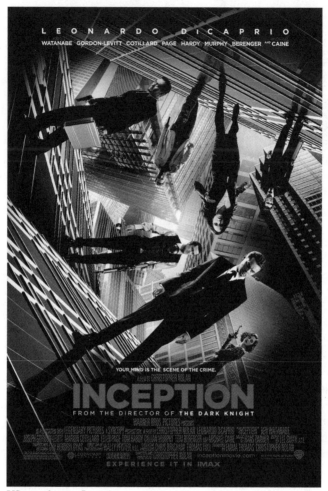

US one-sheet—*Inception.*

tailing Cobb, sent from Cobol because of the botched Saito job. Dom runs, and the men give chase through the streets. Protecting his investment, Saito arrives to pull Cobb and Eames to safety.

Just as Cobb said, Ariadne returns to the warehouse, where Arthur offers some tips in dream architecture. He points out the paradox of the Penrose steps—an endless staircase that, while possible in a two-dimensional concept, is impossible in reality. Arthur stresses the value of maze designs, which can disguise the dream.

Eames introduces Saito and Cobb to Yusuf, a local chemist who has developed a powerful sedative. With it, Cobb believes three levels—a dream within a dream within a dream—would be possible. The drug is effective, as Yusuf uses it to keep a dozen men under a deep, restful sleep in the basement of his shop. Dom tries the drug for himself, and Yusuf joins the team.

Inception target Robert Fischer is the CEO of Fischer Morrow, an energy conglomerate that controls as much as half of the world's energy. Saito believes his company is the only thing that stands between the free market and total dominance by Fischer Morrow. The younger Fischer is heir to the business, to be assumed when his dying father Maurice passes on.

Peter Browning, Robert's godfather and partner, offers advice to his charge but is ignored. Eames aims to get at Fischer through Browning, by means of imitation. Meanwhile, Ariadne chooses her totem—a brass chess piece—and continues to design mazes for the inception.

The team inspects elements of the inception as they strategize that a positive suggestion for Fischer would be more effective than a negative. It's also decided that a three-level dream will be used, with the inception located in the third level—which could be as long as ten years.

One challenge will be to develop a simultaneous and effective kick to bring the team out of the dream. Another is to find ten uninterrupted hours where the inception can take place. Fischer travels from Europe to LA often, a trip that is perfect for the task. Saito ensures the privacy of the flight by purchasing the entire airline.

One evening, Cobb takes a dream trip with the Somnacin machine. Ariadne finds him alone, and she hooks in. She finds herself in an elevator, watching Dom and Mal as they share a tender discussion. Noting the invasion of privacy, Cobb takes Ariadne away and confesses that his dreams allow him to remember when he and Mal were together.

Ariadne escapes to the basement, where she finds a disheveled hotel room and Mal on the couch. Angered at the intrusion, Mal strikes out at Ariadne, but Cobb arrives to take the young woman away in the elevator, while his wife screams at him about broken promises. Cobb and Ariadne wake in the warehouse, as Saito and Arthur enter with news of the elder Fischer's death. His son will accompany the body to LA, and the team will be on the plane.

In the first-class cabin, Eames lifts Fischer's passport and quietly hands it to Cobb. Using it as an introduction to Fischer, Dom hands it back and slips Yusuf's sedative into the rich man's water glass. The team quickly hook Robert and themselves to the Somnacin machine.

Yusuf, drenched from standing in the rain, gets into the team's car in New York City. Arthur, Eames, and Saito carjack a taxi and pick up Fischer as a fare. Saito pulls a gun on Robert, who believes he's the victim of a holdup.

Ariadne jumps into Dom's car, and the riders find themselves immediately jarred by a runaway diesel locomotive thundering down the street. Ambushed and stuck in traffic, the taxi comes under gunfire from Fischer's security team. Cobb and Arthur both adroitly drive out of harm's way and find safety in an empty warehouse.

But Saito has been shot, and Eames prepares to wake him out of the dream by killing him. Cobb stops him, as killing someone on the heavy sedation sends them to limbo—an area of raw, empty subconsciousness that could last forever.

Cobb's team resent being put into such a risky situation and want out. Dom insists on continuing with the plan, completing it as quickly as possible. Wearing masks, Cobb and Arthur press Fischer for the combination to his safe. He claims ignorance and listens as his godfather screams in pain—actually, Eames' impersonation of Browning. Posing as Fischer's surrogate uncle, Eames is handcuffed next to him and urges the young man to reveal the combination.

Saito's condition worsens, but he still intends to get Cobb's clearance to return to his family when he wakes. Cobb knows otherwise—trapped in limbo, Saito will become an old man when he wakes, never even remembering the agreement.

Eames implores Robert to give up the combination to the safe. Its content is a final will, splitting the conglomerate into separate companies, destroying the Fischer Morrow empire and leaving Robert with only a basic living. Eames tries to convince Robert that his father did love him. But Fischer knows there was only disappointment in the old man's heart.

Ariadne fears that Dom's preoccupation with Mal could bring the locomotive thundering through the warehouse at any minute. She must know what happened with Mal and him.

They were working on a job of dreams within dreams, but didn't realize that hours in real life become years in a dream. Lost in the subconscious for fifty years, Mal and Dom built their own world. While Dom came to dislike that make-believe dreamworld, Mal embraced it.

When they returned to the real world, Mal refused to accept it and killed herself, in the misguided belief it would bring her back to reality. Before she plunged from a tall building, Mal confessed she filed a false statement with an attorney, fearing for her safety. In her mind, that freed Dom from any guilt in leaving the children that she thought were only projections in the dream. But the guilt remains inside Cobb.

Fischer's security men from his dream close in on the warehouse, and Cobb needs the safe's combination without any more delay. Robert spits out six random numbers, then he's drugged and thrown into a van. The rest jump in and pull away into the rain.

About to enter the second dream, it is necessary that Fischer's anger at his father be redirected toward Browning. The team hook up to Somnacin, and Fischer is immediately sitting at the bar of a hotel, surrounded by his security and chatting with a pretty blonde woman—once again, Eames in disguise. Cobb introduces himself and the blonde leaves, dropping her phone number on a napkin with Robert. The security men tail the woman.

But Cobb notes it's only six numbers—the numbers Fischer spit out in the previous dream. Arthur and Ariadne watch from nearby, with Arthur disliking this scheme as it unfolds. He knows it requires informing Fischer he is in the midst of a dream, always a dangerous move.

Cobb reveals to Fischer that he is Mr. Charles, the head of his subconscious security, and the blonde has just lifted Robert's wallet. Losing the disguise, Eames connects with Saito in an elevator and leaves Fischer's security behind.

Cobb points out the dreamlike qualities of the surroundings to Fischer, reassuring him that his job is to protect Robert from an extraction. They leave the bar, and Dom is distracted by images of his children playing in the lobby. Fischer and Cobb duck into a washroom, while two of Fischer's security follow. Cobb quickly disarms them and urges Fischer to remember where he was before the dream began and what someone might be trying to extract from his mind.

In room 491—the second set of numbers Fischer revealed in the warehouse—Arthur and Ariadne set blocks of plastic explosives. They are directly under room 528—Fischer's first set of numbers.

Cobb and Fischer meet up with Arthur and Ariadne in 528, preparing to attach themselves to the Somnacin machine. Arthur pulls Browning—a projection of Fischer's—into the room, where he urges Robert to make Fischer Morrow into something even greater than it already is.

Eames and Saito enter, as Dom convinces Fischer that Browning is hiding something and, by hooking him into the Somnacin, they can find out what it is. Actually, Fischer has allowed the team to enter his own subconscious—Fischer will think his own security belongs to Browning. Everyone goes under, with Arthur staying back.

Dressed in white winter gear, Cobb and Ariadne stand at the edge of a snow-covered hospital, heavily guarded.

Meanwhile, gunmen attack Yusuf and the team in the van, as Arthur grapples with similar villains in the hotel's hallway. The van swerves off an incline, as the hallway tips and veers wildly. As the vehicle tumbles, Arthur and his adversary fight on the floor, walls, and ceiling as they roll. Arthur shoots the thug as the van, amazingly, comes to an upright halt.

Yusuf begins to cue the kick at the hotel, which might be too soon. Yusuf drives the van onto a rising drawbridge, while Arthur confronts a gunman in a stairwell. As they are Penrose steps, he throws the shooter down to his demise. Yusuf slams the van into the barrier of the bridge, slowly falling over the edge, and Arthur is tossed into midair in the hallway.

Back in the mountains, Eames fires a flare to draw the attention and gunfire of the hospital guards. An avalanche tumbles down the mountainside, causing Fischer and Saito to abandon their rope climb to the hospital complex. It is a kick, which everyone has missed. But there is still time to finish the job before the next kick—when the van hits the water.

Saito, slowly succumbing to his gunshot wound, still makes his way into the medical fortress through an air duct with Fischer. Eames distracts the snowbound guards as the van slowly descends toward the water. Arthur wrestles with one of the security detail in a freefall state in the hotel hallway.

With Ariadne, Cobb takes his position in a high guard tower, picking off projections of guards with his sniper rifle. Saito and Fischer approach the doors of an enormous safe, but the Asian collapses from his gunshot wound. Robert moves ahead, and Mal quietly drops in behind him. She shoots Fischer, and Cobb shoots Mal.

Dom believes the scheme has died with Fischer, but Ariadne reasons the team can find Robert in limbo, then bring him back when the hospital blows up as a kick. Cobb and Ariadne hook up to the Somnacin machine and enter limbo on a desolate beach with crumbling buildings—the decaying world built by Dom and Mal. They find Mal in an apartment, where she challenges Dom to choose her world—or his. He must get back to the children she left behind.

Cobb also admits the entire concept of inception works because he first used it on Mal, implanting the idea that her world didn't exist. He convinced her that death was her way of escaping, but Cobb never expected the thought would grow like a cancer.

He agrees to stay with Mal in exchange for Fischer's return. Ariadne finds Robert and improvises his kick by pushing him off the ledge of the building. Cobb rethinks his choice to stay with Mal, and she stabs him with a knife. Ariadne shoots Mal.

Eames sets plastic explosives around the base of the complex, while Saito holds off guards that try to make their way in. As he tosses a grenade into an air duct, he dies. Eames shocks Fischer back to life with a defibrillator, as music cues him it is time for the kick.

Arthur thinks quickly and removes the explosive charges from the hotel room. Moving in weightless ease, he uses phone cord to tether everyone together, pulls them into an elevator, and sets the explosives in the shaft above. Arthur waits for the precise moment to detonate the charges.

As the van touches the water, the elevator shaft explodes in a ball of fire, while Fischer keys the combination that opens the safe. Inside, his father lies dying in his bed. Robert's notion that the elder Fischer was disappointed that he couldn't be like him was wrong. The disappointment was that Robert tried to be like his father.

Crying in appreciation, Robert keys 528491 into a small bedside safe. Inside is the final will, but, more importantly, there is a child's pinwheel the elder Fischer kept for many years.

Eames triggers the charges around the complex as the elevator reaches the bottom of the shaft and the van begins to enter the water. The buildings in Dom and Mal's world begin to blow away—the kick has begun. But Cobb must stay to find Saito in limbo.

Mal dies in Dom's arms, and, suddenly old, they hold hands as the couple lie down on railroad tracks. The van continues to sink under the water, and Fischer pulls Browning—really Eames—to safety. The young man vows to live as he should, an independent man.

The rest remain underwater, breathing with scuba gear. Cobb's body sits, lifeless, as the others surface. Arthur fears for his friend, but Ariadne knows he'll be all right.

Guards drag an older Cobb from a beach to Saito in his castle, now an ancient man waiting to die. Cobb's brass-top totem spins, as he urges Saito to leave limbo and be young once more.

Dom and Saito, indeed young once more, quickly wake in the first-class cabin of a jet, surrounded by Fischer and the rest of the team. Upon deboarding the plane, Cobb is welcomed by an immigration agent back to America. Passing his dream partners, Dom hands his luggage to Miles and arrives home to the happy faces of his children. On a nearby table, the brass top still spins.

Afterwords

Christopher Nolan established his reputation in the film industry early on: a no-nonsense, thinking person's director. No one would ever mistake him as a dreamer, but dream-snatching was the theme that motivated him to write an eighty-page treatment in 2002. Then films like 2005's *Batman Begins*, 2006's *The Prestige*, and 2008's *The Dark Knight* came along, pushing the project of *Inception* to the back of the pack.

Fortunately, with Nolan and wife Emma Thomas as coproducers (as well as the massive success of the *Batman/Dark Knight* films), getting the eventual green light for *Inception* was not a problem. However, the problem was how to make it.

Nolan's original thought of *Inception* being a small, low-budget film quickly disappeared as he considered the process needed to properly tell such a complex story. Sure, it was a heist film, but not featuring your typical booty, like cash, jewels, or gold bullion. The vault being broken into was the mind, and the loot was its dreams.

With Warner Bros. firmly behind the project (to the tune of a $160 million budget), Nolan brought in an international cast that included Leonardo DiCaprio, Joseph Gordon-Levitt, Marion Cotillard, Michael Caine, Tom Hardy, Cillian Murphy, and Ken Watanabe. Production would find itself in Morocco, France, Japan, the UK, Canada, and California. Hopefully, the money would be well spent on a film that some called a cross between *Mission: Impossible* and *The Matrix*.

The director wound up with a brilliant film, as complex as anything ever to come out of Hollywood. Running nearly two and a half hours long, *Inception*, and its ending, left many filmgoers wondering if Cobb wound up in a real or dream world. Actor Michael Caine admitted that the brass top eventually stopped spinning—unseen—because the character of Miles only existed in the real world. But director Nolan remained adamant about the film's ambiguity, noting that Cobb didn't even care that the top remained spinning at the film's close.

As his usual choice, Nolan largely stayed away from computer-generated effects, opting for massive sets and practical FX whenever feasible. He called on Chris Corbould, a veteran of Nolan's *Batman* films as well as fifteen James Bond flicks, to supervise the special effects. One such example was a gravity-shifting set of corridors, measuring more than one hundred feet long. Mounted on a gimbal, it resembled an enormous rotating hamster cage.

Another case of Nolan's old-school philosophy of special effects was the construction of an enormous miniature (apologies for the oxymoron) in a studio parking lot of the snow-covered, mountaintop medical facility. More than forty feet tall, the model was based on an area of forty by fifty feet and weighed an incredible seven thousand pounds. It was covered in more than a ton of salt (to represent snow) and then blown sky-high.

Warner Bros. tried to convince the director to shoot *Inception* in three-dimensions, but Nolan wisely begged off. Remembering Hollywood's first feeble attempt at 3-D during the 1950s, he believed a well-shot film had no need for gimmicks like that. Once the process is perfected—or at least when the funny glasses are gone—Nolan will consider making his films in 3-D.

Inception fulfilled everyone's dreams, grossing more than $290 million in America. With $532 million overseas, the film pulled in a buxom $825 million around the world, placing it in the Top Forty of all-time highest-grossing films. What's more, *Inception* earned seven Academy Award nominations, including Best Picture, and took home four in the categories of Best Cinematography, Best Sound Editing, Best Sound Mixing, and Best Visual Effects.

Contagion

Synopsis

- 2011—American/Warner Brothers—106 min./color
- Director: Steven Soderbergh
- Original music: Cliff Martinez
- Film editing: Stephen Mirrione
- Production design: Howard Cummings

Cast

- Marion Cotillard (Dr. Leonora Orantes)
- Matt Damon (Mitch Emhoff)
- Laurence Fishburne (Dr. Ellis Cheever)
- Jude Law (Alan Krumwiede)
- Gwyneth Paltrow (Beth Emhoff)
- Kate Winslet (Dr. Erin Mears)
- Bryan Cranston (Radm Lyle Haggerty)
- Jennifer Ehle (Dr. Ally Hextall)
- Elliott Gould (Dr. Ian Sussman)
- Chin Han (Sun Feng)

- John Hawkes (Roger)
- Anna Jacoby-Heron (Jory Emhoff)
- Monique Gabriela Curnen (Lorraine Vasquez)
- Griffin Kane (Clark)
- Brian J. O'Donnell (Andrew)
- Dan Aho (Aaron Barnes)

On Day 2, Beth Emhoff waits in Chicago's O'Hare Airport during her layover from a Hong Kong to Minneapolis flight. She chats on the phone with John Neal, a former boyfriend with whom she's just spent a few hours of bedtime. She coughs, but thinks nothing of it.

In Hong Kong, a young man moves through the city, arriving home feeling ill. In London, a young office worker collapses dead on her bathroom floor. In Minneapolis, Beth reaches her home after her long trip, where her son Clark and husband Mitch warmly welcome her. In Tokyo, a businessman feels ill, sweating and feverish on his bus ride. He tumbles to the floor, dead.

In Atlanta, Dr. Ellis Cheever arrives at his office in the Centers for Disease Control (CDC), while in San Francisco, activist blogger Alan Krumwiede discusses the Tokyo incident with Lorraine Vasquez, an editor at the *Chronicle* newspaper. Back in Minneapolis, Mitch picks up Clark from school, with his stepson coughing and running a fever.

On Day 4, Beth collapses in her kitchen with convulsions and dies in the emergency room. Understandably, the news stuns Mitch, and doctors have no clue as to the cause of her illness. Tragically, Mitch gets home to find his stepson has also died.

On Day 5, at the World Health Organization (WHO) in Geneva, Dr. Leonora Orantes reviews the mysterious outbreaks around the globe. In China, a boy dies suddenly, and his sister is found dead on the bus. In Chicago, Beth's paramour becomes stricken, as doctors in Minnesota open the dead woman's skull during an autopsy. They are stunned at their findings.

On Day 6 at the CDC, Dr. Cheever assigns Dr. Erin Mears to begin a thorough investigation of the rapidly growing cases of sickness and deaths. Her first stop is Minneapolis. Jory, Mitch's daughter from a previous marriage, finds her dad at the hospital. Despite his exposure to his wife and son, he has not gotten sick.

Dr. Mears briefs local health officials, identifying the outbreak as respiratory in nature and easily transmitted by physical contact—the disease can spread as infected people touch their faces, then touch another surface. When someone else touches that surface, referred to as a fomite, the bug can now infect that person. The rate of spreading—called the R-naught factor—could be enormous. The public should be warned, but, unfortunately, health officials don't know what from.

Heavily protected in biohazard gear, doctors at the CDC inspect Beth's tissue samples. Puzzled, they believe Dr. Ian Sussman might have an idea as to

Jude Law plies flyers in *Contagion*.

what they've found. Sussman angrily rebuffs a surprise blindsided meeting with Krumwiede, who continues to seek the truth about the virus.

On Day 7, agents from the Department of Homeland Security summon Dr. Cheever to a meeting with Rear Admiral Lyle Haggerty, who fears the virus may be a terrorist act. Minneapolis schools begin to close as a precaution.

Dr. Mears meets with Beth's coworkers at Aimm-Alderson, the company where she worked. They are scared, realizing their everyday activities may have left them exposed to what she had. Mears urges Aaron Barnes, an ill work associate, to leave his work-bound bus immediately, for fear of contaminating others. Wearing protective clothes, a medical crew picks up Barnes.

Mitch remains in hospital isolation, answering questions about his wife and her trip. Retracing her path, Mitch realizes that his wife may have had an affair with Neal in Chicago. At the CDC, Cheever reviews his doctors' findings, which reveal there are components of pig and bat DNA in the virus and it can mutate quickly. He orders Sussman's research stopped immediately and all samples destroyed.

On Day 8, Cheever addresses the press with what is known so far. Dr. Orantes arrives in Hong Kong to continue her investigation and takes part in a worldwide teleconference with the CDC and WHO. Sun Feng, Orantes' contact in Hong Kong, seems concerned, as the virus has attacked his family's village. Meanwhile, despite orders otherwise, Sussman continues to run tests. Cheever is not pleased, although the insubordinate Sussman succeeds in replicating the virus called MEV-1.

On Day 12, estimates for worldwide infection reach eight million. Krumwiede thinks he has a cure from a plant called the forsythia and plans to go worldwide with the news. Amid crowds at a Minnesota hospital, Mitch discovers he is immune to the virus but fears Jory could still become infected. Dr. Mears makes plans for a treatment center in a huge armory, with plans for more.

Dr. Orantes reviews surveillance tapes of Beth Emhoff in a Hong Kong casino, casually associating with the Tokyo man who died on the bus, and believes Hong Kong is where the virus started. Fearing a general panic, local officials are not yet ready to admit that.

On Day 14, Dr. Mears seems to be infected with the virus. The news devastates Cheever, since he feels responsible for her condition. At a Minneapolis funeral home, a director regretfully refuses to handle the burials of Mitch's wife and stepson, citing health concerns.

Continued review of the videotape in Hong Kong shows Beth coming in contact with other people, an ongoing pattern of contamination. Dr. Orantes surmises that Emhoff is the first victim, and initiator, of the virus—Patient Zero—while Sun Feng mourns the death of his mother from the disease.

Feng orchestrates Orantes' abduction, holding her as hostage to acquire the first doses of the cure—once discovered—for use in his village. Mears continues to suffer, while Cheever unsuccessfully attempts to get her out of Minnesota. In extreme confidence, Haggarty shares with Cheever the news that a massive shutdown of cities and systems across the country is imminent.

Krumwiede, sickened with the virus, presents a video blog showing him drinking the forsythia cure. Breaking the confidence of Haggarty, Cheever urges his wife, Aubry, to leave Chicago before the shutdown. But Roger, a custodian at the CDC, hears it all and chastises the doctor for his selfishness. Aubry stocks up on supplies and shares the shutdown secret with a friend.

On Day 18, pharmacies are jammed with customers desperately seeking forsythia, available in limited amounts. When restricted, the patrons riot and storm the counters for the drug. Mitch and Jory watch as frantic citizens loot stores and steal vehicles. National Guard troops block the couple's effort to escape to Wisconsin.

Dressed in a hazmat suit, Krumwiede distributes flyers that claim the CDC lies and states that forsythia works. He finds Lorraine waiting for him on the steps of his home, sick and pregnant. Despondent, she offers money for the supposed cure, but Alan has none.

Dr. Mears dies and is buried in a mass grave in Minnesota. Cheever and Krumwiede appear together on a TV show moderated by Dr. Sanjay Gupta, where gonzo journalist Krumwiede guest accuses the CDC and WHO of profiteering by withholding the cure and being in cahoots with drug companies. Cheever counters by claiming that Krumwiede's rumors and accusations are much more harmful than the disease itself.

Krumwiede then drops a bomb by revealing that Cheever's preferential warning about the shutdown showed up on Facebook, hours before the news actually broke. Krumwiede angrily defines the R-naught factor, explaining its exponential possibilities of more than a billion infected around the world. Cheever is speechless.

On Day 21, the CDC discovers the virus mutating once again, now an African strain with an R-naught factor higher than ever. The search for a vaccine continues, with no positive results. Many places around the world have become deserted and people continue to die, including Lorraine.

On Day 26, Mitch watches while a crowd riots after waiting for food distribution, only to find the allotted amount becomes exhausted. In his neighborhood, Mitch hears gunfire and sees robbers leaving a nearby home. His call to 911 is useless.

On Day 29, finding his neighborhood nearly deserted, Mitch breaks into one of the houses for food and a rifle as protection. Jory is missing, and Mitch finds her with Andrew, her boyfriend, in their backyard. Still fearing for his daughter, Mitch sends the boy home.

Cheever and Dr. Ally Hextall at the CDC consider the months of activity and red tape finding an effective cure would take. Homeland Security suggests putting it into America's water supply, much like fluoride. Hextall's experiments find vaccine number fifty-seven seems to have worked on a test monkey and injects herself with the serum. It appears to be effective, so Hextall visits her infected father in the hospital. He cries out of pride for his daughter's success.

With the world's death toll estimated to be twenty-six million people, efforts speed up to facilitate the approval, production, and distribution of the MEV-1 vaccine. Hopefully, it can be ready within ninety days.

On Day 131, looters break into the Cheever household in search of the vaccine. Home alone, Aubry denies having any, since they have to wait like everyone else. Meanwhile, Krumwiede makes no apologies for profiting from his promotion of forsythia and knows he has the eyes and ears of twelve million followers. The blogger ends up caught in a sting operation and charged with securities fraud, conspiracy, and possible manslaughter.

On Day 133, Haggarty supervises the lottery that will randomly select the order of vaccine recipients, based on their birth date. Hextall refuses to take any credit for discovering the vaccine, despite Cheever's insistence that she do so.

Jory anxiously watches the lottery, finding that her birth date selection will keep her isolated for nearly five months. Understandably, she's not happy with the results and shares her displeasure with Andrew via a text message.

In Sun Feng's village, Orantes teaches a class of young children. Finally, she will be freed in exchange for one hundred doses of the vaccine. The swap is made, but Sun Feng was given a case of placebos. Orantes runs from her associate, unhappy with the deception.

Blood tests show that Krumwiede never had the virus. His hoax earned him $4.5 million. What's more, his Internet campaign influenced many people to not count on the vaccine that could save their lives and to trust forsythia instead—which might not work at all. Incredibly, his twelve million followers post bail for the man and he walks out, without any remorse or apology for his actions.

Cheever receives two vaccine doses from Haggerty—one for himself and one for his wife. Secretly, Cheever administers his dosage to Roger's son, then vaccinates his wife.

On Day 134, the vaccination process continues, as does Krumwiede and his blog. Samples of the MEV-1 virus are placed in cold storage, joining others like SARS and swine flu virus.

Jory receives a gift from her dad—a prom dress. Despite her isolation, she attends a dance in her living room, with Andrew as her tuxedo-clad date. Finding a camera to record the moment, Mitch reviews pictures of Beth's trip overseas and cries.

On Day 1, a bulldozer begins deforestation of trees in China, dislodging some bats from their nests. In turn, they innocently drop their food into a pig farm. Then the pigs are sold as pork, ending up on a chef's cutting board in a Hong Kong casino. The chef welcomes Beth and warmly shakes hands.

Afterwords

As the husband of someone who works in the field of public health, I am keenly aware of concerns about proper hygiene, transmittable diseases, and the threat of a pandemic. The implications of 2011's *Contagion* can't be taken lightly, but there's no need to panic. It hasn't had any effect on my lifestyle (I've always gone out wrapped head to toe in plastic wrap and dripping with hand sanitizer).

Seldom can a film come along that tells its story in a thorough, intelligent, and engaging way, while—perhaps without intention—providing a map of safety and instruction for the masses. *Contagion* walks the tightrope between entertainment and education with incredible ease, never becoming preachy or forgetting its place as a popcorn movie.

Screenwriter Scott Z. Burns and director Steven Soderbergh successfully collaborated on 2009's *The Informant!* Looking to continue their working relationship, Burns suggested doing a thriller about a deadly transmittable virus. But instead of some bio-threat from outer space, he wanted a believable film based in reality.

Realizing he needed input from a brilliant scientist, Burns consulted Dr. Larry Brilliant (really!). The doctor and epidemiologist (someone who studies the impact of disease on the public) had done extensive research on the prevention of a pandemic. The good doctor pointed Burns toward another expert, Dr. Ian Lipkin. The CDC and WHO were also consulted. Everyone agreed that the issue of a deadly pandemic isn't "if," it's "when." With the continuing prevalence of HIV, swine flu, and SARS, Burns knew he was on to something.

Such a strong concept called for a strong cast. Soderbergh (one Oscar) assembled an ensemble of award-worthy performers, including Marion Cotillard (one Oscar), Matt Damon (one Oscar), Laurence Fishburne (Oscar nomination), Jude Law (two Oscar noms), Gwyneth Paltrow (one Oscar), Kate Winslet (one Oscar), Elliott Gould (Oscar nom), and Bryan Cranston (one Golden Globe, three Emmys). That's a lot of hardware.

The director made some interesting decisions since he felt the story was so compelling. Unlike many major productions, Soderbergh did not storyboard any of the scenes, usually a valuable tool to effective cinematic storytelling. (For example, Hitchcock was known to storyboard every single shot in his films.)

Soderbergh acted as his own director of photography (although the credits read Peter Andrews—his father's first and middle names). Keeping the film's focus on the story, the director avoided any complex camera moves, special lenses, or excessive editing. He also shot exclusively on location, staying away from the surreal appearance of studio sets and lighting.

With a budget of $60 million, *Contagion* opened in regular and IMAX theaters for the Labor Day weekend in 2011. The results were good but not great, as domestic grosses totaled more than $75 million. The take overseas was less at nearly $60 million. The worldwide gross of over $135 million meant that a fair number of moviegoers were entertained, while being reminded about the dangers of poor hygiene.

Time for a Lube Job

Robots and Robot Wannabes

Do You Worry About Rust?

The word "robot" is Czech in origin. Their word, "robota," refers to drudgery, and, in general, a robot is a device designed to perform tasks usually done by a human (apparently, my time spent up to my elbows in dish soap would make me a "robot"). As such, robots tend to appear in humanoid form, at least in the cinematic world.

The concept of a humanoid robot made sense in Hollywood, as the easiest way to portray one was to build a stiff metallic costume that could be worn by an actor or stunt man. That is, at least, until robots became reality in the 1960s and 1970s. Function overtook form, as the real robots of the world—such as the Stanford Cart—looked more like overloaded tea carts than mechanical men.

The miniaturization of technology took the "man-in-suit" out of the equation in many movies that featured robots. Still, actors Anthony Daniels and Kenny Baker served robots C-3PO and R2-D2 well from inside their stuffy confines in the *Star Wars* epics. Ditto Peter Weller in *RoboCop*.

Stop-motion animation and computer-generated graphics made non-humanoid robots an alternative to men in suits. Take, for example, 1984's *The Terminator*. Once stripped of its cyborg flesh, the T-800 skeleton was presented by way of a full-sized remote-controlled figure built by Stan Winston, as well as stop-motion animation by Doug Beswick, Gene Warren Jr., and the Fantasy II effects team.

The Terminator

Synopsis

- 1984—American/Orion—108 min./color
- Director: James Cameron
- Original music: Brad Fiedel
- Film editing: Mark Goldblatt
- Art direction: George Costello

Cast

- Arnold Schwarzenegger (Terminator)
- Michael Biehn (Kyle Reese)
- Linda Hamilton (Sarah Connor)
- Paul Winfield (Lt. Traxler)
- Lance Henriksen (Det. Hal Vukovich)

In 2029, a raging conflict persists between an army of war machines and guerrilla soldiers. The machines send one of their own back to 1984 Los Angeles, where they intend on killing Sarah Connor. If they don't, she will give birth to John Connor, who is the leader against the machines in the future war. This killing machine, a "terminator,"—Model T-800—is an incredibly sophisticated cyborg. It's constructed of human tissue, with a high-tech hydraulic skeleton and a single mandate—to kill Sarah. It arrives in a flash of lightning and immediately clothes its nude body by killing a group of toughs and taking their clothes.

But the Terminator is not the only time traveler. Kyle Reese also arrives from the future, sent by John Connor to save Sarah. She is a young single girl who seems dependent on many people. Looking in a phone book, the Terminator finds three Sarah Connors listed. He seeks them out, coldly killing the first two. Going to Sarah's apartment, the Terminator kills her roommate and roommate's boyfriend.

Sarah is not home, and she is disturbed when she hears on the news that two Sarah Connors have been murdered. She becomes even more fearful when she observes Reese following her. She calls her apartment from a disco, but only gets her answering machine. Not realizing the Terminator is still there, she leaves a message telling her roommate where she is. She then calls police, and Lt. Traxler tells her to stay put.

In the disco, the Terminator arrives and zeroes in on Sarah, but Reese saves her by firing a salvo of shotgun blasts into the cyborg. It doesn't faze him, and he responds with fierce gunfire, killing dozens of innocent patrons. Sarah and Reese escape in the fray, but the Terminator takes off after them. They duck him in a car chase, where Reese lets Sarah in on the whole story. He tells of the nuclear war that has erupted between man and machines, and how she has borne John Connor as mankind's savior. Sarah is pretty incredulous at the entire premise, since she doesn't see herself as a bold sort of person.

The pair finally find refuge at the police station. A staff shrink pegs Reese as a lunatic, and the Terminator tries to see Sarah, claiming to be her brother. He's turned away by the desk officer, but the cyborg warns, "I'll be back." He makes good on his promise, driving a car through the front doors and shooting everyone in sight. Once again, Reese and Sarah slip away, hiding in a small motel.

Sarah calls her mom and tells her where they are. She doesn't know her mom is dead and the Terminator is on the other end of the line, mimicking her mom's voice. Reese makes a trip to the local grocery store, where he buys

T-800 cyborg in *The Terminator.*

household items that can be made into explosives. He tutors Sarah in guerrilla tactics and tells her how important she is to the future, how the life of John Connor depends on her survival. Reese has a picture of her, taken in the near future, and it has been an inspiration for everyone. (Is it possible that Reese *is* actually John Connor?) The two realize they are in love and consummate their love. At that moment, Reese/Connor may have just become his own father.

The Terminator reaches the motel, just in time for Sarah and Reese to escape in a pickup truck. He follows on motorcycle, and Reese hangs out of the truck, hurling pipe bombs at the cyborg. The vehicles crash, with Reese sustaining some serious wounds. The Terminator commandeers a huge tanker truck and continues to pursue the couple down a quiet side street. Reese tosses a pipe bomb into the exhaust pipe, and the truck lurches forward in a fiery explosion. Sarah and Reese take cover and embrace, seemingly safe.

But from the blaze rises the Terminator, now nothing more than a charred mechanical skeleton, still intent on killing Sarah. Reese seems too wounded to move, but Sarah, like a drill sergeant, assertively orders him to action. They make their way into a factory, just steps ahead of the relentless cyborg. It powers its way in, and Reese engages in a lopsided hand-to-hand battle with the Terminator. Defeated, he slips a final pipe bomb into the Terminator's pelvis. The explosion kills Reese, but the Terminator, with just his upper body remaining, crawls onward toward Sarah. The relentless juggernaut follows her between the plates of a hydraulic press, where she terminates the Terminator by pulverizing it to a metallic pulp.

Some months later, Sarah is pregnant and travels across the Mexican desert by jeep. Recording cassette tapes for her yet-born son John Connor as she drives, Sarah stops for gas. A young boy takes her picture, and she keeps it. The picture will inspire a revolution. SEQUELS: *Terminator 2: Judgment Day* (1991), *Terminator 3: Rise of the Machines* (2003), and *Terminator Salvation* (2009).

Afterwords

Arnold Schwarzenegger took a huge chance, turning down the heroic role of Reese for that of the wicked Terminator. The Austrian-born actor had made an impact in the 1970s as a champion bodybuilder, winning titles of Mr. Universe, Mr. Olympia, and others. His physicality played against the concept of an assassin sent from the future to blend in to society to find and kill Sarah Conner—it's hard *not* to notice the beefed-up man once called "the Austrian Oak."

Linda Hamilton effectively presented the character arc of Conner, taking her from the simple life as a waitress (and not the best at that) to the woman tasked with guiding her not-yet-born son, John, in saving the world. As filming was set to start, the actress broke her ankle—a situation that was hard to shoot around, considering the amount of running required in the script. Even with schedules rearranged, Hamilton still gamely ran on the healing but still-broken ankle.

Director James Cameron proved he could create an effective and successful sci-fi film for under $7 million, returning many millions more. Even better, in 2008, the Library of Congress' National Film Registry chose *The Terminator* as one of America's films deserving preservation for its aesthetic and cultural significance, joining timeless entries like *The Birth of a Nation*, *Citizen Kane*, and *Casablanca*, among others.

Pulling off the special effects was crucial to the movie's success. For that, financial backers insisted on hiring award-winning makeup artist Dick Smith to handle the creation of the cyborg. After reading the script, Smith realized he wasn't the best person for the job, but recommended Stan Winston as ideal for the task. Smith was right on the money.

Winston convinced a dubious Cameron that a full-sized animatronic T-800 was possible, while the director imagined the figure to be accomplished with stop-motion animation (which was eventually used in some scenes). A torso and head puppet of the Terminator, mounted on the shoulders of its operator, was also employed.

The sequel, *Terminator 2: Judgment Day*, came out seven years later, although the character reversed roles and became a hero in the film. A second sequel in 2003, called *Terminator 3: The Rise of the Machines*, found Schwarzenegger receiving a reported $30 million to reprise his role of the T-800 robot. The actor traded in his cyborg role for a podium, as he was elected governor of California in the same year. He did, however, make an appearance in 2009's *Terminator Salvation*, thanks to a digitally created makeup of the actor's face pasted on an actor with a body similar to Schwarzenegger's. Plans for *Terminator 5* moved forward in 2013 after legal and bankruptcy issues delayed it. Schwarzenegger, now ex-governor of California, has confirmed he will appear in the film, although no firm release date has been established.

Robo Cop

Synopsis

- 1987—American/Orion—103 min./color
- Director: Paul Verhoeven
- Original music: Basil Poledouris
- Film editing: Frank Urioste
- Production design: William Sandell

Cast

- Peter Weller (Officer Alex J. Murphy/Robocop)
- Nancy Allen (Officer Ann Lewis)
- Ronny Cox (Richard Jones)
- Kurtwood Smith (Clarence Boddicker)
- Miguel Ferrer (Bob Morton)
- Daniel O'Herlihy (The Old Man)

In the future, Detroit's police force is managed and operated by Omni Consumer Products (OCP), a large business conglomerate managed by Richard Jones. The seedy area known as Old Detroit is run by crime boss Clarence Boddicker, who's been linked to the death of thirty-one police officers.

Young and handsome Officer Alex Murphy is transferred to Metro West, where his fellow officers tell him, "Welcome to hell." He meets Ann Lewis, his pretty and tough partner, and they hit the streets. At OCP, plans are unveiled to build Delta City, replacing the vile and decaying Old Detroit. They also plan to replace law enforcement officers with automated robots called ED-209, looking something like ten-foot headless mechanical birds.

But a demonstration malfunctions, and one of OCP's junior executives is gunned down by the robot. Jones is in hot water with OCP's owner, called "the old man," as the development of Delta City hinges on the success of the ED-209s. But the ambitious and ruthless Bob Morton steps in, offering his department's contingency plan called "RoboCop." Murphy and Lewis chase Boddicker after a bank robbery, tracking him to an abandoned industrial plant. But Murphy is cornered and massacred by Boddicker and his thugs.

Morton revives the dead cop as his prototype RoboCop. Murphy is now made of steel and titanium, controlled by a computer brain. But some of his internal organs and face remain human. Lewis watches RoboCop on the pistol range and notices the android possesses Murphy's trademark fancy gun handling. RoboCop hits the street and immediately thwarts a stickup and a rape. He follows up by saving the mayor, who's being held hostage by a maniac.

Peter Weller is *RoboCop*.

Morton's success makes him a VP with OCP, but Jones resents his style. RoboCop experiences a violent recollection of his demise, and Lewis tells him that he's Murphy. Using police files, RoboCop discovers that he, indeed, was Murphy and Boddicker killed him. Morton is gunned down by Boddicker, but not before revealing that the crime boss is in cahoots with Jones.

RoboCop interrupts a meeting at an illegal drug processing plant and arrests Boddicker, who spills the beans that Dick Jones is the kingpin and the one who *really* should be under arrest. RoboCop goes to OCP headquarters to apprehend Jones, but a secret directive has been programmed into the android's brain that prohibits him from doing so. Jones summons an ED-209, and the heavily armored and armed robot attacks RoboCop. He escapes, but is assaulted by police, who have orders to destroy RoboCop. Lewis rescues the battered android, and they escape.

Jones bails out Boddicker and demands that he kill RoboCop. Labor negotiations between police and OCP break down, and the officers go on strike. Equipped with military artillery, Boddicker and his gang track RoboCop and Lewis to an abandoned steel mill. One by one, Boddicker and his thugs are eliminated.

Jones tells OCP executives that ED-209s can easily replace the striking police force. RoboCop enters the meeting and digitally plays back the evidence that shows Jones to be a murderer. The old man fires Jones, and RoboCop's prohibitive directive now becomes obsolete. He shoots Jones and kills him. The old man admires the fancy gun work, asking the cyborg, "What's your name?" RoboCop replies, "Murphy."

Sequels: *RoboCop 2* (1990), *RoboCop 3* (1993), plus syndicated TV series (1994) and Canadian TV Miniseries, *Robocop: Prime Directives* (2000).

Afterwords

The Motion Picture Association of America originally rated this film "X" due to language and, specifically, the violent murder of Officer Murphy. Considered the "kiss of death" for any commercial film, some quick and judicious editing brought a new rating of "R" and much success for *RoboCop*. With a budget of only $13 million, director Paul Verhoeven was hard pressed to deliver a sci-fi film with any impact. No worries, as the domestic box-office return was more than $53 million.

Special makeup effects designer Rob Bottin created the foam latex, plastic, and fiberglass RoboCop outfit, while makeup artist Stephan Dupuis took more than six and a half hours to apply the "Murphy face" every day (which really didn't fit under the helmet, so there were "helmet on" and "helmet off" shooting days).

Stop-motion animation expert Phil Tippett brought the squat ED-209 robot to life by means of a fourteen-inch articulated model. There was also a full-sized (seven feet tall) version built for a few scenes, but most of ED-209's action was shot in miniature against rear-projected images, a system pioneered by the great Ray Harryhausen.

As is often the case in the movies, the high-tech weapons in *RoboCop* were modified from real guns. The cyborg's thigh-holstered weapon was called an Auto-9, based on the real-life Italian-made Beretta 93R. Made in the 1970s for police and military, the Beretta fired single-shot or three-shot bursts with a twenty-round magazine, making it a formidable sidearm for RoboCop. Propmakers added the boxy barrel extension with vents (to emphasize the flames created by the three-shot bursts), as well as the rear sight.

The evil Boddicker presented his thugs with a big and bold weapon called the Cobra Assault Cannon. He demonstrated its flair by destroying one of their new SUX 6000 sedans. The basis of the Cobra was a Barrett 82A, a fifty-caliber semiautomatic rifle. No lightweight, the weapon fired a shell that was half an inch in diameter and four inches long. For *RoboCop*, a faux computer sighting system was mounted on top of the gun.

Among other reasons, actor Peter Weller was chosen for the role of Officer Murphy/RoboCop because of his slim build. The film's creators felt an actor with a normal-sized build would have looked too bulky once the RoboCop outfit was put on. Weller took his part very seriously, even seeking out the head of the movement department from Juilliard, one of the top teachers of mime in the country. The actor spent seven months training with the instructor to develop the unique mechanical yet fluid movements of the cyborg.

The well-worn ploy of rebooting a successful film brought a brand-new *RoboCop* to theaters in early 2014, with Joel Kinneman cast as Murphy and the redesigned RoboCop suit looking much like the Batman outfits from the Christian Bale films.

I, Robot

Synopsis

- 2004—American/Twentieth Century-Fox—115 min./color
- Director: Alex Proyas
- Original music: Marco Beltrami
- Film editing: William Hoy, Richard Learoyd, and Armen Minasian
- Production design: Patrick Tatopoulos
- Based loosely on the short story collection by Isaac Asimov

Cast

- Will Smith (Del Spooner)
- Bridget Moynahan (Susan Calvin)
- James Cromwell (Dr. Alfred Lanning)
- Bruce Greenwood (Lawrence Robertson)
- Chi McBride (Lt. John Bergin)
- Alan Tudyk (Sonny)

Del Spooner is a Chicago homicide detective in 2035. Robots are now part of the everyday world, handling mundane jobs like dog-walking, trash collection, and helping around the house. The androids are governed by the Three Laws of Robotics (paraphrased here), as cited earlier: One—They can never directly or indirectly harm a human; Two—They must obey human commands, as long as they don't conflict with the First Law; and Three—They must protect themselves, unless that conflicts with Laws One or Two.

Spooner detains a robot running with a purse, although it is no thief; the humanoid was hurrying with an inhaler for its asthmatic owner. This isn't Spooner's first mistake in collaring a robot; he has something against them. His commanding officer, Lt. Bergin, insists it be the last time.

Spooner is summoned to the headquarters of US Robotics, where he finds his friend and cofounder of the company, Dr. Alfred Lanning, has committed suicide. A meeting with Lawrence Robertson, president of US Robotics, reveals more of Spooner's prejudice against robots and Robertson as a very distant person. But he's quite occupied with a major rollout of the new NS-5 robots to every home in America.

Company robotic psychologist Dr. Susan Calvin joins Spooner in his investigation of Lanning's death. They tap into VIKI—Virtual Interactive Kinetic

Will Smith in *I, Robot.*

Intelligence—a supercomputer of Lanning's design that has, among other data, surveillance video of the entire building. It shows nothing out of the ordinary.

But while searching Lanning's lab, a robot jumps from hiding, shows aggression toward Spooner, and ignores Calvin's orders—directly against the first two Laws of Robotics—and escapes into the streets. At a USR assembly plant, Spooner and Calvin flush the rogue robot from an inventory of a thousand NS-5 models. Captured by a police SWAT team, the robot denies killing Lanning. But it also shows emotions and insists on being called "Sonny." Robertson and his attorneys show up, and since a robot cannot be charged with murder, it is released to USR—much to Spooner's dismay.

The detective pokes around Lanning's home, scheduled for robotic demolition the next morning. But the demo robot goes to work early, nearly killing Spooner. A late-night visit to Calvin sheds no light on why robots would try to kill Spooner.

The detective requests confidential files on Lanning from VIKI, who immediately informs Robertson of the inquiry. As Spooner reviews the data in his car, two USR transport vans unload dozens of robots in an attempt to cause a fatal accident. Spooner barely escapes, leaving damaged robots and vans behind him. When a robot assaults him, the detective reveals he has a robotic arm, which stops the attacking android in his tracks. Bergin arrives and demands Spooner's shield.

At USR, Calvin finds Sonny is unlike any other robot. It has a secondary processing system that allows it to override the Three Laws if it so chooses—it can reason. When Calvin visits Spooner's apartment to reveal this news, she discovers how he knew Lanning—it was Lanning that gave Spooner the robotic arm. Years back, a semi truck crashed into Spooner and another car, sending both into the water. A robot saw the crash and saved Spooner, leaving a young girl to drown by calculating the detective's chances for survival were greater—the reason for Spooner's contempt for robots.

Dr. Calvin and Spooner are amazed as Sonny tells of a dream he's had, where thousands of robots wait patiently for their leader—Del Spooner. Sonny even fashions a drawing of the scene. When the pair are brought to Robertson's office, the CEO insists there is no robot conspiracy and Sonny is a rogue robot built by Lanning. Calvin agrees to destroy Sonny.

As Calvin prepares to inject system-destroying nanites into Sonny, Spooner surveys the dry bed that once was Lake Michigan. It is filled with thousands of storage containers, each holding dozens of older robots. The NS-5s are eliminating the older bots and Spooner escapes, phoning Calvin to tell of the destruction. But her NS-5 intercepts the call, claiming it was only a wrong number.

The mass rollout of NS-5s has created an imprisonment of the city, with people under a robot-enforced curfew. Spooner's police station is overrun by the rebelling bots, and the media is shut down. Calvin and Spooner think Robertson is behind it all, but when they get to USR, they find him dead in his office. Sonny greets them—Calvin's conscience wouldn't allow her to complete the deactivation of this unique robot.

Spooner now knows that VIKI developed the plan. As she evolved, her ability to think independently grew, and the Three Laws took on a different meaning. Fearing man's wars and injustices would kill too many people, VIKI logically reasoned that a robot revolution would save more of mankind in the long run. Sonny grabs Calvin at gunpoint, claiming to now agree with VIKI's plan, but the wink of his android eye tips Spooner off—he'll help them escape.

First, they have to shut VIKI down. Sonny ignores VIKI's claims of logic and takes a vial of nanites as hundreds of NS-5s surround and attack Calvin and Spooner. Sonny saves Calvin as Spooner slides down thirty stories to VIKI's core, using his robotic arm as a brake. He injects the nanites, and VIKI shuts down, destroying herself.

The NS-5s return to their docile design as the crisis ends. Sonny admits that Lanning forced the bot to kill him, knowing it was the only way for Spooner to uncover VIKI's plot. Spooner now has a better appreciation for the robots, even shaking hands with Sonny.

The remaining NS-5s gather in the dry bed of Lake Michigan. It seems Sonny's dream is destined to come true, but it isn't Spooner who will guide the robots—it is Sonny.

Afterwords

I, Robot was a film that mixed its genres well. Of course, its roots were firmly based in sci-fi, but it was also a drama of morals and an action "popcorn" film, too. Released in the summer of 2004, the movie had a budget of $120 million and recouped $140 million of those dollars in the US. With more than $200 million from overseas, *I, Robot* did quite well with filmgoers.

Like most modern sci-fi and action-adventure films, *I, Robot* was loaded with CGI, with good reason. Scenes featuring hundreds or even thousands of moving robots just would not have been feasible—by either live-action or stop-motion animation. The lead robot role of Sonny, however, did use the convincing process of motion capture.

Actor Alan Tudyk wore a green spandex suit, adorned with dozens of targets placed at various joints. His full action in a scene as Sonny the robot was captured into a computer. The targets were then assigned to a digital model of the robotic Sonny—when Tudyk ran, the model of Sonny ran in the same fashion. The green suit allowed the digital replacement of the actor with the rendering of Sonny. Such a process allowed real interaction between actors—Will Smith and Bridget Moynahan talking with Sonny was shot as the actors talking with Tudyk. A similar setup was used by actor Andy Serkis as Gollum in the *Lord of the Rings* trilogy and *Hobbit* films, as well as *King Kong* in the 2005 version and Caesar in 2011's *Rise of the Planet of the Apes*.

Other than the title, several character names and plot points, the film of *I, Robot* bore no real connection to the collection of short stories with the same title by Isaac Asimov. The concept of a robot killing its maker and being arrested may have come from another story known as "I, Robot," written by Earl and Otto (Eando) Binder for the *Amazing Stories* pulp magazine in 1939—more than ten years before the Asimov stories.

Real Steel

Synopsis

- 2011—American/Dreamworks—127 min./color.
- Director: Shawn Levy
- Original music: Danny Elfman
- Film editing: Dean Zimmerman
- Production design: Tom Meyer
- Based loosely on the short story "Steel," by Richard Matheson

Cast
- Hugh Jackman (Charlie Kenton)
- Dakota Goyo (Max Kenton)
- Evangeline Lilly (Bailey Tallet)
- Anthony Mackie (Finn)
- Kevin Durand (Ricky)
- Hope Davis (Debra)
- James Rebhorn (Marvin)
- Karl Yune (Tak Mashido)

Hugh Jackman in *Real Steel*.

- Olga Fonda (Farra Lemkova)

In the year 2020, down-and-out ex-boxer Charlie Kenton tours the states with a large and powerful boxing robot called Ambush. As the sport with humans has been replaced, specially designed bots fill in, fighting in state fairs and other exhibitions. Charlie owes a lot of money to a lot of people and can't keep up with paying his debts.

At the Ambrose County Fair, Ambush squares off against an enormous bull called Black Thunder, while Kenton bets Ricky, the fight's promoter, $20,000 that Ambush will win. Although the bot initially handles itself well against the bull, Kenton lets his attention stray to a pretty blonde in the crowd, and Black Thunder tears a leg off Ambush. The bull makes quick work of the robot, and Charlie takes off before settling the bet with Ricky.

Kenton's ex-girlfriend has died, leaving their eleven-year-old son Max at the mercy of the courts. The boy's rich aunt and uncle, Debra and Marvin, desire custody, and Charlie has little interest in Max. But for $100,000, the conniving Kenton will take Max for the summer, then allow Debra and Marvin to adopt Max—half the money up front and the other half at the end of the summer.

Kenton agrees to buy a used bot, Noisy Boy, a sharp-looking, once-promising Japanese fighter designed by phenom Tak Mashida. He picks it up at Tallet's Gym, run by an old friend named Bailey, who took over the gym from her dead father—Charlie's one-time coach. He also picks up his son, who resents his father's abandonment.

At the underworld fight venue called the Crash Palace, Kenton meets up with his friend Finn, who puts Noisy Boy in the main event against Midas for a $50,000 purse. But Max thinks Charlie should just take an undercard match and leave. Max is right, as the overconfident Kenton has a hard time with his robot's voice-recognition software, and Midas knocks Noisy Boy's block off—Charlie's robot is destroyed.

Charlie and Max slip into a boneyard to pull some parts to build a new robot. Max slides down a dangerous cliff, but gets hooked onto the arm of a discarded robot. Charlie pulls the boy to safety and embraces his son for the first time. Having saved his life, Max salvages the robot, against Charlie's objections.

With parts from Ambush and Noisy Boy, along with Max's bot called Atom, Kenton fashions a new fighter. Originally an old sparring robot, it has a shadow function that mirrors the movements of its handler. Max takes a late-night run with Atom and seems to bond with it.

Charlie and Max hit the road, arriving at an arena where Zeus, the World Robot Boxing (WRB) champion, is appearing. Handled by inventor Mashida and backer Farra Lemkova, Zeus is monstrous and undefeated.

Finn sets Charlie up with a match at the Zoo, another underworld venue. Max puts a big bet on Atom and controls the bot while Charlie gives boxing advice. When Atom makes it through one round, Max doubles the bet to take the bot through another one. Atom takes its opponent down with a double uppercut and wins the bout.

Max sets up Atom with voice recognition, and the bot continues to win matches, with Kenton adding his boxing skills and knowledge to the robot's strengths. Charlie starts paying off his debts and gets Atom into a WRB match.

Lemkova offers to buy Atom for $200,000, but Max steadfastly refuses. Atom faces off against a tough two-headed bot called Twin Cities. The bigger opponent takes control of the fight against Atom, but Charlie picks up a flaw in Twin Cities' punching movements. Using that knowledge, Atom knocks the bot out. Max, flush with victory, challenges Lemkova to put Zeus and its belt up against Atom.

Looking for money and revenge, Ricky and his thugs beat Charlie and take his cash. Seeking safety for his son, Kenton leaves Max to stay with his aunt and uncle, with Charlie refusing the remaining $50,000 from the deal. Discouraged, he goes to stay with Bailey.

Charlie reconsiders the situation and reclaims Max, with a five-round championship fight set between Atom and Zeus.

With the arena packed to the rafters, Atom steps into the ring with Charlie and Max at its side. Outside, Finn takes a $100,000 bet from Ricky that Atom will go down in the first round. Zeus quickly puts Atom to the mat, but the smaller bot recovers and mounts its own attack, making it through the first round.

The rounds that follow are brutal, yet equal. By the end of the fourth round, Atom's voice-recognition system is damaged, and despite his own doubts, Charlie takes over Atom with the shadow function. Zeus punches itself out, and Atom takes the advantage, to the cheers of the crowd. Put down for a seven-count, only the final bell saves Zeus from defeat.

While the judges rule in Zeus' favor, the crowd crowns Atom as the people's champion. Max, Charlie, and Atom all raise their hands in victory.

Afterwords

Real Steel is light on the technology and heavy on the pathos, creating a *Rocky*-with-robots type of film. With an estimated budget between $80 million and $110 million, the movie grossed only $85 million in the States, but more than $200 million overseas.

Unlike *I, Robot*, which relied primarily on motion capture and CGI, *Real Steel* included full-sized animatronics built by Jason Matthews and his team at Legacy Effects—previously the Stan Winston Studios. More than twenty-six live-action robots were constructed, many commanded with radio-controlled remotes, much like hobby R/C cars, planes, and helicopters.

Director Shawn Levy shot many of the boxing scenes at Detroit's Cobo Center, home to Joe Louis Arena, the site of many championship boxing matches and pro-wrestling cards over the years. Much of the motion capture was accomplished with real boxers hooked up to the computers, as former world champion Sugar Ray Leonard acted as consultant. The winner of titles in five different weight classes drew on his years of experience in the ring, giving Hugh Jackman and each fighting robot a distinct style in boxing. For example, with Zeus being so enormously strong, Leonard immediately thought of heavyweight champ George Foreman. Atom, on the other hand being smaller and faster, received much of Leonard's own style.

The original short story, "Steel," that influenced *Real Steel* was written by sci-fi author Richard Matheson in 1956. Eight years later, it was adapted by the author for an episode of TV's *The Twilight Zone*, starring Lee Marvin.

The actor plays Steel Kelly, an ex-boxer who now manages a run-down android fighter called Battling Maxo, since human boxing has been outlawed in the near future. When the robot falls apart, it's up to Kelly to disguise himself as Maxo and fight another robot. Kelly is beaten badly and gets only half the purse because Maxo did so poorly in the ring. But the winnings will be used to repair Maxo and keep on fighting.

In still another example of life imitating art, the SyFy television network tapped into the concept of *Real Steel* by producing the reality competition show *Robot Combat League* in 2013. Much like the film, gargantuan mechanical humanoids squared off against each other, operated by teams of engineers, gamers, and geeks. But like many reality shows, the truth was exaggerated, with special-effects devices emitting sparks as the robots wailed away at their metallic midsections.

But Where Do You Keep the Spare?

Sci-Fi Spaceships

Rocket History 101 (Real and on Celluloid)

Wernher von Braun, Nazi German-turned-American rocket designer, created the V-2 single-stage rocket in 1942. Soaring into the sky from a launch site in Peenemünde, in northeastern Germany, the V-2 delivered death and destruction across Europe during World War II. After the war, von Braun and his stockpile of rockets were brought to America, where he eventually headed up the US space program. The smooth, cigar-shaped V-2, with its quadrangle tail fins, became the picture that everyone imagined when they thought "spaceship." Even Hollywood joined in, with productions from 1950's *Destination Moon* to the 1948 Warner Bros.' Bugs Bunny cartoon *Haredevil Hare* using the V-2 as a model for their movie missiles.

Spaceship design changed drastically once man actually reached outer space. Much of the success of the V-2 was due to its cone-shaped nose and contoured body, which cut easily through the air as it rose into the blue. The need for aerodynamics—in the real world—ceased to be a necessity once spacecraft escaped the Earth's dense atmosphere. In the cinematic world, there was no need for sleek, low-friction and low-drag vehicles when traveling from one galaxy to the next. The V-2 had become a quaint and simple memory.

Experts may disagree on the mainstream Hollywood film that actually broke the tradition of utilizing a spaceship with the standard and long-established concept based on the V-2 appearance (UFOs and flying saucers, not included). Stanley Kubrick's *2001: A Space Odyssey*, released in 1968, featured deep-space probes like the Discovery One and lunar landers like the Aries 1B, both of which clearly steered away from the norm. The Valley Forge, the outer space greenhouse in 1972's *Silent Running*, had an appearance similar to those in *2001: A Space Odyssey* (no coincidence, as Doug Trumbull, the effects supervisor on *2001*, was the director of *Silent Running*).

All things considered, it could very well be the armada of oddly shaped spacecraft featured in George Lucas' 1977 mother of all blockbusters, *Star*

Wars, which shattered the paradigm of smooth-skinned, conical vehicles in outer space. Consider the horseshoe-shaped *Millennium Falcon*, or the uniquely-shaped TIE Fighters and X-Wings, or the spherical Death Star—all were truly original concepts in the cinematic world of spaceflight.

Let's Look Under the Hood

Alien—Nostromo

Think of the *Nostromo* as a haunted house in deep space. The 1979 film *Alien* created chills and thrills worthy of any spook joint found on terra firma, except it was millions of miles in space. The crew had its hands full trying to survive after the fearsome alien was discovered on board.

Built sometime around the start of the twenty-second century, the *Nostromo* was originally an interstellar crusader. But the craft was rebuilt as a working-class starship, designed as a tug to haul loads of ore and oil from other planets. Powered by a fusion reactor (that sucker was nuclear), the *Nostromo* was manned by seven members. The ship was equipped with seven hyper-sleep capsules for long-duration flights and controlled by a master computer known as "Mother."

The *Nostromo* was no small ship, measuring 800 feet long, 540 feet wide, and more than 240 feet high—picture an area big enough to fit nearly five football fields. But it apparently wasn't big enough for the feisty Ripley and the alien, so the lieutenant first-class set the self-destruct circuit in the reactor to blast the

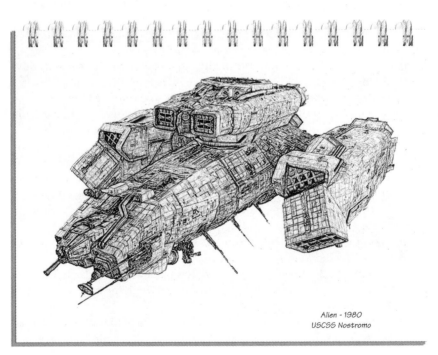

Alien - 1980
USCSS Nostromo

Nostromo to bits. Ripley escaped in a shuttle (along with the crafty alien) and finally sent the monster into deep space with the help of the airlock and a blast from the engines.

Director Ridley Scott and writer Dan O'Bannon looked to artists Ron Cobb and Chris Foss (having made his mark by expertly illustrating the world-famous *The Joy of Sex* book in 1972) to design the *Nostromo*. It had to look real, and it had to look lived in—nothing flashy. Essentially, Cobb would create the interior, while Foss fashioned the ship's exterior.

Expert model builder Terry Reed of Otter FX fashioned a six-inch model of the *Nostromo* for starters. Director Scott worked with the artists and FX team to further develop the craft. With changes suggested and made, the spaceship finally received the green light for construction.

Hardly qualifying as a miniature model, the main *Nostromo* for production was eleven feet long, seven feet wide, and weighed more than five hundred pounds. The craft was assembled from steel, wood, and plastic (parts taken from hundreds of model kits of military tanks, space shuttles, and *Star Wars* vehicles). Even when finished, Ridley Scott insisted on making more changes to the *Nostromo*—to the frustration of the model builders who thought their jobs were done.

Although it was originally designed to be bright yellow, the *Nostromo* wound up a dingy gray, keeping with Scott's desire to make everything appear used and abused. And when Spielberg's *CE3K* hit the screens—complete with a light-filled mother ship—Scott requested a retrofit for his *Nostromo*, adding more lights to the bottom of his craft.

Along with the massive model, a full-scale twenty-five-foot landing leg and a seven-foot miniature were built for detail shots. To increase the impressive scale, Scott put small kids into spacesuits for some scenes, making the leg appear bigger still.

And what happened to the *Nostromo* after the success of *Alien?* The trip of the main model was varied and exciting. Its first stop was at Hollywood's foremost film historian, curator, and master makeup artist, Bob Burns, who welcomed the *Nostromo* from Twentieth Century-Fox with open arms and driveway—since there was no way it would fit into his basement. It would sit there for nearly twenty years, somewhat protected under tarps but suffering the heat and rains of Southern California.

In the early 1990s, Burns realized he was not doing the *Nostromo* any favors by keeping it out in the elements. To the rescue came makeup artists Greg Nicotero and Howard Berger of KNB Effects, who took the spaceship and, despite its need for restoration, gave it an indoor home in their storage site.

Fast-forward to 2007, where Stephen Lane—movie prop collector extraordinaire and owner/operator of London and LA's Prop Store—arranged to take the *Nostromo* from KNB and display it for film fans everywhere. But there was one problem—the exposure to the elements had left the ship near total collapse.

The FX shop known as Grant McCune Design—formerly Apogee Inc. and run by Academy Award–winning visual effects expert John Dykstra—was charged with the task of restoring the *Nostromo* to its original appearance. Interestingly, the model had a stowaway—just like the real *Nostromo* in the movie. But instead of a slime-dripping, spindly alien creature, the model had an opossum inside— in fact, two of them. However, their days had come and gone, as only their bones remained.

More than two thousand man-hours were spent in the restoration across a year's time, shoring up the worn wood substructure, identifying and replacing the thousands of plastic model parts, and repainting the *Nostromo* to its original gray and worn finish.

These days, the *Nostromo* starcraft model resides in the Los Angeles offices of the Prop Store, under the care of General Manager Brandon Alinger. Fans of *Alien* and sci-fi in general can view the ship (by appointment) where it sits— under the watchful eye of a full-sized *Alien* mannequin.

Blade Runner—Police Spinner

Some futurists are of the opinion that, as the Earth's population continues to grow, ground transportation for individuals will be crowded and difficult— picture a really bad traffic jam, all day, every day, times a hundred. While mass transit may solve part of the problem, some suggest looking skyward.

The concept of personal transportation in the sky is not new to the world of sci-fi. The great German film of 1927 *Metropolis* envisioned a future where flying cars were common. Even the cartoon TV world of *The Jetsons* in the 1960s featured a flying vehicle with a clear bubble top that the whole family—even Astro the dog—could enjoy.

Ridley Scott's 1982 *Blade Runner* offered police protection in dingy Los Angeles, courtesy of a not-so-normal blue-and-white vehicle. Called a spinner, the two-person craft could maneuver on the streets like a regular car, then rise in the air via VTOL technology—vertical-takeoff/landing. The car was twenty-one feet, nine inches in length, with a width of eight feet, two inches at the cockpit and nine feet, ten inches at its widest point.

Scott called on industrial illustrator Syd Mead, who began working on sc-fi concepts for movies like 1979's *Star Trek: The Motion Picture*, and *Tron* in the same year that *Blade Runner* was made, to design the future city of LA and its vehicles. Knowing the director had a vision of a futuristic film noir, Mead created cars from influences like Philippine jitneys—small, taxi-like vehicles—and autos from the 1950s and 1960s.

Once designed, Gene Winfield and Rod and Construction Inc. were con- tracted to build the spinners. Producers originally wanted a fleet of fifty-four cars, but with a construction budget of a bit more than $600,000, the final number was twenty-five spinners. Using a Volkswagen chassis, Winfield used everything from aluminum to body bondo to dress up the finished vehicles.

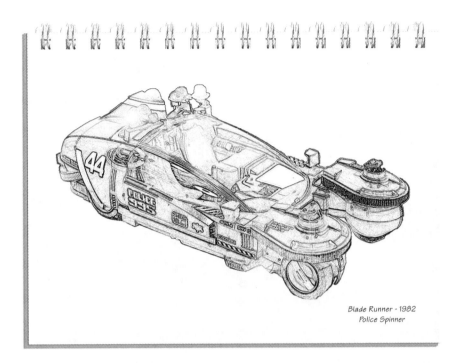

Blade Runner - 1982
Police Spinner

Scott turned to special-effects director Doug Trumbull to incorporate full-sized and model versions of the spinners into scenes of the city. Having just finished working with Steven Spielberg on *Close Encounters of the Third Kind*, Trumbull used similar light, smoke, lens flare, and reflection effects on the *Blade Runner* spinners.

Spinners wound up as background vehicles in films like 1985's *Trancers*, 1989's *Back to the Future II*, and 1990's *Solar Crisis*. A full-sized prop police spinner hangs from the ceiling at the EMP Museum in Seattle, Washington.

Close Encounters of the Third Kind—Mother Ship

The varied levels, towering extensions, and glowing pinpoints of light on the *CE3K* mother ship just might remind you of an oil refinery. And that's okay, since an oil refinery in India was part of director Steven Spielberg's inspiration for the original concept. He also envisioned the myriad of dazzling lights that shone from the San Fernando Valley of LA.

Discarding the idea of a long, cigar-shaped spacecraft, Spielberg and FX supervisor Doug Trumbull decided on a ship with two distinct sides—one would be dish-shaped and the other like the skyline of a major metropolis. Thousands of lights would illuminate both sides. They then turned to conceptual illustrator Ralph McQuarrie to detail the design.

The mother ship was imagined to be more than seventeen hundred feet across its main dish—more than one-third of a mile—and its revelation at

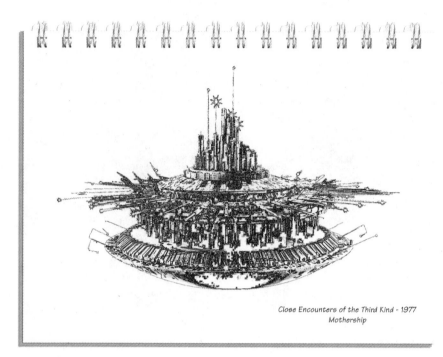

Close Encounters of the Third Kind - 1977
Mothership

Devil's Tower satisfied Spielberg's desire to have a craft that could blot out the sky. McQuarrie completed a simple ten-inch by eighteen-inch painting and then handed it off to model maker Greg Jein. He built a small wood and metal model as a road map for constructing a full production item.

Various materials, including Plexiglas, fiberglass, aluminum, neon tubing, and wood, were used to build a model that was more than five feet across, three feet high, and weighed four hundred pounds. Thousands of tiny modeling lights, along with fiber optic lights, were added as well. Using the well-known habit of kitbashing (adapting parts from plastic model kits), along with custom fabrication, Jein and his crew added more details—including mini versions of R2-D2 and a TIE fighter from *Star Wars*, a mailbox, a VW bus, model train signal towers and cranes, a cemetery, a fire hydrant, a silhouette of Mickey Mouse, and a number of tiny people figures, among other things. Working twelve hours a day, six days a week, the mother ship took nearly ten weeks to build.

Mounted on a crane and a gimbal joint, the mother ship was shot rising from behind the Devil's Tower, as Roy Neary, Jillian Guiler, and hundreds of military and scientists watched in amazement. Impressive enough at first sight, the ship then slowly turned over, revealing the smoothly curved underbelly. Hundreds of lights appeared—an effect created by projecting pinpoints of light on the bottom from underneath the ship.

A ring of pulsating lights surrounded a gangplank walkway that opened from the center of the underside. Once opened, long-lost aviators, sailors, and other folks returned to Earth. A wiry-thin alien made a cameo appearance from inside the mother ship, exchanged nonverbal pleasantries with Lacombe, took on a load of Earth volunteers, closed up the ship, and rose majestically into the night sky.

Spielberg kept the mother-ship model for a number of years, then turned it over to the US government—sort of. The five-foot model is nicely displayed these days at the Udvar-Hazy Center of the Smithsonian National Air and Space Museum in Chantilly, Virginia.

District 9—Drop Ship

Director Neill Blomkamp didn't reveal much information about the mother ship in 2009's *District 9*. The same wasn't true for the vehicle known as the drop ship. Along with being the basis for Christopher Johnson's basement (sure beats a pool table), it was the planned escape vehicle to return to the mother ship—although that didn't go too well.

Looking something like a grasshopper with a three-color paint job, the drop ship had a forward cockpit and was equipped with two VTOL—vertical takeoff and landing—engines. Much like the Harrier jet, the drop ship could gimbal its engines to direct their thrust in a downward direction, allowing takeoff without any taxiing.

Much of the flying and navigation was computer controlled, but maneuvering the drop ship was so simple, even a child could do it (assuming your spawn was a prawn). As for Wikus, he had very little time to prove his aviator chops

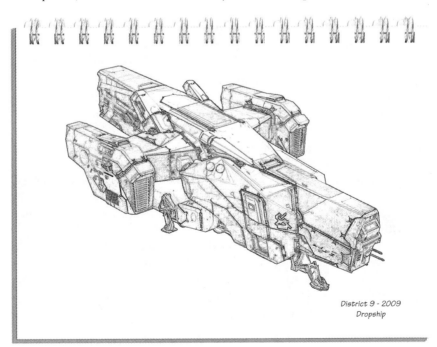

District 9 - 2009
Dropship

when he took off in the drop ship, as the PMC missiles disabled the ship and it crashed back to Earth.

Lead concept designer Greg Broadmore worked closely with Blomkamp to create the mother ship and drop ship. Starting from an original design from the director, Broadmore spent long and hard hours and drew many variations to come up with the final concept for the mother ship. Conversely, the drop ship was conceived and approved in only one afternoon.

The artist used conventional software such as Google SketchUp and Photoshop to draw his designs (proving once more—it's not the wand, it's the magician). Broadmore's completed sketches were passed along to Embassy VFX and ImageEngine in Vancouver, Canada, and WETA Digital Studios in New Zealand to make them appear real. Instead of relying on miniatures and models, the drop ship was completely digital in its creation, integrated with live-action backgrounds.

The resulting scenes were amazingly seamless, as CG artists combined live footage of the landscape and actors with not only the drop ship but its shadow, explosions, debris, and even dust from the engine turbulence.

E.T. the Extra-Terrestrial—Spaceship

> Who launched E.T.'s ship from space?
> Do you know their name? Do you know their face?
> Who was the spark for the Berg of Spiel?
> Were they make-believe? Was it someone real?
> Here's the story—is it any use?
> The inspiration was . . . Dr. Seuss!

(See? This is why I don't write children's stories.)

Director Steven Spielberg's take on the innocence of youth amid an alien left behind on Earth in 1982, *E.T. the Extra-Terrestrial*, required a different kind of spaceship. His floating city of a mother ship from *CE3K* offered high tech, but *E.T.'s* vehicle was quaint—perhaps something from the pen of Jules Verne.

Conceptual artist Ralph McQuarrie at ILM picked up on the director's suggestion that the spaceship look like it was designed by Dr. Seuss. Spielberg selected one rendering from five sketches, from which McQuarrie then created a painting. The ILM model team used that piece to build models in various scales for production.

In the film, the egg-shaped alien craft was fifty feet in height and about thirty feet across at the widest point of the body. It had a single engine at the base, with three landing pads surrounding it. Arranged around the body were eight gimbaled lights that also acted as attitude thrusters, with an egress hatch and extendable ramp under one of them. At the top of the body was an antenna array.

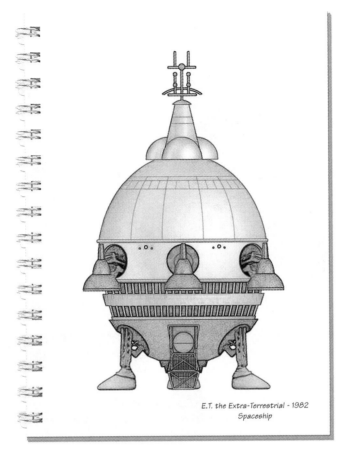

E.T. the Extra-Terrestrial - 1982
Spaceship

ILM model maker Charlie Bailey made the initial drawings for construction and built the main model with Mike Fulmer and Randy Ottenberg. Stainless steel, epoxy-graphite cloth, fiberglass, steel and brass gears, and halogen lights made up the final model. It was two feet high, eighteen inches in diameter, and weighed forty-five pounds. A smaller, eight-inch-diameter spaceship was built from vacuformed plastic, as well as a four-foot fiberglass ship and a simplified ten-inch model, for preview trailers on TV and in theaters.

The focus of the film was the alien itself, with the spaceship taking a backseat at its beginning and end. Even so, the simple yet unusual design of the craft made a big contribution to the overall ambiance of *E.T.*

Galaxy Quest—NSEA *Protector*

The clever 1999 film told the story of stars from a defunct sci-fi television show suddenly thrust into a real world of spaceflight and aliens. *Galaxy Quest* took a lot of its good-natured spoofing and inspiration from *Star Trek*, a defunct

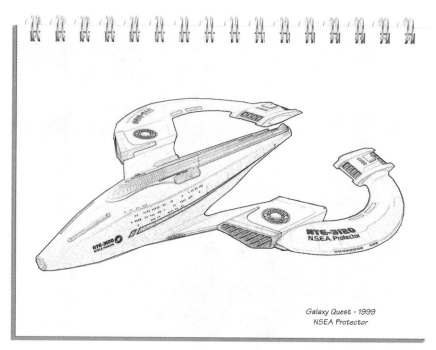

Galaxy Quest - 1999
NSEA Protector

sci-fi-television show. At the forefront was the starship *Protector*, the gem of the NSEA—the National Space Exploration Administration.

At sixteen hundred feet in length, the *Protector* was large but graceful, looking something like a dove in flight. It was powered by a quantum flux drive (whatever the deuce that is) and armed to the teeth as an offensive war craft. Curiously, the *Protector* also had the Omega-13, a device capable of turning time back a full thirteen seconds—enough to rectify a single mistake (perhaps handy around closing time at the local watering hole).

ILM FX supervisor Bill George, along with production designer Linda DeScenna, concept artist Eric Wrigley, and FX supervisor Stefen Fangmeier, collaborated on a starship design that was clearly influenced by *Star Trek's* USS *Enterprise.* Yet, in order to avoid any legal hassles, the *Protector* had to be somewhat unique (its prefix designation of NTE-3120 stood for "Not the *Enterprise*"). Hundreds of test sketches were made before then-director Harold Ramis (to be replaced by Dean Parisot), and producer Steven Spielberg chose the final design.

Model makers at ILM—including future Discovery Channel Mythbuster Grant Imahara—built *Protector* models of several different sizes. A one-foot model was first created as a guide for the other ships. A simplified three-foot model was used for the television scenes—clearly intended to look like a miniature on a TV screen. An eight-foot highly detailed model was built, using materials like lightweight aircraft metals, vacuformed plastic, and hundreds of neon and LED lights. The final paint job tapped into the color scheme of the *Star Trek's Enterprise*.

Even though the NSEA *Protector* established itself as a flight-worthy craft, standing alongside sci-fi ships like the USS *Enterprise*, many fans felt *Galaxy Quest* was actually one of the better *Star Trek* films.

Independence Day—Mother Ship, City Destroyer, Alien Attacker

Creatives Dean Devlin and Roland Emmerich did not hesitate to go big (read: BIG) when it came to the alien spaceships in 1996's *Independence Day*. Individual fighters were equal in size to F-18 Hornets, while the ships that carried them were as big as cities. And those ships came from the mother of all mother ships.

The mother ship that emerged from behind the moon was estimated as being an amazing five hundred miles across—imagine a spacecraft that stretched from Chicago, Illinois, to Dallas, Texas. Obviously occupied by millions of aliens, the mother ship was capable of deploying more than eighty enormous disk-shaped craft to carry out their evil plan to take over the Earth.

Those disk-shaped craft were known as destroyers, spanning fifteen miles across. Literally flying cities, the ships had a devastating weapon called the Schism that released a beam of disastrous power that spewed from the center of the underbelly. A series of flower-petal-like panels opened to reveal the Schism and unleash its force on iconic American buildings like the US Bank Building in Los Angeles, the Empire State Building, and the White House.

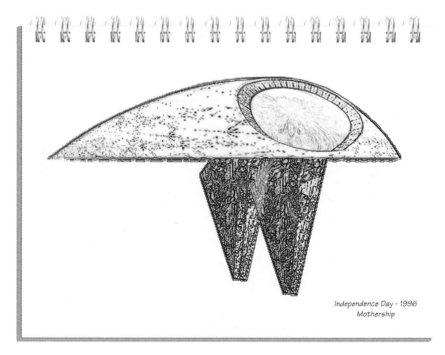

Independence Day - 1996
Mothership

The destroyers acted like carriers for individual attack ships. Occupied by two spindly aliens, the nearly seventy-feet-across attackers were fast and highly agile in the skies over Earth. Little was known about the propulsion unit, but it was capable of keeping up with an F-18. Air Force pilot Steven Hiller proved himself to be a superior flyer, as the alien attacker crashed in the desert after being blinded by Hiller's parachute. What's more, the US government had kept an alien attacker under wraps at an underground Area 51 bunker, since recovering it from Roswell in 1947.

While computer graphics played a major part in the visual FX in *ID4*, the budget was kept under control by using physical effects with miniatures and models wherever possible. A model shop run by Mike Joyce and effects photography stages were set up on the old Howard Hughes airplane plant in Culver City, California. As usual, spaceships of various sizes and scales were built for specific uses.

A twelve-foot model of the beetle-shaped mother ship was used for most of the scenes, with a twenty-foot modular tunnel built for the scenes of Levinson and Hiller flying the captured attacker into the depths of the mother ship. Interiors were detailed with a maze of columns, although only a few were actually three-dimensional. Background columns were merely enlarged photos of a column, attached to plywood.

The city destroyers owed part of their design to the Warner Bros. cartoons of the late 1940s. A Bugs Bunny cartoon called *Haredevil Hare* featured an alien villain called Marvin the Martian. His spaceship, the X-2, was a simple flying

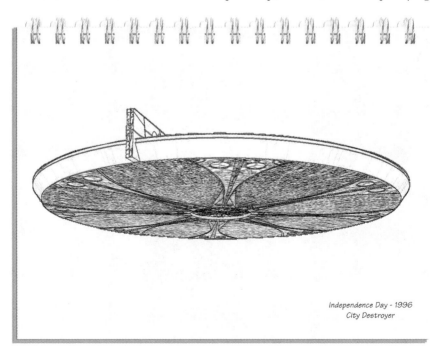

Independence Day - 1996
City Destroyer

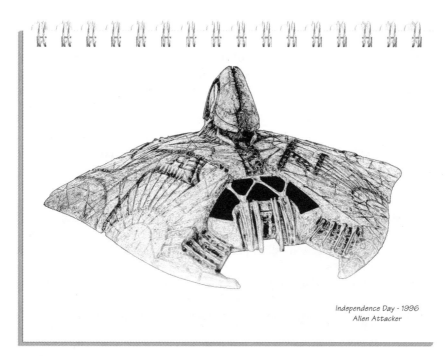

Independence Day - 1996
Alien Attacker

saucer with a single vertical fin. *ID4's* destroyers closely resembled the X-2, although the vertical extension on the destroyer was at the front of the craft, rather than the rear.

Destroyer models were built as four-foot and twelve-foot models, as well as a gargantuan thirty-foot piece that was so large it had to be constructed directly on the effects stage where it would be shot. Built from aluminum and fiberglass, the large model weighed nearly three tons. The twelve-foot model had hundreds of individual urethane parts glued to its top, and photo-etched metal plates were attached to provide even more detail. Ten thousand fiber optic lights were installed inside, providing a myriad of pinpoints of illumination.

The Attacker came in three convenient sizes—two-foot, four-foot, and a full-sized sixty-five-foot mockup—complete with interior and exterior—for the scenes in the Area 51 hangar. A two-foot master attacker was sculpted in clay, then cast in plastic for assembly and detailing. The models were attached to motion-control camera rigs, allowing for precise computer-controlled shooting.

Mars Attacks!—Martian Flying Saucer

Simply put, the term "flying saucer" is quite descriptive. Picture a saucer (although today's Starbucks and Dunkin' Donuts coffees come without one) floating in the air. Voila: a flying saucer. (Up next, we'll answer the burning question: What color is an orange?)

The 1996 film *Mars Attacks!*—directed by the king of kitsch, Tim Burton—was based on the gruesome Topps bubble gum card series from 1962. While many of the film's concepts came directly from the cards, the Martian saucer eschewed the original design in favor of an homage to 1950s sci-fi saucers. Specifically, Burton leaned heavily on the Ray Harryhausen creation from 1956's *Earth vs. the Flying Saucers*, with a sprinkle of inspiration from the C57-D spaceship in *Forbidden Planet* in the same year.

The Martian ship was ultra-simple in design—two convex disks with a diameter of two hundred feet placed together, topped by a bulging dome. The top half spun counterclockwise, while the bottom half spun in the opposite direction. Assumingly aerodynamic in flight, the craft extended six spindly spiderlike legs to land. A long ramp unrolled to provide access from underneath the center of the ship. In flight, that portion of the craft was capable of deploying a disc-shaped ray gun for mass destruction or a large mechanical hand for even more mass destruction (like taking down the large mo'ai statues on Easter Island with a gigantic bowling ball).

In another tribute to the genius of Harryhausen, Burton originally wanted to present the Martians and flying saucers by means of stop-motion animation. But after tests by an English animation team, it was decided to produce almost all of the FX via computer-generated graphics. Warner's new Digital Studios split the work with ILM.

Acme Models created physical effects scenes, including the final scene of a disabled Martian saucer crashing into the Potomac River. They built a

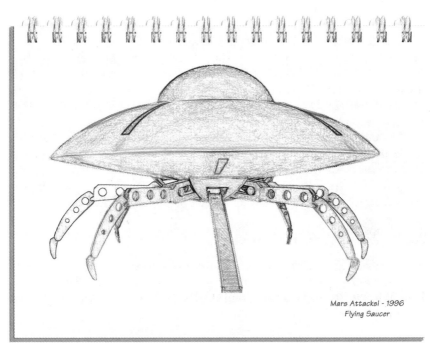

Mars Attacks! - 1996
Flying Saucer

twenty-five-foot-wide model out of steel, wood, and fiberglass, with a final weight of nearly two tons. Using the Falls Lake on the Universal Studios backlot, the Martian saucer was suspended with a one-hundred-ton crane and dropped into the water as cameras rolled.

Small six-inch saucers were used in the war room scenes with Jack Nicholson as the president. One of the saucers was placed up for auction by the prestigious Julien's Auctions in November 2010. Expected to fetch between $600 and $800, the final sale of the disk confounded experts—and showed the popularity of *Mars Attacks!*—by going for more than $1,500.

Prometheus—Spaceship *Prometheus*

The United States Commercial Star Ship (USCSS) *Prometheus*, built by the Weyland Corporation in 2091, was an FTL (faster-than-light) vehicle intended to set the standard for deep-space scientific exploration. Its first mission was to seek the genesis of man on a distant moon called LV-223.

With a crew of seventeen, the Prometheus was more than 575 feet long, 440 feet wide, and 170 feet high—imagine a spacecraft the size of five side-by-side US Navy destroyers soaring through deep space. It was powered by four gimbaled, nuclear-based ion plasma engines, making it capable of vertical takeoffs and landings (VTOL).

The ship held a variety of vehicles, including an exploration rover, a two-person transport, a crew escape module, and additional ejection pods. To ease

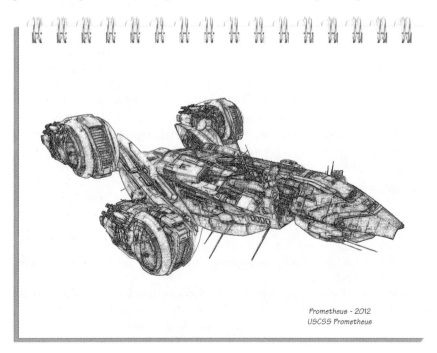

Prometheus - 2012
USCSS Prometheus

the boredom of long trips at the speed of light, hypersleep chambers allowed the crew to catch forty million winks. Health issues were addressed with a Med-Pod, capable of medical diagnosis and surgical procedures.

Crew quarters included the lavishly appointed room for mission director Meredith Vickers. She had her own grand piano, bar, private Med-Pod, and an enormous wall screen depicting comforting scenes of nature.

Unfortunately, no ship is indestructible. When an alien Engineer intended to release a deadly liquid on Earth with its spaceship, the *Prometheus* was sacrificed by crashing into it and destroying both crafts.

The design of the USCSS *Prometheus* was one of production designer Arthur Max's many tasks on the 2012 film of the same name. He relied heavily on NASA and European Space Agency vehicle concepts for a state-of-the-art spaceship that could really exist in the next eighty years. He then designed the ship's interiors as they would relate to the exterior dimensions. Director Ridley Scott insisted on having a clean look to the ship, rather than the worn-out, lived-in appearance that the *Nostromo* featured in *Alien*.

The *Prometheus* was largely realized as a computer-generated image, with initial concepts created by artists like Steve Burg before being handed off to 3-D illustrators like Ben Procter for final rendering. Some exteriors, however, were accomplished the old-fashioned way: using real sets (Horrors!).

The landing scene of *Prometheus* on LV-223 was staged on a huge outdoor set. A thirty-foot-tall landing leg and egress ramp were built, with a sixty-foot expanse of gravel leading to a large green screen. The background was digitally replaced with images of volcanic landscape from Iceland. Functional and operating rover vehicles were created to maneuver across the terrain.

Many of the *Prometheus* interiors were built on the sound stages of Pinewood Studios in London, including the world-famous 007 Stage. With nearly sixty thousand square feet of space, it still wasn't enough, so the building was temporarily expanded by another 30 percent.

A two-level bridge set featured large viewing windows to the wonders of space. Computer graphics artists added holographic displays and touch-screen controls, although director Scott insisted on a compliment of real knobs, gauges, switches, joysticks, and monitors.

Sky Captain and the World of Tomorrow—Flying Wing

One of the deadly devices from the brain (and not much else) of the diabolical Dr. Totenkopf, the flying wings menaced New York City and the Flying Legion, led by Sky Captain Joe Sullivan. Flapping their massive wings like some sort of gigantic metallic bats, the ornithopter drones buzzed the canyons of skyscraping buildings in Manhattan.

With a broad wingspan, the airships had a central cockpit with weapon pods on either side, connecting with the accordion-like fittings for the wings. Each teardrop-shaped pod had four recoiling machine guns. Despite its enormous

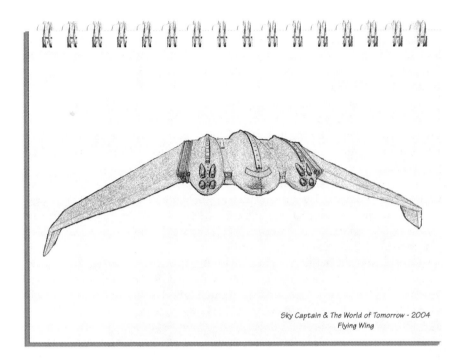

Sky Captain & The World of Tomorrow - 2004
Flying Wing

size and bulk, the flying wing was incredibly agile, with the ability to turn sharply and change altitude in very little time.

At the suggestion of director Kerry Conran, brother and production designer Kevin drew several sketches of "a plane with flapping wings." Once selected, the flying wing design was passed along directly to the CG artists for detailing and creation.

Once a detailed computer-generated model of the flying wing was built, as many copies as needed could be made as quick as one could say "copy and paste." Then those images were composited with various digital layers of background shots of New York City, individual buildings, clouds, and anything else the scene called for.

In a film famed for shooting its live action entirely in front of a green screen (save for one office shot in the beginning), it was clear no models or miniatures would be needed. As such, literally every shot in the film would be a visual effect.

Starship Troopers—Rodger Young

With a scientific background, director Paul Verhoeven put that knowledge to good use when dreaming up the battle cruisers for *Starship Troopers*. Realizing that something as massive as the *Rodger Young* would never have to fly anywhere other than deep space, Verhoeven figured there was no need to apply sleek aerodynamics.

Mainly designed for use as a troop carrier, the *Rodger Young* was more than eighteen-hundred feet long—over twice the length of the *Hindenburg* airship and nearly four hundred feet longer than the Empire State Building. The craft, with fifteen decks of activity, was capable of deploying troops via drop ships and shuttles. And it looked like a whale.

Despite its massive girth, cocky pilots like Carmen Ibanez had no problem controlling the *Rodger Young* (probably rack-and-pinion steering). Its agility was put to the test when weaving its way through an asteroid field—although it did lose its communications array like a twenty-foot semi going under an eighteen-foot viaduct.

The pride of the Federation Fleet came to an end when deadly bug plasma spewed from Planet P. The caustic nuclear juice tore into the hull of the *Rodger Young*, splitting it in two and killing hundreds of soldiers. A quick jump into an escape pod saved Ibanez and her partner, Zander, although it crashed into the planet below for more dramatic action.

Conceptual artist Jim Martin provided renditions of the battle cruiser. Although much of *Starship Troopers* employed CGI effects, most of the *Rodger Young* footage was shot using models. One eighteen-foot and two nine-foot models handled the brunt of the work, although a dozen models in the foot-and-a-half range were used for fleet shots.

Master model makers like George Willis worked with Thunderstone Model Shop—part of the Sony Pictures Imageworks FX company—to build the *Rodger Young*, along with the various drop ships, shuttles, and other space vehicles. With

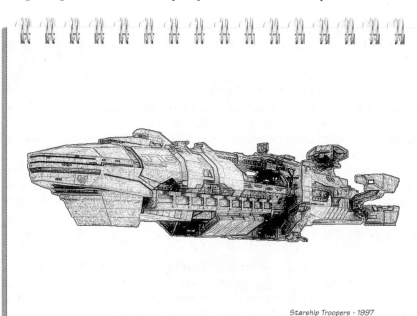

Starship Troopers - 1997
Rodger Young 176

the advent of CGI quickly ramping up, Sony still didn't have enough computers to render the thousands of frames of space battles and bugs, so they turned to miniature photography to accomplish the tasks at hand.

In fact, the standard practice of stop-motion animation was used to create the devastating destruction of the *Rodger Young*. Willis designed a mechanical rig, using brass rods and bass guitar tuning machines, to lower the decks of the split eighteen-foot model of the battle cruiser by small increments during the frame-by-frame animation. The five-second scene took more than two hours to shoot.

While the whereabouts of the big *Rodger Young* models are unknown, the foot-and-a-half models were distributed among executives, producers, cast members, agents, and other folks. When the model makers themselves felt left out, the word was sent down for them to help themselves to additional copies of the *Rodger Young*, suitable for fireplace mantles everywhere.

Star Trek: The Motion Picture—USS Enterprise

Trying to cover the history of the USS *Enterprise* as an entry to a chapter of spaceships is like trying to encapsulate the history of the United States in five hundred words or less (or, as the old adage goes, like trying to fit two pounds of baloney into a one-pound bag). In any case, one ends up needing a smaller baloney or a bigger bag. In the case of the *Star Trek* ship, we will focus only on the ship found in the 1979 feature film (and that's no baloney).

Of course, that *Enterprise* was considered to be a retrofit of the same ship from the 1960s TV series. Designated NCC-1701, the USS *Enterprise* (United Space Ship) was an impressive one thousand feet in length, with a crew of more than four hundred. Built in 2245, the renovations took a year and a half, with the ship returned to active duty in 2270.

The NCC-1701 was equipped with twin propulsion units capable of taking it to speeds past Warp 6 (a logarithmic function of faster-than-light velocity—never mind, it's a sci-fi film, for God's sake!). Offensive weapons included photon torpedoes and phasers, with defensive deflector shields as well. (No mention of whitewall tires, but there were plenty of radios to go around.)

The original design of the *Enterprise* came from the mind of TV art show director Matt Jefferies. Producer Gene Roddenberry was vague in what he wanted, but very clear on what he didn't want in the spacecraft design. It had to be something never seen before (so what else was new?), and it could not have fins, wings, rockets, or fire trails. Jefferies' final concept came from numerous sketches and revisions.

By 1979, the renewed *Enterprise* was first tackled by its original creator—Jefferies—then enhanced with input from FX house Robert Abel and Associates' Richard Taylor and concept artist Andrew Probert. The major changes included sweeping back the propulsion unit struts and eliminating the dish-shaped sensor at the front of the secondary hull.

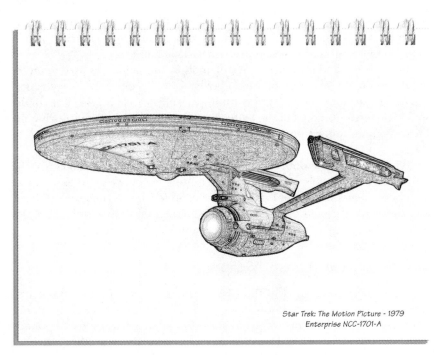

Star Trek: The Motion Picture - 1979
Enterprise NCC-1701-A

More importantly, the *Enterprise*'s migration from the boob tube to the silver screen required a much greater level of detail in the overall design of the ship. What was OK for TV would never pass muster on enormous screens around the world. Thus, hundreds of windows, hatches, and a complete internal lighting system were added.

Several models were made for production by Magicam, a subsidiary of Paramount. The major *Enterprise* was eight feet long, weighed eighty-five pounds (lightened by using newer plastics rather than fiberglass), and cost $150,000 to build. A smaller model, only twenty inches in length, was used for long shots.

Since the first *Star Trek* film in 1979, the one dozen entries in the film franchise (not to mention the four television series that followed the original) brought all sorts of retrofits, upgrades, rebuilds, and reimaginings of the USS *Enterprise*. Yet all remained tied in design to the original TV and film concepts of one of the greatest spacecraft in sci-fi history.

Star Wars—Death Star, X-Wing Fighter, *Millennium Falcon*, TIE Fighter, Darth Vader TIE Advanced XI Fighter

The film that started it all in 1977, *Star Wars* delivered a fleet of imaginary spacecraft from the fertile grey matter between the ears of creator George Lucas. The variety of large and small vehicles became reference guides for many films to follow, least of which were Lucas' own sequels and prequels.

The massive Death Star—nearly one-hundred miles in diameter—was the ultimate weapon in the arsenal of the Galactic Empire. The moon-sized space station was equipped with a high-powered superlaser, capable of obliterating a planet with one shot. Drawing its power from the hypermatter reactor of the Death Star, the superlaser needed nearly a full day to charge before firing a single blast. The weapon was used to destroy Princess Leia's home planet of Alderaan.

With the evil Darth Vader in close pursuit, Luke Skywalker raced along a trench in the Death Star. Using instinct and "The Force," Skywalker unloaded two proton torpedoes down a port leading to the reactor core. Speeding away, Skywalker escaped the massive explosion that resulted, a blast that sent Vader tumbling into deep space.

Skywalker's vehicle was an X-wing fighter, so named for the crossed configuration of the wings. Just over forty feet in length, the X-wing was a steadfast starfighter ship for the Rebel Alliance. Relying on a droid for guidance and navigation, the single-pilot craft was powered by four main engines and capable of jumping to hyperspeed. The X-wing fighter was armed with laser cannons and two proton torpedoes.

The dingy but effective *Millennium Falcon* was a consistent craft for Han Solo and his Wookie copilot, Chewbacca. At nearly 115 feet long, the light freighter had been through many hands before Solo won it from Lando Calrissian in a card game. Like a chopped-up street hot rod, the *Falcon* had been modified

Star Wars - 1977
The Death Star

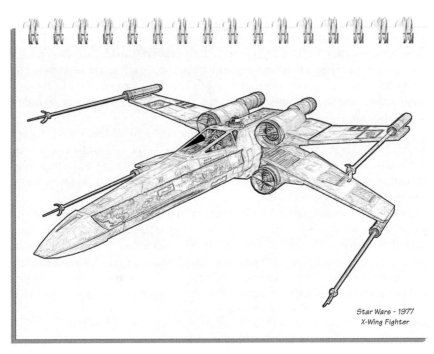

Star Wars - 1977
X-Wing Fighter

many times with many extras—some not considered legal, in terms of power plant and weaponry.

The *Millennium Falcon*, like the X-wing, had hyperdrive capability. Its armament included turret-mounted laser cannons and concussion missile launchers. And, like many customized vehicles, the *Falcon* had a fickle personality. A jump to hyperspeed was sometimes a smooth event and sometimes required a smack on the gear from Solo.

The TIE (Twin Ion Engine) Fighter was a standard for the Galactic Empire, designed to be mass produced and mass deployed against the Rebel Alliance. Not even thirty feet in length, the TIE Fighter was small and light, a plus for maneuverability, kind of like a flying phone booth. Manned by a single pilot, it had twin laser cannons and a large panel on either side of the cockpit for heat exchange coils.

An advanced X1 TIE Fighter was custom built for Darth Vader, adding special refinements for the Galactic Empire's chief enforcer. Just over thirty feet in length, it had twin blasters, cluster missiles, and a deflector shield. The X1 was also equipped with a hyperdrive option, making it infinitely faster than the standard TIE Fighter.

Like many of the vehicles in *Star Wars*, the Death Star was born from the minds of George Lucas and concept artist Ralph McQuarrie. Although the artist crafted a detailed painting for use in *Star Wars: A New Hope*, it was decided to build a miniature for even more depth. A three-foot Plexiglas sphere was assembled, with its signature crater created by cutting a segment from the globe,

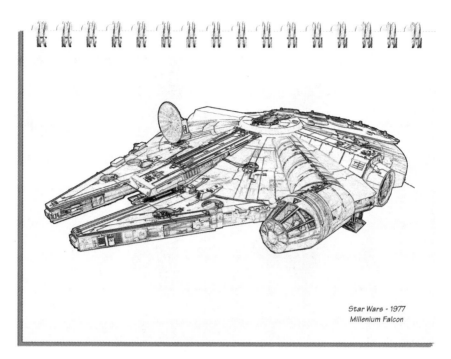

Star Wars - 1977
Millenium Falcon

flipping it, and reattaching it to the hole it made. Hundreds and hundreds of tiny holes were drilled into the entire orb—lit from inside, they represented the myriad of windows and levels on the space station.

The Death Star surprisingly looks like the real-life moon of Saturn known as Mimas, even down to the eighty-eight-mile crater on Mimas, known as Herschel. Many fans believe Mimas was the inspiration for the Death Star, but it's purely coincidence. The tiny moon wasn't even seen in detail until the deep-space probe *Voyager* got a good look in 1980—three years after *Star Wars* opened.

When Industrial Light and Magic moved its facilities from Van Nuys to Marin County in 1978, the Death Star model was unceremoniously tossed into the trash. Fortunately, some savvy garbage pickers saw the iconic piece and saved it for their own collection.

In 2012, more than thirty-five thousand Americans signed and filed a petition with the White House requesting funding to begin construction of a real Death Star by 2016. The document argued that such a weapon would create many jobs for the United States and strengthen the national defense. The White House actually responded, citing an estimated cost of more than $850 quadrillion (yes, with fifteen zeros) and the affirmation that the current administration (fortunately) does not support blowing up planets.

The design of the X-wing fighter was the work of effects designer Joe Johnston (later director of 1991's *The Rocketeer*, 2001's *Jurassic Park III*, and 2011's *Captain America: The First Avenger*, among others). Johnston reasoned the mainstay spacecraft for the Rebel Alliance would have been old and made

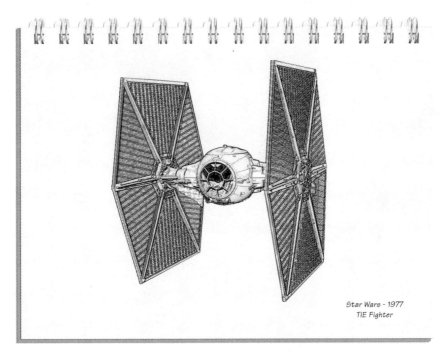

Star Wars - 1977
TIE Fighter

from cast-off parts from other fighters. So it didn't matter how they looked, just as long as they worked.

X-wing fighter miniatures were built from cast plastic parts, along with brass tubing and real glass windows. A full-sized mockup of the ship was created for the scene in the Rebel hangar, as well as fully detailed cockpits.

The *Millennium Falcon* came to the party late, as Joe Johnston originally designed a craft for Han Solo that looked too much like the *Eagle Transport* from British TV's *Space: 1999*. That ship became the Rebel blockade runner, and the new design was influenced by a lunchtime view of a hamburger with an olive on the side (you can't make this stuff up).

The main five-foot miniature of the *Millennium Falcon* was built from wood, steel, and clear acrylic plastic. It had details made from brass, along with dozens of spare parts from model car and tank kits. (A model of thirty-two inches and a tiny two-inch version were built for *The Empire Strikes Back*.)

An ambitious fan in Tennessee has shown his fascination with the *Millennium Falcon* by starting construction on a full-sized, 114-foot-long replica of the ship. Located on an eighty-eight acre plot of rural land, the *Full Scale Falcon* (as it is known) will have every light, switch, grill, and grommet found on the original.

Originally a one-person operation, people from around the world have become involved in building various components of the craft, thanks to the power of the press and the Internet. The builder hopes the finished exhibit will become a centerpiece for a facility that will encourage do-it-yourself skills and creativity.

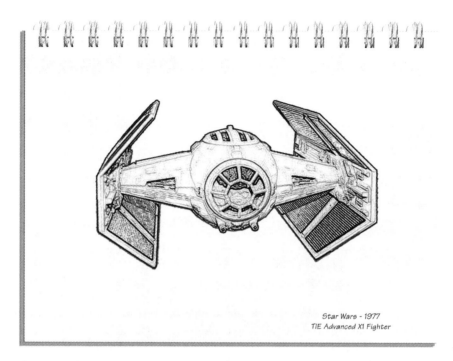

Star Wars - 1977
TIE Advanced X1 Fighter

The TIE fighters were thought up by Colin Cantwell, spaceship designer for *A New Hope*. Knowing there had to be a large number of vehicles, they were designed to be simple and easily constructed, with few details. Plastic was the base material of the TIE fighters, unless they had to be destroyed. In that case, prescored foam was used. A few lights were added, and that was it.

The TIE fighters were built in two sizes for *Star Wars*. An eighteen-inch model was fashioned for close-ups and detail shots, and when long shots and large numbers of the vehicles were needed, a seven-inch model filled the bill.

Looking somewhat harmless, it was decided to make the TIE fighter fearsome by revving up the sound of its engines. Sound designer Ben Burtt took the bellow of a stampeding elephant, slowed it down, and mixed it with the swooshing sound from a car splashing through a rainy street. When the TIE fighter approached on-screen, everyone immediately knew that sound meant trouble.

One of the eighteen-inch TIE fighters was placed up for auction by the Hollywood-based Profiles in History auction house in August 2008. Used in the exciting finale in the assault on the Death Star in *A New Hope*, the model was expected to fetch between $150,000 and $200,000. The winning bid was $350,000—enough money to buy a 2012 Ferrari 599 GTB Fiorano, with enough left over for a 2012 Hyundai Elantra GLS.

Of course, neither are good defenders against a Rebel X-wing.

How Do They Do That?

The Sci-Fi Magicians

Pay Some Attention to Those Folks Behind the Curtain

There's an organization in Beverly Hills, California, that is dedicated to the many facets of the film industry. According to their website, they are committed to providing a broad variety of activities in "education, outreach, preservation, and research." They also give out something called the Oscar. They call themselves the Academy of Motion Picture Arts and Sciences.

It's important to note the two stated fields of their focus—arts and sciences. For everyday filmgoers, it's mostly the arts that put them in their seats—the art of a fine performer like Johnny Depp or Gwyneth Paltrow. Or it's the art of a great writer like David Mamet or Lawrence Kasdan. And, there's no doubt they certainly do.

But for many, it's the combo of art AND science that draws audiences to screens. Technicians who blend the creative arts and precise sciences of filmmaking to produce a truly exciting film are the ones who make it happen. Their work is vital to the genre of sci-fi, as they use their technical toolkits with an artistic mind and eye to deliver unique and often never-before-seen-or-heard visual and aural elements for the viewer's enjoyment.

Masters of What You See and Hear

Special effects (often acronymed as FX) are the cornerstones of sci-fi films. Generally broken into sound and visual categories, FX are tricks to the ear and eye that filmmakers use to create imaginary, unreal, or distorted scenes in the context of telling their story. Yet the creativity and resourcefulness of the tech cannot be understated, as they go to extremes to convince the viewer that something unreal is real.

For example, consider the light saber from the original 1977 *Star Wars* film. Sound designer Ben Burtt imagined an ominous buzzing for the deadly weapon. Therefore, the art of imagination began the process. But where does one get a buzz never before imagined? (Drinkers and druggies can leave right now!) Using the science of sound recording and mixing, Burtt took several motors in a projection system and combined their hums with the raspy signal produced by interference on a television set. The result (enhanced by the pitch-changing physics phenomenon known as the Doppler Effect) was the light saber that everyone wished they had.

Visually, the light saber was a combination of a prop, something known as a "practical effect," and visual enhancement in postproduction. Effects supervisor John Stears took a tube-shaped Graflex battery pack from an old press-style camera, added some details and the handheld light saber was born. For the dueling scenes, a four-sided blade was attached to the handle and motorized to spin. Two sides of the blade were black, and two were painted with the reflective paint one sees on highway signs at night. When lit on the set, the blade appeared to glow with a stroboscopic effect. Once "in the can" (completed and processed film, not the other thing you're thinking of), a South Korean animator named Nelson Shin added to the light saber images by rotoscoping (hand-drawing) over them. Later films in the series took advantage of the development of computer-generated imagery (CGI) and created the effects digitally.

Without turning this into a textbook on movie special effects, there are basic areas of FX that should be explained in general terms (in no particular order, and, bear in mind, there's a lot of overlap)

- *Practical effects*—Also referred to as mechanical effects, these include things like squibs (small charges that explode on a performer, usually with a small blood pack to simulate gunshot wounds), explosions and other pyrotechnics, breaking glass, rain and wind machines, and other actual on-set simulations and events. More modern applications include puppetry and animatronics; the craft of creating life-sized creatures that are controlled off-screen by levers, cables, motors, servos; and stuff that looks like a radio-control-car fan gone mad.
- *Miniature effects*—These include model making in various scales, often reducing entire cities to the size of a backyard swimming pool or the great eight-hundred-foot airship, the Hindenburg, to the length of the family auto. Also part of miniatures is stop-motion animation, the tedious task of building small figures with an internal metal skeleton called an armature, then moving them a small fraction at a time, while exposing one frame of film. When the frames are projected at normal speed (usually twenty-four every second), the figures seem to move on their own.
- *Optical effects*—These are effects that usually involve some sort of manipulation of the film product itself. In the nascent days of filmmaking, optical effects were often achieved "in-camera." For example, a double exposure (perhaps a scene where the performer is playing against him- or herself) was accomplished by shooting the first portion, then rewinding the film "in-camera" back to the beginning, then shooting again with the performer in the second position, When processed, the film showed both performances.
- The optical printer was developed by film pioneer Linwood Dunn in the mid-1930s, and it became possible to combine or "composite" multiple

films into a single shot. Along with compositing, the optical printer allowed effects like fancy transitions between scenes, slow and fast motion, and mattes (combining live action with skillfully painted scenes on glass or other materials, allowing a performer to be filmed walking through an empty lot, only to seem on film like they're walking through the valley of a great mountain range).

- Other variations of optical effects included rear projection (literally projecting a preshot scene onto a screen behind the performers), front projection, blue- and green-screen (sometimes called a "traveling matte," it's a process of performing in front of a colored screen, with a hue that later would be replaced by a preshot sequence).

It is important to note that many of these techniques are still used today, although the advent of computers has adapted some of them and made others obsolete. Think back to the *Star Wars* light saber example. With no computer technology developed for film use in 1977, it took practical and optical effects for Darth Vader's weapon to cut Obi-Wan Kenobi in half. Subsequent films in the series used CGI to create the glow and sizzle of the weapon.

Nowadays, computers are used in many, many ways to enhance the sci-fi film experience. Set pieces, locations, characters, vehicles, and fiery explosions are just a small sample of images generated or enhanced by computer. Stick around for the credits of the next big-budget sci-fi film you see in a theater, and take notice of the hundreds of artists and animators needed to feed CGI into what are known as "render farms"—stacks and stacks of linked computers that digitally pump out the individual frames of film.

Computers can also be programmed to control camera movement, allowing precise motions to be repeated with exact accuracy. First developed for (once again) 1977's *Star Wars* by a team headed by special photographic effects supervisor John Dykstra, the motion control system (appropriately known as Dykstraflex) took the viewer deep into the trench of the Death Star as Luke Skywalker attempted to blow it to Smithereens (a galaxy not far from "Kingdomcome.).

Another use of computers in film combines the actual movements of a performer with the ability to load those actions into a computer and apply them to a CGI. The performer wears multiple sensors on a special suit, most located on joints and other moving points on the human body. When the performer moves, the sensors input the physical activity as digital data into a computer. The action can then be transferred to an imaginary creature created in the computer. Not-so-cleverly called "motion capture," it has allowed actors like Andy Serkis to translate the arts and skills of body control and expression into memorable characters like Gollum in the *Lord of the Rings* trilogy and Caesar in 2010's *Rise of the Planet of the Apes*.

While there are and have been hundreds of talented men and women in the fields of special effects in the last forty years or so, a few tend to stand out as pioneers in what is seen on the screen.

Masters of Special FX

Dennis Muren

Creators of visual effects aren't normally considered to be multiple Oscar winners and have their own star on the Hollywood Walk of Fame. Obviously, Dennis Muren is not a normal creator of visual effects, since he holds both of those distinctions. His work on the *Star Wars* film series, as well as other high-profile sci-fi cinema, has placed him in an elite class of FX pioneers.

Born in Glendale, California, in 1946, Muren found himself attracted to special-effects films during the 1950s, when every other sci-fi movie title had *Amazing*, *Incredible*, or *Giant* in it. As a teen, he was driven by his mom to visit with effects great Ray Harryhausen, whom he had befriended. But, thinking he had no chance of ever getting into the field, he earned an associate degree in business from Pasadena City College.

The desire to create special effects stayed with him, so Muren teamed up with friends Mark Thomas McGee and David Allen with the naïve intention of making a sci-fi film and selling it to a local Los Angeles TV station. Muren took his Bolex 16mm camera, $6,500 from his grandfather, and the trio spent more than two years shooting *The Equinox ... A Journey into the Supernatural*. At only seventy-one minutes in length, the film was ten minutes too short for theatrical release, and TV stations hardly ever purchased programming on a one-shot basis, preferring packages of films or series of shows.

Enter producer Jack Woods, who reworked the script, shot ten minutes of additional footage, transferred the 16mm film to 35mm, reduced the title to *Equinox*, and—five years after Muren and his friends began the project—the movie made its way into theaters. The effects maker was on his way.

Muren continued to work in the field, making commercials and adding FX to the soft-core, sci-fi cult fave *Flesh Gordon* from 1974. Hearing about an upcoming film called *Star Wars*, he obtained an interview with effects supervisor John Dykstra. Director George Lucas had created an FX shop called Industrial Light and Magic for the film, and Muren became one of its first hires.

With the success of *Star Wars* under his belt, Muren joined with FX master Doug Trumbull and director Steven Spielberg (both featured in bios that follow) to work on *Close Encounters of the Third Kind*. The mother ship became Muren's baby, and he spent five months shooting the FX involving it.

Muren quickly moved from FX camera operation to supervising visual effects, returning to the *Star Wars* franchise for *Episode V: The Empire Strikes Back* in 1980 (winning a Special Achievement Oscar). He continued with films like 1981's *Dragonslayer*, 1982's *E.T. the Extra-Terrestrial* (working with Spielberg again and winning an Oscar for Best Visual Effects), and returning home once again for 1983's *Star Wars—Episode VI: Return of the Jedi* (and another Special Achievement Oscar). Through the 1980s, Dennis Muren worked movie magic on other sci-fi and fantasy films like *Indiana Jones and the Temple of Doom* in 1984 (another Oscar), *Captain EO*—a 3D film, directed by Francis Ford Coppola and

Dennis Muren checks a light meter reading from the Death Star in *Star Wars*.

starring Michael Jackson, for exhibition at Disney theme parks around the world—in 1987, and *Innerspace* (still another Oscar) in 1988.

Director James Cameron's *The Abyss* in 1989 posed a real challenge to the FX expert. Cameron wanted a snake-like tube of water to come alive. After first considering the options of cel and stop-motion animation, it was decided to use motion-control photography and computer-generated images. Muren supervised the creation of the computerized water creature at ILM—six months of work for slightly more than a minute of screen time. And, yes, Muren received another Oscar.

Following the film, Muren realized he needed a much firmer grasp of what computer graphics could do. He took a year off and worked his way through a twelve-hundred-page textbook on the subject, adding a valuable body of knowledge to his already formidable skills as an FX master. His study paid off, as he entered the 1990s by supervising the visual FX for films like *Terminator 2: Judgment Day* in 1991 and *Jurassic Park* in 1993 (and winning two more you-know-whats).

Muren has lent his FX expertise to a wide variety of films, from *Casper* in 1995, *Mission: Impossible*, and *Twister* in 1996, to director Woody Allen's

Deconstructing Harry in 1997. Staying with the *Star Wars* and *Jurassic Park* series, he supervised FX for several of their sequels through 2002, as well as Spielberg's *A.I. Artificial Intelligence* in 2001 and *War of the Worlds* in 2005. He also headed the visual FX for *Hulk* in 2003 and *Super 8* in 2011.

Considered to be one of the real pioneers in the FX field by marrying old-timey visual and optic effects with digital imagery and manipulation, Dennis Muren received his own star on the Hollywood Walk of Fame in 1999 (a first for a visual effects artist) and the Lifetime Achievement award from the Visual Effects Society in 2007. He still keeps an office at ILM as Senior Visual Effects Supervisor.

Selected Filmography

Special Photographic and Visual Effects
- *Equinox*—1970
- *Flesh Gordon*—1974
- *Star Wars*—1977
- *Close Encounters of the Third Kind*—1977
- *Star Wars: Episode V—The Empire Strikes Back*—1980
- *Dragonslayer*—1981
- *E.T. the Extra-Terrestrial*—1982
- *Star Wars: Episode VI—Return of the Jedi*—1983
- *Innerspace*—1987
- *Ghostbusters II*—1989
- *The Abyss*—1989
- *Terminator 2: Judgment Day*—1991
- *Jurassic Park*—1993
- *Star Wars: Episode I—The Phantom Menace*—1999
- *A.I. Artificial Intelligence*—2001
- *Star Wars: Episode II—Attack of the Clones*—2002
- *Hulk*—2003
- *War of the Worlds*—2005
- *Super 8*—2011

Full-Motion Dinosaurs
- *Jurassic Park*—1993
- *The Lost World: Jurassic Park*—1997

Douglas Trumbull

Another of the genuine pioneers in visual effects, Doug Trumbull's vision for a truly unique cinematic experience has thrilled and amazed filmgoers for more than forty years. His work has won many awards, but more, Trumbull has received several patents on his groundbreaking technical research in filmmaking.

Born in Los Angeles in 1941, Trumbull came from an influential family, since his father, Donald, had done special-effects work on 1939's *Wizard of Oz*.

By his early twenties, Doug Trumbull was a technical illustrator for a small media production house called Graphic Films. Some of his work was featured in documentaries shown at the New York World's Fair in 1964 and caught the attention of director Stanley Kubrick, who was in the first stages of developing a sci-fi film with noted author Arthur C. Clarke.

Originally titled *Journey to the Stars*, the film consumed three years of Trumbull's life and was released in 1968 as *2001: A Space Odyssey*. The young FX wizard's work with the brilliant and temperamental Kubrick resulted in radically new visuals, while requiring the development of special camera equipment.

Like many scenes in sci-fi films, the director's Stargate sequence posed a problem in how to show something that had never been seen and most likely didn't even exist. Trumbull created a technique called "slit-scan photography," with resulting images that, indeed, had never been seen before. With washes of brilliant colors, extended perspective, and rapid motion, the slit-scan technique found itself in lockstep with audiences of the day. As hallucinogenic drugs and psychedelic artwork had become de rigueur in the late 1960s, Trumbull's Stargate visuals of *2001* filled the bill completely.

Following the success of *2001*, Trumbull's slit-scan effects found their way onto American TV. He created a small company that produced the unique visuals for *Movie-of-the-Week* intros on ABC, as well as commercials. He also supervised the visual effects for *The Andromeda Strain* in 1971.

Trumbull moved quickly into the director's chair for the sci-fi feature *Silent Running* in 1972. He also watched over the film's visual effects, as well as writing the original story treatment. Shot on a slim $1 million budget, the movie received generally favorable reviews from audiences of the day. With a focus on ecology and saving the Earth's plant life that was years ahead of its time, *Silent Running* has since become a cult favorite.

Trumbull teamed up with director Steven Spielberg in 1977 to make *Close Encounters of the Third Kind*, starting the Future General Corporation production house (FGC) to provide the impressive visual effects. Trumbull was one of the first to create massive cloud effects by injecting ink and paint into salt- and freshwater tanks, then compositing the resulting images.

He then joined director Robert Wise and the crew of *Star Trek: The Motion Picture* in 1979, after the Robert Abel and Associates effects company was unable to produce suitable footage for the film. Facing a tight deadline, Trumbull agreed to complete the complicated FX schedule in return for getting a release from his FGC contract, which had become a subsidiary of Paramount Pictures. He got the job done, but wound up with ulcers and ended up in the hospital, suffering from exhaustion.

Trumbull opened a new effects house, Entertainment Effects Group (EEG), and hooked up with director Ridley Scott to create the dark and gritty future world for *Blade Runner* in 1981. But Trumbull broke off halfway through the project to begin work on a film of his own that he had nurtured for quite a while called *Brainstorm*.

Intended as a showcase for his Showscan film process—a combination of large-format motion picture film stock and high-speed shooting and projection—*Brainstorm* was bounced from Paramount to MGM, only to see the latter balk at such a revolutionary system and insist on a standard production (although the FX would be shot in a big 70mm format). With Trumbull producing and directing, the film starred Christopher Walken, Natalie Wood, Louise Fletcher, and Cliff Robertson.

Doug Trumbull with detailed model of the Tyrell pyramid in *Blade Runner*.

When Wood drowned under suspicious circumstances during the production, the studio, strapped for cash, saw the opportunity to back out of their commitment to *Brainstorm*. Although the actress had completed shooting her scenes, production was shut down, and Trumbull was locked out from any access to the film.

MGM hoped to collect on an insurance policy from Lloyd's of London for the unfinished film, claiming it was unfixable. But after their investigation, the insurance company determined there was no reason to pay MGM. Lloyd's, however, did furnish enough money for Trumbull to finish *Brainstorm*, and it was released two years after Wood's death.

Trumbull succeeded in getting *Brainstorm* into America's theaters, but the whole experience completely soured him on Hollywood's ways of making movies. He moved to Massachusetts to focus on developing new and exciting technologies for media production.

One project in 1991 found him directing *Back to the Future: The Ride* for producer Steven Spielberg and Universal Studios theme parks. Hardly a simple trip on the Tilt-a-Whirl, the amusement attraction combined motion simulation with large-format film projection under a seventy-foot dome. Trumbull created a similar experience for visitors to the Luxor Hotel in Las Vegas in 1993. He reluctantly returned to Hollywood in 2011 to provide special visual effects for director Terrence Malick's *The Tree of Life*, as the director convinced Trumbull that he wanted effects that didn't look generated by a computer.

Trumbull's efforts have resulted in him being awarded more than a dozen patents, as well as receiving five Academy Award nominations and the Gordon E. Sawyer Award—an honorary Oscar for his lifetime of technical work in the cinema. He was also inducted into the Science Fiction Hall of Fame in 2010 as "an innovative master of special effects."

No doubt.

Selected Filmography

Special Photographic Effects
- *2001: A Space Odyssey*—1968
- *The Andromeda Strain*—1971
- *Silent Running*—1972
- *Close Encounters of the Third Kind*—1977
- *Star Trek: The Motion Picture*—1979
- *Blade Runner*—1982

Director
- *Silent Running*—1972
- *Brainstorm*—1983

Stan Winston

Stan Winston's role in the world of sci-fi films was truly unique, as his career spanned both fields of visual effects and makeup. As a result, he won Oscars for both categories, along with a crateload of nominations in each domain. His brilliant work spanned four decades and was at the center of some of the biggest sci-fi films in the last forty years.

Winston was born in Arlington, Virginia, in 1946. His interests as a boy aren't surprising: drawing, making masks and puppets, and watching classic horror movies. He attended the University of Virginia, Charlottesville, graduating with degrees in fine art and drama. Having intentions of becoming an actor, he moved to California in 1969.

With acting jobs nowhere to be found, Winston began a three-year internship as a makeup artist under Robert Schiffer at Disney Studios. Completing that, he began Stan Winston Studios in the garage of his Northridge home and within two years, received Emmy Awards for his makeup work on the made-for-TV movies, *Gargoyles* and *The Autobiography of Miss Jane Pittman*. He continued his makeup work on a wide selection of projects, including turning Rod Steiger into W. C. Fields in the 1976 feature *W. C. Fields and Me*, designing a new vision of the *Wizard of Oz* characters for the movie musical *The Wiz* in 1978, and transforming Maximilian Schell into the title misshapen musician in the 1983 CBS-TV version of *The Phantom of the Opera*.

Winston combined his makeup mastery with special visual effects in 1984's *The Terminator*, turning Arnold Schwarzenegger into the juggernaut cyborg—first as a disfigured humanoid, then as the high-tech nuts-and-bolts robot. Based on a concept painting by director James Cameron, the T-800 endoskeleton quickly became an image recognized around the globe.

The exciting chase scene climax featured a combination of Winston's full-sized, puppet-like figure (fashioned largely with heavy steel), and a stop-motion miniature, animated by the team at Fantasy II Film Effects. Winston was inspired by the puppetry pioneered by Muppets creator Jim Henson and also tapped into the evolving technology of animatronics—the use of motors, gears, and servos to control a creature remotely.

He followed up his work on the T-800 with *Aliens* in 1986, the first sequel to Ridley Scott's 1980 success *Alien*. Once again teaming up with director James Cameron, Winston and his crew created the immense fourteen-foot-tall Alien queen, first by building a full-sized mockup from black garbage bags in his shop parking lot. Two operators were placed inside the bags and hung by a crane to manipulate the spindly arms, with everyone pleased with the results. Winston's efforts paid off, as he won his first Oscar for Best Visual Effects.

In 1987, Winston was able to hook up with Arnold Schwarzenegger once more for *Predator*. The makeup/FX artist was brought in to redesign the creature after Jean Claude Van Damme—originally cast to play the monster—left the project. Early on, Winston was traveling on an international flight with James Cameron to promo *Aliens* and making some *Predator* sketches. Cameron mentioned he'd never seen a movie ET with mandibles, and with that suggestion, the Predator would have its signature toothy jaws.

Stan Winston with full-sized figure and maquette of *Pumpkinhead.*

In the same year, Winston had the rare opportunity to reimagine the classic Universal monsters for a little-seen film called *Monster Squad*. The challenge was to create the Frankenstein monster, Count Dracula, the Mummy, the Wolfman, and the Creature from the Black Lagoon in recognizable forms, without infringing on the original copyrighted Universal images. Winston succeeded and the film has since become a huge cult classic. He also had the chance to direct his first film, the horror-themed *Pumpkinhead*.

Winston's work in the 1990s began with a revisit to his creations for *Predator 2* in 1990 and *Terminator 2: Judgment Day* the following year, as well as other films like 1989's *Leviathan* and 1990's *Edward Scissorhands*, starring Johnny Depp. *T2* earned Winston an amazing double-winning hand of two Oscars—one for Best Makeup and another for Best Visual Effects. In 1993, Winston partnered with Cameron and former GM from Industrial Light and Magic Scott Ross to start Digital Domain, a production house for state-of-the-art digital effects.

Keeping his dance card full, Winston joined Steven Spielberg in the same year to create the most realistic-looking dinosaurs since the Mesozoic Era itself. *Jurassic Park* relied on CGI for many of its scenes, but some required real interaction with real people (although some may wonder if actors are "real" people). Winston Studios built a full-sized Triceratops, the head and neck of a Brachiosaur, and, of course, a full-blown version of the mighty T. rex. All were brought to life by rod and cable manipulation, remote-controlled servos, and computer-aided hydraulics.

Another featured dinosaur was the clever and cunning velociraptor, again relying on cable-controlled puppets. For some shots, however, it was decided to use the old "man-in-a-suit" standard, established in 1954's *Godzilla*. With Winston Studios' John Rosengrant and Mark "Crash" McCreery assuming modeling positions that resembled downhill skiers, full Raptor suits were designed and sculpted. Foam latex outfits were built and detailed, while Rosengrant and McCreery rehearsed the motion needed, with Winston supervising the activity and paying attention to the details. Again, the efforts paid off, as he won another Oscar for Best Visual Effects.

Winston continued to make major FX contributions to feature sci-fi films like 1996's *Island of Dr. Moreau*, 1999's *End of Days* and *Galaxy Quest*, as well as staying with the franchises of the Terminator for *Terminator 3: Rise of the Machines* and Jurassic Park for *Lost World: Jurassic Park* in 1997 and *Jurassic Park III* in 2003. He also worked with Spielberg once more in 2001 on *A.I. Artificial Intelligence*. Winston also handled the visual effects in 1996 for James Cameron's twelve-minute short film that accompanied the *T2 3-D: Battle Across Time* attraction for the Universal Studios theme parks around the world. In the same year, he directed Michael Jackson in the forty-minute music video, *Ghosts*.

In 2001, Stan Winston produced a series of five films for the Cinemax cable channel. Starting with the titles of fan-favored B movies from the 1950s, he delivered *The She Creature, How to Make a Monster, Earth vs. the Spider, The Day the World Ended*, and *Teenage Caveman*, although none bore any resemblance to the originals.

Winston pitched in with animatronic FX for films like 2005's *Constantine* and 2006's *Benchwarmers*. When director Jon Favreau brought Marvel Comics' *Iron Man* to the screen in 2008, Stan Winston's team was charged with the daunting task of making the comic book suits of Tony Stark become reality.

Sadly, Stan Winston had spent most of the twenty-first century fighting the real monster of cancer. He had multiple myeloma, which targets the plasma cells in bone marrow. He died in June 2008, having worked right to the end on films like *Terminator Salvation* and *Avatar*, released in 2009, and *Shutter Island* the following year.

Along with Ray Harryhausen and Dennis Muren, Stan Winston is the only visual effects artist to receive a star on the Hollywood Walk of Fame. After his passing, four of the supervisors from Stan Winston Studios formed their own effects and makeup/creature design company, called Legacy Effects, in memory of their mentor.

Selected Filmography

Makeup Effects

- *Heartbeeps*—1981
- *The Thing*—1982
- *Starman*—1984
- *Edward Scissorhands*—1990
- *Terminator 2: Judgment Day*—1991
- *Island of Dr. Moreau*—1996
- *Galaxy Quest*—1999
- *A.I. Artificial Intelligence*—2001
- *Terminator 3: Rise of the Machines*—2003

Special Effects Creator

- *The Terminator*—1984
- *Invaders from Mars*—1986
- *Aliens*—1986
- *Predator*—1987
- *Leviathan*—1989
- *Terminator 2: Judgment Day*—1991
- *The Relic*—1997
- *End of Days*—1999
- *Galaxy Quest*—1999
- *A.I. Artificial Intelligence*—2001
- *Jurassic Park III*—2001
- *Terminator 3: Rise of the Machines*—2003
- *Iron Man*—2008
- *Terminator Salvation*—2009
- *Avatar*—2009

More Than Putty and Paint—Makeup Marvels

Rick Baker

Gifted artists have awed audiences for hundreds of years, dating back to the Old Masters of Europe. Their works hang in museums and galleries around the world, where they bring pleasure and inspiration to those who view them.

And then there is Rick Baker.

A modern-day Old Master, Baker's skill and genius as a movie makeup artist has rewritten the rule book originally laid down by Lon Chaney Sr., Jack P. Pierce, and Dick Smith. In the forty-plus years of his career, Baker has shown a keen eye for detail, a steady hand for application, a fertile mind for imagination, and the ability to innovate.

In other words, Rick Baker is the "stuff."

Born in Binghamton, New York, in 1950, Baker and his family moved to Southern California while he was still an infant. Like many in his field, growing up in the fifties meant a lot of time spent in front of the TV, watching vintage Universal monster movies on *Shock Theater*, and reading *Famous Monsters of Filmland* magazine.

Although his dad made a living as a truck driver, he was also an artist and taught his son the basics of drawing and sculpting. As a natural next step, Baker began playing around with horror makeup—usually with himself as the model. Before long, he started referring to himself as "Rick Baker—Monster Maker."

While still in high school, Baker got a job with Clokey Productions, the stop-motion clay animation company that created *Gumby* (dammit) as well as *Davey and Goliath*. He soon began palling around with another young animator, who knew a guy, who knew a guy. Normally, that wouldn't be any big deal, except the guys had names like Doug Beswick, David Allen, Dennis Muren (profiled earlier in this chapter), and Phil Tippett. Each one would go on to make a major impact on the world of cinema FX.

Baker and Beswick got their first break creating the latex-tentacled suit for the ultra-low-budget *Octaman* in 1971. Written and directed by Harry Essex (who had penned the scripts for *It Came from Outer Space* and *The Creature from the Black Lagoon* in the 1950s), the final result was a reminder that everyone has to start somewhere. One-time Golden Globe winner, actress Pier Angeli, starred in *Octaman* and (perhaps to no one's surprise) committed suicide upon its completion.

A young director named John Landis put together a paltry budget of $60,000 in 1971 and directed a film he had written called *Schlock*. It was a parody of the "monster runs amok" movies, and he enlisted the twenty-year-old Rick Baker to create the hairy, ape-like creature known as "schlockthropus." With such a small budget, Landis himself played the monster. Baker and Landis would meet again down the road.

Eager to learn, Baker had sent a letter to makeup master Dick Smith, enclosing some pictures of his makeups. Smith was duly impressed and, in 1973,

Teenage Rick Baker with his handmade masks.

offered the rare opportunity for Baker to move in with him as he worked on *The Exorcist*. Smith's lab was in the basement of his Larchmont, New York, home, and the budding artist jumped at the chance.

At the recommendation of Dick Smith, Baker was quietly brought in to create some special makeup effects for the James Bond film *Live and Let Die* in the same year. One challenge was to create a head and torso replica of actor Geoffery Holder, which mysteriously rises from the ground at one point in the movie. As 007, Roger Moore shoots the figure to prove it's only a big dummy, splitting the head open and causing the eyes to roll back. The other makeup effect involved the film's climax, where Bond forces a compressed gas pellet into the mouth of the villain Kananga, played by Yaphet Kotto. The gas expands inside him, causing his head and body to swell up like someone who's eaten a few too many beans. Every man has his limit, and Kananga finds his, exploding into little criminal cube steaks. Baker's work was uncredited but no less effective.

Word of producer Dino De Laurentiis' big-budget remake of *King Kong* in 1976 reached Baker, and, with his lifelong affinity for anything ape, he convinced the producer that he could effectively create Kong. Dismissing the obvious choice of stop-motion animation, the producers initially envisioned Kong as a missing link (an early trade paper ad callously sought "tall black men" to play the beast, until claims of racism moved them to consider using a mechanized creature instead).

Baker was challenged to build a convincing gorilla suit, while Italian special-effects artist Carlo Rambaldi was asked to create a mechanical suit. Rambaldi's result was, as director John Guillermin described, "A two-hundred-thousand-dollar disaster." Baker's suit was a winner, and, to his credit, he convinced the powers-that-be that only he could fill the suit and the role of King Kong. The makeup artist had spent many hours studying apes in books and zoos, becoming intimately familiar with their motion and personality.

In the end, Baker's work turned out to be the only redeeming factor for *King Kong*, although Rambaldi won a special Oscar for building a forty-two-foot-tall "robot Kong." The creature, which weighed more than six tons and cost nearly $2 million to build, occupied all of fifteen to twenty seconds of actual screen time (the absurdity of the award prompted stop-motion animator Jim Danforth to resign from the Academy).

Baker hit the big time in 1977 with a "little" film called *Star Wars*. Director George Lucas had already shot the cantina scene, with aliens created by British makeup artist Stuart Freeborn. But the director later wanted to sweeten the scene with additional aliens. FX artist Dennis Muren, already working on the film, recommended his friend from the old Clokey days, Rick Baker. He filled the bar with thirty new aliens, including the bulb-headed musicians in the cantina band. Even though the new footage was shot half a world away, six months later than the first cantina scene with a completely different crew, the final edit with Baker's aliens integrated seamlessly with the original creatures.

Rick Baker found himself in higher demand, doing FX makeup for films like *The Incredible Melting Man* in 1977, *The Fury* and *It Lives Again* in 1978, *The Howling* and *The Incredible Shrinking Woman* in 1981. Baker also worked with his protégé Rob Bottin (featured elsewhere in this chapter) on an ape suit for a simian character called Blue in *Tanya's Island* in 1980.

Having played a gorilla known as Dino for John Landis in the silly but satisfying *Kentucky Fried Movie* in 1977, Baker crossed paths with the director for a third time in 1981 for *An American Werewolf in London*. Based on a script that Landis had written back in 1969, the film challenged Baker to transform actor David Naughton into a four-legged wolf in a way never before seen in cinema. The makeup expert used a combination of techniques to boldly present the transformation in a brightly lit room, rather than dark shadows as had often been the case in other werewolf films.

To replicate hair growing rapidly out of the character's body, Baker fashioned foam latex body parts from a cast of Naughton, then punched individual hairs through their back side. While cameras rolled, the hairs were pulled into the body part. But when processed, the shot was reversed, so the hair appeared to be growing out of the skin. Along with making up the actor in various stages of change, Baker also built mechanical faces, hands, and feet—all rigged with cables to allow extension and distortion of the body parts during the painful metamorphosis.

Often forgotten from the film is the character of Jack, played by Griffin Dunne, and his gruesome decay as a deceased victim of a werewolf. Baker put in some gory overtime to create Jack's torn neck and face. For the later scene of Jack and David in the movie theater, Baker fashioned a grisly puppet to show Jack's advanced state of rot. Cleverly, Dunne was allowed to operate the jaw when the puppet spoke, voicing the lines at the same time and giving the actor the chance to be involved, despite the mechanical head being used.

The innovation and effort demonstrated in *An American Werewolf in London* paid off for Baker, as he was honored with the first-ever official Academy Award for Best Makeup.

Over the next fifteen years, Rick Baker became known as the "go-to guy" for special makeup effects. During that time, his work was seen in films like *Videodrome* in 1983; *Greystoke: The Legend of Tarzan, Lord of the Apes* and *Starman*, both in 1984; *Harry and the Hendersons* in 1987; *Gorillas in the Mist* and *Missing Link* in 1988; *Matinee* in 1993; *Wolf* and *Ed Wood* in 1994; *Batman Forever* in 1995; *The Nutty Professor*, with Eddie Murphy in seven different roles; and *Escape from L.A.* in 1996. In that period of time, he was nominated for five Oscars, winning three.

Director Barry Sonnenfeld took on the sci-fi comedy *Men in Black* in 1997, despite never having seen a sci-fi film in his life. With aliens of all sorts secretly living on Earth, it was obvious who could deliver a wide variety of unworldly beings—Rick Baker.

Since the artist had formed Cinovation Studios in 1993, he was now spreading out the work between himself and his team. One member, Aaron Sims, thought up the quirky "worm guys." Clearly not makeup, the worm guys were rod puppets and CGI that once more demonstrated how the line separating makeup and special effects often became blurred.

Baker remained involved in *MIB* by creating makeups for characters like Edgar, the farmer whose body became a disguise for the alien bug; Jeebs, the alien arms dealer whose head seemed to morph into something a little different every time Agent Kay blew it away; and Mikey, a fleeing extraterrestrial whose appearance was accomplished with both makeup and costume, and CGI sequences. As no surprise, Baker took home Oscar number five for *MIB*.

Nearing the new millennium, Rick Baker took on more projects, including *Mighty Joe Young* in 1998 (another ape), a return with Eddie Murphy to *Nutty Professor II: the Klumps* in 2000, as well as *How the Grinch Stole Christmas* in the same year, which earned him his sixth Oscar. Then (guess what?) more monkeys with director Tim Burton's *Planet of the Apes* in 2001, back to *Men in Black II* in 2002, and films like *Hellboy* in 2004 and *X-Men: The Last Stand* in 2006.

Baker and Cinovation Studios welcomed new talent, just as Dick Smith had done with Baker in the early 1970s. One exceptional artist was Japanese native Kazuhiro Tsuji—known as Kaz—who worked with Baker on a special age makeup

Rick Baker receives his star on the Hollywood Walk of Fame.

for Adam Sandler in 2007's *Click*. They also teamed in the same year with old friend Eddie Murphy for *Norbit*, creating three separate make-ups for Murphy's three separate characters. Both films earned Academy Award nominations for their work.

For 2008's *Tropic Thunder*, Baker designed a unique makeup for actor Robert Downey Jr., who played a white actor who had himself surgically altered to look like a black man in order to really get deep into a movie role. At the same time, Baker began to ease back on some of the intense projects he was committing to. He cut back on his crew at Cinovation and decided he would be more selective in the jobs he took on.

One film that he keenly desired to do was director Joe Johnson's *The Wolfman* in 2010. With Benicio Del Toro cast as the troubled Lawrence Talbot, Baker knew he wanted to stay close to Jack Pierce's original makeup but update it as well. The result was a combination of physical makeup and CGI images for both Del Toro and Sir Anthony Hopkins, who was also a werewolf. Baker's work—naturally—won him a seventh Oscar.

A revisit to the computer world of *TRON: Legacy* in 2010 and *Men in Black 3* in 2012, as well as special makeup for Angelina Jolie in *Maleficent* in 2014, gave Rick Baker more breathing room in recent years. He received his own star on the Hollywood Walk of Fame in 2012, with friends Dennis Muren and Dick Smith at his side.

Fittingly, when mentor Dick Smith was given the Governors Award in 2011 at the Academy Awards, it was Rick Baker who presented it to the man who had given him his start in movie makeup nearly forty years before.

Selected Filmography

Makeup Designer and Artist
* *Star Wars*—1977
* *The Incredible Melting Man*—1977
* *Videodrome*—1983
* *Starman*—1984
* *Matinee*—1993

- *Escape from L.A.*—1996
- *Men in Black*—1997
- *Mighty Joe Young*—1998
- *Planet of the Apes*—2001
- *Men in Black II*—2002
- *Hellboy*—2004
- *X-Men: The Last Stand*—2006
- *TRON: Legacy*—2010
- *Men in Black 3*—2012

Rob Bottin

The community of FX and makeup artists in Hollywood is a close one, evidenced by the fact that many come from similar interests and backgrounds. In the case of Rob Bottin, his entry into the makeup world mirrored that of his mentor, Rick Baker.

Born in El Monte, California, in 1959, Bottin was fortunate to grow up not far from Hollywood and the center of the film world. His interest in monster movies and *Famous Monsters* magazine (I hope this story isn't getting old ...) prompted Bottin to start making sketches of his own creatures.

As a fourteen-year-old high school freshman, Bottin sent a fan letter to Rick Baker. He enclosed a drawing of Lon Chaney for Baker to review. The makeup artist did more than that—he was so impressed with the quality of the sketch that he offered an apprenticeship to the young phenom. Before long, Bottin was attending his classes at Arroyo High in the morning and indulging his dreams with Baker in the afternoon.

The experiences were invaluable for Bottin, as he worked on *King Kong*, *Star Wars*, and *Tanya's Island* with Rick Baker. On his own, Bottin's reputation became quickly known, as he worked with director Joe Dante on *Piranha* in 1978 and John Carpenter on *The Fog* in 1980.

In 1981, Dante began work on a werewolf film called *The Howling*. He enlisted Rick Baker and Rob Bottin to do the FX makeup. As fate would have it, shortly after the design process had begun, John Landis contacted Baker with the news that *An American Werewolf in London* had finally been green-lighted, and production was ready to begin. The director was none too pleased to find Baker toiling away on another werewolf film, so Baker moved on to do *American Werewolf*, leaving Bottin to handle the makeup for *The Howling*. As Dante's film actually made it to the screen before Landis' film, Bottin's amazing makeup FX thrilled moviegoers before Baker's.

On his own at age twenty-two, Bottin reconnected with John Carpenter for the 1982 remake of *The Thing*. The director entrusted the young artist with creating things (or a "thing") never seen before, desperately seeking to avoid the "man-in-a-suit" techniques so often used in sci-fi films.

Rob Bottin with oversized rodent built for *Rock 'n' Roll High School.*

Bottin did not disappoint, as he provided a gorefest of distorted humans, a shape-shifting alien, all with a combination of FX makeup, rod and cable puppets, and plenty of imagination. This *Thing* was clearly not James Arness as that *Thing*. But Bottin, who toiled seven days a week on the film, even sleeping at his shop, paid heavily for his efforts. He wound up hospitalized for exhaustion after completing *The Thing.*

Joe Dante kept Rob Bottin close at hand, as the makeup FX expert created the amazing cartoon-like characters in the third segment of 1983's *Twilight Zone: The Movie*, which was directed by Dante. The duo followed that up with *Explorers* in 1985. Bottin's work on *Legend*, the fantasy film directed by Ridley Scott and starring Tom Cruise the same year, earned the artist an Oscar nomination for Best Makeup.

In 1987, *The Witches of Eastwick* and *Innerspace* (directed by Dante) found Bottin lending his talents for special makeup effects. Later the same year, the artist took on a new challenge, with spectacular results.

Director Paul Verhoeven (profiled elsewhere in this chapter) picked up the sci-fi project of *RoboCop* after others had passed on it. Set in the near future, crime is too much for the local police, so big business decides to take over with a cyborg known as RoboCop. Rob Bottin came on board, spending eight months of back-and-forth discussions with Verhoeven on the design of the iconic RoboCop suit.

The result was a black inner suit made of foam latex, with polyurethane plastic sections making up the outer suit, attached with a combination of Velcro, hooks, and snaps. A fiberglass helmet, gloves, and boots completed the outfit, which weighed about forty pounds. In all, Bottin and his crew built seven complete RoboCop suits for the film.

Equally stunning was the brutal scene of Officer Murphy's killing, actually shot after the rest of the film had wrapped. Bottin created prosthetic copies of actor Peter Weller's arm, pre-segmented to blow apart with compressed air when "shot away." A detailed and complex replica of Murphy's torso and head was built, capable of facial expressions and extensive motion. Much of the gory assassination, however, was left on the cutting-room floor, as censors wanted to slap an "X" rating on the film as originally submitted. The very believable FX had to be excessively trimmed to achieve a more acceptable "R" rating.

Bottin stayed with Verhoeven to make *Total Recall*, starring Arnold Schwarzenegger, in 1990. Once more, Rob Bottin and his crew delivered an incredible array of visual makeup FX, with a full animatronic figure creating the effect of a man with a child growing out of his midsection; a combination of computer-based, optical-processed, and precision-built practical effects to replicate a "fat lady" mask worn by Ahh-nold; not to mention prosthetics for scarred mutants and a three-breasted woman. The amazing results ended up with Bottin and his crew receiving a Special Achievement Oscar for Visual Effects.

The nineties saw Rob Bottin creating special makeup effects for films like *Basic Instinct* in 1992, *Mission: Impossible* in 1996, and *Fight Club* in 1999, among others. He continued with *Charlie's Angels* in 2000 and *Mr. Deeds* in 2002.

But since then, Rob Bottin has all but disappeared from the cinema magic that he has made. As far as anyone knows, he has retired and disappeared from public life.

Selected Filmography

- *Star Wars*—1977
- *The Fog*—1980
- *The Howling*—1981
- *The Thing*—1982
- *Twilight Zone: The Movie*—1983
- *Innerspace*—1987
- *RoboCop*—1987
- *Total Recall*—1990
- *Mission: Impossible*—1996

Ve Neill

In an industry dominated for decades by a "males-only" attitude, makeup FX master Ve Neill stands out as one of the first women to break into the "boys' club." In a career that has spanned more than thirty-five years, her spectacular work has earned her seven Oscar nominations, with three wins to her credit.

Born Mary Flores in Riverside, California in 1951, Neill thrilled to monster movies on TV and quickly showed her interest in makeup by applying lipstick, shoe polish, and other household materials on the faces of her cousins. By great fortune, her next-door neighbor happened to be Leo Lotito, a Hollywood makeup artist who had endless credits in film and television. Early on, Neill knew she wanted to do what Mr. Lotito did for a living.

As a teen, Neill designed costumes for a local rock band. Attending a sci-fi convention some years later, she had the fortune to meet Fred Phillips, a makeup artist who had worked on 1939's *Wizard of Oz*, as well as acting as makeup supervisor on TV's *Outer Limits* in the mid-1960s. What's more, Phillips had been the makeup artist for producer Gene Roddenberry and TV's *Star Trek* in the late 1960s. He offered to keep Neill in mind for future gigs.

Ve Neill did makeup for films like 1977's *Kingdom of the Spiders*, *Laserblast* in 1978, and *The Day Time Ended* in 1979. That same year, Fred Phillips brought Neill in to work on director Robert Wise's *Star Trek: The Motion Picture*. From there, she hooked up to do makeup for Lily Tomlin in 1980's *Nine to Five*, 1981's *The Incredible Shrinking Woman*, as well as the 1982 CBS-TV special *Lily for President?*

With movie and TV work through the mid-1980s, Neill got the chance to do sexy vampires years before *The Hunger Games*, making up Jason Patric, Corey Haim, and Kiefer Sutherland in *The Lost Boys* in 1987.

The next year, Ve Neill worked with director Tim Burton on the dark comedy *Beetlejuice*, with Michael Keaton as the undead title pest with wild hair, sunken eyes, and mossy facial growths. Additional characters included a disfigured football team killed in a plane crash, a chain-smoking counselor for the recently deceased, and a grisly cinder of a man who died while smoking in bed. Behind all the wonderful makeup was Ve Neill, who won her first Academy Award for her efforts.

Neill continued with films like *Dick Tracy*, *Flatliners*, and *Edward Scissorhands* (for director Tim Burton once more) in 1990. Among other flicks, she worked on *Batman Returns* and *Hoffa* in 1992, with another great challenge in 1993. *Mrs. Doubtfire* told the story of a man who masqueraded as an elderly English nanny in order to see his kids. Neill applied a multiappliance foam latex makeup,

designed by Greg Cannom, on actor Robin Williams. Her work was rewarded with a second Oscar for Best Makeup.

In 1994, with a makeup designed by Rick Baker, Neill turned actor Martin Landau into Count Dracula himself, Bela Lugosi, for Tim Burton's biopic *Ed Wood*. At Oscar time, Ve Neill won her third statue.

In the years to follow, Neill worked her makeup magic for films like *Batman Forever* in 1995, *Mars Attacks!* (as artist to Jack Nicholson) in 1996, *Batman & Robin* and *Gattaca* in 1997, *Stigmata* and *Man on the Moon* in 1999, among others. She worked with Rick Baker on *How the Grinch Stole Christmas* in 2000 and *A.I. Artificial Intelligence* in 2001.

Starting in 2003, Neill began the first of three turns as makeup department head for the *Pirates of the Caribbean*

Ve Neill tends to Lenny Kravitz in *The Hunger Games*.

films, making up Johnny Depp as Captain Jack Sparrow. She also headed the makeup crews for *The Chronicles of Riddick* in 1994 and *Constantine* in 2005. She teamed up with Johnny Depp and Tim Burton again in 2007 for the quirky musical *Sweeney Todd: The Demon Barber of Fleet Street.*

Ve Neill has headed the makeup for more recent films like *John Carter, The Hunger Games,* and *The Amazing Spider-Man,* all in 2012, plus *The Host* and the *Hunger Games* sequel in

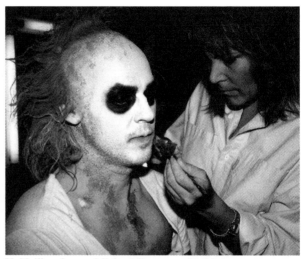

Ve Neill makes up Michael Keaton as *Beetlejuice.*

2013. At the same time, she has shared her skills and experience by acting as judge and mentor for up-and-coming makeup artists on the Syfy Channel reality series *Face Off.*

Selected Filmography

Makeup Designer and Artist

- *Kingdom of the Spiders*—1977
- *Laserblast*—1978
- *Star Trek: The Motion Picture*—1979
- *Beetlejuice*—1988
- *Edward Scissorhands*—1990
- *Mars Attacks!*—1996
- *Gattaca*—1997
- *A.I. Artificial Intelligence*—2001
- *The Chronicles of Riddick*—2004
- *John Carter*—2012
- *The Amazing Spider-Man*—2012
- *The Host*—2013

Elite Directors of Sci-Fi

Steven Spielberg

Long passed up by critics as a "popcorn movie" director, Steven Spielberg finally received his due accolades in winning several Oscars for gritty wartime films like 1993's *Schindler's List* and 1998's *Saving Private Ryan.* Of course, audiences knew all along about his ability to tell a story, including several in the sci-fi genre, with exciting images and a sharp narrative. Today, he simply is one of the industry giants, famed for knowing how to make a blockbuster film.

Spielberg was born in Ohio in 1946, moving with his family to New Jersey and Arizona. As a young teen, he earned his Boy Scout merit badge in photography by shooting a nine-minute western with his father's 8mm movie camera. Just a few years later, he wrote and directed *Firelight*, a 140-minute sci-fi epic with a $500 budget. Its only showing sold out the Phoenix theater where it played, and the film would serve as an indication of his future success in sci-fi movies.

Despite being twice refused admission to the film school at the University of Southern California, Spielberg became an unpaid intern at Universal Studios while attending California State University, Long Beach. When an exec at the studio saw *Amblin'*, a short film made by Spielberg, he signed on the twenty-one-year-old as a staff director for TV shows like *Marcus Welby M.D.* and *Rod Serling's Night Gallery*. *Duel*, a thrilling made-for-TV movie in 1971, gave Spielberg a shot at proving his potential for directing something feature length.

In 1975, Spielberg turned moviegoers on their heads and made everyone afraid to go into the water with *Jaws*. A spine-chilling flick featuring an enormous great white shark with a taste for swimmers, the movie was nominated for a Best Picture Oscar and won three statues for Best Sound, Best Editing, and Best Original Music Score. Shot for $8 million, *Jaws* grossed nearly half-a-billion dollars worldwide. Despite the opinions of USC, Spielberg obviously knew something about making movies.

For his next film, Spielberg decided to indulge what he once referred to as his "hobby": aliens. The 1977 *Close Encounters of the Third Kind* presented a view of an alien visit that had not been seen before. Historically, films that featured "little green men from outer space" invariably featured "big green men from the military" whose first response was to blow the visitors to bits. In *CE3K*, scientists were anxious to greet, not beat, the aliens.

In a stroke of what seemed to be genius, Spielberg cast famed foreign film director François Truffaut as one of those scientists. In reality, Spielberg was merely a huge fan of the French New Wave director, and, even though he had conceived the part of Claude Lacombe with Truffaut in mind, he never really expected him to accept the offer to act in an American sci-fi film.

To no one's surprise, *Close Encounters of the Third Kind* was another huge success for Spielberg. With a big budget (for the day) of $22 million, it brought in more than $300 million around the world, winning two Oscars and a Best Director nomination for Spielberg. In a rare demonstration of the massive leverage he had quickly gained in Hollywood, Spielberg rereleased the film as *Close Encounters of the Third Kind: Special Edition*, with newly shot footage added, just three years later.

In regard to the 1979 World War II farce known as *1941*, it's important to remember that even baseball great Babe Ruth struck out more than a thousand times at the plate. Directed by Spielberg, with a script written largely by Robert

Zemeckis, *1941* was in need of a good psychiatrist—Was it a comedy? Was it a drama? Just what the heck was *1941*?

Critics ripped it; the *New York Times* said it was "as fun as a 40-pound wrist watch." Spielberg himself called *1941* "a demolition derby." The cast was assembled as if someone took folks from *Saturday Night Live, Jaws, Laverne and Shirley*, along with every bit and character actor in Hollywood, shoved them all into a studio, and told them to make a movie (after adding international stars like Christopher Lee and Toshiro Mifune for spice). Apparently, Steven Spielberg was human.

Of course, great filmmakers survive, and Spielberg quickly rebounded. With the success of *Jaws* and *CE3K* under his belt, he approached Albert "Cubby" Broccoli—producer of the James Bond film franchise—and offered to direct a 007 movie, one of his lifelong dreams. But the producer declined, wanting someone with a longer resume. Years later, after the success of *Schindler's List*, Broccoli once more denied Spielberg's offer to direct a Bond film. Now, Broccoli claimed, he could no longer afford to hire Spielberg.

The director forged ahead, with a story from friend and *Star Wars* creator George Lucas (profiled elsewhere in this chapter). In 1981, Spielberg directed *Raiders of the Lost Ark* and Indiana Jones was born. With an opening sequence that was more thrilling than most movie climaxes, Spielberg slapped action and adventure—with a hint of sci-fi—together into a major summertime movie blockbuster. Budgeted at $18 million, *Raiders of the Lost Ark* grossed nearly fifteen times that in American box offices alone. With overseas numbers added, it was nearly a $400 million movie—thirty years before that kind of film income was common as an impressive figure.

Back to his hobby of aliens, Spielberg directed *E.T. the Extra-Terrestrial* in 1982. Showing a knack for working with children as his main characters, the director told the story of neighborhood kids who befriend an alien when it is left behind on Earth. In order to get the right emotional reactions from his young stars, Spielberg shot the film in order, from start to finish (unlike most movies, which are shot out of sequence according to location, cast availability, schedule, and other factors). When E.T. had to leave at the end, everyone's tears at separation were real.

The movie (here's a surprise—with sarcasm added) made its $10.5 million budget back on the opening weekend alone. All in all, *E.T.* grossed nearly $800 million worldwide. With nine Oscar nominations (including Spielberg for Best Director), it took four (excluding Spielberg, once again).

A screening of *E.T. the Extra-Terrestrial* was presented at the White House for then-president Ronald Reagan, along with wife Nancy and others, including Neil Armstrong, the first man on the moon. With Spielberg in attendance, the president thanked him for the film and then told everyone in the room that the whole story was true. Although Spielberg was sure Ronnie was just kidding, he also noticed there was not even a hint of a smile on the president's face.

After directing a segment of *Twilight Zone: The Movie* in 1983 and the first sequel to *Raiders*, called *Indiana Jones and the Temple of Doom* in 1984, Spielberg took on the Alice Walker novel *The Color Purple* in 1985. He also directed the film version of the World War II novel *Empire of the Sun* in 1987.

Another *Raiders* sequel, *Indiana Jones and the Last Crusade*, followed in 1989, as well as *Always*, a remake of 1941's *A Guy Named Joe*. Spielberg also tackled a musical version of Peter Pan called *Hook* in 1991.

With the novel of *Jurassic Park* not yet released in 1990, producer Kathleen Kennedy and Universal Pictures purchased the film rights from author Michael Crichton, with only one director in mind. Spielberg quickly decided to bring in Stan Winston to provide full-scale animatronic dinosaurs, while Phil Tippett would provide stop-motion animation for the additional dinosaur sequences.

Even though Tippett delivered top-notch test footage of the animated dinosaurs, Spielberg wasn't completely happy with them. When Dennis Muren showed the director an example of newly developed computer-generated dinosaurs, it looked like the prehistoric world had just entered the digital world.

Even though Spielberg's given middle name is Allan, it might just as well have been Midas, as he showed his golden touch once more with *Jurassic Park*. With a bulging budget of $63 million, the film grossed nearly $50 million on just its opening weekend. Overall, *Jurassic Park* brought in $350 million in the US, with another $500 million overseas, for a total of nearly $1 billion. A 3-D-enhanced version of the film was released in 2013, adding another $57 million to the overall gross.

While postproduction was ongoing for *Jurassic Park* in 1993, Spielberg directed *Schindler's List*. A gripping three-hour film about a German business owner who saved more than a thousand Polish Jews during the Holocaust of World War II, it won seven Oscars out of twelve nominations. Along with a Best Picture statue, Spielberg was finally honored with a win for Best Director.

Having spent a solid twenty-five years directing and producing some of Hollywood's most memorable films, Spielberg decided to take a break in 1995 so he could be with his family and start up his own business. DreamWorks SKG, founded with former Disney Studios chairman Jeffery Katzenberg and music magnate David Geffen, provided Spielberg with a studio that would develop, produce, and distribute media projects like movies, TV, and video games.

Desiring to direct a diverse group of films in 1997, Spielberg handled a sequel to his dinosaur epic, *The Lost World: Jurassic Park*, and *Amistad*, a true story of a mutiny aboard a slave ship bound for America in the 1830s. In 1998, he brought *Saving Private Ryan* to the screen, telling the true story of American soldiers in the Normandy invasion during World War II. It won five Academy Awards, including Spielberg's second for Best Director.

Entering the twenty-first century, Spielberg took on two sci-fi stories. *A.I. Artificial Intelligence* originally was the project of Stanley Kubrick, who had worked closely with Spielberg in its development. When Kubrick suddenly passed away in 1999, Spielberg made sure *A.I.* was completed by directing, as well as writing the screenplay. Like a futuristic Pinocchio story, the movie told of a young boy android who dreamt of being a real boy.

The second film was *Minority Report*, based on the short story by Philip K. Dick. In this near-future action film, Tom Cruise plays a police officer accused of a crime he hasn't committed—yet. Years back, Spielberg had been set to direct Cruise in *Rain Man* in 1989, but took on *Indiana Jones and the Last Crusade* instead. They finally connected with this film.

Both *A.I.* and *Minority Report* did fairly well, although both

Steven Spielberg with *E.T.*

were far more popular overseas than in America. *A.I. Artificial Intelligence* grossed $235 million in 2001, with about a third of that in the US. *Minority Report* took in $358 million around the globe in 2002, with $132 million in America.

Spielberg directed *Catch Me If You Can* in 2002 and *The Terminal* in 2004, both starring Tom Hanks. Both movies were relatively successful, taking in $350 million and $219 million, respectively, worldwide.

In 2005, Spielberg directed an updated version of H. G. Wells' *War of the Worlds*, budgeted at more than $130 million and once again starring Tom Cruise. Unlike the director's first two films about an alien landing, the visitors in *War of the World* weren't cute, cuddly, or friendly. They were mean, ugly, and had one goal—killing as many humans as they could. And they certainly slayed audiences at the box office, as *War of the Worlds* grossed nearly $600 million around the world.

The same year saw Steven Spielberg direct *Munich*, the dramatic story of the aftermath from the massacre of Israeli athletes at the 1972 Olympics in Munich. A powerful film, *Munich* was an acquired taste for moviegoers, grossing $130 million worldwide.

In 2008, the long, long, long-awaited fourth installment in the *Indiana Jones* franchise arrived, with Spielberg teaming up with Harrison Ford again. *Indiana Jones and the Kingdom of the Crystal Skull* brought the story into the 1950s, with Dr. Jones facing off against Commies, aliens, an old girlfriend, and a son he didn't know existed. It was a big ol' popcorn film all the way and collected more than three-quarters of a billion dollars around the world.

Since then, the director has helmed the computer-animated *The Adventures of Tintin* in 2011, based on the European comic strip, and *War Horse*, the film version of a popular dramatic novel and stage play of the same name, also in 2011.

Spielberg also finished his long-awaited biopic of *Lincoln* in 2012, although it more accurately focused on only a small portion of the life of Abraham Lincoln and his presidency. The film pulled twelve Oscar nominations, winning two.

Spielberg remains committed to producing and directing films and media projects in all genres, as he is connected to a fourth *Jurassic Park* film, as well as a fifth *Indiana Jones* entry. In forty-plus years of directing, Spielberg movies have grossed an astonishing $4.155 billion.

Take that, USC.

Selected Filmography

Director

- *Jaws*—1975
- *Close Encounters of the Third Kind*—1977
- *E.T. the Extra-Terrestrial*—1982
- *Twilight Zone: The Movie* ("Kick the Can")—1983
- *Jurassic Park*—1993
- *The Lost World: Jurassic Park*—1997
- *A.I. Artificial Intelligence*—2001
- *Minority Report*—2002
- *War of the Worlds*—2005

Producer and Executive Producer

- *E.T. the Extra-Terrestrial*—1982
- *Poltergeist*—1982
- *Twilight Zone: The Movie*—1983
- *Gremlins*—1984
- *Back to the Future*—1985
- *Innerspace*—1987
- **batteries not included*—1987
- *Back to the Future II*—1989
- *Back to the Future II*—1990
- *Gremlins 2: The New Batch*—1990
- *Men in Black*—1997
- *Deep Impact*—1998
- *A.I. Artificial Intelligence*—2001
- *Jurassic Park III*—2001
- *Men in Black II*—2002
- *Transformers*—2007
- *Transformers: Revenge of the Fallen*—2009
- *Super 8*—2011
- *Transformers: Dark of the Moon*—2011
- *Cowboys & Aliens*—2011
- *Real Steel*—2011
- *Men in Black 3*—2012

Writer
* *Close Encounters of the Third Kind*—1977
* *Poltergeist*—1982
* *A.I. Artificial Intelligence*—2001

George Lucas

Known as one of the most powerful and influential people in the film world, George Lucas' visibility is somewhat amazing, considering he's directed only five big-time films—four of which are part of *Star Wars*, an incredible and vast cinematic and marketing franchise.

Lucas was born in the northern California town of Modesto in 1944. Along with an interest in fast cars, the teenage Lucas was drawn to the work of European filmmakers like Godard, Truffaut, and Fellini. Also, as fate intervened at an auto racetrack, he happened to meet Hollywood cinematographer Haskell Wexler—who would go on to win Oscars for shooting films like *Who's Afraid of Virginia Woolf* in 1966 and *Bound for Glory* in 1976, as well as lensing *One Flew over the Cuckoo's Nest* in 1975, *Coming Home* in 1978, and many more. Wexler was impressed with Lucas' way with a camera and encouraged him to pursue his interest in movies.

The teen attended Modesto Junior College for two years, focusing on social sciences. Enrolling in the USC film school (he obviously showed something that Spielberg seemed to lack), Lucas became friends with future filmmakers like John Milius, who would write *Dirty Harry* in 1971, *Magnum Force* in 1973, and *Apocalypse Now* in 1979, as well as direct *Conan the Barbarian* in 1982 and *Red Dawn* in 1984, among others; Walter Murch, a multiple Oscar-winning film editor; and Robert Zemeckis, director and screenwriter of the *Back to the Future* films, *Contact*, *Cast Away*, as well as winning an Oscar for *Forrest Gump*.

In 1967, Lucas wrote and directed a seventeen-minute student film at USC called *Electronic Labyrinth THX 1138 4EB*. Pre-*2001*, the film offered a look at a dystopian, computer-based world and one of its citizens who sought to escape. It was obvious that the young Lucas had a firm grasp on his craft, as the film took first-place honors at the National Student Film Festival the following year.

With an internship at Warner Bros. Studios, Lucas had the chance to observe director Francis Ford Coppola as he worked on the 1968 film musical *Finian's Rainbow*. Among his other experiences in the late 1960s, Lucas was a camera operator on the 1970 Maysles Brothers' documentary on the Rolling Stones, *Gimme Shelter*.

The association with Coppola was only the beginning, as Lucas joined the director to found American Zoetrope, a film production studio, in 1970. Wishing to avoid the hassles and bureaucracy of the established Hollywood studios, the duo opened their own independent venture in San Francisco.

One of their first projects was a revisit to Lucas' story from his USC student film. With a title shortened to *THX 1138*, the film was remade in 1971 with

Robert Duvall in the title role. Warner Bros. Studios, partnered for the film's distribution, didn't care very much for Lucas' final edit and recut it. It still had little impact upon release, although it has gained major cult status since.

Lucas returned to his memories of life in California in the early sixties and his love of street racing with *American Graffiti* in 1973. It was a tough shoot, with a tight schedule, all-night filming, and little time for rehearsals. He called upon his old friend Haskell Wexler to consult and help get his story on film. The result was pure dynamite.

American Graffiti, made on a budget of a bit more than $750,000, raked in $115 million. It launched the careers of actors Richard Dreyfuss and Harrison Ford and influenced the creation of the long-running hit ABC-TV show *Happy Days*. It also earned five Oscar nominations, including one for George Lucas as Best Director.

With the success of *American Graffiti*, Lucas set his sights on his next film, targeting the sci-fi genre once more. Long enamored with the *Flash Gordon* serials of the 1930s and 1940s, the director imagined making what he called "2001 meets James Bond."

As a matter of fact, if the rights for the Flash Gordon character had been available, that would have been Lucas' cinematic subject. Instead, he began writing the screenplay for what he would call *Star Wars* right after shooting *American Graffiti*. The writing was nonstop for more than three years, with draft after draft completed—seven in total—until Lucas began his shoot in March 1976.

From the very start, Lucas realized that no special-effects facility existed that could realize the never-before-seen images that spun around in his head. Not so simply, he formed Industrial Light and Magic in an empty warehouse in the San Fernando Valley north of Los Angeles. With a crew of as many as seventy-five techs, working two shifts, ILM helped to make Lucas' future vision a reality.

The result was more than anyone could have imagined. *Star Wars* opened on Memorial Day weekend in 1977 in a limited release to only forty-three theaters. With a budget of $11 million, the film made that back within the month and was still playing in nearly six hundred theaters by Thanksgiving. By the year's end, *Star Wars* had grossed almost $200 million in America. In total, the film thrilled audiences around the world for more than $775 million.

The impact of *Star Wars* wasn't lost on voters from the Academy, as it was nominated for ten Oscars, including another for Lucas as Best Director. The film won six: Best Art Direction, Best Costume Design, Best Visual Effects, Best Film Editing, Best Original Music Score, and Best Sound. Ben Burtt won a seventh Special Achievement Award for developing the sound effects and voices of the aliens, creatures, and robots.

The full title of the film was actually reminiscent of the Flash Gordon serials that influenced Lucas—*Star Wars Episode IV: A New Hope*. The director originally envisioned a series of nine films in total, with three trilogies telling the stories of Jedi Knights and Luke Skywalker. Uniquely, *A New Hope* was the first of the middle triad.

Between the creative and technological aspects of the franchise, George Lucas quickly found that *Star Wars* would take over his life, something he didn't expect. *Episode V: The Empire Strikes Back* hit the screens in 1980, with *Episode VI: Return of the Jedi* coming out in 1983. Although he wrote and produced both films, he turned the directing chores over to Irvin Kershner and Richard Marquand, respectively. Together, the two sequels grossed $1 billion worldwide.

Sixteen years separated the release of *Return of the Jedi* and the first film of the initial trilogy, *Episode I: The Phantom Menace*. In the time between them, Lucas kept busy by being a father to his three adopted children, as well as writing stories for Spielberg's *Indiana Jones* films. He also remained very involved in writing stories for numerous TV and video-game projects in the *Star Wars* and *Indiana Jones* worlds. Additionally, Lucas executive produced films like *Willow* and *Tucker: The Man and His Dream*, both in 1988. He also exec produced what is considered to be one of the worst films of all time, 1986's *Howard the Duck* (much like Spielberg's fiasco with *1941*).

With the first trilogy of *The Phantom Menace*, *Episode II: Attack of the Clones* in 2002 and *Episode III: Revenge of the Sith* in 2005, Lucas returned to the director's chair, as well as writing and producing.

Alec Guinness takes a break with George Lucas on *Star Wars*.

Part of Lucas' delay in returning to the *Star Wars* films was based on the need for FX technology to achieve what he felt was required to tell the story. The strides made between 1985 and 1999 in terms of CGI, motion control and other aspects of digital filmmaking were enormous—often spearheaded by ILM.

In fact, Lucas revisited his fist three *Star Wars* films at the time of the release of *Episode I*, replacing physical effects like Jabba the Hutt, matte paintings of the Cloud City of Bespin, and the celebrating creatures following the destruction of the Empire with CGI, among many others. Lucas made edit changes, including recutting the shootout between Han Solo and Greedo the bounty hunter. Also, the original print of *Star Wars* was in need of physical restoration, since so many copies had been made since 1977.

Many fans objected to the "reenvisioning" of the original films, believing Lucas was tampering with films that needed no tweaking, enhancing, or additional editing. Some compared his actions to altering classic works like *The Mona Lisa*. In his defense, the director believed he was just trying to make the best films possible, despite their "landmark" status as anointed by the fans.

With the completion of *Episode III* in 2005, Lucas wrote the story for Steven Spielberg's return to *Indiana Jones and The Kingdom of the Crystal Skull* in 2008. There is more than just speculation that Lucas will be involved in *Indiana Jones 5*, whenever it gets underway.

It goes without saying that the "prequel" trilogy of *Star Wars' Episodes I, II,* and *III* was successful, pulling in more than $1 billion in total. At the time of the release of *Episode I*, however, Lucas had decided that he was getting a bit too old to consider making his third trilogy. Figuring *Episodes VII, VIII,* and *IX* would take him past the age of seventy, the director announced in 1999 that *Revenge of the Sith* in 2005 would be the final entry to the *Star Wars* saga.

Just as Sean Connery learned that one should "never say never again," Lucas found a way to enjoy his semiretirement while still seeing his vision of nine *Star Wars* films coming true. In late 2012, Disney Studios bought LucasFilm from George Lucas for more than $4 billion. Almost immediately, they announced that the next three entries to the *Star Wars* series would be released in 2015, 2017, and 2019.

Perhaps Lucas will be sitting in the first row, with a box of popcorn in his lap. Why not? He earned it.

Selected Filmography

Director
- *THX 1138*—1971
- *American Graffiti*—1973
- *Star Wars*—1977
- *Star Wars: Episode I—The Phantom Menace*—1999
- *Star Wars: Episode II—Attack of the Clones*—2002
- *Star Wars: Episode III—Revenge of the Sith*—2005

Producer and Executive Producer
- *Star Wars*—1977
- *Star Wars: Episode V—The Empire Strikes Back*—1980
- *Star Wars: Episode VI—Return of the Jedi*—1983
- *Howard the Duck*—1986
- *Star Wars: Episode I—The Phantom Menace*—1999
- *Star Wars: Episode II—Attack of the Clones*—2002
- *Star Wars: Episode III—Revenge of the Sith*—2005

Writer
- *THX 1138*—1971
- *Star Wars*—1977
- *Star Wars: Episode V—The Empire Strikes Back*—1980
- *Star Wars: Episode VI—Return of the Jedi*—1983
- *Star Wars: Episode I—The Phantom Menace*—1999
- *Star Wars: Episode II—Attack of the Clones*—2002
- *Star Wars: Episode III—Revenge of the Sith*—2005

Paul Verhoeven

In his native home of the Netherlands, director Paul Verhoeven was well established in film long before he assaulted moviegoers with *RoboCop* in 1987. But his Dutch films were love stories and war stories, often using the acting talents of Rutger Hauer and Jeroen Krabbé. Reluctantly, he tackled the sci-fi genre several times, usually with great success.

Born in Amsterdam in 1938, Verhoeven grew up under Nazi occupation and recalls watching the launching of deadly V-2 rockets from very near his home. He attended the University of Leiden, receiving doctorate degrees in math and physics. Yet he was more interested in making movies, and when drafted into the Royal Dutch Navy, Verhoeven made documentary films for the military.

After three years of service, Verhoeven became a director for Dutch television, where he first worked with Rutger Hauer on a very popular series called *Floris*. From there, he moved to directing feature films, including *Turkish Delight* in 1973, earning an Oscar nomination for Best Foreign Language Film. Other Dutch features included *Soldier of Orange* in 1977 and *Spetters* in 1980.

With a Dutch government that was restricting his style of filmmaking, Verhoeven came to America to make *Flesh+Blood* in 1985, a Middle Ages epic starring his oft-used Rutger Hauer and Jennifer Jason Leigh. With big-budget Hollywood films now part of his world, the director took his next major step.

When Verhoeven first received writer Ed Neumeier's script for *RoboCop*, he felt it was just a bit silly and didn't even finish reading it. Fortunately, his wife did and suggested the director give it another review. When he did, Verhoeven saw the humor and social satire among the challenge of a rough and violent sci-fi film.

Paul Verhoeven lines up a shot in the camera viewfinder.

The script had been turned down by many Hollywood directors, some who couldn't even get past the cartoonish title. But with the help and support of Neumeier and executive producer Jon Davison, Verhoeven tackled the futuristic story of a police officer turned into a crime-fighting robot after a savage and deadly shooting. Mixing ultra-violent images with humorous scenes of a goofy TV show host, the director also incorporated stop-motion effects from Phil Tippett. He cast actors Ronny Cox and Kurtwood Smith—usually seen in "good guy" parts—against type as villains.

When submitted to the MPAA (the Motion Picture Association of America) for approval, *RoboCop* was given the "kiss of death," an X rating for graphic violence. With Verhoeven making cuts in the gore, the MPAA still marked *RoboCop* with an X eleven times before finally giving it an R.

The result was a very popular film with audiences in 1987, and the director was ready to move on to his next film, another sci-fi story called *Total Recall*. Based on the Phillip K. Dick short story "*We Can Remember It for You Wholesale*," the film starred Arnold Schwarzenegger as a man in the near future who tries to realize his troubling dreams by having the memories of a trip to Mars implanted in his brain.

Once again, Verhoeven's over-the-top take on violence earned the film an X rating from the MPAA. And once again, with appropriate cuts, *Total Recall* eventually received an R rating and took in more than $260 million worldwide.

After sexy non-genre films (and, not surprisingly, more struggles with the MPAA) like 1992's *Basic Instinct* and 1995's *Showgirls*, Verhoeven returned to form with the sci-fi flick *Starship Troopers* in 1997. Despite accusations of presenting a positive spin on a fascist and militaristic society, the movie was basically a big-bug film with—as usual with the director—plenty of action, violence, and satirical humor.

Based on the Robert Heinlein novel and with a screenplay by Ed Neumeier, *Starship Troopers* was a $100 million film that struggled to make half of that back at the box office in America. It fared slightly better overseas, but was still not considered to be successful for Verhoeven, although it has a strong cult following today and resulted in two—albeit inferior—sequels and an animated TV series.

Verhoeven followed up with *Hollow Man* in 2000. As an updated retelling of *The Invisible Man*, the film starred Elisabeth Shue, Kevin Bacon, and Josh Brolin. Even though the $95 million film brought in more than $193 million around the world (only $70 million in the US), the director admits he had little interest in it. He found that directing a sci-fi film strictly for the FX was no reason to make a movie, and *Hollow Man* was the last he made in the genre.

Selected Filmography
Director
• *RoboCop*—1987
• *Total Recall*—1990
• *Starship Troopers*—1997
• *Hollow Man*—2000

James Cameron

A self-proclaimed "King of the World" (more on that in a moment), writer/producer/director James Cameron finds himself connected to some of Hollywood's biggest sci-fi blockbusters, and an amazing historical drama to boot. Part scientist and part filmmaker, Cameron has used his cinematic acumen to influence worldly activities, from NASA in outer space to the deepest parts of the ocean.

Cameron was born in Canada, near Niagara Falls, in 1954. At age sixteen, he and his family moved to Southern California, where the young Cameron attended Fullerton College. Aiming for a career as a scientist, he majored in physics and English, but he knew he really wanted to make films.

A rabid fan of sci-fi films, Cameron—like many—was floored by 1977's *Star Wars*. When some friends offered him the chance to pitch a low-budget space opera movie, he quit his truck driver job and learned everything he could about filmmaking. He wound up attending the same school that many other aspiring filmmakers had—the low-budget academy of Roger Corman films.

Working on Corman's *Battle Beyond the Stars* in 1980, Cameron made matte paintings, operated the FX camera, designed and built the sets as art director, built miniatures, and created a front projection system (most likely, he also emptied the trash containers). Without even realizing it, Cameron had assembled a very competent and complete visual effects department.

Competent and complete enough to convince John Carpenter to let him create twenty-five effects shots for the director's 1981 *Escape from New York*. Cameron continued to produce FX out of Corman's facility and at the same time began writing a sci-fi script of his own.

By July 1982, the young man had written a screenplay treatment based on a fever-borne nightmare he experienced in a cheap Italian hotel; a dream where a metallic man relentlessly chased a woman who couldn't run away.

Cameron's agent thought the concept was a bad one, so the young film-maker fired his agent and forged ahead. With a script and $6 million budget in hand, Cameron insisted on directing his vision called *The Terminator*.

The original Terminator role went to O. J. Simpson (funny how life works sometimes), with Arnold Schwarzenegger in the hero's role of Reese. Eventually, Michael Biehn became Reese, Schwarzenegger became the Terminator, and Simpson became inmate 41144. Linda Hamilton took the part of Sarah Connor and began running for her life.

As they say (whoever "they" are), the rest of the story is history. *The Terminator* brought in an amazing thirteen times its original budget in 1984 and became the first film in a franchise that grossed more than $1.4 billion around the world.

What's more, *The Terminator* established James Cameron as a filmmaker to be reckoned with as time went on. His first follow-up was writing and directing *Aliens*, the 1986 sequel to Ridley Scott's terrific 1979 flick *Alien*. Knowing how iconic the initial entry had been, Cameron headed into new territory, making a film with a faster pace, more action, and—literally—plenty of bang for the buck.

The Abyss was next in 1989, as Cameron wrote and directed a film that allowed him to indulge his fascination with deep water and diving. With computer graphics still in its infancy, Cameron reached new heights (or depths) in creating a believable CG liquid alien known as a pseudopod—a fluid with a face. Unfortunately, the $70 million budget (big bucks for the late eighties) was not earned back in America, and the overseas take was even less.

He returned to the Terminator saga in 1991 with *Terminator 2: Judgment Day*, once more pressing CG FX to the limits. The villainous, shape-shifting T-1000 took on the traits of liquid chrome, based on the writer/director's desire to do something never done before. *T2* was another big hit.

In 1994, Cameron took his Terminator star and turned him into a spy with two lives. *True Lies*, with Arnold Schwarzenegger, Jamie Lee Curtis, Tom Arnold, and Art Malik, was a huge summer blockbuster. It grossed nearly $400 million worldwide and did nothing to tarnish Cameron's Midas touch at the movies.

After penning the screenplay for the dystopian 1995 drama *Strange Days*, Cameron set his sights on a massive undertaking—weaving a romantic story throughout the events surrounding the sinking of the *Titanic*. Simply titled *Titanic*, the 1997 film was what the title said.

The budget was titanic, at an unheard-of $200 million. The cast was titanic, with Leo DiCaprio, Kate Winslet, Kathy Bates, and an amazing eighty-seven-year-old Gloria Stuart—with a film career that spanned more than sixty-five years—playing Rose, the centenarian survivor. The running time, at three hours, fourteen minutes, was titanic.

Of course, the results were . . . you know. Fourteen Oscar nominations resulted in eleven wins, including Best Picture. A Best Director Academy Award led Cameron to excitedly exclaim "I'm king of the world!" during his acceptance speech.

Even more titanic were the box-office results, as the film grossed well over $600 million in the US, with an incredible $1.5 billion overseas. The total take of $2.1 billion pegged *Titanic* as the number one, all-time-grossing film. It would stand for twelve years, until Cameron broke his own record.

During that time, James Cameron continued to develop Digital Domain Inc., the effects company he had started in 1993 with makeup and animatronics master Stan Winston and former ILM executive Scott Ross. Cameron also immersed himself in his underwater interests, producing several documentaries on deep-sea exploration and inventing a propulsion device for underwater photography.

Director James Cameron.

Cameron spent much of that time developing a film project unlike anything seen before. It would incorporate three-dimensional cinematography, realistic human characters created via motion-capture and CG technologies (some of which hadn't yet been invented), and would embrace a strong ecological theme.

Released in 2009, the film was called *Avatar*. The King of the World would soon become the King of the Universe, as *Avatar* turned out to be bigger than *Titanic*. It pulled in a myriad of awards and recognition, including nine Oscar nominations and three Oscar wins (although Best Picture and Best Director eluded Cameron this time around).

Avatar was a huge hit with audiences, as it collected three-quarters of a billion dollars in America and an unprecedented $2 billion overseas. The total of nearly $2.8 billion worldwide established *Avatar* as the all-time box-office champion.

Any doubts about the man's ability to make successful and entertaining films can be quickly quelled, considering the top two all-time entries were written and directed by James Cameron. As a director alone, Cameron's films have grossed enough money to truly make him "The Six-Billion Dollar Man."

Selected Filmography

Director
*   *The Terminator*—1984
*   *Aliens*—1986
*   *The Abyss*—1989
*   *Terminator 2: Judgment Day*—1991
*   *Titanic*—1997
*   *Avatar*—2009

Producer and Executive Producer
*   *Terminator 2: Judgment Day*—1991
*   *Titanic*—1997
*   *Avatar*—2009

Writer
*   *The Terminator*—1984
*   *Aliens*—1986
*   *The Abyss*—1989
*   *Terminator 2: Judgment Day*—1991
*   *Titanic*—1997

Rate or Rate Not ... There Is No Try

Top Five Modern Sci-Fi Films

Land of the Free, Home of the Faves

As an author who writes about movies of all sorts, the inevitable question is posed: Which is the best (insert genre here) film? (Followed by a close second of: Does this look infected to you?) It strikes me that "best" can mean "favorite," and vice versa.

A favorite pastime around pub tables, lunch tables, and kitchen tables alike is the ongoing argument for one's "favorite" films. The problem is that the argument often becomes confused with the concept of "best" films. For example, in my own case, my all-time favorite film is the 1941 classic *Citizen Kane*—I've seen it at least 200 times (really). Conveniently, it is a film that—in the opinion of many, if not most—is also considered to be the best film ever made. But that begs a distinction between "favorite" and "best."

"Favorite" needs no quantification, other than HOW GOOD it makes you FEEL. "Best," while still requiring some personal opinion, is much more measurable and objective, stating HOW GOOD the movie IS—ignoring one's personal feelings. Consider two other films that loom large in my DVD collection—*Plan Nine from Outer Space* and *The Godfather*.

US insert—*Slaughterhouse-Five*.

The first, released in 1959 (or did it escape?), is full of cheesy sets, cheesier dialogue, and the cheesiest spaceships this side of Cheetos. Many consider it to be the worst film ever made, and I might even agree (still, there's always *Bubble Boy* and *Kangaroo Jack* . . .). Yet, it truly is one of my favorites. No qualification needed. I always get a kick out of watching it.

Now, *The Godfather* boasts superior execution (in more ways than one) in many areas—script (Oscar), acting (Oscar for Brando, despite his refusal, as well as three additional nominations), overall production (Oscar for Best Picture), plus a Tommy gun full of additional nominations and accolades. My opinion means nothing here—the recognition for its greatness is overwhelming. Hence, one way (among others) of measuring "best." And, guess what? I always get a kick out of watching it.

So, on to the business of modern sci-fi films. As I was writing this book, many people asked, "Which is your favorite?" If time allowed, the conversation would eventually drift from "favorite" to "best." Even before writing the book, I had both established in my head. Afterward, my research had given me that much more info on which to base my list of "favorite" sci-fi films and "best" sci-fi films from the last forty years.

Oh, I could quit right now and leave the reader summarily "cheesed off," but I'm not that kind of person. So, here: Let it

WOODY ALLEN TAKES A NOSTALGIC LOOK AT THE FUTURE.

Woody Allen and Diane Keaton in "Sleeper"

A JACK ROLLINS—CHARLES H. JOFFE PRODUCTION

Produced by JACK GROSSBERG • Executive Producer CHARLES H. JOFFE
Written by WOODY ALLEN and MARSHALL BRICKMAN • Directed by WOODY ALLEN
United Artists
A Transamerica Company

International one-sheet—*Sleeper.*

start your own discussions around the water cooler and corner tap—my five favorite sci-fi films from the last forty years. (Please, no wagering. . . .)

Number Five—*Slaughterhouse-Five*

I've always liked George Roy Hill's films. This was his only foray into the sci-fi genre, and I think he handled a difficult story in a very satisfying way. Instead of casting a big Hollywood name as Billy Pilgrim, Michael Sachs was chosen and his underplayed, everyman approach to the character worked very well.

Number Four—*Sleeper*

Funny is funny, and Woody Allen was still in full "yuks to the wall" mode with this story of some poor schlub stuck two hundred years in the future. His scenes where he masquerades as a service robot never fail to make me laugh—pummeling the instant pudding with a broom? Priceless.

Number Three—*Back to the Future*

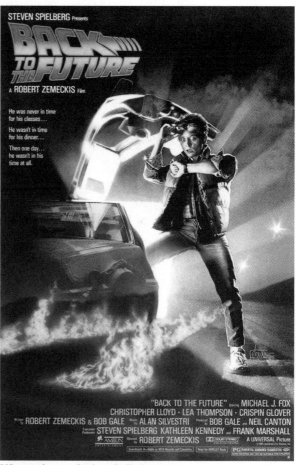

A different treatment of time travel. I've always wondered what my neighborhood looked like before houses sprang up in the post-WWII years. There were farms (from what I've been told), so Marty's trip back to 1955 rang a bell for me. Everyone gave entertaining performances, and, as a musician, the side story of Marvin Berry calling his cousin—Chuck—with a new sound, cracked me up.

US one-sheet—*Back to the Future.*

Number Two—*The Terminator*

There's a lot for me to like about this movie. The way James Cameron told the story doesn't leave time for breathing—lots of action, lots of tension. The T-800 is still an amazing villain, wonderfully realized with a combination of animatronics, puppetry, and stop-motion animation. Plus, the score is a pulsing success, too.

US one-sheet—*The Terminator*.

Number One—*Starship Troopers*

Remember, I said "'favorite," not "best." Director Paul Verhoeven's wry sense of humor, some of the over-the-top acting, and great CG bugs never fail to amuse and entertain me. Where many people see Verhoeven embracing a militaristic society, I see him condemning it—with a knowing wink.

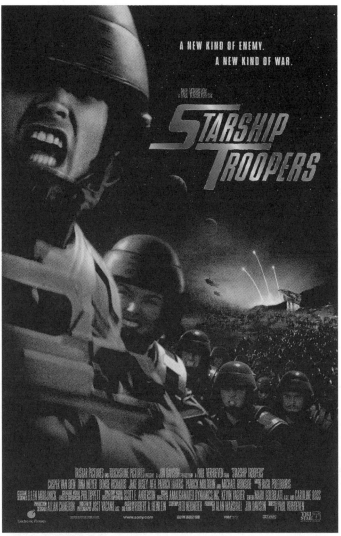

US one-sheet—*Starship Troopers.*

One Man's Meat Is Another Man's Wurst

Put succinctly—"favorite" is emotionally based, and "best" is based on logical analysis and measurable qualities. And while anyone can have "favorites," choosing "bests" might require a more experienced person, possessing the background and knowledge to separate emotion from the facts. Then who in the name of Yoda am I to say what's "best"?

For the record, I have written about the film world for more than twenty years, publishing in books and magazines (including the *James Bond FAQ* for this publisher), as well as being a former college major in TV/film, a technician for broadcast television, and a makeup artist for stage, film, and live performance. As actor Walter Brennan used to say in his 1960s TV show *The Guns of Will Sonnett:* "No brag, just fact."

With those principles established, here are what I feel are the five best sci-fi films of the last forty years. (I can hear you screaming already . . . calm down.)

US one-sheet—*The Matrix.*

Number Five—*The Matrix*

A dystopian future where reality was not what it seemed to be, the Wachowskis' film had great action, great and innovative effects, and a great look. Laurence Fishburne and Carrie-Anne Moss gave excellent support to Keanu Reeves, and Hugo Weaving, seldom acknowledged for his stoic role as Agent Smith, was just right.

Number Four—*Star Wars*

This was the film that put everyone in the cockpit of an X-wing starfighter. The first entry of an epic space saga, combining proven themes from western and war movies with thrills from deep space. Iconic characters and a big music score that contributed to big-time fun at the flicks.

US one-sheet—*Star Wars.*

Number Three—*Jurassic Park*

Steven Spielberg showed filmgoers that it's not nice to fool Mother Nature. A fine ensemble cast, plenty of action, and scenes that made us believe that real dinosaurs were used in the picture. A prime example of what an entertaining film should be.

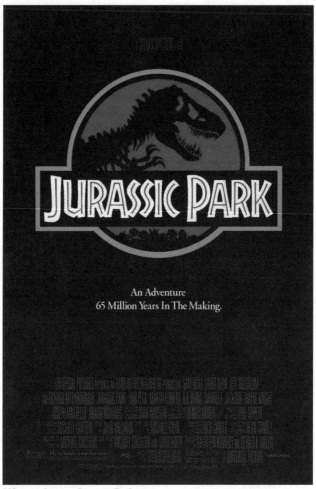

US one-sheet—*Jurassic Park.*

Number Two—*District 9*

Neill Blomkamp explained the shameful stigma of South African apartheid by way of science fiction and aliens. Great FX that never got in the way of the bigger picture, and newcomer Sharlto Copley played a man who paid a big price to see how the other half lived.

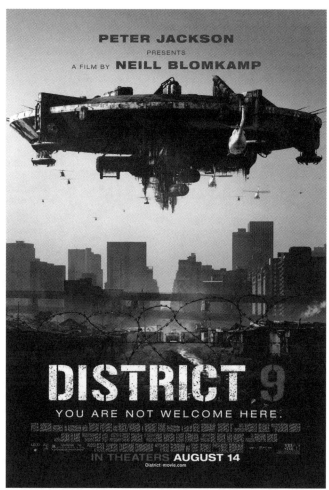

12_09 US one-sheet—*District 9.*

Number One—*A Clockwork Orange*

Proof that a sci-fi film doesn't need a big FX budget to be great. Stanley Kubrick took a rough but compelling story and told it with a great visual sense and performances. Malcolm McDowell never lost his "bad boy" temperament as Alex, seasoned with an unsettling touch of lunacy. The film also had tight editing and a wonderful classical score, brought into the future with the newfangled synthesizer.

British quad—*A Clockwork Orange*.

Bibliography

Books

Anderson, Craig W. 1985. *Science Fiction Films of the Seventies*. Jefferson, North Carolina. McFarland and Company.

Asimov, Isaac. 1979. *In Memory Yet Green: The Autobiography of Isaac Asimov, 1920–1954*. New York, New York. Doubleday Publishing.

Brooker, Will. 2009. *BFI Film Classics: Star Wars*. London, England. Palgrave Macmillan.

Bukatman, Scott. 2012. *BFI Film Classics: Blade Runner*. London, England. Palgrave Macmillan.

Burton, Tim, 2006. *Burton on Burton, Revised Edition*. London, England. Faber and Faber.

Capua, Michelangelo. 2006. *Yul Brynner: A Biography*. Jefferson, North Carolina. McFarland and Company.

Clover, Joshua. 2007. *BFI Film Classics: The Matrix*. London, England. Palgrave Macmillan.

French, Sean. 1997. *BFI Modern Classics: The Terminator*. London, England. Palgrave Macmillan.

Glintenkamp. Pamela. 2011. *Industrial Light & Magic: The Art of Innovation*. New York, New York. Abrams Books.

Hanson, Matt, 2005. *Building Sci-Fi MovieScapes*. New York, New York. Focal Press.

Hardy, Phil, 1984. *Encyclopedia of Science Fiction Movies*. Minneapolis, Minnesota. Woodbury Press.

Heaphy, Maura, 2009. *Science Fiction Authors: A Reference Guide*. Westport, Connecticut. Greenwood Publishing Group.

Horton, Andrew. 2010. *Films of George Roy Hill, Revised Edition*. Jefferson, North Carolina. McFarland and Company.

Lax, Eric, 2007. *Conversations with Woody Allen: His Films, His Movies, and MovieMaking*. New York, New York. Knopf Books.

Morton, Ray. 2007. *Close Encounters of the Third Kind: The Making of Steven Spielberg's Classic Film*. Montclair, New Jersey. Applause Theatre and Cinema Books.

Peterson, Lorne. 2006. *Sculpting a Galaxy: Star Wars*. San Rafael, California. Insight Editions.

Raw, Lawrence. 2009. *The Ridley Scott Encyclopedia*. New York, New York. Scarecrow Press.

Roddenberry, Gene, and Susan Sackett. 1980. *The Making of Star Trek: The Motion Picture*. New York, New York. Pocket Books.

Rogin, Michael. 1998. *BFI Modern Classics: Independence Day*. London, England. Palgrave Macmillan.

Salisbury, Mark. 2012. *Prometheus: The Art of the Film*. London, England. Titan Books.

Sammon, Paul M. 1996. *Future Noir: The Making of Blade Runner*. New York, New York. It Books.

Scalzi, John. 2005. *The Rough Guide to Sci-Fi Films*. London, England. Rough Guides Ltd.

Shail, Andrew, and Robin Stoate. 2010. *BFI Film Classics: Back to the Future*. London, England. Palgrave Macmillan.

Shay, Don. 1985. *Making Ghostbusters*. New York, New York. New York Zoetrope.

Smith, Thomas G. 1987. *Industrial Light & Magic: The Art of Special Effects*. New York, New York. Ballantine Books.

Periodicals

Benidt, Jennifer. 1985. *The Terminator*. *Cinefex*. Riverside, California. (April 1985)

Cronenweth, Jordan. 1981. Behind the Camera with *Altered States*. *American Cinematographer*. Hollywood, California. (March 1981)

D'Angelo, Carr. 1988. Mandy Patinkin—They Call Me Mr. Potato Head. *Starlog*. New York, New York. (November 1988)

Duncan, Jody. 2010. *Avatar*—The Seduction of Reality. *Cinefex*. Riverside, California. (January 2010)

Duncan, Jody. 2011. *Cowboys* and *Aliens*—Invasion of the Body Snatchers. *Cinefex*. Riverside, California. (October 2011)

Duncan, Jody. 1994. *Demolition Man*—Fire and Ice. *Cinefex*. Riverside, California. (March 1994)

Duncan, Jody, and Estelle Shay. 2000. *Galaxy Quest*—Trekking into the Klaatu Nebula. *Cinefex*. Riverside, California. (April 2000)

Duncan, Jody. 2008. *I Am Legend*—Urban Legend. *Cinefex*. Riverside, California. (January 2008)

Duncan, Jody. 2004. *I, Robot*—Ghosts in the Machine. *Cinefex*. Riverside, California. (October 2004)

Duncan, Jody. 1993. *Jurassic Park*—The Beauty in the Beasts. *Cinefex*. Riverside, California. (August 1993)

Eisenberg, Adam. 1984. *Ghostbusters*. *Cinefex*. Riverside, California. (June 1984)

Fordham, Joe. 2001. *A.I. Artificial Intelligence*—Mecha Odyssey. *Cinefex*. Riverside, California. (October 2001)

Fordham, Joe. 2009. *District 9*—Slumdog Aliens. *Cinefex*. Riverside, California. (October 2009)

Fordham, Joe. 2013. *Elysium*—A Tale of Two Cities. *Cinefex*. Riverside, California. (October 2013)

Fordham, Joe. 2002. *Minority Report*—Future Reality. *Cinefex*. Riverside, California. (October 2002)

Fordham, Joe. 2012. *Prometheus*—Alien Genesis. *Cinefex*. Riverside, California. (July 2012)

Fordham, Joe. 2004. *Sky Captain and the World of Tomorrow*—Brave New World. *Cinefex*. Riverside, California. (July 2004)

Horizon Staff. 1997. UC Goes Hollywood—Special Effects—Seeing Is Believing At ILM. *Horizons*. Cincinnati, Ohio. (Fall 1997)

Kaufman, Debra. 1997. SPI Makes Digital Contact. *American Cinematographer*. Hollywood, California. (July 1997)

Lee, Nora. 1988. *Alien Nation*—Buddy Film with a Twist. *American Cinematographer*. Hollywood, California. (September 1988)

Lofficier, Randy, and Jean-Marc. 1992. Detective Future Past. *Starlog*. New York, New York. (November 1992)

Magid, Ron. 1988. *Alien Nation*—A Planetful of Aliens. *Cinefex*. Riverside, California. (November 1988)

Magid, Ron. 1997. Cruising the Cosmos. *American Cinematographer*. Hollywood, California. (December 1997)

Martin, Kevin H. 1999. *Matrix*—Jacking into *The Matrix*. *Cinefex*. Riverside, California. (October 1999)

Oppenheimer, Jean. 1994. Stargate: Adding Layers in *The Outer Limits*. *American Cinematographer*. Hollywood, California. (December 1994)

Prokop, Tim. 1996. *Independence Day*—Fireworks. *Cinefex*. Riverside, California. (September 1996)

Roberts, Paul. 1990. *Total Recall*—Ego Trip. *Cinefex*. Riverside, California. (August 1990)

Robley, Les Paul. 1995. H. R. Giger—Origin of Species. *Cinefantastique*. Oak Park, Illinois. (March 1995)

Rubin, Steve. 1978. *Invasion of the Body Snatchers*. *Cinefantastique*. Oak Park, Illinois. (January 1978)

Sammon, Paul M. 1983. *E.T.: The Extra-Terrestrial*—Turn on Your Heartlight—Inside E.T.
Cinefex. Riverside, California. (January 1983)

Sammon, Paul M. 1987. *RoboCop*—Shooting *RoboCop*. *Cinefex*. Riverside, California. (November 1987)

Sammon, Paul M. 1998. *Starship Troopers*—Bug Bytes. *Cinefex*. Riverside, California. (April 1998)

Satian, Al, and Heather Jackson. 1974. Make Up Man: From Schlock to *The Exorcist*. *Monsters of the Movies*. New York, New York. (December 1974)

Shay, Don. 1980. *Star Trek: The Motion Picture*—Into the V'ger Maw with Douglas Trumbull. *Cinefex*. Riverside, California. (March 1980)

Shay, Jody Duncan. 1985. *Star Trek: Cocoon*—Creating the Wonder of *Cocoon*. *Cinefex*. Riverside, California. (November 1985)

Sturhahn, Larry. 1974. The Filming of *American Graffiti*. *Filmmakers Newsletter*. Andover, Massachusetts. (March 1974)

Swires, Steve. 1988. John Carpenter and the Invasion of the Yuppie Snatchers. *Starlog*. New York, New York. (November 1988)

Vaz, Mark Cotta. 1996. *Mars Attacks!*—Martial Art. *Cinefex*. Riverside, California. (December 1996)

Vaz, Mark Cotta. 1995. *Stargate*—Through the Stargate. *Cinefex*. Riverside, California. (March 1995)

Vitale, Joe. 1978. An Interview with America's Most Brilliant Science-Fiction Writer (Philip K. Dick.) *The Aquarian*. Little Falls, New Jersey. (October 11-18 1978)

Warren, Bill. 1995. Breeding *Species*. *Starlog*. New York, New York. (September 1995)

Whitney Jr., John. 1973. Behind the Scenes of *Westworld*. *American Cinematographer*. Hollywood, California. (November 1973)

Williams, Paul. 1975. The Most Brilliant Sci-Fi Mind on Any Planet: Philip K. Dick. *Rolling Stone*. Little Falls, New Jersey. (November 6 1975)

Recordings

Allen, Tim. 1999. *Galaxy Quest: 20th Anniversary, The Journey Continues*. E! Entertainment Network. (1999)

Black, Shane. 2001. *If It Bleeds We Can Kill It: The Making of Predator*. Twentieth Century-Fox Home Entertainment DVD. (2001)

Burton, Tim. 1996. *Plan of Attack: The Making of Mars Attacks*. Sci-Fi Channel. (1996)

Conran, Kerry. 1998. *The World of Tomorrow*. Warner Bros. Home Entertainment DVD. (2005)

Craig, Daniel. 2010. *Cowboys & Aliens Interviews*. Universal Studios/Dreamworks. (2010)

Warner Bros.Ford, Harrison. 2010. *Cowboys & Aliens Interviews*. Universal Studios/Dreamworks. (2010)

Lucas, George. 2004. *Artifact from the Future: The Making of THX 1138*. Warner Bros. Home Entertainment DVD. 2004)

Pantoliano, Joe. 1999. *HBO First Look: Making of The Matrix*. HBO. (March 1999)

Philip, Kavita. 1992. *Interview with Carl Sagan*. Bookpress. (July 2)

Piper, Roddy. 2012. *Q and A with Roddy Piper—Making They Live*. New Beverly Cinema. (June 10 2012)

Schwarzenegger, Arnold. 2001. *Imagining Total Recall—The Making of Total Recall*. Artisan Home Entertainment DVD. (2001)

Smith, Will. 2008. *I Am Legend: Creating a Legend*. Warner Bros. Home Entertainment DVD. (2008)

Snipes, Wesley. 1994. *Late Nite with David Letterman: Interview with Wesley Snipes.* CBS (February 1)

Spielberg, Steven. 2002. *Creating A.I.* Dreamworks/Warner Bros. Home Entertainment DVD. (2002)

Verhoeven, Paul. 2002. *Backstory: RoboCop.* American Movie Classics Channel. (2002)

Websites

http://articles.latimes.com/1985-06-12/entertainment/ca-6289_1_ron-howard

http://www.benprocter.com/prometheus/

http://cinefantastiqueonline.com/2008/06/interview-stan-winstons-creates-creature-features/

http://collider.com/inception-christopher-nolan-explains/

http://www.clubhaunt.net/01essman_neill.html

http://www.digitalartsonline.co.uk/news/video-post-production/behind-scenes-on-prometheus-vfx/

http://www.douglasadams.se/biography/

http://douglastrumbull.com/key-fx-sequences-blade-runner-spinner-vehicles

http://entertainment.time.com/2011/06/06/super-8-director-jj-abrams-interview/2/

http://filmschoolrejects.com/features/comic-con-interview-rick-baker.php

https://www.fxguide.com/featured/children_of_men_-_hard_core_seamless_vfx/

http://www.giantfreakinrobot.com/scifi/favreau-cowboys-aliens-failed.html

http://www.heinleinsociety.org/rah/biographies.html

http://www.hollywoodreporter.com/heat-vision/george-lucas-star-wars-interview-288523

http://www.ldsfilm.com/directors/Cameron.html

http://moviesblog.mtv.com/2011/06/13/super-8-credits-the-case/

http://ottens.co.uk/forgottentrek/designing-the-first-enterprise/

http://www.pinewoodgroup.com/our-studios/uk/pinewood-studios/stages/007-stage-pw

http://project.cyberpunk.ru/idb/gibson_interview.html

http://www.psacard.com/Articles/ArticleView/5822/1962-topps-mars-attacks-set-martians-still-have-hobby-appeal

http://sarahsbackstagepass.com/karen-allen-exclusive-interview/

http://www.sci-fi-online.com/Interview/04-08-16_DennisMuren.htm

http://www.slashfilm.com/elysium-set-for-imax-release-august-9/

http://www.telegraph.co.uk/culture/music/rolling-stones/9647047/Andrew-Loog-Oldham-The-Svengali-who-set-the-Stones-rolling.html

http://www.theasc.com/magazine/oct04/skycaptain/index.html

http://www.theasc.com/protect/nov97/interstellar/index.htm

http://www.thefamouspeople.com/profiles/carl-sagan-155.php

http://www.theguardian.com/film/2013/aug/17/elysium-neill-bloomkamp-interview

http://www.thehugoawards.org/hugo-history/1958-hugo-awards/

http://www.vfxhq.com/1997/men.html

http://voyager.jpl.nasa.gov/spacecraft/goldenrec.html

https://www.worldswithoutend.com/books_year_index.asp?year=1962

Index

THE FAQ SERIES